CW00670103

ISBN: 9781290518611

Published by:
HardPress Publishing
8345 NW 66TH ST #2561
MIAMI FL 33166-2626

Email: info@hardpress.net
Web: http://www.hardpress.net

MEMOIRS

OF

SIR ELIJAH IMPEY, Knt.,

FIRST CHIEF JUSTICE OF THE SUPREME COURT OF JUDICATURE,
AT FORT WILLIAM, BENGAL;

WITH

ANECDOTES OF WARREN HASTINGS, SIR PHILIP FRANCIS,
NATHANIEL BRASSEY HALHED, ESQ.,

AND OTHER CONTEMPORARIES;

COMPILED FROM AUTHENTIC DOCUMENTS,

· IN

REFUTATION OF THE CALUMNIES

OF THE

RIGHT HON. THOMAS BABINGTON MACAULAY:

BY HIS SON,

ELIJAH BARWELL IMPEY, ESQ., M.A.,

FACULTY STUDENT OF CHRIST CHURCH, OXFORD.

LONDON:

SIMPKIN, MARSHALL, AND CO., STATIONERS' COURT,
D. BATTEN, CLAPHAM:

1846.

INTRODUCTION.

THE fortune and after-fame of public men, often depend rather upon the spirit of the times in which they live, and the state of political parties, to whose influence they are exposed, than upon their own intrinsic merits or defects. This is an axiom, approaching indeed to a truism, applicable to all times and countries, but more especially to our own; where, for so many generations, government has avowedly been carried on upon the principle of balancing party against party; and where, until quite recently, no public man seems to have thought that we could be governed in any other manner.

It was the lot of my father to enter the service of his country, at a period when party heat and violence had attained to their greatest height; and it was his misfortune to excite the personal enmity of a man, who became, in a manner, the oracle and prompter of a faction, the most intemperate, and, at the same time, the most able, persevering, and influential, that ever sate upon the Opposition benches: I allude to Sir Philip Francis. This is not the place to descant upon the character of that gentlemen; it will be fully developed hereafter. But I think it highly important, thus early in this work, to premise, in a summary way, what manner of man he was, who originated these proceedings. I shall assume, then, without stopping to prove, the following facts:—
Sir Philip Francis was the author of many anonymous libels;

principally, the "Letters of Junius;" a pamphlet entitled "Extract of an Original Letter relative to the Administration of Justice by Sir Elijah Impey, dated 1780;" a book, in two octavo volumes, called "Macintosh's Travels in Europe, Asia, &c.," published two years after; and a pamphlet entitled "The Answer of Philip Francis, Esq., to the Charges exhibited against him, General Clavering, and Colonel Monson, by Sir Elijah Impey, Knight, when at the Bar of the House of Commons, &c."

His identity with Junius, I maintain to be established on the united testimony of many able writers.* I will even venture, in addition, to submit my own, *valeat quantum valere potest*. I know, and can swear to Sir Philip's handwriting, as compared with the *fac-similes* preserved in Woodfall's last edition. The three other publications above-named, have been brought home to him by Sir Elijah. I cannot affirm that my father ever declared any positive opinion on the authorship of Junius's Letters; but his exposure of the other three above-named is upon record. Now Sir Philip was in the habit of denying that he was the author of any one of these libels; but if he was convicted of the last three, it approaches to something like presumptive evidence of his being equally guilty of the first. However, I will not argue hypothetically on facts assumed to be already proved; I would rather hazard the chance of contradiction, when I assert, that in habitually disclaiming the authorship of all or any one of these publications, Sir Philip Francis stands convicted, at the very least, of having been an habitual — dissembler.

Lord Brougham, in his "Historical Sketches," grants that

---

* Mere trifles sometimes tend to corroborate more weighty proofs. There was an old monkish writer, mentioned in the Biographical Dictionary, Franciscus Junius by name. It appears to me not altogether unlikely that this circumstance may have suggested to Francis, who was a great reader, the name of Junius, in conjunction with his own : but the question, in my mind, has been completely set at rest. a good many years ago, by Mr. Taylor, in his "Junius Identified."

"Francis's nature was exceedingly penurious;" but, drawing a nice distinction between penuriousness and avarice, he has nevertheless asserted, that he "never stooped one hair's breadth to undue gains;" that he "had been an Indian satrap in the most corrupt of times, and retired from the barbaric land washed by Ormus and Ind, the land of pearls and gold, with hands so clean, and a fortune so moderate, that, in the fiercest storms of faction, no man ever for an instant dreamt of questioning the absolute purity of his administration."* To these remarks I oppose the testimony of men, who, at an early period of his career, knew Francis better than his Lordship, happily for himself, can ever have done. It was notorious among many of his trustworthy contemporaries, that he returned from India enormously rich, having gone out positively poor. This I have heard accounted for, by an illicit participation with his brother-in-law, Macrabie, in salt and opium contracts. It was in allusion to this, that Major Scott, in 1787, said openly in the House of Commons—"Before I join in applauding the honourable gentleman's integrity, I require it to be proved by this test: let him state, that he left England in debt, that he was six years in India, that his expenses at home and abroad were so much, and his fortune barely the difference between the amount of his expenses and the amount of his salary. Until he shall submit to this test, as Lord Macartnay did, I shall pay no attention to the animated panegyrics of his friends." To this Francis made no reply, nor did he ever show the least disposition to acquiesce in such a criterion. If this proves no more, it must be admitted, at least, to disprove the assertion, that "no man ever dreamt of questioning," &c. Nor was Major Scott the only member of the House who publicly questioned the *purity* of Francis's administration. That the noble writer never dreamed of the absolute falsehood, sor-

* See Lord Brougham's Historical Sketches, Vol. II. pp. 96-7.

didness, and vindictive spirit, of Sir Philip Francis, may be accounted for, by the well known elevation and generosity of his Lordship's own character.

I will not now pursue this topic; enough is here stated, by way of preface, to point out how little Sir Philip Francis was to be relied on for the groundwork he supplied, and to what extent the leven of his evil passions may be presumed to have worked upon the enthusiasm of better men.

It was that truly formidable party, which, headed by Burke, and followed by Fox, Windham, Sheridan, and others of like ability, laboured for well nigh fifteen years to ruin the illustrious Hastings; and which, with Sir Gilbert Elliot for their mouthpiece, determined, from the beginning, to couple the judicial conduct of the Chief Justice with the political administration of the Governor General,—a combination which never existed in the sense alleged, and which it is my object, unequivocally to disprove.

It was this party, which, under the dictation of such a prompter as Sir Philip Francis, and such a leader as Mr. Burke, claimed an exclusive knowledge of Indian affairs. Having succeeded in establishing this preposterous claim, they proceeded to electrify, dazzle, and mislead the nation, by a series of such brilliant harangues, as were never before or after surpassed in Parliament, and by a controul or monopoly of the press, such as is now difficult to be conceived.

In our great popular representative assembly, the efforts of declamatory genius have never failed to produce deep and lasting impressions; and so much collective genius, and so much genuine elocution, have never, perhaps, been brought to bear upon one unassisted man, as were levelled at my father, in the House of Commons. In society, few or none took the trouble of investigating facts, or of comparing Parliamentary reports and debates, with examinations before select or general Committees. Few pretended to understand, and fewer still to unravel, the intricacies of the

Regulating Act, to reconcile the discrepancies of the Charter, or to define, precisely, how both were meant to carry into effect the law of England, statute and common, over the provinces of Bengal, Bahar, and Orissa; but all admired the orators who declaimed on these intricate questions,—all were prepared to take upon trust the infallibility of their leaders. Such a statement was to be implicitly believed, because it was suggested by Francis, and confirmed on the authority of Burke; such a denunciation fixed itself upon the memory, because it had been uttered by the glowing eloquence of Fox ; and such a charge, however outrageous or absurd, could not be forgotten, because it had been pointed by the epigrammatic wit of Sheridan. Against such fearful odds,—so brilliant an association,—what success could have been expected from a sober, dry, and somewhat tedious defence ? The assailants, moreover, were always on the alert, in motion and in speech; they perpetually filled the public ear and eye ; while the accused stood upon the defensive, but once for all: and that, before an assembly shamefully prejudiced against him.

Sir Elijah Impey, standing at the bar of the House, alone *with his innocence,* and unsupported by any party, did, indeed, refute, and triumphantly crush, the only charge which the House ever entered into; and, this being done, he printed and published his "Speech," verified by an appendix of documents and vouchers, so full, so thoroughly authenticated, and so convincing, that one would imagine no rational man could read them, without concurring in the vote of acquittal which the Commons had pronounced; or without feeling that my father's impeachment and ruin had been attempted upon no higher or purer motives, than those of personal malignity, and party rancour.

But the printed defence found but a very limited number of readers, compared with those who had read the spirit-stirring speeches of Burke, Fox, Elliot, and Sheridan ; my father's numerous documents were, of necessity, almost as dry and un-attractive, as other mere legal papers are to all but lawyers ; his modest octavo volume was soon withdrawn from circulation, and lost sight of ; not, as I believe, without some active underhand agency on the part of Sir Philip Francis, whose web of artifice, as it gradually expands, will prove him by no means incapable of every secret and surreptitious practice.

How otherwise can it be accounted for, that almost every trace of Sir Elijah Impey's justification should have disappeared where so much defamatory matter affecting his character has been carefully accumulated and preserved ? I will not affirm what I cannot prove ; but what is not improbable I have a right to conjecture; namely, that Francis bought up the copies of my father's defence. Another work equally scarce, I believe him to have suppressed. It is entitled, "A Refutation of a Pamphlet entitled the answer of Philip Francis, Esq., &c. London : Stockdale, 1788." Of both these books the reader will find an epitome in its proper place in this volume.

Sir Elijah's enemies, in the course of the proceedings against Mr. Hastings, audaciously, though not without correction, revived and repeated the charge which he had triumphantly refuted, and of which he had been declared innocent. I refer to the vote of censure of the House of Commons upon Mr. Burke on the 27th of April, 1788, on the petition of Sir Elijah Impey. The vote of censure was moved by the Marquess of Graham, and carried by a majority of more than two to one, the numbers being 135 to 66. Nevertheless the revived calumny came recommended with the same passion, wit, and rhetoric, which had originally given it so much poignancy. Thus, it fixed itself still more firmly upon the popular mind; and, while impartial lawyers who had examined the matter, laughed scornfully at the monstrous fiction, and while easy people of no party slighted it as some gross, ridiculous exaggeration, it became an indestructible article of belief

among the whole body of the blind followers of the oppo-
sitionists.

Dr. Samuel Johnson, who was at this time but recently
dead, had said, thirty years before: —

"Of all kinds of credulity, the most obstinate and wonderful is that of
political zealots; of men, who, being numbered, they know not how, or
why, in any of the parties that divide a state, resign the use of their own
eyes and ears, and resolve to believe nothing that does not favour those
whom they profess to follow."*

By this "most obstinate and wonderful" credulity, by the
untiring malice of faction, and, by the carelessness, indolence,
presumption, and averseness to research of public writers—
journalists, annalists, reviewers and essayists—the exploded
calumny of sixty years ago has been kept alive, and outrages
and indignities have, at intervals of time, continued to be
heaped upon my father's memory.

It is as the reviver, and re-propagator, of slander and
falsehood, that I address myself to the Right Honourable
Thomas Babington Macaulay. This popular writer has
originated no charge, has made no new construction, has invented nothing beyond a few rhetorical embellishments; he
found the structure built, roofed in, and finished, but something the worse for time and wear. All that he has done, or
attempted to do, has been to prop the dilapitated edifice,
re-chisel some of its broken scrolls and cornices, re-paint, re-
plaster, and make it more conspicuous to the public eye.

As far back as the year 1818, the late Mr. James Mill
published a history of British India, which contains every
charge that was brought, or attempted to be brought, against
Sir Elijah Impey, and every evil and malignant construction,
that was ever put upon his conduct as Chief Justice in India.
Although rather more research might have been expected from
a writer holding a foremost situation in the East India House
and having access to all its stores of documents, Mr. Mill

* Idler. No. 10.

collected nearly all the materials for his history of the administration of Warren Hastings, out of inflamed parliamentary
reports, drawn up by Committees most hostile to the Governor
General, and out of the pages of the *Annual Register*, which
was the organ of a party, and which, for many years
had been entirely under the controul of Mr. Burke,—the
accuser, and irreconcilable foe of Mr. Hastings.   Like him,
this *soi-disant* historian of British India confounds two cases
which have nothing necessarily in common with each other;
like him, he never discriminates between the motives of the
Chief Justice and the acts of the Governor General, takes
no pains to ascertain what might have been said on the other
side of the question, and seems never so much as to have
known of my father's printed defence: and yet it had been as
openly made as the accusation itself; it had quashed the proceedings in Parliament, and had thus become an historical fact.
In the face of all this, Mr. Mill puts the accused out of court,
and out of all consideration; takes charges for proofs, and
speculative opinions for the decisions of law; and, finally,
imposes his own unauthenticated conclusions upon the public,
as indisputable history.

I am told that Mr. Mill disclaimed any adherence to party;
that he affected independence; or that, if he consented to wear
the Whig favours, it was only with the admixture of some
Radical ribbons of his own: that he aspired to be chief and
sole ruler of a distinct party, who were variously called, " Phi-
losophical Radicals," " Utilitarians," " Millites," &c.; and,
that he had, at one time, a little knot of young disciples, who
fancied that the whole world, would, inevitably, be altered,
and reformed, and turned into a sort of Utopia, by his political
philosophy. But with Mr. Mill's theory I have little to do. I
only affirm that he selected his materials essentially from *a*
party, however he may have pretended to repudiate it; that he
was negligent of documentary evidence, though it lay at his
hand in Leadenhall Street; that he had neither the research nor

the impartiality which becomes an historian; and, that it was his humour to fly out against all constituted authorities, and, more especially, against all Governors General and Chief Justices of India. I have been assured, however, by a gentleman, likely to know the fact, and incapable of propagating, a falsehood, that Mr. Mill, some years before his death, confessed, in private society, that he had committed many errors in his book; and that, although he had done nothing in malice, he had given not a few persons just reason to complain of him. Yet—whether from want of candour, or from want of what he might consider a proper opportunity, I will not decide—Mr. Mill never put forth any public retractation, but left his history behind him with all its misrepresentation and imperfections unrevised. That such is the fact, there is far better authority than I pretend to, or than can be safely assumed from what the author is reported to have said of himself.

In the preface to the fourth edition of Mill's history, published by Mr. Wilson, in 1840, the learned member of the Asiatic Society, and Boden Professor of Sanscrit in the University of Oxford, with his usual moderation and good-nature, thus qualifies his opinion of Mr. Mill's claim to the " merits of patient and laborious investigation."

" Besides the defects occasioned by *incompetent materials*, the ' History of British India' presents *inaccuracies, both of fact and opinion*, which have arisen from the author's imperfect knowledge of the country, and unacquaintance with any of the languages spoken in it. He has taken great pains to prove that these deficiencies are of no consideration, and that his never having been in India, and his possessing but a slight and elementary acquaintance with any of the languages of the East, are to be regarded rather as qualifications than disqualifications, for the task which he had undertaken. His arguments are ingenious: they will carry conviction but to a few."

But, besides this, Mr. Mill had none of the graces and vivacities which constitute what is called a popular writer. His book, therefore, though often named, was seldom read; and all the slanders therein contained, lay, for a great length of time, sealed up and forgotten: the rather, perhaps, as nobody, except Mr. Macaulay, thought it worth while to notice so dull a writer; and when, upon another occasion, he *was* noticed by Mr. Macaulay, it was, at first, in such abusive terms, as to induce a quarrel between the reviewer and the reviewed. Afterwards, it seems, they were reconciled; for what reason does not appear; but, in the preface to his " Critical and Historical Essays contributed to the Edinburgh Review," the right honourable re-publisher has these words: —

" Serious as are the faults of the 'Essay on Government,' a critic, while noticing those faults, should have abstained from using contemptuous language respecting the historian of British India. It ought to be known, that Mr. Mill had the generosity, not only to forgive, but to forget the unbecoming acrimony with which he had been assailed, and was, when his valuable life closed, on terms of cordial friendship with his assailant."

This quarrel, reminds me of what I have read or heard quoted somewhere: —" *Ctesias mendacissimus Herodotum mendaciorem arguit;* " while the reconciliation brings to my mind the Rovers in the "Antijacobin: "—"A sudden thought strikes me; let us swear an eternal friendship!" How far this friendship was cemented by their enmity to other characters, may be gathered from the sequel; but when, from whatever motive, Mr. Macaulay condescended to rouse the drowsy calumnies of Mr. Mill; when one of the most popular writers of the day—writing for that great party organ, the *Edinburgh Review*—exerted all his ingenuity to revive them; it was then that falsehood and defamation took a new and wider range; and I began to feel that something must be done to rescue from dishonour the good name I inherit.

But the production, on its first appearance, was, like all review articles, anonymous. The well-known peculiarities, indeed, the smartness and antithesis, of Mr. Macaulay's style—which, by the way, has in no degree improved since the writer was a student at Trinity College, Cambridge—left little doubt as to the authorship; and, in every society I frequented, the article was unhesitatingly attributed to that Right Honourable gentleman. But still it was " a deed without a name; " and there are mocking birds in the field of literature, as well as in the forests of America. Both before and since, I have seen the right honourable reviewer's mannerism so closely imitated, that it has been difficult to tell which was the copy and which the original—which the voice and which the echo. I could not commit myself upon an uncertainty, or combat with a phantom. From that moment, however, I began to collect and arrange materials, for a vindication of Sir Elijah Impey, who had thus been evoked from the sanctuary of the tomb, to be re-produced to the world, as a monster of meanness and iniquity.

At that time, besides myself, there were four children of Sir Elijah yet surviving. We were all most tenderly attached to his memory, and deeply wounded by its desecration. Though not altogether unknown in the world, it is just possible that the reviewer knew nothing of our existence; but it is highly probable, that he would not have deranged the symmetry of a single sentence, once constructed, to save five affectionate hearts from anguish. I abstain, as much as possible, from mixing up the sanctity of domestic sorrow with resentment of a public wrong; but, if there be *a slanderer base enough to find pleasure and triumph in having tortured the feelings of delicate and sensitive women, aged and honourable men, he may take my assurance for the fact, that these calumnies have not only embittered the remnants of life, but mingled with the sharpness of death.* But I scorn to rest my claim to popular sympathy upon any but popular grounds. It is only upon those grounds that I pause to exemplify, in one instance, the baneful effects—the wide-spreading pestilence, of a libellous pen. Other examples are not wanting, where provocations of this nature have resulted, both to individuals, and to communities, in the most disastrous consequences—in brutal assaults, and sanguinary challenges;

in frenzy, and assassination! And therefore it is, that defamatory libels, in which I include libels on the dead, have been always considered, by the soundest lawyers, and still stand upon our statute-books, as directly tending to an overt act of the breach of the peace.* However, Time has a lenient wing, and mitigates the resentments as it blanches the hairs of old age. If I have thus slightly glanced at worldly consequences and responsibilities, let it not be thought that I am unaware how much more consistent it is, with my time of life, and present disposition, to admonish and remind the slanderer and false witness, of higher and holier obligations, than were ever suggested by human vengeance, or sanctified by merely human law.†

About the time when the *Edinburgh Review* article was first making a noise in the world, there were two other writers who were treating largely of Indian affairs; who were publishing their works periodically, or in parts; and who were both approaching the difficult subject of Mr. Hastings's administration. One of these gentlemen was Mr. Charles Mac Farlane, who was then writing the civil and military narrative in the "Pictorial History of England," published by Messrs. Charles Knight & Co.; the other was Mr. Edward Thornton, who was producing his "History of the British Empire in India," published by Messrs. Allen & Co., booksellers to the Honourable East India Company.

Fully aware of the strenuous efforts which had been made to falsify that portion of our history, knowing that I was the sole possessor of many papers which could alone restore it to the

---

* See "Blackstone's Commentaries," vols. 3 & 4 ; and 32 George III. cap. 60. For a remarkable conversation between Dr. Johnson and Solicitor General Murray—afterwards Lord Henderland,—concerning libels on the dead, see "Boswell's Life of Johnson," and the note on the passage where he quotes the case of "Rex *versus* Topham," tried in the King's Bench, Trinity Term, 1790; when defendant was found guilty of a libel, published in *The World* newspaper, against Lord Cowper, deceased.

† Deut. xix. 18—21.

light of truth, and feeling that I should render an acceptable service to those two authors, if they aimed at impartiality, by affording them the means of attaining to it, I determined to put myself in communication with them, and to offer them both the free use of my materials. In so doing, I resolved to ask from them no other return or condition, than that they would carefully peruse my books and papers, and then judge for themselves.

In the first instance, because, of the two, he was more nearly approaching to the critical point in his narrative, and for no other reason, I addressed myself to Mr. Mac Farlane. Personally, I knew nothing of this gentleman, nor he of me; but I had read parts of his history, and from them I judged that he had no party bias, and was sincere in his pursuit of truth. I was not disappointed. Mr. Mac Farlane gladly accepted my offer, acknowledging that he found himself involved in doubts and difficulties; that he had sought in vain for a copy of Sir Elijah Impey's defence; and that he was wholly unacquainted with the contents of that volume. I placed it in his hands, together with ten folio volumes of manuscript letters, and all such other documents and vouchers as I had, at that time, procured from public offices. The result was, that he not only lost no time in correcting many old errors, and inserting many facts new to him into the history upon which he was then employed, but that he afterwards made free use of my materials in the compilation of another work, entitled, "Our Indian Empire," in two volumes, bearing his name, and published likewise by Messrs. Charles Knight & Co., in 1844.

It is due from me to Mr. Mac Farlane, most unequivocally to state, that he performed this task under no compact or agreement whatever; but at a very considerable expense, and inconvenience to himself; that he scrupulously examined the whole mass of evidence which I put into his hands; and that, through his generous medium, I have thus been enabled to influence the cause of historical truth in two well-written, and widely-circulated publications. It is equally due to myself to make it clearly understood, that I left the historian entirely to the guidance of his own judgment and good feeling in this matter; I could never, for a moment, have thought of insulting him, or debasing myself, by an attempt at any unworthy compromise of his opinion. I would as soon have crouched to Mr. Macaulay himself for a favourable article on this present volume, as have attempted to tamper with the author of the "Pictorial History," and of "Our Indian Empire." His own unbiassed conclusion was, that my father had been an honourable and cruelly misused man. This opinion he expressed with honest warmth and earnestness; and there are various points in both his narratives, which he has cleared up, and substantiated, by reference to unquestionable documents; to the advantage of Sir Elijah's fame, and to the conviction of Mr. Mill and his followers, either of wilful misrepresentation, gross ignorance, or want of common research. In a *general* history of the eventful reign of George III., and in a *general* account of "Our Indian Empire," it is obvious that to have inserted more details must have been considered disproportionate and out of place; but, for what the author of these volumes has done, towards the elucidation of truth, it behoves not only *me and my relatives,* but every honest reader of his country's annals, to be grateful.

Mr. Mac Farlane and I are no longer strangers to each other; and I trust that an acquaintance which began under circumstances painful to me, but assuredly not dishonourable to either of us, will terminate in a lasting friendship.

My intercourse with Mr. Edward Thornton was not quite so satisfactory. I waited, in person, upon that gentleman, at his office in the East India House, and offered him the use of the same documents which I had submitted to Mr. Mac Farlane. Politely, but coldly enough, he declined accepting my offer. I spoke of the difficulty of finding any copy of Sir Elijah Impey's defence, and of the importance and conclusive nature of the arguments and vouchers contained in that volume. But he wanted not the loan of my book; and I left him upon receiving his assurance that "*full justice would be done, by him, to Sir Elijah.*" Within a short space of time *his* part also came out. The *justice* which Mr. Thornton had done my father, had been to take upon trust the charges of his persecutors, to repeat the slanders of Mr. Mill, and to modulate his abuse in the manner of Mr. Macaulay. With documents at his elbow, or to be seen by merely moving a few steps, from his own to the adjoining offices, where I myself found them,—with proofs, the most clear and accessible, of my father's most honourable and disinterested conduct, Mr. Thornton, without bestowing a thought upon such evidence, repeated the dishonouring construction which Mr. Mill had put upon that conduct, and even exceeded Mr. Macaulay in his invectives against it. I allude here principally to the charge of the Chief Justice having accepted the presidency of the Sudder Dewannee Adaulut; but, in other very serious matters, Mr. Thornton had been equally indolent, careless, ignorant, and intemperate. His great rhetorical Paragon had infected him,—had transported him out of the mediocrity of his own style,—and it is quite clear, that, for information on a most important part of our Indian history, involving the character of the dead and the feelings of the living, he had never looked beyond that chronicle and repertory of party, the old *Annual Register*, the ponderous tomes of Mr. Mill, and the frivolous article in the *Edinburgh Review*. In the heat of the moment *that* was done which I now regret. My eldest brother, Admiral John Impey, and myself, presented an ineffectual memorial * to the Honourable East India Company. We ought rather to have despised so impotent an attack. The dullness of Mr. Thornton's book was quite sufficient to limit its circulation. It is already consigned to merited oblivion. I have not met the person that has read it.

* This memorial will be found in the Appendix to this volume.

The *Edinburgh Review* article first appeared in 1841. In 1843, Mr. Macaulay published, with his name on the title-pages, three volumes, entitled, "Critical and Historical Essays contributed to the Edinburgh Review." They were nothing but reprints of the several original publications in that periodical work; and, as a matter of course, the libel in question was among them.

In that interval of time, Mr. Mac Farlane, with the aid of my papers, had published in the History of England his account of my father's administration of justice in India. That account had been very generally read, and had made many converts to the truth. That the right honourable gentleman had read it, appeared from his own acknowledgment *in a foot-note* appended to his essay. He had therefore learned, if he knew it not before, that numerous documents on the subject were extant; that my father had triumphantly defended himself against the only charge that was ever pressed against him; that there existed, in print, the copy of that defence, of which he might possibly have had no previous knowledge, but of which well nigh one-third had now been re-published; and that there were still living, children of Sir Elijah Impey, whose hearts had been harrowed by the original article. Finally, I will add, that, by this time, and through this means (if not long before, through Mr. Gleig's book), Mr. Macaulay must have learned, that of those descendants of Sir Elijah Impey, there was one, at least, not likely to let an avowed libel against his father, under the author's own name, pass unnoticed. Therefore it became the Right Honourable gentleman, before he determined to convert his anonymous review into an essay acknowledged by himself, carefully and soberly to have re-considered the whole matter; it became him, for the sake of his reputation *as a writer*, and from dread of further exposure of his inaccuracies, thenceforward to have commenced that historical research which he had hitherto neglected; it became him, *as*

a gentleman, and from a regard to filial feeling, to have expunged that which had been proved to be false, and to have
apologised for that which had justly given offence. With
these considerations, it may surely then be asked, did not
Mr. Macaulay's re-publication appear in a form and temper
widely differing from those of the original review article? If
not retracted, surely it must have been softened, moderated,
or explained? No such thing. The review article of 1841,
and the essay of 1843, were substantially the same! No
research had been instituted, no documents consulted, no
violent denunciation altered or qualified, no error acknowledged or amended, *except one,* and that bearing on the most
trifling part of the whole subject. This sole confession, that
he had in one instance been caught tripping, was thrust into
a foot-note, in small type, and was accompanied by an arrogant
sneer. The injustice and impertinence of that insult, I have
taken good care to expose, in its proper place. Meantime, in
justice to Mr. Mac Farlane, I may here remark, that it is matter
of common courtesy among literary men, that, when a work is
referred to, the title of the book, or the name of the author,
or both, should be given; but the critical and historical essayist, named neither the author nor his work; still less did
he deign to treat with any deference the source from which
the information had been derived: though he seems to refer
it to one of Sir Elijah Impey's family. But this omission,
I take it, did not proceed so much from discourtesy as from
calculation. Mr. Macaulay was not willing that his *foot-note*
should serve as an advertisement, either to my papers, or to
Mr. Mac Farlane's book; because, in the former, the reader
was sure to find an index to those documents, which he had
either ignorantly or dishonestly suppressed; and, in the latter,
a mortifying detection, of not simply *one* trifling error, but of
many gross, infamous, and abominable mis-statements. It
was for that reason, that, *ex abundanti cautelâ,* Mr. Macaulay
smuggled through a *foot-note* his nameless allusion to Mr.

Mac Farlane, and took care not to betray even so much as a knowledge of my existence.

The Right Honourable Thomas Babington Macaulay, having thus re-published his original *libel*, without any qualification or apology, though ample time and opportunity had been allowed for both, I was no longer in any doubt as to the course I ought to pursue. I resolved to refute him publicly, and upon public grounds. He had committed two great national outrages: the falsification of history for party purposes; and the invasion, beyond all allowable liberty of language, of a character belonging to the State. I felt, therefore, that he had given me a twofold advantage over him ; I felt myself justified in pursuing these advantages; and, with the aid of incontrovertible facts, and authenticated documents, opposed to mere assertion, with the utter absence of all proof, I did not despair of bringing the truth to light; neither would I shrink from competition with my brilliant adversary, so long as I was conscious of a better cause, and of a mind superior, at least, to his habitual prejudice, and infinitely better informed, by means of patient investigation, on a subject, which, it is plain, he had undertaken without the remotest pretension to research. Feeling, moreover, that, sooner or later, I might be called upon to repel this unwarrantable, unprovoked, and worse than personal attack, I girded myself for the task.

Nor had I been altogether idle in the interval: I had arranged some of my materials, cautiously examining papers already in my possession, and searching for more; I had solicited information in many quarters, especially from gentlemen whose lives had been spent in India, or in the service of the Company; and, to the best of my ability, I had studied the whole subject anew; so as to make myself, more than ever, thoroughly master of it. At first, I had thought of confining myself to a pamphlet; but I soon found that nothing like justice to my father's memory, could be done within such narrow limits. My materials accumulated,—and the final result has been the present volume.

In this pursuit I have been aided by many of my friends, both private and official, in a manner too kind and effectual not to call forth my most grateful acknowledgments. There is a reverence due to exalted names, which should protect them from being unnecessarily cited upon occasions of inadequate importance; yet I persuade myself that, in a case involving the character of a dignified servant of the Crown, though long deceased, there will be no impropriety in availing myself of the sanction of such names, *alike* connected with the public service, and therefore *alike* liable to fall upon "evil days and evil tongues." Having first sought, in vain, among the more intimate of my private acquaintance, or those upon whom I thought myself best entitled to call for documents indispensible to my work, I was induced to apply for them in higher quarters. On application to Sir Robert Peel, I was instantly supplied with a circular letter of introduction to the Government offices, dated May 8, 1842, and addressed to the Keeper of the State Papers, the Clerk of the Privy Council, and the President of the Board of Controul. The terms in which this circular is expressed, conveyed a recommendation so personally flattering to myself, that though I have not the vanity to print it, yet have I pride and gratitude sufficient to preserve it among my most precious testimonials. The exact success with which I presented myself at all these offices, it is not necessary to state. Enough that I left none of them unsearched, and that my reception at each deserves my warmest thanks.

At first, and of my own accord, I had solicited the inspection of papers at the India House; and, with the accustomed liberality of the Honourable the East India Company, I was favoured with immediate permission to consult them. I have already signified my regret at having, on a later occasion, presented an ineffectual memorial to the Court of Directors. But

I would have it clearly understood, that I do not by any means consider their unfavourable answer to that memorial as detracting from the previous obligation which I owe them. With much thankfulness I acknowledge their ready assent to my former petition; and that I am more particularly obliged to their respectable officials, Mr. Peacock, Mr. Lawford, and Mr. Cottle, for all the accommodation and facility of reference obtained at their several departments, in Leadenhall Street and Drapers' Hall. To their learned librarian, Professor Wilson, I am equally thankful for the favour of having been admitted to the advantage of his conversation, during my attendance at the India House in July, 1842. It may be asked, then, why the memorial alluded to should be published in my Appendix ? Simply, and for no other reason, than because it is my purpose to give publicity to every proof of the general merits of this case; and at all times, and in all places, to cause a register to be made of my protest against these execrable calumnies. I was besides warranted, by no light authority, in pursuing this course.

Before I presumed to memorialise the Court of Directors, I submitted to my friend, the late Lord Fitzgerald, then President of the India Board, the propriety of addressing the Chair. His lordship, with an affability and good nature which ever marked his conduct towards me, attentively read my memorial; and though he professed not to give an opinion, either on its merits, or upon its probable result, he did, nevertheless, most expressly approve the motive, and encourage the design, with which I presented it; adding, with some compliments on the *"piety of my task,"* a strong recommendation that I should put it upon every possible public record ; and that, as both the memorial and the answer to it, must, in the course of business, come before him, he should have been sorry if I had petitioned the Court of Directors, without having first communicated with him. In the end, his lordship desired me to leave a written minute of my application at his office;

and directed, in my hearing, that it should be placed among the documents at the India Board. Before I quit this portion of my subject, let me take this opportunity of offering my tribute of gratitude to the memory of that accomplished nobleman, not without an expression of sorrow that I should have obtruded upon his attention a matter which may have caused some pain and trouble, at a moment not long preceding his lamented death.

Let me, likewise, not omit to express my sense of obligation for the civilities bestowed upon me by the under-secretary, and junior officers of the Board ; particularly to my young friend Charles Phillimore, to whom I am indebted for having called my attention to a very valuable document at the India House.

By the authority of the present eminently learned Master of Trinity College, Cambridge, I am enabled to authenticate my father's academical career in that University: and I feel obliged to Dr. Whewell for his kind alacrity in replying to my inquiries.

And, finally, I must not forget the obligations I am under to my hereditary friends of the Sutton family, and to their venerable medium of communication with me—the Rev. I. T. Becher, Prebendary of York—for the very acceptable anecdotes imparted to me, at the eve of this publication.

That the book should not have appeared until *three* years after the publication of Mr. Macaulay's Essay, has been owing to various circumstances and considerations, in few of which the general reader will take much interest. I may say, however, that I was far more anxious for correctness than for speed ; that some of my researches in public offices consumed much time ; that I was frequently delayed by waiting for information from distant friends and correspondents; and not seldom retarded by an indifferent state of health. No time, at least, has been wasted in *elaborating fine sentences, or seeking after far-fetched illustrations and fanciful effects.* Nevertheless

I never contemplated, nor do I contemplate now, that the interest of my book should be merely of a momentary and personal nature. My intention, on the contrary, was, and is, that it should have an interest for all times, and for all men capable of feeling the value of historical truth; that it should prove that repetition of falsehood, however long and obstinately continued, can never accumulate into fact; that, in history and biography, research—industrious, scrupulous research—is of far more account than exquisite writing; that the characters of public men are not to be everlastingly sacrificed to the purposes of faction; and that, eventually, detection, exposure, shame, will await those who deliberately print and publish, in a daring contempt of facts long since passed into legitimate history, and established upon parliamentary proof. And is not this a lesson needed, from time to time, in this writing and reviewing age? And is not the memory of many a just man, as dear to his descendants as my father's is to me, equally exposed to the risk of atrocious defamation? Is not every man who makes himself at all known in the world, who excites the enmity of a party, or the jealousy of a *powerful, fashionable* writer, liable alike to be assailed in his life-time, and, when he can no longer defend himself, to be calumniated in his grave?

If I have adequately performed my task, then have I done a public as well as a private duty; I have not only vindicated Sir Elijah Impey individually, but I have thrown a shield between a host of other innocent men, and the attacks of future slanderers. At the very least, I have raised a beacon for the warning of future historians; and it would be no less than to meditate a libel upon this high-minded nation if I could bring myself to believe that Englishmen are indifferent to the sacred principle of historic truth; or that they will long mistake a tinsel embroidery of rhetoric on a coarse ground-work of faction and falsehood for the annals of this glorious land. Mr. Macaulay, I am told, is now writing a full history, wherein is to be included the substance of nearly all the articles he has contributed to the *Edinburgh Review*, from the commencement of the Revolution, to the end of the reign of George III. What sacrifices of public reputation, what immolation of private character may not be expected in such a work from such a pen! But is there a reader in his senses, who—after being made acquainted with his mode of writing, and the specimens hereinafter to be exhibited and exposed— will attach any value to Mr. Macaulay as an historian? Is there one of our truth-seeking, candid, and ingenuous country-men that will ever think of looking for impartiality in *his* book? or that will attach the slightest importance either to *his* condemnation or applause?

But if anonymous reviews, avowedly written for party purposes, and republished verbatim with their authors' names, are not to be regarded as impartial history; so neither are passionate invectives, coarse epithets, and cruel personalities to be substituted for sober reasoning on the conduct of public men: and were it not that our evil passions are often, but too succesfully stimulated by these means, it would be almost incredible that so many experienced writers, and declaimers, should trust to such precarious and unworthy methods of persuasion. Too much intemperance, whether real or simulated for the sake of effect, has already been lavished on this subject. It has been my endeavour to divest myself of every similar passion; but if, in the course of this investigation, I may have been betrayed into any unbecoming heat, some deduction will surely be made, on account of the more than individual provocation I have received. *Tametsi causa postulat, si non planè cogit, in iram non soleo descendere.*

E. B. I.

Clapham Common,
    September, 1846.

$*_*^*$ In the course of my work, I have repeatedly announced my intention of depositing the Family MSS. and other papers (upon which this volume is mainly founded), in the Library of the British Museum.

I have now only to announce that those books and papers have been so deposited, and that they are now accessible to every man of letters, that may wish to study an important chapter in Indian history, or to test the correctness of my numerous quotations and references.

CONTENTS.

CHAPTER XIV.

CHAPTER XV.

CHAPTER XVI.

CHAPTER XVII.

CHAPTER XVIII.

CONTENTS OF APPENDIX.

ERRATA.

Page 4, line 3, in note, for "twelve" read *nine;* line 4, for "1804" read *Feb.* 4, 1805.

  ,, 13, line 15, in note, for "Colyten" read *Colyton.*

  ,, 24, line 16, for "1824" read 1818.

  ,, 50, line 8, for "Syrian" read *Persian;* line 3, in note, for "as well by" read *as well of.*

  ,, 69, line 34, for "the were" read *they were.*

  ,, 87, line 32, for "berefaced" read *barefaced.*

  ,, 91, line 20, for "admissable" read *admissible;* line 34, for "and Hyde, Lemaistre" read *Hyde, and Lemaistre.*

  ,, 92, line 3, for "is his" read *in his.*

  ,, 139, line 20, at commencement, omit "some."

  ,, 233, line 18, for "country" read *Company.*

  ,, 251, line 32, for "Barber" read *Baber.*

  ,, 257, lines 1 & 10, for "cap. 64" read *cap.* 63.

CHAPTER I.

―――

EARLY LIFE OF SIR ELIJAH IMPEY.

OF the immediate parentage and early history of Sir Elijah Impey, there is little of any public interest to be recorded, beyond the fact that he was born and bred a gentleman and a scholar. Yet some short biographical notice may be expected to precede a work like the present. Moreover, as Sir Elijah's reputation has been assailed from its very earliest years, it is fit that, from its very earliest years it should likewise be vindicated; in order that the general reader of this day, who is not likely to devote time, and still less the labour of research, to such a subject, may be as carefully disabused, as he has been ignorantly and uncharitably, if not maliciously misinformed; and that it may plainly appear from beginning to end, whether Mr. Macaulay is justified in representing the character of an able, honourable, and amiable man, as he has presumed to do. So unambitious was my father of any posthumous fame to be achieved by memoirs or biographical sketches, and so averse to the publication of correspondence unconnected with public affairs, that the materials which have come down to me, whether of his early private life, or professional efforts, are very scanty; but such as they are, I possess them, while Mr. Macaulay, his pretended critic and historian, has not the slightest authority or shadow of proof for his

daring, off-hand, unwarrantable assertions. Some most
important materials, indeed, there were, accessible to this
ingenious writer, in printed books; but neither he nor
the author* whom he has followed for his facts, have ever
looked at these memorials. If it can be proved to demonstration, that Mr. Macaulay, in his very first mention of
Sir Elijah Impey, couples his name with what is slander-
ous, and has assumed a character for him in his boyhood which is utterly false, there will be little credit left
to cement the structure which he raises on such a
foundation.

> " Let him in nought be trusted,
> For speaking false in that."

Assuming my own name and person, in the execution
of a filial duty, I therefore commence with the commencement of my father's career, and shall attempt to
bring it to a close with brevity and truth.

In the male line, Sir Elijah sprang from that middle
class of society, which, in this commercial land, has supplied so many able lawyers and enlightened statesmen.
He was the third and youngest son of Elijah Impey, Esq.,
of Butterwick House, Hammersmith, by his second wife,
Martha Fraser. He was born at Hammersmith, on the
13th of June, 1732, and was baptised in St. Paul's Chapel,
in the parish of Fulham, on the 24th of June, as appears
by the parish register.† His father, like many of his predecessors, was a merchant, engaged in various traffic, but
chiefly connected with the East India and South Sea trade.
He died in 1750, and was buried in the family vault at
Hammersmith, as recorded on a monument erected against
the inner wall, on the north-west side of the church. From
this commercial connection, my father's mind was, at an
early period, familiarised with Eastern affairs. His mother
was nearly related to the noble Scottish family of Lovat,
being the daughter of James Fraser, LL.D. Dr. Fraser
was author of a Life of Nadir Shah, held an official
situation in Chelsea Hospital, and was uncle to
Amelia, Baroness in her own right, and married,
in the strange manner recorded in history, to Simon,
the twelfth Lord Lovat, beheaded for the part he had

---

* Mr. Mill.
† See Lyson's Environs of London.

taken in the Rebellion of 1745. My paternal grandfather left behind him both a good name, and a considerable estate, in and about Fulham, Uxbridge, and
the parish of St. Mary-le-bone in London. Of Sir Elijah's
two brothers, Michael the eldest, succeeded to his father's
business, and the greater part of his estate at Hammersmith, where he resided till his death in 1794. The
second, James, was educated at Westminster, and
Christ Church, Oxford; being at the former a King's
Scholar, and at the latter a Faculty Student. At both
places he was highly distinguished, as well by his amiable disposition, as by his scholastic acquirements.
Among his intimate friends at Oxford, who afterwards
obtained eminence in the world, were Dr. William
Markham, afterwards Archbishop of York, and that
distinguished lawyer, who eventually became Chief
Baron Skinner. Having taken the degree of M.D.,
James Impey began to practise as a physician, residing
chiefly at Richmond. Possessing an independence, and
with it the desire of travelling so common to scholars,
he indulged it in the capacity above-mentioned; visiting
many foreign climes in pursuit of science. He died at
Naples, in 1756. Having no issue, he left a considerable
property to his youngest and favourite brother, the
subject of this Memoir. It is to be regretted, that the
reputation he acquired for learning, is but scantily attested by some elegant Latin verses printed in an early
edition of the "CARMINA QUADRAGESIMALIA," by a
published treatise on Comparative Anatomy, and by a
few other manuscripts which do not appear to have
been printed. His common-place books, however, which
are in my possession, denote an inquisitive, industrious,
and highly cultivated mind, combined with a turn for
the humorous, which was an equally remarkable feature
in the character of my father at every period of his life.
To this brother, who was about eleven years his senior,
Sir Elijah was chiefly indebted for the superintendence
of that education, which, aided by his own industry and
abilities, procured for him, without either high connection
or patronage, the distinguished post he held in his profession. From this brother he likewise imbibed that
love of classical literature, which, like his wit and
pleasantry, never forsook him either in prosperity or
B 2

tribulation ; in the bustle and incessant toil of middle
life, or in the retirement of old age. Of his brother
James he always spoke with tenderness and gratitude ;
but, like most other eminent men, he always declared
that he owed most of all to the early tuition of his
mother, and to the tender care she took to instil into his
bosom early principles of religion and morality. He
never wrote or spoke of her but as his "*pious mother.*"*

In his seventh year, he was placed at the lowest form
of Westminster School, then under the able direction of
Dr. Nicoll. He proceeded to the end of his academical
course, the favourite of his master, and the friend of
many of his school-mates, who were afterwards men of
note, and of honour in the world. I have sufficient
evidence before me to show that, though quick and
industrious at his studies, the future Chief Justice of
India, was a joyous, light-hearted, and spirited
"Westminster boy," much addicted to sportive exercise,
and not less to sportive verse. From this last practice
he scarcely weaned himself until his last hour ; although
he never took up poetry otherwise than as an exercise,
or pastime, nor ever attached the slightest value to the
things he struck off (at times in no unhappy vein of
poetry) for the amusement of his children, or of some
old and familiar friend. Some droll doggrel which
left an echo behind it in Westminster School, and which
will still be familiar to many an old King's Scholar, I
believe to have been his. The joke is nothing without
the story. The celebrated Dr. Arne, at that time residing
near Westminster Abbey, where he had probably some
professional engagement, requested some of the boys to
write him a copy of verses, that he might set them to

* I cannot better exemplify the force and duration of this sentiment,
than by extracting a paragraph from a letter addressed to me by my father,
dated Ryde, in the Isle of Wight, June 18, 1800, about ~~twelve~~ years before his decease. It relates to his parting with my lamented brother
Hastings Impey, who died in India, 1804. " At present," he writes, " the
wind is in the west, and will not permit him to sail. . . .I may confess my
weakness to you ; I am fond enough to wish it may remain in that quarter :
for every day and hour that my dear boy remains with me, seem to be
added to my life. My mother, when approaching the age of ' threescore
years and ten,' used to tell me that every morning when she saw daylight,
she piously returned thanks to God for having permitted her to see it.
I feel sentiments of a similar kind for every day I behold my Hastings."

music.   The Doctor, if we may trust to his portraits, was a grave and solemn person, as professors are apt to be; but there ran a story, that his wife was accustomed to bathe in the river Thames, with her servant-maid; be that as it may, the verses which they presented to the composer, began,

"Dr. Arne, Dr. Arne, it gives us consarn,"

and ended in cautioning Mrs. Arne against the great risk she ran of catching cold.*

Some of my father's exercises in Latin verse, are exceedingly creditable to a boy of his age; having more meaning and point than are usually found in such juvenilia.   The following epigram was written when he was about sixteen or seventeen years old, under the following thesis—given, as is usual, a little before Easter, preparatory to the recitation of similar compositions, which form part of the examination of candidates by the electors deputed from either University:—

"DECUS ET TUTAMEN."

"Hæc coma quam spectas duplicem mihi servit in usum,
    Tutamen capiti nocte, dieque decus."†

The double office of the wig, will remind the reader of the idea of Goldsmith in his description of the distressed poet:

"A night-cap crowned his head instead of bay,—
    A cap by night, a stocking all the day."

Yet I hardly think it possible that my father could have taken the thought from Goldsmith.   The first allusion to the "Distressed Poet," occurs in a letter to

* I have been reminded by a contemporary, that the song ended thus:
"Dr. Arne, Dr. Arne, it becomes your consarn,
    These matters may chance to make you sick;
You ask for a song, and we mean nothing wrong,
    But beg you'll set this to your music."

† So general was the fashion of wearing wigs in those days, that even Westminster schoolboys wore them; and it may well be supposed, that in their rough dormitory of St. Peter's College, they converted them occasionally into nightcaps.

the Rev. Henry Goldsmith, dated in February, 1759; and the verses were not published until some years later.* My father quitted Westminster School in 1751. His epigram must have been produced in 1748 or 1749. In Latin verse he was the pupil of Vincent Bourne, then an usher at Westminster.

There appears to have been no sport or frolic in which the future Judge did not take his full share: the reputation he enjoyed among his contemporaries, and which had a little traditionary existence in the school many years after he had quitted it, was that of being a right merry and hearty companion. The most remarkable of his school-fellows, as well as one of the most remarkable of men, whether of his own day or of any other, was Warren Hastings, who was very nearly of his own age, being his junior by about one year. This trifling difference is, however, something in the boyish age, and it is fair to presume that, from my father's seniority, from his more muscular frame, from his being first at the school, and from his having enjoyed advantages, as well in education as in other particulars, which Hastings, through his father's misfortunes or imprudence, had been denied, his lively friend and playfellow figured, for a time, as the protector and champion of the future Governor General of India. As much as this, indeed, appears to be signified in fragments of letters and memoranda, written many years after both had quitted school. But what is quite positive, is, that Elijah Impey and Warren Hastings were bosom friends as schoolfellows, and that the friendship thus commenced, *faustis sub penetralibus,* continued till old age and death, being never for a moment interrupted, except for a short interval at Calcutta, by the political and professional differences which will be hereafter discussed.

The illustrious Hastings, as I, who have enjoyed so much of his society and confidence, can well witness, was a man of the most engaging manners,—one that could not be known without being beloved. I can well fancy that this power of captivation was strong in him, even as a boy; and that a person of my father's dis-

* See Mr. Prior's minute and interesting Life of Goldsmith.

position and tastes, must have been strongly attracted towards him; I can also conceive that my father's penetration, of which he gave many striking proofs in his maturer age,* may have enabled him, even as a youth, to read the future high fortunes of Warren Hastings; or, at the least, to conjecture that a comrade so richly endowed with ingenuity, wit, industry, and energy, would not long be depressed by the heavy burdens of poverty and dependence, or remain hid in obscurity among common men; but what I cannot conjecture, or find any authority or ground for believing, is, that my more fortunately circumstanced father, with the character, disposition, and habits he possessed, should ever have made himself " a serviceable tool," † or how " we may safely venture to guess that, whenever Hastings wished to play any trick more than usually naughty, he hired Impey with a ball or a tart to act as a fag in the worst part of the prank."

The confession previously made by the writer of this flippant and illiberal passage, that he knew little about their schoolboy days, might have taught Mr. Macaulay more caution. Happily there are those still living, who, if not of their own knowledge, yet from authoritative record as well as tradition, can testify of the early friendship of Warren Hastings and my father, that it was founded upon honourable and noble principles; and of my father's character, that it was always frank and manly, incapable of being bribed by great things or by small, and abhorrent of trickery and meanness. Both he and Hastings were favourite scholars of Dr. Nicoll. Stimulated by the same generous emulation, they were friendly rivals in every boyish exercise, whether of play

---

* A good many years after his own return from India, and when he was well advanced in the vale of years, my father chancing to be upon some business at the East India House, in Leadenhall Street, saw and conversed with an engaging and energetic youth, who had just entered the Company's service, and was making the necessary arrangements for his passage to India. He saw little of him then, and never before or after that morning. "That active and intelligent boy," said he, " is sure to become a great man in India." The boy is now Lord Metcalfe.

† Mr. Macaulay, who puts what immediately follows as a *guess*, gives this as a direct assertion, saying,—" *The Chief Justice was Sir Elijah Impey. He was an old acquaintance of Hastings; and it is probable that the Governor General, if he had searched through all the Inns of Court, could not have found an equally seviceable tool.*"

or study.   They swam in the Thames, and rowed upon
it with each other; they played at cricket, and capped
verses together.   There might, doubtless, in some few
things, besides scholarship or school exercises, have
been a disparity in favour of Hastings; but there was
no dependence or base submission on either side.   Few
minds could, in any pursuit, have kept pace with
Warren Hastings.   My father appears to have been
once, at least, distanced by his competitor; for in 1747,
when they stood out for College, and were admitted as
King's Scholars, the name of Impey stood fourth upon
the list of which Hastings was the head : but they
were both monitors in the same election.   This, in the
palmy days of Westminster School, was considered
no trifling proof of scholarship in either.   It was
otherwise with my father; but Hastings's classical
studies terminated at Westminster; for his uncle died,
and the distant relation who took charge of his maintenance and education, having it in his power to obtain an
East India writership, instead of leaving him to proceed
to the University, removed him to a commercial school,
to acquire the necessary arts of arithmetic, and book-
keeping.   Besides Churchill, Colman the elder, Lloyd,
Cumberland, Cowper, whom Mr. Macaulay mentions
as contemporaries of Hastings, and consequently of
Impey, they had for their schoolfellows, Lords Stormont
and Shelburne, R. Sutton, afterwards Sir Richard,
Samuel Smith, afterwards Head Master and Prebendary of Westminster, and the two Bagots, Richard and
Walter (Richard changed his name to Howard, and
Walter became the Incumbent of Blithfield and Leigh,
in Staffordshire, and afterwards Precentor of St. Asaph).
Of the latter it is recorded, by his immediate descendants, who are among my most honoured friends,
that, late in life, being casually absent in London from
his benefice, he affectionately abstained from presenting himself at Hastings's trial, lest he should witness
the humiliation of his early friend ; nor have I ever
heard that he expressed greater delight at the persecution of Sir Elijah Impey.   Next to Hastings, many of
these distinguished men were my father's most intimate
friends ; and here again, and in every case, their friendship for him lasted through all the storms and maligni-

ties of life, and ended only in death. Would this have been the case if Sir Elijah Impey had been, as a school-boy, that which Mr. Macaulay represents him to have been? Has this brilliant and unhesitating writer, who has so neglected obvious sources of information, any unknown, and hitherto undiscoverable source from whence to produce facts subversive of this more than circumstantial evidence? He has none, and he cares for none. His object is not to investigate facts, but to write a stirring article. His constructive ingenuity is even more conspicuous than his rhetorical power. He knows the truth contained in the line of the most meditative and philosophic of our modern poets,—

" The child is father to the man."

He knows that the monster Zeluco begins his career of cruelty as a child, by twisting off the neck of a bird; and, as he starts with the pre-determination of making a judicial monster, a suborner, an ermined murtherer, of Sir Elijah Impey, he begins by describing him as a base bad boy at Westminster School. Before I take leave of Westminster, let me be allowed to make one more remark. Mr. Macaulay, in his most graceful manner, speaks of a friendship which Warren Hastings contracted with the poet Cowper; " *a friendship,*" he says, " *which neither the lapse of time, nor a wide dissimilarity of opinion and pursuits could wholly dissolve;*" but he abstains from mentioning that Elijah Impey was equally, or perhaps more, the friend of the poet. This omission may be considered as a trifle; it is, however, a thing of some significance; inasmuch as the whole prelude to Mr. Macaulay's laboured defamation is purposely made up of a few preliminary trifles, that they may with the greater plausibility be magnified into matter of very serious importance, by way of inference hereafter. The lamented Southey, in his life of Cowper, thought it no derogation to the subject of his biography, to include the name of Impey among the early associates of the amiable poet at Westminster School.

In January, 1750, Warren Hastings sailed for Calcutta. On the 28th December, 1751, Elijah Impey was admitted pensioner of Trinity College, Cambridge; having on

the preceding 8th December, entered as law student at
Lincoln's Inn.   His career was distinguished at the
University, as it had been at Westminster; each year
bringing with it some new academical honour.   In 1752,
he gained a scholarship; for he left school without being
elected to Cambridge; and he therefore earned both that
and the fellowship afterwards, by his own merit as an
independent member of the University.   In 1754, he
gained the college prize for a Latin declamation, of
which I possess a copy.   In 1756, in the Cambridge
Calendar, under the head of Tripos, the second name on
the column is "* Elijah Impey (B.), Col. Trinit."   The
marks designate that he was Fellow of a College, and
had obtained the junior Chancellor's medal, instituted
in 1752, and for which none were qualified to contend,
who had not previously won a mathematical prize.
In other words, Impey was a junior Wrangler, and
Chancellor's Medalist.   The large gold medal is among
the relics I preserve of my father.   The Chancellor at
the time was the Duke of Newcastle.   I possess also
some college exercises in Latin, which, if not otherwise
very remarkable, are stamped through and through with
a generous, frank, and manly feeling.   On the 3rd of
October, 1757, he became junior Fellow of Trinity
College; and, on the 4th of July, 1759, he was senior
Fellow.   The friendships he made during his residence
at Cambridge, were as lasting as the rest; and there
was this in my father's nature,—whether their fortunes
proved brilliant in the world, or otherwise, he always
clung tenderly to the associates of his early days.
Dishonour and vice might efface this kindly feeling,
but neither misfortune nor mere imprudence could
destroy it.   In the meantime (on the 23rd of November, 1756) he had been called to the bar.   There he
soon became associated with all the most eminent
or rising characters in the profession at that day:
with Thurlow, Kenyon, Heath, Mansfield,† Wallace,
and Dunning.   With the last-named of these distinguished men he contracted a close friendship, attested
by a long and intimate correspondence, which lasted

† Sir James, afterwards Solicitor and Attorney General, and lastly,
Chief Justice of the Common Pleas.

throughout the whole of his arduous career in India, and terminated only in the decease of his friend, in August, 1783, just nine months before his return to England. If the faithful and highly-gifted Dunning had but lived a few years longer, until the furor of impeachment set in, Sir Elijah Impey would not have been left, as he in a manner, was, " naked to his enemies." Few men had ever a larger share of religious resignation; yet was he often heard to lament that Dunning did not survive to welcome him back to his country, and to stand by him in the perilous hour of persecution.

In 1766-7, he made an extensive tour on the continent. His travelling companions were Alexander Popham* and John Dunning. At Naples he visited, with the deepest feeling of fraternal love, the grave of his brother James, who had been the instructor and guide of his boyhood. My father was not a correct artist, but I have now hanging before me a little drawing he made of his brother's last resting-place, which I value more as a proof of his affectionate nature, than I could do were it a masterpiece by the ablest hand.

When at Rome, my father, Dunning, and Popham, sat for their busks to Nollekens, who was then beginning his career as a sculptor. This bust of my father, in his thirty-fifth year, bears the same expression of frankness, gentleness, and kind-heartedness, not without a mixture of pleasantry, which exists in a portrait painted many years later, and which characterised his living countenance to the last.†

In such mixed society as he found time to frequent, his amiable disposition, and conversational talent,

---

* Alexander Popham was elected Fellow of All Souls, Oxford, in 1750, and was afterwards made Master in Chancery. He was a near relation of Major Popham who distinguished himself in Sir Eyre Coote's campaign, against Hyder Ali, in 1780.

† Whilst on the subject of pictures, it may not be amiss to notice, that the frontispiece to this volume is engraved from an original, painted by Kettle, in 1776, being a duplicate of one which now hangs in the Court House, at Calcutta. There is another, in the attitude of speaking, in some other public building. The former was presented to Sir R. Sutton, in return for Sir Richard's likeness by Sir Joshua Reynolds, which my father took to India, with two others,—one of Lord Shelburne, by Gainsborough, still in our family; the other, of Dunning, by Sir Joshua, and now in the possession of Mr. Baring. The portraits of Sir R. Sutton, and Sir Elijah Impey, were afterwards interchanged by their widows.

made him a great favourite. Dunning, it is well known, was a rich humourist, and Sutton and his friends were either witty themselves, or content to be " the cause of wit in others." Not long ago, a lady* who lived to a very advanced age, and who had a memory very retentive of the circumstances of her youth, used to relate, how, in large London parties, she and some young friends of congenial taste, would quit the ball-room, to gather round the card-table where Dunning, Impey, Sutton, and Popham, were playing at whist, and making puns faster than points in the game. "The table of those facetious lawyers," she said, " was the centre of attraction to all who relished an intellectual treat."

On the 18th of January, 1768, in the thirty-sixth year of his age, my father was married to Mary, a daughter of Sir John Reade, Baronet, of Shipton Court, Oxfordshire. For some time after his marriage, he resided in a very quiet manner, at a house in Essex Street, Strand; living sparingly, and working very hard, as became a barrister who had to make his way without patronage or extraneous support. I have often heard my dear mother say that this was by far the happiest period of their lives. An increasing family was a stimulus to exertion; and his warm affections rendered toil easy. In all the cares, crosses, and vexa-tions, attendant on an always harassing profession, he was never known to lose his sweetness and cheerful-ness of temper. At the bar, and on the Western Circuit, though he had to contend with many a for-midable rival, he was considered, as a pleader, second to none but Dunning. In those days, which are made to appear more remote than they really are, by the rapid improvement of material objects (though it may be doubted whether there has yet been an equal improvement in things more intellectual), when there were no railways, and the posting roads were worse than the poorest cross-country lane now is, it was the custom of most barristers who went the circuit, to ride from one assize town to another on horseback. My father was fond of horsemanship, and had a fa-vourite nag, which would come at his call, and follow

* The late Dowager Lady Sutton; the second wife and widow of Sir Richard.

him about like a dog. By going year after year to the same places, this horse was as well known on the circuit as his rider. Only a short time ago, some old people in the west of England, remembered how lawyer Impey's horse would follow him into the town, and even walk after him into the inn where some of the great lawyers would be sitting, with a solemnity ludicrously contrasted with the freedom of so extraordinary an intruder. If I mention these trifles, it is simply because they help to throw light upon the genial character of my beloved parent. And, surely, when the assailant of my father's fame preludes his atttack with the romance of a fictitious " *ball or tart*," I may be allowed to speak of a real, not an imaginary creature, whose generous nature could have been so tamed only by patience and gentleness. But, to be more serious, let me remind the right honourable gentleman, that it is the " *merciful man* " who is proverbially " merciful to his beast."

Having distinguished himself in a difficult cause,[*] business began to flow in apace; and of that more profitable kind which is reserved only for the fortunate few. My father was a barrister of seventeen years standing, and in good practice, when, in the year 1773, he was thought worthy of filling the new and important post of Chief Justice of Fort William, Calcutta. His recommendation to this office

[*] The circumstances of the trial alluded to are now but faintly remembered; thus far, however, I have been fortunate enough to ascertain. The cause of action was an assault of a very aggravated nature,—" Head *versus* Mullins and others," tried before Chief Justice Willes, at the Exeter Assizes in 1769. My father, as counsel for plaintiff, was opposed by no less an adversary than the great John Dunning. The defendants, therefore, made sure of their acquittal; for Dunning, as usual, had involved the cause with subtleties so ingenious, as nearly to have secured a verdict for his clients; when one of his witnesses broke down under the cross-examination, or examination, in chief by his opponent. The exact point at issue I have been unable to ascertain; but the fact, with these few particulars, of Mullins's sentence to fine and imprisonment, I gathered by personal inquiry in August, 1844, from the late plaintiff's daughter, Mrs. Mary Ann Head; at that time a very old inhabitant of Seaton, near Colyton, which last place had been the scene of the assault. Mrs. Head died only the year after my interview with her; but there are those still living in and about that neighbourhood, who can testify not only this event, but also my father's general reputation on the western circuit.

proceeded from the Lord Chancellor, Henry Bathurst Baron Apsley, who, in the course of the next year, succeeded his father in the title of Earl of Bathurst. But my father, who had previously argued before committees of both Houses of Parliament, had also attracted the notice and esteem of Lord North, the premier, and of Lord Shelburne, afterwards first Marquess of Lansdowne, one of the two Secretaries of State. His appointment was made out by Lord Shelburne, who had the department of the colonies, &c.; and to that nobleman Sir Elijah Impey was accustomed to look up as to a friend.

Seeing the career that lay open to him in England, and dreading for him the effects of the burning and enervating climate of Bengal (at that time a much greater object of dread than it now is), many of his friends either advised him not to accept the offer, or thought that he acted unwisely in accepting it; but, on the other hand, it was difficult to refuse what was so honourably offered. His family was already numerous; his private patrimony not large; his friend and school-fellow, Hastings, was at the very head of affairs in India; and his own mind, as I have already hinted, had been turned at an early period towards the glowing East. He therefore accepted that appointment, which has made his name and character a part of the history of our Indian Empire. But in taking this hazardous step, it must ever be regretted that Sir Elijah seems not sufficiently to have reflected upon the danger which, especially at that time, attended a man who took upon himself such a novel, difficult, and responsible situation, without the support of any political party at home; for, at that period, when Cabinet Ministers were so miserably divided among themselves, it was hardly to be expected that any minister or premier would stand forward in fair defence of any servant of Government, even though appointed by himself; nor could the first Chief Justice of India have been at that time aware of the violent factions about to break out in Calcutta, so soon as the three newly-appointed members of council who were to accompany him, should arrive with an ill-defined authority which must necessarily conflict with that of the new Governor General of India. True, indeed, it is, that much of this knowledge was not to be acquired otherwise than by painful experience in watching the operation of the Regulating Act in the country to which it was applied. All preceding legislation had been vague, unstable, and contradictory. The recent enactment, which was to regulate everything, in its very first application threw all things into worse disorder than before: and even after three explanatory acts had been passed, during my father's residence in India, to modify and alter what was otherwise unintelligible, the said amended Act remained a very defective piece of legislation after all; an opprobrium to Government, a puzzle to lawyers and statesmen both at home and abroad; and, though an inexplicable riddle to all men besides, yet a sure weapon in the grasp of a tyrannical faction hereafter. Meanwhile it was by turns a nullity, or a bewildering and cruel embarassment to every responsible servant, whether of the Supreme Court established by Government, or of the East India Company, who acted under it in the Indian presidencies. But the die was cast: my father prepared for his voyage to India; all his fortunes were embarked in that crazy ark, and all his prospects of professional advancement in England wrecked and ruined for ever. Years after his return from the East, as he was passing one day through the Court of King's Bench, Chief Justice Kenyon, who was then presiding, said to him, "Ah, Impey! had you stayed at home, you might now have been seated here."* Such were the convictions of all the friends who best knew him, and who were most capable of estimating his personal accomplishments and professional qualifications.

Now, confining myself to a view of the less remarkable portion of his history up to this period, I think it may "*safely*" be left to the decision of any honest and unprejudiced man, whether there is anything in the early life of Sir Elijah Impey to justify the insinuation of Mr. Macaulay, that, from his youth upward, Sir Elijah was a mean and vicious character. I trust I have, on the contrary, shown that, as a boy, he was high-spirited,

---

* For this anecdote I am indebted to the late eminent barrister, Mr. Adolphus, who heard this honourable testimony pronounced in open court.

amiable, and industrious; that, as a youth, he was an
accomplished scholar; that, as a man, he had earned
among his contemporaries the reputation of a learned,
able, and eloquent lawyer.   May it not, then, be safely
assumed from all these combinations, that the new
Chief Justice entered upon his arduous duties in
India with a character for virtue and wisdom fairly entitled to the respect of all good men?   But without
this logical inference, I know and can prove, what is in
fact matter of notoriety to many who are yet living,
that he did enter upon office with the full enjoyment of
that respect which nothing he did in office ever made
him forfeit; and that after his recall from Calcutta, and
after the defamatory processes which were carried to
such a length against him, he both retained the esteem
of all who had previously known him, and formed
many new friendships with others who were themselves
both good and able men, and somewhat better qualified
to judge of his judicial character and general conduct
than Mr. Macaulay, who never knew, nor could have
known him, being not much beyond the precincts
of the nursery when Sir Elijah died: not but that
something more might have been expected from a late
English barrister, who afterwards, for several years,
had held the appointment of Law Commissioner in
India!   But it is plain that the right honourable gentleman has never taken the trouble to inform himself
of the facts connected with my father's legal administration, nor even of the nature and bearings of the
statutes under which he acted; all which he might
have done, while at Calcutta, from records preserved on
the very spot.

And here, although I anticipate what must be said
on a future occasion, I shall quote my father's own
words from the speech he delivered in his defence at
the bar of the House of Commons, on the 4th of
February, 1788; that defence which was utterly unknown, or has been deliberately suppressed by his
calumniator.

   " It is hardly conceivable," said my father at the Commons' bar, " that any man whose constant habits of life have
been known to be such as mine have been—and there are not
wanting members in this house who know both how, and with

whom, the earlier part of my life, down to the time I quitted this country, had been spent,—that I—a man I will assume to say, who left this country with a character unimpeachable, who maintained that character till May, 1775, should, in the course of the next month, have been so totally lost to every sense of shame, every principle of justice, every duty of office, every feeling of humanity, to have been at once so deeply immersed and hardened in iniquity, as to be able deliberately to plan, and steadily to perpetrate, an outrage with all the circumstances with which it is charged and aggravated. *Nemo repente fuit turpissimus.*"

The assailants of my father's fame hold as the key of their position, that he was greedy after money, and had all the meanness of character attendant on that sordid passion. With my hand upon my heart, or upon the Evangelists, in the awful solemnity of an oath, I can declare that, in my long intercourse with the world, I have never known a more generous man, or one less animated by the love of lucre. As well in the prime of life, as afterwards in his old age, he carried his liberality to an excess which at times amounted to imprudence. I cannot for a moment suspect that, in making these statements, I am misled by any filial partiality. The facts which are vividly impressed on my memory, and the private documents that lie before me, do more than bear me out in what I have said on this point. I find his heart and hand always open to the appeals of distress and misfortune; I find him paying debts to a large amount for which he was not liable by law or in equity, but which he paid out of a delicate sense of honour, and a regard to the ties of blood which connected him with the deceased debtor: and this I find him doing at a time when his fortune was diminished by a most unfortunate investment of capital. In fact to do this deed he was compelled to sell out of the English Stocks, and to reduce his domestic expenditure; which last circumstance he regretted only inasmuch as it might curtail the enjoyments of his wife and children. Simple and unexpensive in his own habits, and finding his chief pleasure in his books and garden, a small annual sum would have been enough for *him.*

Touching his liberality and kindness to his family, and his generosity to those who were dependent on

c

him, my recollections are likewise aided by documentary
evidence, and that, too, of a nature which goes to establish far more than I will endeavour to express, or venture to obtrude upon public notice. The domestics who
once entered his service generally remained in it until
they died, or until his death gave them their discharge,
together with some substantial token of his good will.
He treated them all as humble friends; solacing them
in their sickness, and not unfrequently causing some
of his children to preside over their little feasts and
periodical pastimes.* These are topics too trivial to be
dwelt upon; yet, as tending to an object of serious
inquiry, they will not surely be considered as altogether
uninteresting, or unworthy of this cursory notice.

Before the Chief Justice quitted England for the
East, he carefully drew up a set of instructions for the
nurture and education of the young family he was
about to leave behind him. The minuteness of these
instructions manifests a degree of attention and tenderness rare even in a good father. I have before me
no less than four draughts of these instructions, so
carefully corrected and transcribed, as to convince me
that more pains were bestowed upon them than on any
other paper, of whatever consequence, in my possession. The guardian appointed for these infants was
his brother, Michael Impey, who continued to reside
at Hammersmith, and who was repaid with no stinted
gratitude for the zeal and affection with which he
undertook and executed the difficult and delicate
charge. During Sir Elijah's long residence in India,
where several other children were born to him, a
very considerable part of a correspondence with his
relatives and friends at home was given to the subject of the education of the children left in England.
There everywhere appears in these letters an earnest
desire, a most tender anxiety, that his infants should

* When living, in the decline of life, in Sussex, he was a great advocate
for the maintenance of the ancient festival of Harvest Home; and often
amused himself, and delighted his domestics and tenants, by writing verses
to be said or sung at their harvest supper. One of these little *jeux d'esprit*
was set to music by the late well known natural philosopher, Tiberius
Cavallo, a frequent visitor at Newick Park, and is affectionately preserved
by Sir Elijah's only surviving daughter.

be diligently trained in religion and morality. This consideration is always made paramount to that of their acquiring the habits and accomplishments of mere scholarship or gentility. Although few men had a greater respect for learning, and all the higher mental graces and acquirements of cultivated society, he considered them as dross when placed in comparison with those of a moral and religious life. When the children could read and write, he corresponded directly with them, mingling his fatherly admonitions with the pleasantry of a playmate. In this way, he could always trace back his steps to the scenes of his own ardent youth, and be once more the brave Westminster boy, or earnest Trinity scholar; and to this I may likewise attribute part of the entire confidence and affection, in which we ever lived together. These letters from India to his children, could have little interest for any other party, and were worth preserving only as family relics; many of them have been scattered and lost, but I have still a good number among my papers. Nor are they the things in this world which I least value. Playful and joyous, and encouraging as they are, they were written for the most part when his health was seriously affected by the debilitating climate of Bengal; when his mind was harassed by official duties, and contentions altogether alien to his nature, and when he was oppressed by a multiplicity of conflicting cares.

CHAPTER II.

HAVING received the honour of knighthood from his Majesty George III., and leaving his children in England, Sir Elijah, with his wife, sailed for India on board the " Anson," in the early part of April, 1774.

Perhaps I cannot better fill up the interval occupied by the voyage, than with a few notes—without however pretending to any complete particulars—I. Upon the political history of the time: II. Upon preceding events in India, and preceding measures concerted in England for the government of that country: and III. Upon the Regulating Act; which, in practical efficacy, turned out to be so lamentably deficient.

I. In 1773, when Sir Elijah was nominated to his Indian judgeship, the administration of Lord North was weak, and though certainly not as yet unpopular with the great body of the nation, it was assailed by an opposition more formidable in talent, and more united in purpose, than any that had been known for many generations. The prosecutions of John Wilkes, his ejection from the House of Commons, and all the well-known storms of the Middlesex election, had discredited and weakened Government. The citizens of London, or at least the bodies corporate, were inflamed by the wealthy and influential Alderman Beckford, who played into the hands of his friend, the discontented and morti-fied, and almost disaffected Earl of Chatham. . Of Wilkes they both made use as of a sharp cutting instrument of offence. Party spirit was perhaps never more violent than at this period; or from 1768 to 1782, when Lord North was driven from his helm, and Sir Elijah Impey recalled from his tribunal in Bengal. I imagine it will be now admitted by all impartial men, that grievous faults and errors had been committed, as well on the part of Government, as on that of Opposition; and that Lord North, though a thoroughly amiable and right-hearted man, an honest statesman himself, and a friend to the liberties and constitution of his country, was occasionally led by his friends, or driven by his foes, to measures which had a tendency to despotism. But what perhaps most injured his ministerial character was a want of steadiness of principle in some of his colleagues.

When Wilkes had acted as a thorn in the side of this ministry for years, and had, in effect, triumphed over it, gaining by its unwise persecution a weight and influence which he could not otherwise have obtained; and when this Government, full of internal heat and irritation, if not scorched by the flames, had been blackened by the smoke of civic conflagration, then commenced those troubles in our American colonies which ended only in their alienation from the British crown. At the time my father took his departure, and indeed during the whole period of his residence in the East, ministers were so occupied with this gloomy aspect of affairs in the West, that it was only by short and un-certain snatches that they could devote any attention to our Eastern Empire. Hence it arose that Sir Elijah Impey, in common with many other men holding re-sponsible situations, was left for years without any con-sistent set of instructions from home; nay, even without a single answer to his numerous and most earnest re-monstrances, and petitions for advice. It is not for me to enter upon the still vexed question whether the war of American independence might have been warded off by concession and conciliation, or by a course of conduct the opposite to that pursued by Lord North. It seems, however, at this day, to be a very general impression among well-informed and thinking men, that no line of policy whatever, on the part of any British government, could long have delayed the American crisis, or the attempt of the colonists to secure a separate and independent national existence. It has been but too common to attribute the war which ensued, to the pride, love of dominion, and self-willedness of George III. (whose historical character is improved almost year by year by some new light thrown upon it, by the publication of memoirs and documents), and to the mean submission of Lord North to the will of his royal master. But the most obvious of truths is, that the American war, not only at its commencement, but for a long time after, was exceedingly popular. The many provocations which preceded those riots, and then the assaults and humiliating insults committed at Boston, inflicted a wound upon English pride, which the English people were unable to bear without having recourse to the arbitrement of arms. No ministry could have stood which should have attempted to resist this national feeling; and so bitter was the hatred borne to the revolutionists and republicans of the western world, that, from the beginning of this war, the popularity of the King began gradually to increase. The people of England became loyal in proportion as the Americans waxed republicans and federalists. Nor did the flagrant mismanagement, and eventual ill-success of this protracted struggle abate one jot of the English feeling; they drove Lord North from power, but they did not affect the regard and respect in which his sovereign was held by the vast majority of the nation.

An attentive perusal of the parliamentary debates, and a study of the history of party at that time, will prove, that our miserable failure in the American war was not entirely owing to Lord North and his incompetent colleagues. The opposition, who started by predicting that all our efforts would terminate in defeat and failure, contributed, in a prodigious degree, to the working out of their own prophecy. They thwarted ministers at every step; they censured or ridiculed their conduct of the war, even when it was spirited and right; they never lost an opportunity of extolling the valour of the republicans, and depreciating the conduct of the King's troops: they turned nearly every American burgher, that took the command of an undisciplined mob, into a hero or great general; and they treated nearly every general of the King, if not as a coward, as a fool: before the Americans had gained a single advantage in the field (a battle they never gained during the whole war) they proclaimed them to be unconquerable, and after the capitulation of General Burgoyne, they set no limits to the expression of their affected despair. Gradually all this, which was enunciated by rare eloquence, told upon the country, and upon the servants of Government both military and civil: officers took their departure for America being disheartened beforehand; ministers, being harassed in all their plans, at last hardly knew what plan to adopt, and became so bewildered, that at last they let the war run on without any plan at all.

When, during the American war, and at the moment in which the embarrassments and difficulties it created, were at the highest, this same formidable opposition began to take up the subject of India—when Mr. Hastings, with an exhausted treasury, and nearly every other circumstance of discouragement, was contending against the power of France, and a combination of native powers, —the King was exceedingly alarmed. I am informed by a friend who derived his intelligence from a near source, that George III. said at this trying crisis,— "These gentlemen have been doing their best to make us lose America, and now they will go on to make us lose India!"

It was during these hot debates on American affairs, that Mr. Burke began first to distinguish himself, and to display that enthusiasm, which, even his warmest friends and admirers will allow, he occasionally suffered to transport him beyond the limits of justice, common-sense, and propriety. Amid these violent political contentions in parliament, the *press* was not idle. An activity was *there* excited, which it had never known before. *There* the newspapers, pamphlets, and other publications of the day, carried on a war of argument, wit, ribaldry, and invective, in support of their respective parties; *there*, as in later times, declamation and rhetoric were often substituted for reasoning, while it was most rare that any scrupulous attention was paid to sober facts. By far the ablest pens were those dipped in Opposition ink.

Even numerically, the writers of this party exceeded those of the ministerialists; for men out of office have more time for writing and printing than men trammelled with official business. Attack is more pleasant and excitable, and, at the same time, much more easy than defence; and it seems to be the natural instinct of literary men, to look up rather to an untried opposition, than to a tried administration. The most considerable of all these writers was Junius; whose letters in the *Public Advertiser* excited general notice, striking the Ministry, at the same time, with astonishment at the unwonted audacity of their attacks. That they continue even now to be an object of some interest, is, I conceive, almost entirely owing to the mystery of their authorship, and to the frequent disputations which have been held thereupon; although, since the year 1824, that question ought ‑ 14 to have been set at rest by Mr. Taylor's laborious and ingenious volume.

After venting his acrimony against the ministers, and other leading men of the time, Junius levelled a shaft at Majesty itself. This outrage, which appeared in the *Public Advertiser* of December the 19th, 1769, gave rise to the prosecution, by the Attorney General, of Woodfall, the printer and publisher of that newspaper. On the 13th of June, 1770,* within four months after Lord North had become First Lord of the Treasury, on the resignation of the Duke of Grafton,† who was said to have been driven from the premiership by the heavy and venomous scourge of this anonymous writer, the trial took place before the great Lord Mansfield; who, in his charge, instructed the jury that all they had to decide was the fact of publication. The jury, presuming to dispute the legality of this direction, found the defendant guilty of printing and publishing only, which verdict annulled the prosecution, and virtually amounted to an acquittal. Encouraged by this, Junius presumed to attack the Lord Chief Justice, on

---

* See " Howell's State Trials."

† His Grace resigned on the 28th of January, 1770, Woodfall's trial came on June 13th following. It is remarkable, *but not surprising*, that there is no mention of the *trial* in the " Annual Register " for the year, while the date of the *resignation* is there very circumstantially recorded.

what he called his new principle of English law.* At the same time, many able men at the bar supported the learned Judge both in his doctrine, and its applications; thus, as a matter of course, making themselves objects of the malice and unextinguishable hatred of Junius. For the space of nearly two more years, Junius went on most remorselessly assailing a number of eminent characters; accusing some of them of heinous personal, as well as political vices, of which it is notorious that they were innocent, and emptying the vials of his wrath upon all the measures of Government. But suddenly, towards the close of 1772, to the wonder of some, and the relief of many, his signature disappeared altogether from the pages of the press. A very short time after this, Mr. (subsequently Sir Philip) Francis, whom I as firmly believe to have been the author of the letters of Junius, as I believe him to have been the first, the most persevering, and the cruellest of my father's enemies, received from Lord North, or at least from Lord North's government, his splendid appointment as member of the Supreme Council of Calcutta, with a salary which amounted to just ten thousand pounds per annum. He had never before held any place under Government except that of a clerk in the War Office, with a salary of two or three hundred pounds. He had no family support, no political connection, no sudden accession of personal importance, except what he may have gained as a pamphleteer, and as the author of the bitterest political satires that had ever before appeared in the newspapers, to account for this sudden and extraordinary rise.† In the same fleet which carried out Sir Elijah Impey, was Mr. Philip Francis, and the two other

---

* It is well known how directly Lord Mansfield was opposed to all those popular contentions, in which Alderman Wilkes, Oliver, and Crosby, encouraged by their parliamentary patron, Lord Temple, and their legal adviser, Pratt (Lord Camden), took so mischievous a part. But it is not so generally known, that my father bore an ample share, with the great Lord Chief Justice, in the obloquy cast upon him by Junius, *though not in his letters;* or that, in Lord George Gordon's riots, the house at Hammersmith, as connected with his name, was threatened with attack, but bravely defended by his brother, in 1780.

† Francis was acquainted with Burke before leaving England; and during his residence in India, he maintained an active correspondence with Burke's cousin. This will be more particularly alluded to in a future chapter.

members of the newly-created council; they all arrived at Calcutta together, and entered upon their duties at the same time. The two colleagues of Francis, were both men of high and old standing in the world; allied to rank, and with those political connections, without which it was most rare, in those days, for any man to attain to eminent employment in the State. But of General Clavering, and Colonel Monson, more will be said in the next chapter.

Unhappily, in the eye of the world, there is too close a connection between my father's public character, and the character and performances of that great professor and teacher of defamation, the author of the letters of Junius, whose school became so extensive. A few more words, therefore, on the writings of Junius, the tone of the political press, and the spirit of party which disgraced those times, may not be considered out of place.

The public and parliamentary language of the time (from 1760 to 1788), was gross, and contemptuous of all authority. Junius had set the example by insulting not only the throne, but the private habits and personal feelings of all classes. If the King was not too high, the obscurest magistrate was not too low for his attack. Junius was the anonymous writer who first assailed all men under their own names; he was the subtle assassin who dropped poison into the cup of not only every public man but of every private individual whom he thought it expedient to injure or destroy. In some cases the poison was administered to his direct personal enemies; but much more frequently it was mixed, and given solely for the purpose of working out a political end, or for the mere oratorical object of producing a startling effect upon the world. In the majority of cases, there was not even the bad excuse of vehement feeling or private passion : he poisoned without hatred or any acquaintance with his victim; he murdered in cold blood. The ability of the writer, though for a long time extravagantly overrated, is indisputable; but its abuses deprive it of all the higher admiration due to the exercise of talents honestly employed in an honest cause. The remorseless and malignant venom of this political serpent, annuls all our praise of its force and beauty. While the school of Junius continued to be the model of English political writing, declamation kept the place of fact, and satire that of research ; the reason was not convinced, but the passions were inflamed ; for what was written in cold blood, was read by the unthinking multitude with fury : a ceaseless perversive war was carried on; festering and enfeebling the public sense of truth, justice, and honour. These dialectics are only in part exploded. Unhappily, the school still exists, and Junius is still the favourite model of too many of our anonymous writers, whether they figure in *Edinburgh Reviews* or *Weekly Despatches.*

It was also during the stormy and exciting period now under consideration, that the practice of reporting fully the speeches and proceedings of Parliament in newspapers, was for the first time admitted ; after the struggle made by the Parliament for privileges, and many strange scenes which tended to raise the popularity of Mr. Wilkes and his friends, and to throw more and more disfavour upon Government and its adherents. Previously to this internal revolution, Parliament pretended to the property or custody of whatsoever was said within its walls, holding it a breach of privilege in any person to print the speeches of its members; and such reports of Parliamentary debates as appeared, were under fictitious names, and generally placed in some remote or imaginary country. Doctor Samuel Johnson, in the earlier part of his literary career, furnished monthly, to the *Gentleman's Magazine,* an article entitled "The Senate of Lilliput." Herein was typified the British Parliament, the speaking members of which figured sometimes with feigned denominations, and sometimes with anagrams of their real names. Johnson drew up these speeches and debates, from scanty notes furnished by persons employed to attend in both Houses; but he told Boswell that sometimes, however, he had nothing more communicated to him than the names of the several speakers, and the parts which they had taken in the debate. " Parliament," says Boswell, " then kept the press in a kind of mysterious awe, which made it necessary to have recourse to such devices." About the year 1770, the proceedings in the House of Commons in the case of John Wilkes, the letters of Junius, the interest felt about the Falkland Islands question, and about the rapid march of federalism in America, the growing curiosity of the people, with the efforts made by the legislation to repress it, all contributed to make the public earnestly long for a full reporting newspaper, and encouraged the printers to venture upon giving the proceedings of Parliament from week to week, or from day to day, instead of giving them, as heretofore, as mere matters of chronicle at the end of the month. On the 5th of February, 1771, Colonel George Onslow, one of the Lords of the Treasury, denounced these proceedings, and moved the reading of the resolutions of the 26th of February, 1728 : "That it is an indignity to, and a breach of privilege of this House, for any person to presume to give in written or printed newspapers any account or minutes of debate, or other proceedings of this House, or any part thereof; and that, upon discovery of the authors, printers, or publishers of any such written or printed newspaper, this House will proceed against the offenders with the utmost severity."

In the debate which immediately followed upon this question, Colonel Onslow was supported by a majority of 90 against 55, and two printers* were called to the bar of the House; who, when committed to the Serjeant-at-Arms, for infringing the standing order, &c., like several others of their fraternity, grew refractory ; and being supported by their popular leaders in the City, finally triumphed over the authority of Parliament, as well as that of the courts of law.

This was the proximate cause of all those memorable civic contentions; involving a long train of events, too well known, and too ably and copiously detailed in a late historical work, to require any recapitulation in this.† It appears to me sufficient, in alluding to those transactions, wherein Mr. Wilkes and his colleagues took so prominent a part, and wherein his subordinates, the proprietors and printers of the *North Briton*, and of the *Daily Advertiser*, gained so signal a victory, if I simply establish a fact, very essentially, though but

---

* Thompson and Wheble.

† See Mr. Mc Farlane's full and candid account of the " Civil Transactions " of this period, in the " Pictorial History of England," published by Charles Knight and Co., London, 8vo., 1843.

collaterally, connected with the right understanding of my subject, always bearing in mind the immense influence of the press, for good or for evil, over the fame and fortune of public men.

This was the era when it was first and most decidedly fixed ; nor would it be easy to name any other period than that between the years 1773 and 1788, in which that predominating influence ever more directly tended to exasperate the spirit of the times, or in a greater measure subserved to the purposes of political faction. But a newly acquired liberty is mostly liable to abuse; and the feeling of triumph is inconsistent with calm discretion. After this victory over a weak government, the press became more virulent than it had previously been ; the imitators of Junius took the field, superseding, by a wholesale monopoly of scandal, all the chronicles of their day, and attacking, not by *anagrams,* but *by name,* every character, whether high or low, personal or official : in short, liberty ran into licentiousness; and thus a school for political writing was established, which consigned to the tender mercies of any prevailing faction, the reputation of all men, as they were more or less inclined to one or other party. Had this state of things remained stationary, it might have been well ; for, hitherto, the principle at least tended to the public good, and the wrong occasionally done to individuals, might be said to be balanced by the benefit bestowed on the many. Some notorious delinquents were justly held up to shame and reprobation; and if here and there a more venial offender was too roughly handled, and the character of a perfectly innocent man misrepresented, the one would probably become more circumspect in future, and the other have the chance of justifying himself by an open defence. But, when the actions of men, good or bad, came to be estimated by an uncompromising spirit of party; when able and spirited writers, and eloquent parliamentary orators, laid it down as their maxim, that nothing could be right but what was in conformity with their measures, and that no respect was due to the character of a political opponent ; then came a state of society so repugnant to justice and morality, that no arguments of public expediency can possibly atone for it.

Such was the state of things in England, as well at the time when Sir Elijah Impey received his Indian appointment, as during his long absence from this country; and such it continued to be many years after his return. This spirit of political prejudice fell with reckless vengeance on other men connected with India; who, whatever their errors might have been—for who is without error ?—had yet deserved better treatment of their country, than to be sacrificed to the fury of her demagogues and partizans.

I have freely admitted that the ablest pens were employed on the side of the opposition. Through the negligence of Lord North, through the harassing and incessant occupation given to him by the American war, and through various other circumstances, this formidable party, some years before the period of Sir Elijah Impey's recall, had acquired almost an entire controul of the press,—by which I understand not only the newspaper press, but also that employed in the production of pamphlets and books.

Long before this period, viz., in 1759, came out the first volume of the *Annual Register*, of which Mr. Burke wrote the historical part. It very soon obtained the extensive notice and circulation to which its literary merits entitled it. The *Register* was an immeasurable improvement upon any work of that kind which had previously been attempted ; nor is it too much to say that, so long as the illustrious Burke was connected with its publication, it maintained a decided superiority over every other work of a similar description. For many years that gentleman continued to write the historical part ; and afterwards, when prevented by parliamentary business from wielding his own pen, he deputed either Dr. Lawrence, or some other political friend, who not only took his tone, but also much of his information from the original great contributor ; himself superintending the whole. I need not refer to earlier portions of that periodical work ; but can confidently affirm, that, from the time when my father went to India, down to his appearance at the bar of the Commons, the historical portions of the *Annual Register* are pervaded throughout by the manner, thought, feeling, and passions of Edmund Burke. Great and grievous as were the wrongs he was led to inflict upon him to whom I owe my birth, and all that makes life valuable, I class myself among this great man's literary admirers; I bow to his transcendent genius; I revere much of his political philosophy, his honesty of purpose, his energy of mind; I look upon him, in short, as one proudly pre-eminent above all his political contemporaries; as one who was as little spoiled at heart by the prejudices of faction, and the demoralizing influences of public life, as any merely mortal man could have been in those times. I would no more defame the writer of the " Reflections on the French Revolution," than I would asperse my own father. I believe Mr. Burke to have been utterly incapable of saying and writing that which he really and positively knew to be untrue : but, when any relation of events accorded with a pre-conceived notion of his own, I believe him to have been impetuous in seizing that relation, and easy in being duped by almost any artful, ingenious, and persevering man : and such a man was Philip Francis, and such were several others who filled his ears with Indian stories, even before he became intimately acquainted with the author of the letters of Junius.

Burke being once convinced of the truth of any statement, however false, was always most difficult to be reclaimed : his conviction became ever after a passion and a principle. He had taken up, at an early period, the history of Lord Clive's conquests, and the woes of the native Indian population; and he never, to the end of his days, could cease to think of these things without the fervour and enthusiasm of youth. While writing or superintending the historical department of the *Annual Register*, every striking account, real or fictitious, of wrongs committed there, was sure to find his ear open to receive it, and his mind not disposed to any severe inquiry into the authenticity of the tale. The enemies of Mr. Hastings, and of my father, knew all this, and took advantage of it to lay that substratum for their secret calumny, which was formerly recommended by one great professor of that art, and which has been more recently adopted by *another*. " La calomnie ! monsieur," says the noted Don Basile, in Beaumarchais' famous comedy,—

" La calomnie ! monsieur, vous ne savez guère ce que vous dédaignez ; j'ai vu les plus honnêtes gens près d'en être accablés. Croyez qu'il n'y a pas de plate méchanceté, pas d'horreurs, pas de conte absurde, qu'on ne fasse adopter aux oisifs d'une grande ville en s'y prenant bien : et nous avons ici des gens d'une adresse ! . . . . D'abord un bruit léger, rasant le sol comme hirondelle avant l'orage, *pianissimo* murmure et file, et sème en courant le trait empoisonné. Telle bouche le recueille, et *piano, piano,* vous le glisse en l'oreille adroìtement. Le mal est fait, il germe, il rampe, il chemine, et *rinforzando* de bouche en bouche, il va le diable ; puis tout à coup, ne sais comment, vous voyez la calomnie se dresser, siffler, s'enfler, grandir à vue d'œil. Elle s'élance, etend son vol, tourbillonne, enveloppe, arrache, entraîne, éclate et tonne, et devient, grace au ciel, un cri général, un *crescendo* public, un chorus universel de haine et proscription. Qui diable y résisterait ? "

In each *Annual Register* that appeared for several years before the party were prepared to begin their impeachments in Parliament, there was some *bruit léger,* some whisper more or less loud, some hint more or less broad, that matters were shamefully managed in Bengal ; that Hastings was acting as a tyrant, and the Chief Justice as his tool. These indistinct murmurs met with no reply ; there was scarcely a possibility of re-plying to them : and to the parties most interested, that is, to Warren Hastings and to Sir Elijah Impey, (the one upheld by the conviction that, at that very epoch, he was saving, or had saved, British India, and the other by the consciousness of his innocence and activity in the same cause), they seemed of little moment ; yet these murmurs were widely spread, and eagerly listened to ; preparing the public mind for the reception of those grosser calumnies which followed. Then, after a long interval, came Francis's Book of " Travels in Asia, &c.," of which, as well as of other matters connected with the adverse influence of the press upon my father's fame, more will be said hereafter.

While the long trial of Mr. Hastings lasted, few took the trouble of reading anything that was written on the other side : the general impression or conviction was made and kept up exclusively by those eloquent and ex-citing speeches, those tremendous and overwhelming charges which came flashing and thundering from the House of Commons, to be re-echoed and re-kindled in

Westminster Hall. If, afterwards, the memory of the hearer or reader failed him as to some particulars during this interminable process, he refreshed it simply by referring to the *Annual Register,* which book, as I have said, was under the controul of Mr. Burke, and the repertory of his vehement feelings.

When that great storm blew over, and the trial and impeachment of Mr. Hastings, together with the defeated attempt to impeach Sir Elijah Impey, became matter of history, still those facts were most rarely, if ever, studied in any other work than the said convenient and compendious *Register.* Even now, at the distance of more than half-a-century, the same accessible and easy source is almost singly resorted to by the dull compiler who fabricates a history, and the vivacious and pains-sparing scribbler who furnishes an article for a *Review.*

Thus, every account of the transactions in which Sir Elijah Impey was concerned, rests upon mere ex-parte evidence, and originated in narratives inflamed with party spirit : and thus it is, that even in this, which is called a reading age, motives the very reverse of those which actuated the conduct of Sir Elijah Impey, are still attempted to be imposed upon the public. Upon no better materials than these have histories been compiled, and articles composed. But, if I mistake not in believing that a very general disgust,—a stern and moral odium,— still attaches to such performances, the attempt will fail.

Insignis est temeritas cum aut falsa, aut incognita res approbatur. Nec hôc quicquam est turpius, quam cognitioni et perceptioni assertionem approbationemque præcurrere.

II. For a long series of years, the British Government bestowed but a small portion of its attention upon the affairs of India. Nearly everything was left to the management of the chartered Company, whose acts had hitherto been rarely questioned in any way. But when the great Clive, by his astonishing victories, and successful policy, had raised the Company from the humble condition of a merely commercial body, trading and residing in the country upon sufferance, and having firm possession of only a few forts, to the condition of a sort of sovereign power, with absolute possession and authority over provinces more populous and extensive than many an European kingdom, ministers were constrained to take somewhat more notice of Hindustan. The jealousies excited by Lord Clive's great wealth and influence, still more the deadly hatred of his reforms in India, had kindled such a commotion among all classes of men, that the ear of ministers was incessantly beset with charge upon charge against him : this led eventually to those bitter parliamentary proceedings, which mainly contributed to bring his life to so melancholy an end.

Lord Clive, as well during his arduous services in India, as after his return, strongly expressed his opinion that our Indian Empire was too vast to be governed as it hitherto had been, by a dozen or two of plain citizens called directors, and some hundreds of shareholders called proprietors. He repeatedly declared, that the cause of misgovernment in England, lay not so much among the resident servants of the Company, as in the Company itself—not so much in India as in Leadenhall Street. Other less experienced but equally reflecting men had come to the same conclusion ; and it was very generally considered, that there was not much reliance to be placed in the disinterestedness or moderation of a body so constituted, and that the Court of Directors were scarcely to be considered competent to the wise, just, and effective management of a population of eighty millions, at the distance of ten thousand miles !

In the year 1767, when Lord Clive was on his return from Calcutta, the affairs of the East India Company attracted the serious attention of Parliament ; and it was then, for the first time, contemplated to place them under the controul of His Majesty's ministers ; a measure which, though partially provided for by the Regulating Act, was not ultimately effected till ten years after, by Mr. Pitt's wise institution of the Board of Controul, in 1784.

But the various difficulties which were then opposed to such an arrangement, and the large amount of revenue (£400,000) which the Government derived from the Company, in compensation for their exclusive charter, with the supposed difficulty or impossibility of making up that large revenue, were enough to relax the efforts of those who were most inclined to the project, and even to postpone its execution for seventeen years!

It was not until after the annual defalcation of that revenue to the state, and the annual increase of dividend to the proprietors, that the leaders of the administration, in 1773, returned in earnest to the subject. It was then that the pecuniary embarrassments of the Company at home, and the abuses arising from its maladministration abroad, seemed to afford a full opportunity of interference; but there can be no doubt, that Lord North and his colleagues looked also to the extensive field of patronage, which the Directors had hitherto monopolised. After some vehement debates, a select committee of the House of Commons was invested with full authority for every purpose of the most searching inquiry. The labours of this committee, after several reports, and many prolonged consultations, in which there was a great contrariety of opinions, and even of fundamental principles, resulted in the bill for regulating the concerns of the East India Company, civil and judicial. This act briefly and commonly called "the Regulating Act," was passed in the month of June, 1773, and commenced its operations in India on the 1st of August, 1774.

III. The only parts of the new constitution—for such it was—which had a direct influence upon the government in India were,—The appointment and powers of the Governor General and Council; and the creation of the Supreme Court of Judicature.

The Act appointed Warren Hastings to be Governor General, a loftier title than he or any of his predecessors had hitherto enjoyed; but it set up, at the same time, a new council of four, who were nominated by the crown, and were not removable except by the king, upon representation made by the Court of Directors. The Act failed to give a distinct limitation of power, or to draw any line whereby to show how the authority was to be divided between the Governor General and these new Members of Council, or how far the one could act without the others.

From these fertile elements of disunion, it almost necessarily followed that, from the very first arrival of the new Members of Council in India, there broke out the bitterest jealousies and dissensions between the Governor General and the majority of his colleagues. These feelings never ceased until the empire which Lord Clive had founded, and which Mr. Hastings had extended and consolidated, was brought into the utmost jeopardy : nor, in truth, were they discontinued even at that crisis, which was concurrent in date with the lamentable issue of our American war.

Hence it could scarcely, by any possibility, happen otherwise, than that the Chief Justice of the newly-constituted Court should be thwarted in his functions, at their very outset, by these commotions, engendered by the defects of the Act itself, at the seat of Indian government, and in the centre of his own jurisdiction. It is true that in India, at least, though cruelly embarrassed, and for a time disunited by their enemies, both Mr. Hastings and Sir Elijah Impey ultimately triumphed over their malice, and thereby, each in his own department, contributed to rescue our Indian Empire; the one by his great reputation and astonishing genius for government, the other by his firm and able administration of English law : but it was not till both law and government had been shaken to their very foundations ; not till their own fame and fortunes had been well nigh overwhelmed in that unequal contest. Both for many years outlived their persecution,—both died long since, lamented and revered by those who knew them best. To this extent their destinies were inseparable ; but when, at the end of more than thirty years from my father's death, the old exploded calumnies are revived ; when it is attempted once more to stigmatize their honourable friendship by connecting it with guilt, it behoves me, both as the friend of Mr. Hastings, and the son of Sir Elijah, to repel the foul aspersion : and this I will endeavour to do, not by vague and unsupported declamation, but by plain and documental proof. With this view, it will be necessary, in the first place, to examine the Act 13th George III. cap. 63 ; particularly that part of it which relates to the Supreme Court of Judicature, for it is this that claims the fullest attention ; nor will it be possible to come to a right understanding of the merits of the case, without reciting the principal clauses of that part of the Act, as the surest guides to explain its general tenor, and to define, as far as possible, the jurisdiction which it was meant to convey.

The preamble to the Regulating Act sets forth, that,

" Whereas the several powers and authorities granted by charters to the East India Company, have been found, by experience, not to have sufficient force to prevent various abuses which have prevailed in the administration of the affairs of the Company, to the manifest injury of public credit, &c., it is highly expedient that certain farther regulations should be provided."

Clause X. Nominates Major General John Clavering, the Honourable George Monson, Richard Barwell, Esquire, and Philip Francis, Esquire, Members of the Supreme Council, to continue in office five years ; counting from their arrival in Bengal.

XIII. Establishes by charter, a Supreme Court of Judicature, at Fort William, with this preamble,—"Whereas His late Majesty George II., by letters patent, dated January 8, of the 26th year of his reign, granted to the said Company his royal charter to constitute Courts of Civil, Criminal, and Ecclesiastical Jurisdiction, and which charter does not sufficiently provide for the due administration of justice, &c., be it therefore enacted, that it shall be lawful for His Majesty to erect a Supreme Court, to consist of a Chief Justice, and three other judges ; which said Supreme Court, shall have full powers to exercise all civil, criminal, admiralty, and ecclesiastical jurisdiction, and appoint such clerks, and other ministerial officers, with such salaries as shall be approved of by the said Governor General and Council, &c., and also shall be at all times a court of record, and a court of oyer and terminer, and gaol delivery, in and for the said town of Calcutta, and factory of Fort William, in Bengal, and the limits thereof, and the factories subordinate thereto.

XIV. Limits the extent of the jurisdiction of the Court to all British subjects residing in the provinces of Bengal, Bahar, and Orissa, or shall then have been directly or indirectly in the service of the said Company, or of any of His Majesty's subjects.

XV. Prohibits the Court from trying any action of indictment against the Governor General and Councillors for any offence not being treason or felony.

XVI. Gives power to try all other persons, being His Majesty's subjects, on all suits and actions against any inhabitant of the provinces aforesaid ; all suits and actions being brought before the Court in the first instance, or by appeal from the sentence of any of the provincial courts.

XVII. Exempts the Governor General and Councillors from arrest and imprisonment.

XVIII. Grants a power of appeal from the judgments of the Court to the King in Council.

XIX. Enacts that so much of the charter of 26th George II. as relates to the establishment of the Mayor's Court at Calcutta, be repealed by the new charter immediately on the publication thereof; but that the said charter of the 26th George II., in all other respects shall continue in full force.

XX. All records, muniments, and proceedings, belonging to the said Mayor's Court, to be delivered to, and preserved by the Supreme Court.

XXI. Appoints the salaries of the Governor General, of the Councillors, and of the Judges : viz., to the Governor General £25,000; to each of the Councillors £10,000; to the Chief Justice £8,000; and to each of the other Judges £6,000 per annum, out of the territorial acquisitions of the Company.

XXII. States these salaries to commence from the time of their appointments, and that they shall be in lieu of all fees, perquisites, and emoluments whatsoever.

Several of the clauses which next follow, relate to the receiving of presents from the native princes, the carrying on of private trade by the servants of the Company or government, &c. The Governor General, and the Members of the Council, were strictly forbidden being concerned in any commercial transactions. Every person holding any civil or military office, either under the Crown or under the Company, was forbidden to accept, receive, or take directly or indirectly, from any Indian princes, or their ministers or agents, or from any of the natives of India whatsoever, any present, gift, donation, gratuity, or reward, pecuniary or otherwise, upon any account or pretence whatsoever. The penalties threatened were sufficiently severe, and were thus clearly expressed,—

"And if any person holding or exercising any such civil or military offices, shall be guilty of any such offence, and shall be thereof legally convicted in such Supreme Court of Calcutta, or in the Mayor's Court, or any other of the Company's settlements, where such offences shall have been committed ; every such person so convicted, shall forfeit double the value of such present, &c., so taken and received, one moiety to the said Company, and the other moiety to him or them who shall inform or prosecute the same : and also shall be sent to England, unless such person so convicted, shall give sufficient security to remove himself within twelve months of the said conviction."

All these servants, whether civil or military, were forbidden to enter into any private commercial transactions.

XXXI. This clause of the Act, subjects persons making composition contrary to the meaning of the Act, to imprisonment, at the discretion of the Court.

XXXIII. Makes the Company's servants liable to fine and imprisonment for breach of trust.

XXXIV. Enacts that all offences shall be tried by a jury of British subjects resident at Calcutta, and not otherwise.

XXXV. Gives the Company the power of compounding or discharging the sentences of the Supreme Court, in cases of debt or penalty due to the Company, on the same being made known to the Directors.

XXXVI. Empowers the Governor General and Council to make all just regulations, which, however, shall not be valid, until duly registered in the Supreme Court ; and grants appeals to the King in Council, to set aside the rules of the Court, a copy of the same being affixed in the India House, and held valid, until it be set aside or repealed upon the hearing or determination of such appeal.

XXXVII. Directs the Governor General and Council, to transmit copies of their rules to one of the Secretaries of State.

XXXVIII. Constitutes the Governor General and Council to act as justices of peace.

XXXIX. Declares the Governor General and Councillors, the Chief Justice and other Judges of the Supreme Court, as well as all other persons holding office under the Crown or the East India Company, liable for offences committed against this Act, to be tried in the Court of King's Bench, in the County of Middlesex.

XL. Recites the manner of procedure in cases of indictments and informations laid in the Court of King's Bench.

XLI. Lays down the particular manner of procedure in the King's Bench, in all cases of offence or misdemeanour, committed by the Chief Justice, and the other Judges of the Supreme Court.

XLII. Enables the Lord High Chancellor, or the Speaker of the House of Commons, to issue warrants for the examination of witnesses, touching all such offences, which shall be deemed competent evidence, to both Houses of Parliament.

XLIII. Enacts that no proceedings in Parliament against offences committed in India, shall be discontinued by prorogation.

XLIV. Empowers the Courts in Westminster, a motion duly made, to award and provide writs, in the nature of a mandamus, to the Chief Justice and Judges of the Supreme Court, when the Company commence suits in law or equity.

XLV. Provides, however, that no such depositions taken and returned as aforesaid, by virtue of this Act, shall be allowed to be given in evidence in any capital cases, other than such as shall be proceeded against in Parliament.

It will be seen that by the letter of this Act, the jurisdiction of the Supreme Court was made very extensive. But, as if the home Government doubted whether the powers thus granted would prove sufficient in India, where the servants of the Company, who would still form so large a portion of the governing power, might find their interests opposed to the Court, the jurisdiction was still farther enlarged by some provisions which closely followed the Regulating Act. Under the date of the 26th of March, 1774, were issued letters patent, establishing the Supreme Court of Judicature, at Fort William, in Bengal. Here the first clause recites so much of the Regulating Act, 13th George III., cap. 63, as regards the Court.

II. Creates, directs, and constitutes a court of record, to be called the Supreme Court of Judicature, at Fort Willliam, in Bengal.

III. To consist of a chief justice, and three puisne judges, appointed by the King under the great seal, to act during pleasure.

IV. To be justices of the peace and coroners in Bengal, Bahar, and Orissa, and to have authority as the justices of the King's Bench in England; the four, or a majority, to concur, and the Chief Justice to have a casting voice.

V. To have a seal, to be kept by the Chief Justice, or by the senior puisne judge.

VI. All writs, summons, rules, precepts, &c., to be issued by the Court in the King's name.

VII. Fixes the salary of the judges as in the Regulating Act, and assigns to them rank and precedence, &c.

VIII. Nominates Elijah Impey, of Lincoln's Inn, Esquire, first Chief Justice, and Robert Chambers, of the Middle Temple, Stephen Cæsar Lemaistre, of the Inner Temple,

John Hyde, of Lincoln's Inn, Esquires, to be first puisne justices.

IX. Appoints the existing sheriff to continue in office until another be appointed, prescribes the future appointment, the oath of office, provision in case of death, his duty, mode of proceeding when a party, &c.

X. Gives the Court power to appoint clerks and officers, with salaries to be approved by the Governor General and Council. Such officers to reside within the jurisdiction of the Court.

XI. The Court to approve advocates and attornies-at-law, and to remove them on reasonable cause.

XII. And to settle the fees, as approved by the Governor General and Council.

XIII. Tables of fees to be hung up in Court, and copies thereof, with a list of the officers, transmitted to England.

XIV. States the power and jurisdiction of the Court in Bengal, &c., in all trespasses against the Company, Mayor's Court of Calcutta, or others in Bengal, or others who have resided there, or who have effects there, or are or have been in the Company's service, or of the Mayor's Court, or of others, but not against such who have never resided there. Also the Court's power to try causes, actions, and suits of Indian inhabitants within Bengal, &c., where the cause shall exceed 500 current rupees. It then prescribes the mode of proceeding in such actions. Plaint or bill, summons, precept, and appearance, to be in writing. Examination of witnesses on oath. Allows reasonable expenses, compels payment, enforces oaths upon witnesses, except upon Quakers. Enables the Court to give judgment on hearing the parties, in case defendant should make default after appearance, or refuse to make defence, and to award costs.

XV. And to issue writs of execution for seizing effects. Debts so seized to be paid as the Court shall appoint. Such interlocutory orders to be made as the Court shall see fit. In failure of appearance, the Court may order the party to be arrested. The sheriff may take bail for appearance. It states also the proceedings thereon.

XVI. Recites former proceedings, either where the Company are plaintiffs or defendants. Grants the Company the appointment of an attorney to act in their behalf, and states the form of proceedings. If the Company refuse to appoint an attorney the Court may.

XVII. Disputes between Indian natives (see ante II.) and British subjects, may, by this clause, be determined in the Supreme Court; and causes of action exceeding 500 current rupees, and suits brought in other courts, either party ap-

pealing to the Supreme Court, it shall cause proceedings elsewhere to surcease, and the Supreme Court shall determine
thereon.

XVIII. Constitutes the Supreme Court a court of equity,
like the Court of Chancery in Great Britain, and empowers
it to compel appearance accordingly.

XIX. And to be a court of oyer and terminer, and gaol
delivery.   The sheriff to summon grand juries, and petit
juries, &c.—And in all respects to administer criminal justice in such or the like manner and form, or as nearly as the
condition and circumstance of the place and the persons will
admit of, as in the courts of oyer and terminer, in that part
of Great Britain called England, and to hear and determine,
and award judgment and execution of all treasons, murders,
felonies, *forgeries*, &c., committed in the districts and provinces
called Bengal, Bahar, and Orissa, by British subjects, or other
persons who shall at the time of committing them, have been
employed by, or shall have been directly or indirectly in the
service of the Company.   It makes it unlawful for offenders
to object to locality, or the Court's jurisdiction, or to juries;
*and orders all offenders to be tried as if their crimes had been
committed in Calcutta.*

XX. Empowers the Supreme Court to reprieve or suspend
execution of sentence, *in cases where there shall appear a
proper occasion for mercy,* until the King's pleasure be known.
In such cases, a state of the case, and of evidence, *and of
reasons for recommending the criminal to mercy, is demanded
of the Court.*

XXI. Makes the court of requests, and quarter sessions,
established by the late charter of the 26th of George II., and
the justices, sheriffs, and other magistrates, subject to the
Supreme Court, as the lower courts of Great Britain are to
the Court of King's Bench.   And grants the power of issuing
writs of mandamus, certiorari, &c., and to punish contempt
by fine and imprisonment.

XXIII. Confers on the Supreme Court, the same ecclesiastical jurisdiction over British subjects as is exercised in the
diocese of London, &c., and the power of granting probates,
and to commit letters of administration of intestates.   And
to sequester the estates of deceased persons.   To allow and
reject accounts, with a proviso, if an executor appears after
administration is granted.

XXIV. Orders administrators to give security to the junior
justice, to the value of the estate, &c.

XXV. Empowers the Court to appoint registers, proctors,
&c.

XXVI. And guardians to infants, &c.

XXVII. Makes the Supreme Court a court of admiralty, with extent of jurisdiction as exercised in England, without the strict formalities of law.

XXVIII. Extends its power in regard to crimes maritime, to punish offenders, to deliver and discharge them, to arrest ships, &c., to compel appearance under penalties, &c.

XXIX. Prescribes the form of affidavits and affirmations in the admiralty court.

XXX. Reserves fines, &c., to the King, and grants satisfaction to prosecutors out of fines set by the Court.

XXXI. Allows an appeal to the King in Council, from the Supreme Court, in civil causes, by petition to that Court, and requires security on such appeal, for costs, and for performance of judgment ; the Supreme Court transmitting a copy of all evidence on such appeal.

XXXII. In criminal suits, the Court is empowered to allow or deny appeals.

XXXIII. Reserves the power to the King to refuse an appeal, and directs the Court to execute the judgments and orders of His Majesty. And restricts the allowance of appeals to within six months of the presentation of the petition, unless the matter shall exceed 1000 pagodas.

XXXIV. Provides against the arrest of the Governor General and Councillors, Chief Justice, and other justices, except for treason or felony, but allows the sequestration of their estates.

XXXV. Establishes a court room, and orders the Chief Justice and puisne justices to be sworn before they act.

XXXVI. Repeals the former charter of the 26th George II., after publication of the Supreme Court. Orders the judgments pronounced by the Mayor's Court to be in force, and the proceedings depending therein not to be abated, but transferred, and the records, &c., to be delivered over to the Supreme Court.

XXXVII. Appoints four terms and sittings after term in each year, the duration of terms and sittings, and two sessions to be held in every year.

XXXVIII. Authorizes the Court to frame rules of practice, &c., and to transmit them to the Privy Council for approval.

XXXIX. Strictly charges and commands all the King's governors, commanders, magistrates, officers, and ministers, civil and military, and all His Majesty's liege subjects in Bengal, Bahar, and Orissa, &c., that they be aiding, assisting, and obedient in all things unto the said Supreme Court of Judicature, in Bengal, as they shall answer the contrary at their peril.

If the reader will compare clause XIII., of the Regulating Act, with clauses XIV. and XXI. of the charter or letters patent, he will see that they differ inasmuch as the two latter clauses extend the jurisdiction given to the Court by the Act. By the words of the Act, the Court was to be a court of record, and a court of oyer and terminer, and of gaol delivery, in and for the town of Calcutta, and factory of Fort William, and the limits thereof, and the factories subordinate thereto. By these words it should seem, that the jurisdiction was intended to be confined to the Company's factories in Bengal, *except where the subsequent clauses specially enlarge the jurisdiction.* But by these subsequent clauses, the Court's jurisdiction is widely extended,—first, over all the British subjects resident in Bengal, Bahar, and Orissa; secondly, over all complaints against the King's subjects in all the provinces, for any crimes, misdemeanors, or oppressions; thirdly, over all suits or actions against the same subjects; fourthly, over suits and actions against the same persons, who, at the time the cause of action arises, shall *be directly or indirectly in the service of the Company, or of any of the King's subjects;* fifthly, over suits and actions by any of the King's subjects, *against any inhabitants of India, residing in either of the three provinces aforesaid,* or any contract in writing, where the cause of action shall exceed 500 current rupees, and where by the contract it is agreed that in case of dispute, the matter shall be determined in the Supreme Court. And it is provided that these latter suits shall be brought in the first instance before the Supreme Court, and by appeal from any of the provincial courts.

On the clause which makes the judges justices of the peace and coroners, in Bengal, Bahar, and Orissa, with such authority as the justices of the King's Bench in England, it is to be observed, that this can only mean the same jurisdiction and authority in the character of coroners and conservators of the King's peace; and here the charter or patent goes beyond the Act of Parliament: for the Act confines the whole jurisdiction, criminal as well as civil, to the Company's factories, except in certain cases specially provided for; but in the charter, the justices of the Supreme Court, are made coroners, and justices, and conservators of the King's peace *in every part of the provinces of Bengal, Bahar, and Orissa, indiscriminately,* and *without any qualification or limitation.*

In respect to the mode of proceedings in actions, I would draw particular attention to the clauses in the charter which relate to *" appearance and pleading,"* and to the clause empowering the Court *to issue writs of execution for seizing effects.* And, still more is it necessary to give attention to the clause which makes it *unlawful to object to the locality of the Court's jurisdiction or to the juries,* and which ordains that offenders shall be tried, convicted, and punished *as if their crimes had been committed in Calcutta.* Nor must attention be denied to the particular words in clause XX. of the charter, empowering the Court to reprieve and suspend execution of any capital sentence, *where it shall appear in their judgment that there is a proper occasion for mercy;* evidently meaning thereby to imply, that, *without a proper occasion for mercy, the Court could not reprieve or suspend execution of any capital sentence.*

On the clauses XXI. and XXII. of the charter, which relate to appeals to the King in council, I would point out that, in civil causes, the appeal from the Supreme Court is allowed only by petition to the Court itself; and that, *in criminal suits,* the power of *denying* appeals and of *regulating the terms upon which such appeals shall be allowed,* is reserved to the King. Finally it must be observed and borne in mind, that clause XXXV. of the charter or patent, which repeals the former charter of the 26th George II., after the publication of the Supreme Court, leaves untouched the power formerly given to the Governor and Councillors to act as justices of the peace. The Regulating Act itself, indeed, expressly reserves to the new Governor General and Council power to act as justices, giving *like power* to the judges of the Supreme Court. This ambiguity, or this unreasonable co-existence of judicial powers must be constantly borne in mind, since it accounts for the different construction put upon the Act of Parliament and upon the charter, during the disputes between the Supreme Council and the Supreme Court as to the extent of their respective jurisdictions.*

---

* See Statutes at large, 13th Geo. III., c. 63, sec. 13, vol. II.

Even upon the most hurried perusal of the Regulating Act and the charter, it will appear, as clear as the sun at noonday, that the intention and command of the British Government was, that English law should be used in India, with English custom and procedure; and that all classes of men were to be brought under the operation of this law. It was not for the Supreme Court collectively to alter or modify this law and practice, or to disobey the command which they were sent out to execute: much less was this competent to Sir Elijah Impey singly and individually; for, though placed at the head of the Supreme Court, he was only *one* out of *four* members of it, and his rank—a mere matter of precedence and increase of salary—gave him no increase of authority over the other judges.   Mr. Macaulay always speaks of my father as if he were everything and the rest of the judges nothing—as if he were absolute dictator, and his three respectable colleagues something less than mere registering clerks.   When the members of the Supreme Court proceeded to India, they had almost every thing to learn with respect to the habits, customs, and prejudices of the natives, and the manner in which they would be affected by the strict administration of English laws. This knowledge, which was wanting, could be acquired only by time and experience in India. Sir Elijah Impey may have discovered after he had been resident for two or three years in Calcutta, that some of our laws and some of our practice demanded extensive modifications in order to be suited to the Hindu and Mohammedan population; but he had no authority to make any changes.   He could only offer suggestions to the home Government.   And this he did; but, during the whole of his residence in the East, that Government was too much occupied by the riots at home, or too much distracted by the contest in America, to attend to any such suggestions, however urgently repeated.   Yet how inconsistent was this neglect; since the authorization given by the charter itself to the Supreme Court, to frame rules of practice, was made subject to the condition that those rules should be approved by the Privy Council! I discover from my father's correspondence while in India, and from papers written by him after his return to England, that he was far from being fully satisfied either with the constitution of the Supreme governing Council, or with that of the Supreme Court of Judicature; that he thought both in need of material alteration ; and that, unless the former were remodelled, and the latter strengthened by authority from England, our Indian Empire, at any great or sudden crisis, might be put in jeopardy. On this last subject he wrote a luminous paper which was deemed worthy of preservation by a very able man, who had devoted much time and study to the best means of governing India, and of securing alike the well-being of the native population, and the British power in that vast peninsula.*

Sir Elijah was not sent out to India to make a code, but to administer, impartially and *strictly*, the English laws as they then stood. I will not allow myself to doubt that, with his natural perspicacity, his well-earned reputation as a lawyer, his steady application to his profession—for he was not a barrister by mere name alone—I cannot, I repeat, bring myself to believe otherwise than that my father, after a few years residence in the East, must have been better qualified for what Mr. Bentham called "codification" than some gentlemen who have since been employed upon that duty, with much emolument to themselves, but no visible profit to the community: but neither Sir Elijah Impey, nor any one of his brother judges, was ever charged with such a task; which had they been—though they might have modestly declined the commission—yet most assuredly *they* were not men ever to have declared that they were *no lawyers,* as Mr. Macaulay blushed not to declare concerning himself in the House of Commons, after his return from the exercise of his functions as a law-reviser and codifier in Calcutta !

Far be it from me to vilify the labours of those great men, who, with better pretensions, have succeeded in reforming the errors or in mitigating the asperities of British jurisprudence; yet it is but just· to estimate lawyers, as we do other men, by the standard of the times

* See among the Hargrave MSS. in the British Museum, a MS. book in quarto, entitled, " A Plan for Bengal," 333, PL. CLVI. B. 12. This plan is discussed under six several questions, the last of which is headed, " How and by what Courts shall Justice be administered ?" And the compiler (Mr. Lind) states in a note, p. 90, " This plan contains the outlines of the heads of the bill, by Sir Elijah Impey."

in which they lived : no man, and especially no lawyer, can practically advance beyond the rules and usages of his own generation. " I am not," said my father, in one of his numerous letters to Lord Weymouth, " I am not gifted with intuition."* Let it, then, ever be borne in mind, that, in Sir Elijah's day, the spirit which has animated our eminent law-reformers lay dormant.   The English community at large, and the great body of our statesmen, politicians, and writers, seemed to think not only that our laws were good, but that they could scarcely be improved.   Only a few years before my father's departure for India, Blackstone had published his popular and captivating book of " Commentaries on the Laws of England," and his optimism became an all-prevailing feeling, more and more closing the eyes and hearts of men to the necessity of any change. Whatever novelties were then introduced in our criminal code, were not, it must be allowed, on the side of *mercy* to the criminal.   Perhaps there never was a time when a belief in the efficacy of capital punishments was more universal than during the first thirty years of the reign of George III.

We are now startled at reading the calendars, and the dreadful lists of executions, often amounting, at the Old Bailey, to twelve or fifteen, or even more, at a time ; but if we refer to the newspapers, monthly magazines, and *Annual Registers* of the period, there is nothing to denote any doubt as to the wholesome repressing effects of these periodical slaughters.

The writers of the day occasionally make some common-place remarks about the awfulness of the scene, but they never hint that the criminals did not deserve that extreme punishment, or that that extreme punishment was failing to produce the contemplated diminution of crime.   The ideas that began to be so ably and energetically expressed by Sir Samuel Romilly in 1809 and 1810, had no place either in the hearts of the English people, or in the heads of those who governed them, thirty-five years before.   The law in cases of forgery was administered with unvarying and unmitigated severity; that crime, in particular, was considered of all " the most dangerous in a commercial country," †

* See Parliamentary Reports.   † Boswell's Life of Johnson.

and to be checked only by the gallows. No intercession, no consideration of his holy calling, not the pen of Johnson himself, could procure from George III., either pardon, respite, or commutation of punishment for Dr. Dodd. He was hanged, accordingly, on the 27th of June, 1777, just two years, one month, and eight days after the execution at Calcutta, for forgery, of the Rajah Nuncomar; who, according to Mr. Macaulay, was most foully murdered by Sir Elijah Impey.

The offence of forgery, which is certainly of dangerous import in all communities, and which goes to the annihilation of trust, credit, and security in commercial ones, had, unhappily, been very prevalent among the natives of Bengal, Bahar, and Orissa; and since the foundation of our empire by the great Clive, various efforts had been made to check it. The Charter of George II., had declared the law of England, civil and criminal, to be the law of Calcutta, and before that Charter passed, forgery had become a capital crime in England. As far back as 1764, a Hindu of rank, like Nuncomar, had been condemned to death for forgery ; and, though he had received the King's pardon, other natives *had been hanged*, for the same crime, years before the execution of the Rajah Nuncomar.*

These punishments might doubtless be considered as excessive, as they were *then* unusual ; but it does not appear, that they excited any great emotion among the native population, or that either Hindus or Mohammedans doubted that the severest measures must be taken, in order to defend their respective property from the far-spreading effects of such offences.

In the rude state of society in which the Koran was composed, forgery was a transgression which could scarcely have entered into the contemplation of the Arabian camel-driver; but muftis and oulemas, the expounders alike of Mohammedan religion and Mohammedan law, in their commentaries and glosses, written at a later period, and in a different state of society, had found their attention called to the subject, and had drawn up very severe laws against falsifyers of deeds, as well as against clippers of coin. In the sum-

---

* Examination of Mr. Barwell, on Hastings's trial. Mr. Barwell deposed that he had himself presided in the Court which had condemned these men.

mary proceedings of Persian and Turkish jurisprudence, it had long been usual to cut off the head of a man convicted of such falsification, or to sentence him to torments more dreadful than death; nor was the custom of strangulation, either by the bow-string, or hanging by the neck, less customary, or more abhorrent to the Asiatic than to the European, from the days of Haman the ~~Syrian~~, down to the Hindu Nuncomar.*

'ersian

The Mohammedan conquerors of India, knew no other law than that of their Koran, and their oulemas; and with very slight, and often merely accidental modifications, this law was administered in Hindustan, much in the same manner as in Persia or in Turkey; the native courts being in India, as in those two countries, notoriously partial, and infamously corrupt.

We have seen in clause XIX. of the Charter, that forgeries are especially named among the offences with relation to which, the Supreme Court, of which Sir Elijah was the president, were ordered to administer criminal justice, according to the law and practice of England; or, as in our own courts of oyer and terminer. Nothing was distinctly left to the discretion of the judges; the mention of " the condition and circumstances of the place and the persons," having no apparent meaning, and the charter making the English law enclose within its ample compass, natives as well as Europeans.

It so chanced, that the very first criminal case which came before the Supreme Court, was that of Nuncomar; and the Rajah being convicted of forgery, was, of course, condemned and executed, according both to the spirit and the letter of our law. The Court could not have acted otherwise than it did, without flying in the face of the Government which had appointed it, and in the face of the law which it professed, and which it was created and purposely appointed to administer. But the particulars of the case will be gradually developed, and fully explained, in a future chapter.

I need not here say more about the Act and Charter; I trust that their spirit and intention, with respect to the

---

* See " Halhed's Translation of the Code of Gentoo Laws." I have to add, that, in this view of the subject, I am amply borne out by the testimony, as well by the present learned Oriental Professor in the University to which I myself belong, as by all other authorities which I have had the honour to consult.

of

Supreme Court, will be clearly understood by any one that will attentively peruse the present chapter. I have here given the clauses of the Regulating Act, which are applicable to the Court over which my father presided, and all the clauses of the Charter, which Charter wholely and solely regards that Supreme Court. The reader who will follow me in the investigations I have undertaken, may refer back to the Charter, and to the clauses of the Act whenever they are named. The justification of my father will be best established by this reference to the authorities under which he acted, and to the spirit of the law which he was bound to execute. In all public matters, I wish it to rest upon no other basis.

With all his colleagues in the Supreme Court, Sir Elijah lived in constant harmony and good-fellowship; notwithstanding many perplexing occurrences which took place in India, and the numerous disputes which arose touching the authority of the Court, and its procedure. The three puisne judges, Chambers, Hyde, and Lemaistre, were all men well known, and honourably distinguished in their profession; and all of them retained their respect and friendship for Sir Elijah Impey until death. His successor, Mr. Justice Chambers— afterwards Sir Robert—had been the intimate friend of Dr. Samuel Johnson, whose esteem, in itself, was an honourable distinction to any man. And of all the judges, Chambers was the most constant associate of my father in India; their occasional, but rare difference in opinion, never creating a moments coolness between them.* A good many records of Chambers's estimable qualities, are found in " Boswell's Life of Johnson." When he obtained his Indian judgeship, Johnson, who was well acquainted with Mr. Hastings, gave Chambers a warm letter of introduction to that great man. The place in Johnson's affection, left vacant by the departure of Chambers, was occupied by the late Lord Stowell.

Of Hyde and Lemaistre, the most honourable testimony is borne, by a very learned and competent witness, who was the common friend, and early companion, of all the four Justices of the Supreme Court nominated under the Regulating Act and Charter.†

* See Mr. Croker's Note to his edition of "Boswell's Life of Johnson."
† See " Nicholls's Recollections."

Of the colleagues of Mr. Philip Francis, in the new
Supreme Council, I need say nothing. Their characters
and conduct will be developed in the course of my narrative, and I shall venture on no comment upon them,
without strict truth, and safe evidence, to support my
assertions. In general, I believe them to have been men
of honour but of no very distinguished ability; and,
that they were carried into evil extremes, solely by the
factious spirit of their leader, Mr. Francis.

The same ship carried out the Judges of the Supreme
Court, and the new Members of the Supreme Council;
Mr. Barwell was already in India when he obtained
his appointment.

Mr. Hastings received my father as an old friend and
schoolfellow. They had been bosom friends in boyhood; and neither the different nature of their pursuits
and struggles in manhood, nor their long separation,
had estranged them from each other; they had corresponded frequently, and during Mr. Hastings's visit
to his native country, in the years 1764-5-6,* they
had met again, and renewed many a joyous recollection
of their Westminster days.

The Governor General knew the Chief Justice too
well to expect from him anything like subserviency, or
connivance in wrong-doing; but, most assuredly, he
might be delighted nevertheless at the appointment, and
receive his old friend with a hearty welcome. And there
is good evidence to prove that he did so.†

His reception of the Members of the Supreme Council,
though conciliatory, could scarcely be expected to be
quite so cordial. They had come to divide, cut down,
or split the authority of the Governor General, and to

---

* Obituary for September, 1818.

† See Warren Hastings's own letters, in his Memoirs, by the Rev.
G. R. Gleig.

"On learning Sir Elijah's appointment to preside over the Supreme
Court, Mr. Hastings had written to him to express his entire satisfaction,
'which,' he said, was 'without a circumstance of regret to alloy it.' 'In
truth, my friend,' he continued, 'nothing else could have reconciled me
to that part of the Act, which, if any latitude is left to you in its first
establishment, may, and I am sure will, be made a source of the most
valuable benefits to this country.' We here see not only the satisfaction
of the Governor General at the appointment of his friend, but also his
dissatisfaction at part of the Regulating Act, together with a very evident
doubt whether the Supreme Court, as constituted by that Act, could work
well at Calcutta."

dispute with him on all points of Indian administration. The love of power is a natural passion, strongly implanted in the hearts of all statesmen like Mr. Hastings : he had passed his life in the country, knew well the native languages, and had signalized himself by many splendid achievements.

With the exception of Mr. Barwell, an old servant of the Company, and long resident in India,* the Members of the Supreme Council, which Lord North's government had been pleased to appoint, knew, practically, nothing of India; nothing of its idioms, nothing of its policy. They had everything to learn,—and some of them never learned anything,—yet they came with a fixed pre-determination of overturning nearly all that Hastings had done. It may be questioned whether any mortal man, situated as the Governor General was, could have been pleased at their arrival. But I know too much of Mr. Hastings's unvarying urbanity, and courteous bearing, to allow me to believe that he received them otherwise than with perfect politeness. It took years of Mr. Francis's coarseness and malignity to shake the equilibrium of the Governor General's mind, or to drive him to any degree of irritability, or ill-temper. Mr. Macaulay, who loves to put everything pointedly and dramatically, and who seldom objects to a loud report or striking effect, says, that the Members of Council expected a salute of twenty-one guns from the batteries of Fort William, that the Governor General allowed them only seventeen, and that this trifle was sufficient to give occasion for dispute.

I have been assured that there was no difference about this matter, and that the salute was loud enough and long enough to satisfy all parties. But could not the historical and political reading of Mr. Macaulay, suggest to his hurried and overtaxed memory, the simple and notorious fact, that these three Members of Council had come out primed and prompted by Lord North to oppose Hastings ? And was not this fact sufficient to explain the cold reserve of the first civilities on the

---

* It may be noted even here, that Mr. Barwell, who knew so much of India, as constantly supported Mr. Hastings as Mr. Francis, General Clavering, and Colonel Monson, who knew so little of it, opposed him. Mr. Barwell was also the constant friend of Sir Elijah Impey.

day of the arrival, and on the morrow the commencement of " that long quarrel, which, after distracting British India, was renewed in England, and in which all the most eminent statesmen and orators of the age, took active part on one or the other side ?" *

In the apprehension of sober-minded readers, Mr. Macaulay's language is often too strong and inflated for his subject ; but the term " *distracting*," as here used, is not excessive, but strictly applicable to the state of the case.   India was not only distracted, but well nigh lost, through the war waged at the Council-board, by Mr. Francis, General Clavering, and Colonel Monson.

The differences which had previously arisen between Lord North's administration, and that of Mr. Hastings, were neither few nor unimportant. There seems, indeed, to have been at no time a good understanding between these parties.   Mr. Hastings, though professing a great regard for Lord North's private character, always complained of him as a statesman, attributing to his indolence and indifference, not only much personal suffering and disquietude, but also many public evils in India. With the exception of Mr. Barwell, who, as an experienced servant of their own, was admitted to conciliate the Company, the Members of the Council owed their appointments entirely to the patronage of ministers. These appointments did not go free from the cavils and criticism of the day.   Men not only wondered at the sudden and great rise of Mr. Francis, but also questioned the propriety of the ministerial patronage in the case of General Clavering and Colonel Monson, who were to be three out of a Council of five, to govern a country which they knew nothing about ; thus out-numbering the two who knew everything.

But even without taking into account the existing differences of the administration of Lord North and the Governor General, or the ministerial prompting and priming which the majority had received, there was quite enough to lead to dissensions and violent quarrels in the Council-room at Calcutta.   The Regulating Act itself, was one great apple of discord ; for it divided a governing authority into parts, without defining or limiting the separate portions.   And then there was

* See " Mr. Macaulay's Critical and Historical Essays."

the dark and hateful temper of Francis, who, from first to last, led Clavering and Monson by the sleeve, precipitating them into the gulf of his own quarrels, whether private or public, with Hastings,—working upon their passions with all his ingenious art of persuasion, and closing their ears to every conciliatory word uttered by the Governor General.

It was on the 19th of October, 1774, that the Members of Council and the Judges landed at our settlement in Bengal.

I cannot affirm that the feud began on the very day after the arrival of the three Members of Council; but there is now most abundant evidence—printed and published to the world—to show that it broke out very soon after their landing; and with this published evidence, that of letters and family papers in my possession, completely agrees.

CHAPTER III.

ON their arrival at Calcutta, Sir Elijah Impey and his
brother judges, without loss of time, proceeded to open
the King's commission, and to organize and establish
the Supreme Court. This was no trifling labour: the
institution was new, and everything had to be either
republished or begun; proper officers to be selected and
appointed; rules applicable to the locality to be laid
down; the records of the old Mayor's Court to be
received, authenticated, registered, and put in order;
and the processes pendent or dormant in that court to be
prepared for trial and decision. This Mayor's Court,
as well as the adauluts, or native revenue courts, had
been managed in a way very perplexing to lawyers;
for no regularly trained English barrister had ever
practised in them, or been concerned in their formation,
or in drawing up the rules of procedure. Mr. Hastings,
in re-organizing these courts, had said to a friend some
years before, that he, and the servants of the Company
at Calcutta, were making laws at a great rate without
having a single lawyer among them.* This law-
making was no doubt very ingenious, for Mr. Hastings did nearly all of it himself, and whatever he
did bore the stamp of ability; but it will readily be

* Rev. G. R. Gleig; Memoirs of Warren Hastings.

conceived, that laws so framed by laymen would not quite satisfy professional men, or suit a bench of judges who were strictly bound to proceed according to the law of England. The proceedings of the Mayor's Court were of course suspended by the formation of the Supreme Court; but it was necessary for the new judges to know what their nature and tendency had been before; what decisions had been given under them, and in what state the different processes in that Court lay at the time of the new establishment of the new Supreme Court of Judicature.

As early as the 25th of March 1775, Sir Elijah wrote to Lord Rochford, the Secretary of State for the Southern Department, as it was then called, to report the progress which had been made. He enclosed to his Lordship " a certificate under the hand and seal of the Chief Justice, and Justices of the Supreme Court, of the full and true account of the several offices and places, and officers and clerks, and of their salaries severally and respectively; and a true copy of the table of fees settled by the said Court, together with the approbation of the Governor General and Council. He likewise enclosed under the seal of the Court, all such rules and orders as had been framed by the Court, for the due administration of justice," praying his Lordship "to transmit the same to his Majesty in his Privy Council, for his approbation, controul, or alteration."*

The King in Council approved of the rules, and of all that had been done by the judges.

Notwithstanding these arduous labours, and other occupations and anxieties arising out of the conflict of authorities in the Supreme Council, my father began to study the Persian, which is the language of business, and the Bengalee, or vernacular of the country. For he saw, and had known beforehand, that Persian was the language of law and diplomacy, that all documents were written in that language, and that all official correspondence was carried on in it. The proceedings of the Supreme Court were to be in English, with the aid— where natives were concerned—of sworn interpreters.

* From MS. Letters in my possession, and from the printed Reports of Parliamentary Committees.

But he would not trust entirely to these hired dragomans and monshees, as so many men in office had done, and were continuing to do ; he felt that a knowledge of the languages used in writing or in speaking by the natives, would become a judge who had to administer the law to them, and that such knowledge was indispensable to one who would obtain a proper insight into their characters, and their habits of thought and action.

He had always had a love for philological studies, and a natural facility in acquiring various dialects.   He therefore set earnestly to work, with books and a Persian master, in the midst of his laborious judicial occupations, and a very sickly season; * while his mind was incessantly harassed by the dissensions in the Government-house.   Men are apt to put off a difficult study, in the fanciful hope of obtaining, at some future day, a perfect tranquility and composure of mind.   If my father had trusted to that fallacious hope, he could never, during his residence in India, have mastered a difficult and delicate oriental tongue.

Soon after his arrival he wrote to his brother, Michael Impey,—"I am labouring hard at the Persian language, and therefore hope you will not neglect sending me Richardson's Dictionary."† In another letter, written to his brother about this time, he speaks cheerfully enough of his heavy official toils, but in a melancholy tone of the dissensions which were raging at the Council-board. "The disputes here," he says, "have so far involved me, that they make my despatches, by every ship, very voluminous. I do not trouble you with a recital of the matters in contest, but I send to Mr. Elliot a copy of all my public letters, that he may make use of them among my friends ; and, as I am obliged to send duplicates, these are as much as I can procure to be copied." ‡   He continued his studies in spite of the

* " This season hath been the most fatal that hath been experienced in Bengal for some years."   General Clavering, one of the Members of the Supreme Council, had had a severe attack.—*Letter to Michael Impey, Esq. in Family Letters.*

† Family Letters.

‡ MS. *Family Letters.*   In this particular letter, which was evidently written at a time of great agitation and anxiety, and in the midst of a chaos of business, there is a good deal about his children left in England. He asks his brother whether he makes them talk of him ?—Whether one of them has duly celebrated his birth-day ?—Whether he had shown to another

political whirlwind, and made himself a very accomplished Persian scholar. The Bengalee he soon spoke fluently.

It was impossible that he should long remain uninvolved in the disputes of the Council-board. Many of these differences of opinion arose about the Supreme Court itself. In other disputes, each party claimed to have the law on its own side, and made application to the judges. The Court could not entirely agree with the one party or the other; and therefore it was alternately exposed to the animosities of both. But there was nothing in these disputes that regarded my father personally or distinctly from his brethren. The quarrels were with the Court not with Sir Elijah Impey; Justices Chambers, Hyde, and Lemaistre, were just as much implicated as the Chief Justice. The judges were unanimous, and quite ready to take in common whatever praise or blame might be meted out to them, and in all measures where they agreed, they were, of course, equally responsible. It was in personal matters—and more especially in one that affected the character and *the purse* of Mr. Francis—that my father drew down upon his head that implacable hatred which operated singly upon him, and which was the proximate cause of so many years of trouble, and of the persevering defamation, which, as it would seem, has not ceased within fifty-eight years after his triumphant defence in the House of Commons.

I can but slightly sketch the war which raged in the Council-chamber at Calcutta; and, in the execution of my filial task, I am only so far concerned with it, as it involved my father.

The indiscretion and rashness of pre-determined and ill-informed innovators and reformers are proverbial; and, when to this madness is superadded a ravenous appetite for patronage and power, with a favourable chance of gratifying that appetite, there are few extremities that may not be apprehended. The three Members of Council deputed by the English Government,

his Cambridge medal, in order to stimulate him to a love of learning? He implores his brother to love them all for his sake; and he sends the most heart-warm thanks to some friends who had shown kindness to them. But similar passages occur in all his private letters, no matter what the state of his mind, or affairs at Calcutta.

had gone out to India as innovators or reformers; Lord North's administration had stamped them with that character, and Mr. Francis, the only man of eminent ability among them, was alike hungry for power, and resolute for change. From the moment of his coming he took the reins. His influence over the minds of his two colleagues was unbounded,—they saw with his eyes, spoke with his tongue, and acted with his hand.

General Clavering I believe to have been a conscientious, honourable, high-minded English soldier ; but he was deplorably ignorant of business ; his mind, as well as his body was weakened by the climate, and he soon became fretful from disease, and passionate and impatient of contradiction. The first sickly season in Bengal appears to have destroyed the better part of him. At an early period Sir Elijah says, " General Clavering's severe illness has totally shattered his constitution, and precipitated him into old age ; his body is emaciated, his strength exhausted, and his spirits sunk. The violence of his disorder, has, in some measure, expended itself ; but he is far from recovering, and the effects of it must, I apprehend, prove fatal at no great distance of time." * I should scarcely feel disposed to hold General Clavering responsible for what was done, or attempted, during his short tenure of office in India.

Of Colonel Monson, I cannot speak quite so gently. He was in good health, and in possession of such faculties as nature had given him, and he had been capable of improving. From all evidence, Monson stands out prominently as a proud, rash, self-willed man ; though easily misled, and very greedy for patronage and power, if not for money. Francis seems to have ruled him, by making him believe that he was ruled by him. It has been said, and, as I believe, with perfect truth, that the temper of Francis alone, was enough to introduce discord into a paradise.

Mr. Barwell, the fourth Member of Council, and the only one of the four who had resided in India, or practically knew anything of Indian affairs, was, a man of very distinguished ability, great firmness of mind, and of indefatigable application to business.

* Letter to Michael Impey, in Family MS. Letters.

I believe that, in the various difficult and delicate situations where he had been placed, he had acted conscientiously and honourably. He was certainly no "tool" to the Governor General. He had frequently disagreed with Mr. Hastings on questions of government, and, unless convinced by discussion, he had manfully supported his own opinions. But, when Mr. Barwell saw that rash opinions were insolently urged by men new in the country, and that one of these men, by misleading and hoodwinking the other two, was aiming at nothing less than a power supreme in this new Council, he took his stand by the side of Hastings, and never quitted it.

Mr. Macaulay, who is on the whole favourably disposed towards the Governor General, and who gives a not unfair account of these quarrels, says, correctly, that " the arrival of the new Members of Council from England, naturally had the effect of uniting the old servants of the Company." It could not be otherwise : in many respects it was a contest between inexperience and ignorance on the one side, and experience and knowledge on the other.

But then came the monstrous pretensions of the new Members of Council from England, to revise all the late treaties and acts of Mr. Hastings's government ; to make an entire change in the civil appointments, both up the country, and at Calcutta ; and to monopolise the entire patronage of Government.

On the 20th of October, 1774, being the day after the arrival of the new Council and the Judges, the existing government was dissolved by proclamation, and the new Council, consisting of the four gentlemen named, and Mr. Hastings, with the new rank of Governor General, took possession of its powers. As the authority at home was still divided, attention was paid not only to the Regulating Act, and the Charter or letters patent of the King in Council, but also to the injunctions of the Court of Directors in Leadenhall Street. The general letter of the Court of Directors, which was read at the first meeting of the new Council at Calcutta, recommended, above all things, unanimity and concord among those to whom the powers of the Government were now delegated ; it required them to do all in their power to preserve peace in India ; it required them to meet in council twice every week at least; it committed to Hastings, as Governor General, the charge of carrying on all correspondence with the country powers; but, at the same time, it prescribed that he should despatch no letters without the previous sanction of the Council : and that all letters received by him from the country powers should be submitted to the Council; it recommended a careful revision of all the Company's affairs, alliances, connections, &c., formed, or likely to be formed with the Indian states ; and as, by the Act of Parliament, they alone had the power of peace or war in the country, it exhorted them to be careful and cautious in the extreme, not to commit themselves by any alliances or compacts, whether with the native powers, or with the Europeans settled in India.

As the Company had fully approved of Hastings's system, which had then only recently been completed, of letting the lands on farm, and of other parts of his fiscal regulations, the Council were instructed to leave those things as they were ; but the Directors, nevertheless, urged an inquiry into all past abuses and oppressions, with the view of preventing the possibility of their recurrence. The letter finished as it began, with an exhortation to unanimity and concord. But unanimity was incompatible with a body so constituted, and with tempers, interests, and views so diametrically opposed. The earnestness and repetition of the injunction, may be taken as indicative of the belief of the Court of Directors, that discord was to ensue.

Mr. Hastings, conscious of his own superior knowledge of Indian affairs, and accustomed, for some time, to an almost undivided authority, was not likely to descend very willingly from the whole, to be only a fifth part of the representative government, or to manifest an implicit deference to the opinions of men who had passed their lives in so different a sphere as Francis, Clavering, and Monson had done. Besides, the natural love of power, the intimate and unselfish conviction, that such a system of government as he had hitherto been pursuing, was the only one that could work well with the native princes, who had no idea of a divided rule, led Mr. Hastings to act upon the recommendation, and after the example of Lord Clive, and in his political negociations at least, to assume a high, and almost single authority.

In conformity with this plan of action, he had, of his own accord, appointed his friend Middleton to be resident and agent at the court of Sujah Dowla, the Nabob of Oude, with instructions, on all secret and important matters, to correspond with himself alone, without communicating to the Council at Calcutta, who did not invariably preserve the secrecy considered necessary to the success of his diplomatic schemes. Mr. Middleton was at Lucnow, with our close ally, the Nabob, when the Members of the new Council arrived at Calcutta.

This was the very first point to which Francis, Clavering, and Monson directed their attack. They demanded that the whole of Middleton's correspondence, from his first appointment, should be laid before them. Hastings very reasonably refused to produce more than a part of it, alleging that the other portions had reference merely to private matters and opinions; and, hereupon, they began to assert, by implication, that he had embarked in an unnecessary and unjustifiable war,— the war with the Rohillas, in waging which, the English were allied with the Nabob of Oude,—for *private and sordid motives,* as they assumed; and that his whole connection with Sujah Dowla, had been a series of *bad actions, fraud, and selfishness.*

The Governor General, who ultimately returned to England with a very limited fortune, was, at the commencement of these charges, a poor, if not an embarrassed man. Power he loved as a possession congenial to his nature, and as a habit which had made it doubly natural to him to possess; but to money he was both habitually and constitutionally indifferent. Not so was Mr. Francis, who led the attack, and spread the reports of the Governor General's avarice and corruption. But I must not anticipate that part of my subject.

As Francis, Clavering, and Monson, constituted the majority of the Council, they assumed all the powers of government; reducing, for a time, Hastings, with his adherent Barwell, to the condition of a cypher. " *We*

three," said Francis, "*are king!*" And, in the pride
of his heart, he made such frequent use of this expression, that other men in Calcutta gave him, in
derision, the nick-name of " King Francis," or " Francis
the First." The kingly trio persevered in their resolution of undoing all that Hastings had done, and of
beginning every thing anew.

By this means, the government, of course, was soon
turned into an anarchy. They voted the immediate
recall of Middleton from Oude, although Hastings
declared that such a measure would be attended with
the very worst consequences, as proclaiming to the
natives, that the English authorities were no longer
agreed among themselves, and that the government of
Calcutta was falling into a state of revolution. The
Nabob Sujah Dowla, who had always looked to
Hastings, and to none other, was utterly confounded ;
and, when Middleton showed him his letter of recall,
he burst into tears, regarding it as the beginning of
hostilities intended against himself.

At every meeting of the Council, some fresh difference arose ; and Hastings began to complain bitterly
of the precipitate violence of the majority.

At the beginning of December, before the new
Members of Council had been six weeks in the country,
he wrote thus to Lord North :—

" The public despatches will inform you of the division which
prevails in our councils. I do not mean, in this letter, to
enter into a detail of its rise and progress, but will beg leave
to refer to those despatches for the particulars, and for the
defence both of my measures and opinions. I shall here only
assure your Lordship, that this unhappy difference did not
spring from me; and that, had General Clavering, Mr. Monson,
and Mr. Francis, brought with them the same conciliatory
spirit which I had adopted, your Lordship would not have
been embarrassed with the appeals of a disjointed administration, nor the public business here retarded by discordant
councils." *

Nor had Sir Elijah Impey been many months in the
country, ere he found himself obliged, in like manner,
to complain to Mr. Thurlow, and other friends in
England, of the pride and insolence of the three Coun-

* Rev. G. R. Gleig. " Memoirs of Warren Hastings."

cillors, and of certain underhand proceedings they were adopting in his regard :—

"I shall always," he said, " think myself strictly responsible for my own conduct. I do most solemnly assure you, that I have, to the best of my abilities, assisted public business in every instance ; though these gentlemen complain of the Court's giving opposition to government. The *hauteur*, insolence, and superior airs of authority, which the new Members of the Council use to the Court, may be partly discernable in the style of their minutes; but, on the spot, they maintain no colour of decency. My conduct to them has been absolutely the reverse; and I believe they are the more angry with me for it. I must beseech you not to let popular prejudices (if their letters and minutes have created any), prevent your attending coolly to the subject; and, I do assure you, that one great line in my conduct has been, to consider how I thought *you* would have acted were you in my situation; and whatever may be the opinion of others, it will be a full satisfaction to me, if I meet with your approbation. *It is to Government I hold myself answerable, and to whom I look up for protection.*" *

Alas ! my father's confidence in the protection of the Government he served, proved, from beginning to end, little better than a mere delusion.

The majority continued to declare the Rohilla war to be monstrous ; and the dispossessed, tyrannical, treacherous, and cruel Afghan tribe, bearing the name of Rohillas, to be a brave, but meek and inoffensive people, who had strong claims on the sympathy of generous minds !†

Even at this distance of time, Mr. Macaulay throws all *his sympathy* into some of his neatest, and most

---

* Letter to Thurlow, from the MSS. in my possession.

† Arrian, who wrote his account of India in the reign of the Emperor Adrian, from the materials compiled by Megasthenes, the physician of Seleucus, speaks of two tribes inhabiting the same range of mountains, but one considered inferior to the other. These mountains were traversed by Alexander, who penetrated no farther south than the Punjaub ; then sailing down one of the five tributary rivers (perhaps the Sutlej) into the Indus, returned to Babylon. It is agreed by modern travellers, that those are the same mountains which to this day are distinguished as the habitation of two separate tribes of the same descent, one still considered inferior to the other—the former Afghans, the latter Rohillas. In whatever else they may have differed, it may be presumed their *morality* was, and is, much the same. See the first 17 chapters of Arrian, in Dean Vincent's Voyage of Nearchus. Oxford, 4to. p. 15, et sequent.

F

emphatical little periods. In speaking of the engagement which—upon weighty considerations, and upon payment of money, which the Company much needed, and for which it had incessantly been calling upon the Governor—Mr. Hastings contracted with Sujah Dowla, to put that Nabob in possession of the country which these Rohillas had conquered and overrun not many years before, he says,—"The fate of a brave people was to be decided. It was decided in a manner which has left a lasting stain on the fame of Hastings and of England." Now, even in the midst of the rage for impeachment, the House of Commons itself failed to make good the Rohilla charge against Mr. Hastings.

The revival of it certainly comes with peculiar grace from a member of the cabinet which authorised the late invasion of Afghanistan. After imprinting that stain upon reputation, with which he seems to love to contaminate his own hands, Mr. Macaulay proceeds to make a kind of " happy valley" of the country where these Afghan tribes were most barbarously oppressing the Hindu people, and constantly waging wars and blood-feuds with one another. The picture is pretty as words and antithesis can make it; it is nothing, however, but a very ingenious fancy-piece, *totally divested of the charm of truth.*

The Rohillas were then, what their congeners, the Afghans, now are, and always have been, turbulent and deceitful, dangerous and vindictive neighbours,—plunderers, usurpers, and marauders. If Mr. Macaulay had spoken of the sufferings of the poor Hindus, living under the contiguous rule of the unmerciful spear and yataghan, and as utterly defenceless in themselves, he might, indeed, have awakened a just cause for commiseration; but he, as well as Mr. Francis, and all the parliamentary orators at home, leaves these poor people altogether out of the question about Rohilcund; pitying the oppressors instead of the oppressed.

In 1774, the Rohillas certainly were brave and powerful; they fought far more resolutely in open field of battle, than any foe with whom the English had hitherto contended in Hindustan; but this bravery and power, only rendered it the more necessary to dislodge them from the advanced and central position which they occupied ; and which, so long as they held it, might serve as an enticement to new invasions of our frontier.   The craft and treachery were exceeded only by the blood-thirstiness of these invaders ; but, according to Francis, though the war was to be reprobated, and the conquered Rohillas spared ; though Colonel Champion and his brigade were to be instantly ordered to evacuate, leaving the fierce clans an opportunity of renewing the contest with the unwarlike Sujah Dowla single-handed ; yet both the calculated expenses of the war, and the actual spoils of the conquest, were to be poured into the Company's treasury ; and the Nabob forced to pay, to the last rupee, what he had promised, and threatened and intimidated into earlier disbursements than he had bargained for.

In vain did Mr. Hastings and Mr. Barwell remon-strate and protest ; they were but two to three, and the determinations of Mr. Francis and his colleagues were carried into execution instantly.   Champion and his brigade were recalled, and the money demanded from Sujah Dowla with something very like the elo-quence and action of highwaymen, who hold out one hand for the purse, and point a pistol at the heart with the other ! This treatment is believed to have hastened the death of Sujah Dowla.

This allusion to the Rohilla charge against Mr. Hastings, may perhaps appear irrelevant to the object of my present investigation; but it is necessary to the continuity of my narrative, and will be found not inap-plicable to the perverted view which Mr. Macaulay takes hereafter of Sir Elijah Impey's conduct, relative to the oppression of the Hindu ryots, by the revenue collectors, in 1778-9.

> " I had not thought to have unlocked my lips,
> *In this unhallowed air*, but, that this juggler
> Would think to charm my judgment and my eyes,—
> Obtruding false rules, prankt in reason's garb:
> I hate when vice can bolt her arguments,
> And virtue hath no tongue to check her pride."

The Nabob-Vizier, Sujah Dowla, died a few months after the arrival of the new Members of Council, at the very beginning of 1775 ; dictating, in his last moments, a letter to the Governor General, to implore his friendship and protection for his son.

Towards this son and successor, Asoff-ul-Dowla, the majority in Council were as harsh as they had been towards his father; they called upon him for prompt payment of all the money that was claimed; and, at the same time, declared that the treaty of alliance was dissolved by the death of the old Nabob.

Mr. Middleton had been succeeded at the Court of Oude, by Mr. Bristow, whom Mr. Macaulay rightly calls *"a creature of their own,"* and of whom it may well be said, that he took his orders from, and acted entirely in the spirit of Mr. Francis, General Clavering, and Colonel Monson. Mr. Bristow extorted from the young, weak, and terrified Nabob, a new treaty, which contained, as an essential article, an incomparably more questionable arrangement than Hastings's subsidy for the expulsion of the turbulent Rohillas, and the annexation of their territory to that of Oude. By this treaty, the Company guaranteed to Asoff-ul-Dowla the possession of Corah and Allahabad; but the Nabob in return, ceded to the Company the dominion of Cheyte Sing, Rajah of Benares, which was not his to cede, and which Hastings had solemnly secured to the Rajah by a former treaty.

The revenue of Cheyte Sing's territory, thus alienated, was estimated at 22,000,000 rupees; but, as this took nothing out of the revenue of the young Nabob of Oude, he was bound, in the same treaty, to discharge all his father's debts and engagements with the Company, and to increase the allowance of the Company's troops which were stationed in his garrison, quite as much for the security of the Company, as for his own. Mr. Hastings indignantly refused to sanction this latter treaty, which, nevertheless, met the warm approbation of the Court of Directors at home; who, as usual, looked at the money clauses, without reflecting on the injustice of the conditions, or the ability of the young Nabob to pay.

Although convinced of the elevation of Mr. Hastings's motives, in all respects, I would not undertake entirely to justify those measures which were often forced upon him by difficult circumstances and conflicting duties; but I may confidently assume, that the policy of these reformers was altogether of a lower standard than that of our first great Governor General.

Mr. Macaulay—with an eye to his own congenial qualities—though he dignifies Junius with the title of " great anonymous writer," &c., nevertheless speaks in plain terms of the conduct of the majority, with whom the same Junius—under the name of Francis—was all in all.

I would not knowingly quote an exaggeration, however much it might tend to expose the persecutors of my father; but all my reading and information in this part of our Indian history, justifies me in saying, that I believe the following passage to be as correct in fact, as it is pointed and striking in expression.

" In spite of the Governor General's remonstrances, they [the majority] proceeded to exercise, in the most indiscreet manner, their new authority over the subordinate presidencies; threw all the affairs of Bombay into confusion; and interfered, with an incredible union of rashness and feebleness, in the intestine disputes of the Mahratta Government. At the same time they fell on the internal administration of Bengal, and attacked the whole fiscal and judicial system —a system which was undoubtedly defective, but which it was very improbable that gentlemen fresh from England would be competent to amend. The effect of their reforms was, that all protection to life and property was withdrawn; and that gangs of robbers plundered and slaughtered with impunity in the very suburbs of Calcutta. Hastings continued to live in the Government-house, and to draw the salary of Governor General. He continued even to take the lead at the Council-board in the transaction of ordinary business; for his opponents could not but feel that he knew much of which they were ignorant; and that he decided, both surely and speedily, many questions which to them would have been hopelessly puzzling. But the higher powers of Government, and the most valuable patronage, had been taken from him." *

In this state of things, the native inhabitants of Calcutta were " hopelessly puzzled," and the Europeans thrown into amazement and alarm. If these were the first fruits of reform, what would follow when the tree should be in full bearing? Mr. Hastings had thanked

* Macaulay.

his stars that, in spite of nature, he had brought his
warm temper under proper subjection and controul;*
but great as was his command over his passions, he
could not bear this personal debasement, and this
prospect of public shame and ruin.   In a letter dated
the 25th of February, 1775, he said—

"These men began their opposition on the second day of
our meeting.   The symptoms of it betrayed themselves on the
very first.   They condemned me before they could have read
any part of the proceedings, and all the study of the public
records since, all the informations they have raked up out of
the dirt of Calcutta, and the encouragement given to the
greatest villians in the province, are for the sole purpose of
finding grounds to vilify my character, and undo all the labours
of my government." †

Irritated, and hopeless of any change of temper
there, Mr. Hastings transmitted a load of papers, containing complete and literal copies of his correspondence with Mr. Middleton, to Lord North, in vindication
of his own character; and announced to his friends in
England, that he should certainly return home by the
next ship unless he received the approbation of the Court
of Directors to his past conduct.

"The natives," says Mr. Macaulay, "soon found this
out.   They considered him as a fallen man; and they acted
after their kind.   Some of our readers may have seen, in India,
a cloud of crows pecking a sick vulture to death—no bad type
of what happens in that country, as often as fortune deserts
one who has been great and dreaded.   In an instant, all the
sycophants who had lately been ready to lie for him, to
forge for him, to pander for him, to poison for him,
hastened to purchase the favour of his victorious enemies
by accusing him.   An Indian Government has only to
let it be understood that it wishes a particular man to
be ruined; and, in twenty-four hours, it will be furnished
with grave charges, supported by depositions, so full and
circumstantial, that any person unaccustomed to Asiatic
mendacity would regard them as decisive.   It is well if the
signature of the destined victim is not counterfeited at the
foot of some illegal compact, and if some treasonable paper is
not slipped into a hiding-place in his house.   Hastings was
now regarded as helpless.   The power to make or mar the

* See Letter to Mr. Sullivan in Mr. Gleig's work.
† Letter to Sullivan, as published by Mr. Gleig.

fortune of every man in Bengal had passed, as it seemed, into the hands of his opponents. Immediately charges against the Governor General began to pour in. They were eagerly welcomed by the majority, who, to do them justice, were men of too much honour knowingly to countenance false accusations; but who were not sufficiently acquainted with the East to be aware that, in that part of the world, a very little encouragement from power will call forth, in a week, more Oateses, and Bedloes, and Dangerfields, than Westminster Hall sees in a century."

Abating somewhat for the exaggerations of rhetoric, and for Mr. Macaulay's peculiar style, I take this to be a tolerably correct picture; and, with a slight reservation as to the "*too much honour*" of Mr. Francis, who led them, I can subscribe to the opinion that General Clavering and Colonel Monson, however unwise, were honourable men. It appears, however, that the charges were not merely poured in by the natives, but that they were diligently sought for by the majority of the Council, or by Francis (which means the same thing); and that, *not a little*, but a great deal of encouragement was offered to every native witness that would bear testimony against the Governor General or his friends. I only follow Mr. Macaulay in stating that it was in this temper of the Council, and in this condition of the feelings of the natives, that the Rajah Nuncomar was brought to bear testimony against Mr. Hastings.

"It would have been strange indeed," says Mr. Macaulay, "if, at such a juncture, Nuncomar had remained quiet. *That bad man was stimulated at once by malignity, by avarice, and by ambition. Now was the time to be avenged on his old enemy, to wreak a grudge of seventeen years, to establish himself in the favour of the majority of the Council, to become the greatest native in Bengal.*"

It is no necessary part of my task to enter into details of the previous life and political conduct of this ill-famed Indian : I have only to show that the crime of forgery with which he was charged, and of which he was convicted by a jury of Englishmen, whose characters were never impeached, was fairly tried; and that Sir Elijah Impey, as well as his brother judges, acted in the only manner in which they were free to act. Yet in order to render the narrative more intelligible and correct, I must relate a few particulars respecting Nuncomar, more clearly to show the manner of man he was, and the degree of consideration in which he was held before he was brought to the bar of the Supreme Court.

The Rajah, as his title imports, was an Indian of high caste. He had been minister and general to Suraj-u-Dowlah, the Nabob of Bengal, who had perpetrated the atrocities of the Black Hole of Calcutta, and who, soon after those atrocities, had been annihilated by Lord Clive. At an early period, he prepared to abandon his prince and master, and to obtain advantages to himself by playing into the hands of the English conqueror. After the fall of Suraj-u-Dowlah, Nuncomar obtained eminent employments, and alternately served and betrayed the English. He was never known to do anything except upon the most selfish and corrupt motives —he was universally regarded as one of the most faithless, the very worst, and wickedest of the Hindu chiefs. But he had a perfect knowledge of the indirect practices of his countrymen, and was supposed to have a far greater influence over them than he really possessed.*

For a long time the Court of Directors were impressed with the notion that business could not be conducted in Bengal without Nuncomar; and they continued to employ him, or to insist upon his being employed. In vain did Lord Clive declare, and in vain did Mr. Hastings repeat the declaration, that the Rajah Nuncomar was the worst man they knew in India,—one that might be employed, but never could be trusted. Hastings even accused Nuncomar of plotting against his life or absolute ruin. He said in one of his letters to the Court—"From the year 1759 to 1764, I was engaged in a continued opposition to the interests and designs of that man, because I judged him to be adverse to the welfare of my employers, and I had sufficient indications of his ill-will to myself." These, and other, and still stronger expressions, were used by the Governor in his correspondence; but still the Company were infatuated in their belief that, in counteracting the falsehood of the native courts, Nuncomar was to them an indispensable

* See Major Rennel's evidence before the House of Commons, during Sir Elijah Impey's Defence in 1788. Appendix, part III. p. 217.

instrument; not but that the Court of Directors admitted the moral obliquity of the man.   Eleven years before the arrival of Sir Elijah Impey at Calcutta, they had declared their conviction that Nuncomar was capable of *forgery*, false accusations, and all other frauds and crimes, and that he ought to be vigilantly looked after. Nevertheless the Directors from time to time availed themselves of the dangerous services of this man ; and he was employed in state intrigues, and *coups d'etat*, which wise men would not have ordered, and which none but bad men would have executed.

The published correspondence of Mr. Hastings (though but a small part of the evidence which might be produced) will sufficiently show that the crooked counsels pursued in India were far more frequently dictated by the Court of Directors in England, than acquiesced in by the Governor in India ; and that it was with reluctant shame and anguish that Mr. Hastings bowed to the commands of his masters and employers, in dealing with Nuncomar.   Hastings, however, partly consoled himself by reflecting that the low estimation in which the Rajah was held by his own countrymen, of all castes, would prevent his being dangerous to the Indian Government, and that as he would remain "a subject of the Company," it would be easy to remove him, or otherwise punish him as soon as it should be proved, or even suspected, that he was abusing the trust.*

It certainly never occurred to Mr. Hastings to doubt that Nuncomar was not, to all intents, a subject of the Company, and as such within the jurisdiction of the courts of law at Calcutta, whatever those courts might be.   Yet, as we shall soon see, it has been made a crime in Sir Elijah Impey to have tried this Rajah in the Supreme Court!—and the foundation of this offence is traced to a fanciful theory, opposed to all fact and precedent, that the Rajah was not amenable to the laws established in Calcutta !

Surely Mr. Macaulay is not quite so ignorant as to believe this.   But no matter; like a veracious historian, and no "idiot or biographer," he is intent upon making my father a judicial murderer, and therefore believes or

* See Letter from Warren Hastings to Josias Dupré, Esq., quoted by Mr. Gleig.

disbelieves whatever he chooses. One only wonders that
he has conjured up no more victims to the alleged conspiracy between the Governor General and the Chief
Justice.   Unhappily for his argument, out of all Mr.
Hastings's accusers, not another had been hanged either
for forgery or any other capital offence, and still more
unluckily, it was proved afterwards before the House of
Commons, that, during Sir Elijah's long residence in India,
not a single prisoner had been sentenced to death except
the Rajah.   Yet if these two functionaries had been capable of the crime he imputes to them, and if the other
judges had been so uninfluential or supine as he implies
them to have been, nothing would have been easier
than to have brought some score of the Governor's
enemies under the same dreadful penalty : and yet, in a
former instance, Fowkes and others, including the Rajah
himself, who had been tried for conspiracy against Mr.
Hastings, were acquitted by the Supreme Court.*   Concerning that transaction Mr. Macaulay keeps a prudential
silence.   Nor does he pretend to deny that Nuncomar was
a most accomplished scoundrel, and one who had committed crimes which would have brought him to condign
punishment in any country under the sun.   He admits
that "this bad man was stimulated at once by malignity,
avarice, and ambition;"   and   that, by accusing Warren
Hastings, he sought " to be avenged on his old enemy, to
wreak a grudge of seventeen years, to establish himself
in the favour of the majority of the Council, to become
the greatest native in Bengal !"   With all this my father
had nothing to do ; for whatever were Nuncomar's evil
motives and propensities, the Supreme Court had only to
try him on a capital charge which had long been pending.   It was, however, in that blessed frame of mind,
which Mr. Macaulay himself has   described,   that
the Maharajah Nuncomar, on the 6th of March,
put into the ever-open and inviting palm of Mr.
Francis, a paper accusing the Governor General of
oppression, fraud, embezzlement, and corruption.
Francis read this precious document in Council.
The Governor General indignantly complained of the
way in which he was treated ; spoke with contempt
of the accusations of so discredited an informer, and

* See Howell's State Trials.

significantly asked Francis whether he had previously been aware of Nuncomar's design in thus standing forth as his accuser. Mr. Francis, with hesitation avowed, that though ignorant of the precise contents of the letter then read, he knew perfectly, when he received it from the Rajah, that it was full of heavy charges against the Governor General.

Warren Hastings denied the right of the Council to receive such accusations against him; and the meeting broke up, as nearly every meeting of Council now did, in storm and anger. Francis retired to confer with his accomplice; and, at the very next meeting of the Board, produced another paper, in which Nuncomar demanded to be heard before the Council, in support of his previous allegations. Francis, as usual, carried along with him Clavering and Monson, thus constituting a majority, voted against Hastings and Barwell, that the Rajah should be called in and heard. The Governor General then said, that although he had no objection to the majority forming themselves into a committee of inquiry, he would not sit as the President of a Council, to be confronted by such a man as Nuncomar, or to see the very refuse of the community brought in, to give evidence at the dictation of his accuser. Mr. Macaulay seems to admit that the Governor General could not have suffered this without betraying the dignity of his post; and that from persons like Francis, Clavering, and Monson, who were heated by daily conflict with him, he could not expect the fairness of judges. But even with such rudiments of a legal education as Mr. Macaulay may confess to have received, or even without ever having eaten his commons in an inn of court, this uncandid writer ought to have seen and stated that the Members of Council could in no case sit as judges upon the Governor General. Mr. Barwell spoke of the Supreme Court as the proper tribunal before which such cases ought to be tried; and Mr. Barwell was right in law and in reason; but it did not suit Mr. Macaulay's dialectics to introduce anything that went in favour of the Court over which my father honourably presided, and so he says not a word about Mr. Barwell's proposition.

In spite of that proposition, and the angry protest of

the Governor General, the majority carried their motion.   Hastings rose, declared the sitting at an end,—
as he had a right to do,—and left the room, followed by
Barwell.

With their ordinary disregard to all legal prescription,
and with an utter contempt of the presidential authority
vested in the Governor General by Acts of Parliament,
and letters patent, the majority, instead of considering
the Court as dissolved, kept their seats, voted themselves
a council, put Clavering in the chair, and ordered the
Rajah Nuncomar to be called in.   He entered with a
flourish about his own integrity, and the purity of his
motives, which must have cost them a struggle to keep
their countenances or repress their laughter.   It was
utterly impossible for any one of this self-voted council
to have been five or six months in Calcutta without hearing of the old grudges which Nuncomar bore to
Hastings, or without knowing in what estimation the
Rajah was universally held.   It should appear, however, that the countenance and demeanour of the Board
were such as to encourage and not disconcert the self-
applauding *honest* Rajah ; for he not only adhered to
the original charges set down in the first paper delivered
to Francis, but—to use Mr. Macaulay's words—after
the fashion of the East, he produced a large supplement
to them.   In particular he stated that Hastings had received a large sum for appointing Goordas—the son of
Nuncomar, the accuser—treasurer of the Nabob's
household, and for committing the person of his highness—then a mere child—to the care of his step-mother,
the Munny Begum.   In urging this charge, Nuncomar,
forgetting the honest character to which he had just
laid claim, admitted that he himself had, in the matter
of this imputed bribe, acted as the Begum's agent.   The
evidence he produced was a letter addressed to himself
by the Munny Begum, in which she expressed her
great satisfaction at the kindness of Hastings, and said
that the Governor had consented to take from her two
lacs of rupees, if she should be pleased to give them.
Of this letter Mr. Macaulay says,—"The seal, whether
forged, as Hastings affirmed, or genuine, as we are
rather inclined to believe, proved nothing.   [Mark the
insidious caution of this innuendo ; for what does it

imply but the writer's belief that Nuncomar was not an habitual *forger*, lest by admitting it now, he should compromise himself hereafter?] Nuncomar, as every body knows, who knows India, had only to tell the Munny Begum that such a letter would give pleasure to the majority of the Council, in order to procure her attestation."* Thus, either way this letter was unworthy of the slightest attention; and even had it been as authentic as gospel, these three Members of Council had not only no legal right to decide upon it, but none whatever to receive it. They, however, with their wonted precipitancy, voted that the charge was made out; that Hastings had corruptly received between thirty and forty thousand pounds sterling; and that he ought to be compelled to refund the same. The injustice, the irrationality, the monstrous absurdity and illegality of such a decision, seem to strike Mr. Macaulay as they must strike every man of common sense; but how, after such an act, such a foul antecedent as this, can he place confidence in any decision or attestation of the majority? how can he believe that rancorous passions were ever absent from their counsels, at least from those of their prompter? or how believe that their unofficial and perfectly unauthenticated accusations were to be received as satisfactory evidence against the characters of two such men as the Governor General and the Chief Justice? *Igitur ne suspicari quidem possumus quenquam horum ab amico quippiam contendisse quod contra fidem, contra jusjurandum, contra rem publicam esset. Nam hoc quidem in talibus viris quid attinet, discere? si contendisset scio, impertraturum non fuisse; cum illi sanctissimi viri fuerint: æquè autem nefas fit tale aliquid et facere rogatum, et rogare.*

I need not enter into Nuncomar's charges against the

---

* But what says Hastings? " The letter produced by Nuncomar as the Munny Begum's is a *gross forgery*. I make no doubt of proving it."— Letters to Mr. Graham and Colonel Macleane, dated 25th March, 1775. Mr. Macaulay speaks of a *seal*, because it looks more oriental and picturesque, but he says nothing of a signature, although the letter certainly had a signature, and very probably bore no seal. These little things are characteristic of the school to which Mr. Macaulay belongs. The signature of the letter was compared with the Begum's signature attached to an authenticated communication just received from that lady, by Sir John D'Oyly, and it was declared not to be in the handwriting of the Begum.

Governor General. In common with every man who
has attentively examined the subject, I believe them to
have been utterly false, and to have been supported by
forgery. This is, and must be, Mr. Macaulay's impression; although for the reason I have alleged he will not
acknowledge it to its full extent. He admits, however,
that after the proceedings in Council which I have just
related, the general feeling among the English in
Bengal was strongly in favour of the Governor General.
He might have added, that the feeling of the far greater
part of the more respectable or wealthier natives sat
in the same direction; and that it was the general
opinion among these Hindus and Mohammedans that
the country would shortly become the scene of war and
of anarchy, if the wisdom and experience of the accomplished Governor General were to be superseded
and overruled by a man like Philip Francis; whom, by-
the-bye, at this point, Mr. Macaulay himself decribes
as "a War Office clerk, profoundly ignorant of the
native languages and the native character." Yet, notwithstanding these feelings of the better part of the
community of Calcutta, the triumph of the Rajah
seemed for a time to be complete.

"Nuncomar," says Hastings, "holds his durbar in complete
state, sends for zemindars and their vakeels, coaxing and
threatening them for complaints, which no doubt he will get
in abundance, *besides what he forges himself*. The system
which they (the majority) have laid down for conducting
their affair is, as I am told, after this manner. The General
(Clavering) rummages the consultations for disputable matter,
with the aid of old Fowke. Colonel Monson receives, and, I
have been assured, descends even to solicit accusations.
FRANCIS WRITES.* Goring is employed as their agent, with
Mohammed Reza Khan, and Fowke with Nuncomar. .   .   .
Was it for this that the legislature of Great Britain formed
this new system of government for Bengal, and armed it with
powers extending to every part of the British Empire in
India!"†

Yet where there existed so many persons, of all conditions and castes, that were terrified at the aspect of
affairs and disgusted at these sanctioned and applauded

* For Francis was Junius.
† Letter to Mr. Graham and Colonel Macleane, as given by the Rev.
G. R. Gleig, in Memoirs of Warren Hastings.

villainies, it could not but happen that the Rajah's triumph should be interrupted. One of the principal native witnesses waited upon the Governor General, and affirmed with the most solemn asseverations, that Nuncomar, Mr. Fowke, Radachurn, and others, were guilty of conspiracy against him, offering to produce satisfactory evidence to that effect. Hastings resolved on the prosecution of these men, and accordingly instituted proceedings in the Supreme Court against them for a conspiracy. The judges, after a long examination of the case, made Nuncomar and Fowke give bail, and bound over the Governor General to prosecute them.

It was immediately after these proceedings—that is to say, after Nuncomar had been charged with a foul conspiracy, and the four Judges of the Supreme Court had seen cause sufficient to hold him to bail—that Francis, Clavering, and Monson made their visit of honour at Nuncomar's durbar, a compliment which had never been paid him before, either by themselves or by the members of any preceding administration.*

Nuncomar was thus out upon bail, when, on the 6th of May—only a few weeks after—he was charged with the private forgery which he had committed long ago. About five years before the arrival of Sir Elijah Impey, and the new English Court, accusations for this offence had been brought against the Rajah by one Mohunpersand, a native and a Hindu, like himself. The prosecution had been registered in the Mayor's Court at Calcutta, over which Hastings then presided; for even this Court, according to the Charter of 26 Geo. II., was bound to administer English law, but no proper judges or law officers had been then appointed, either by the Crown or the Company; the Governor's functionaries had made a medley of English, Hindu, and Mohammedan; and whether sitting in the Court or not, the Governor himself often interfered in the proceedings and decisions of that Court. These facts were well known in England when the Regulating Act was framed, and in a great measure for the purpose of preventing their recurrence. The Mayor's Court considered the charge so grave, and the evidence so good, that it arrested and committed

* See Hastings's own letters in Mr. Gleig's Memoirs, and " Our Indian Empire," by Mr. Mac Farlane.

Nuncomar; but Hastings, who had at that time been ordered by the secret committee of the Court of Directors to avail himself of the services of the Rajah, commanded the Court to release the already half-convicted villain, and the Mayor's Court had released him accordingly.

As there then existed no other criminal court to resort to, and as the Governor had interposed between the law and the offender, it followed, of course, that the prosecutor, Mohunpersand, neither did nor could take any further steps in the prosecution before the arrival of the Supreme Court, which was to supersede the Mayor's Court, and to be wholly independent of Warren Hastings and the Council. Moreover, the forged instrument, the capital evidence of the Rajah's guilt, was kept in the Mayor's Court, and could not be procured from thence. In conformity with the Regulating Act, the new Supreme Court, which sat for the first time towards the end of October 1774, demanded the records and papers of the Mayor's Court, and these records and papers were forthwith delivered up. Among them was found the document alleged to have been forged by Nuncomar. The Judges of the Supreme Court restored this document to Mohunpersand, the party entitled to it, thus putting the prosecutor in a condition to proceed against the Rajah. In doing this the Court did that which it was bound to do. And it must be noted that this was done some months before Nuncomar, under the encouragement of Francis, Clavering, and Monson, preferred his charges against the Governor General. With good ground to go upon, Mr. Mac Farlane says—

"It seems proved, by every possible variety of evidence, that the Supreme Court could neither have tried the forgery *sooner* than it did, nor *later* than it did; and that, with the startling coincidence of time and facts (which years afterwards was turned to such account by Francis and the other numerous enemies of Hastings and Impey, and which made so deep an impression on the public mind in England) proceeded from natural and almost inevitable causes and circumstances over which neither the Supreme Court collectively, nor Sir Elijah Impey individually, had any sort of controul. It further appears that Impey, though subsequently selected out of that body as the sole object of prosecution, had less to do with the measures which preceded the trial and condemnation of Nuncomar, than any of the four members of that Supreme Court. Judge Chambers did indeed suggest that the indictment should be laid under an Act of Queen Elizabeth,* when forgery was not held as a capital offence; but the other three judges all agreed that the said Act of Elizabeth was obsolete; that the Charter of George II.,† and the Regulating Act, left them no choice, binding them to administer English law at Calcutta as it was administered in England; and that, therefore, the indictment of Nuncomar must be laid under the statute which made forgery an offence punishable with death. The whole amount of Chambers's difference of opinion was this, and no more. This old associate of Dr. Samuel Johnson sat on the bench during the whole trial, concurred in the sentence, and approved of whatever was done. It was not Impey, but Judge Lemaistre, who issued the warrant upon which Nuncomar was arrested, and thrown into the common prison of Calcutta.‡

Thus, if there had been a conspiracy against Nuncomar between Hastings and my father, his private friend and schoolfellow, the Chief Justice, must have had the art of inducing Judge Lemaistre to take the first step in it, while in the conclusion of the affair, Chambers, Hyde, Lemaistre, and himself, must have been equally concerned, and equally guilty. There is no separating them, except by that rhetorical and reviewing process, wherein law and common sense are set at defiance.

But Mr. Macaulay, as if he considered it too daring a flight to accuse four English judges of a detestable conspiracy with the Governor General to take the life of an obnoxious Hindu, singles out my father as the only offender, never mentioning any other name than that of Sir Elijah Impey, and placing all the power, and all the assumed iniquity in that one Judge. And yet, he knew, or ought to have known, that Sir Elijah could do nothing at all without the knowledge, and very little without the concurrence of his three colleagues—all men of approved worth, and unblemished reputation.

* The 5th of Elizabeth.
† 2 Geo. II., c. 25, having made forgery to be a felony, became the only law by which forgery was any crime at all : the Court, therefore, must have proceeded on that statute, or not at all.
‡ Our Indian Empire.

In describing what he considers to have led to the
arrest of Nuncomar, the right honourable gentleman
does indeed speak of the Calcutta bench collectively;
but he cannot do even this, without holding up my
father as an especial mark. He says,—

"The Supreme Court was, within the sphere of its own
duties, altogether independent of the government. Hastings,
with his usual sagacity, had seen how much advantage he
might derive from possessing himself of this stronghold; and
he had acted accordingly. The judges, *especially the Chief
Justice*, were hostile to the majority of the Council. The
time had now come for putting this formidable machinery in
action."

Now the judges were of no party, and only " *hostile* "
to the majority of the Council, inasmuch as that
majority were " *hostile* " to law, and passionate and unconstitutional in the conflict they were waging against
the Governor General; and neither Mr. Macaulay,
nor any other man, whether writer or parliamentary
orator, or both in one, had ever a shadow of evidence to prove, that the hostility of Sir Elijah Impey
was greater than that which Justice Chambers,
or Justice Hyde, or Justice Lemaistre, entertained against the majority in the Council. In
good truth, the elements of hostility were wanting in
my father's disposition. He was the worst—that is to
say the feeblest—hater I ever knew. But had it been
otherwise,—had his disposition been hot and impetuous,
instead of calm and conciliatory as it was,—he could
never have indulged his *hostility* to the majority of the
Council at the expense of the life of a human being, to
the outrage of the laws he revered, and to the offence
of the God he adored !

Mr. Macaulay speaks as if the arrest of the Rajah
followed immediately upon his denunciations of the
Governor General ; in the first place, let it be remembered, that two good calendar months elapsed between
those two events. But I shall hereafter show distinctly,
not only in the words of my father's defence, but from
the evidence of various English witnesses taken upon
oath, that the coincidence, if such it can be called, was
indeed inevitable, and that there was no connection
whatever, between Nuncomar's insidious attack upon

Warren Hastings, and his trial and condemnation for forgery. Mohunpersand, who had been wronged by the Rajah, and who was a Hindu, and probably as prone to revenge as any of his countrymen, stood in no need therefore of any prompting: he was bound to prosecute the charge he had brought, and he did prosecute it at the very first moment that he could do so, or that the terms and rules of the Court allowed.

The right honourable critical and historical essayist, with an unmannerly and unwarrantable sneer at Mr. Hastings's biographer, says,—"the ostensible prosecutor was a native. But it was then, and still is, the opinion of everybody—idiots and biographers excepted—that Hastings was the real mover in the business." This is flippant,—this is indecent,—this is *cowardly*,—if regard be paid to the sacred profession of the biographer ; neither is it true, and far from amounting to anything like proof : it does not afford matter for a sober hypothesis, —not even for a rational guess.*

The Governor General on the trial of Nuncomar, deposed upon oath, that he had never, directly or indirectly, countenanced or forwarded the prosecution for forgery against Nuncomar. The solemn oath of Warren Hastings is assuredly worth more than the hazardous assertion of Mr. Macaulay, who can produce no manner of evidence to support his sharp dictum.

In regard to the alleged conspiracy against the prisoner, let it here and hereafter be borne in mind, that though the fact had been for eleven years the subject of parliamentary investigation, nothing either then or since was ever brought to light, to prove any such combination between the parties. How, then, can it be averred, at the present distance of time from those transactions, that "it was then, and still is, the opinion of every body —idiots and biographers excepted—that Hastings was the real mover in the business?" That it was not

---

* Mr. Gleig is far too able and spirited a writer, to require any advocacy of mine, and has, perhaps, done well, to treat *his insulter* with the silent contempt which he deserves. Had our cases been parallel, I might have done the same. But Mr. Macaulay has not insulted me, but my father, whose reputation is more sacred to me than my own, because he no longer lives to defend it for himself. By this act of double cowardice—though entitled to a double portion of contempt—Mr. Macaulay has no right to expect the same forbearance from me as from Mr. Gleig.

the opinion of contemporary lawyers, is proved by the letters produced, at the time of his persecution, by Sir Elijah Impey, from Lord Ashburton and Sir W. Blackstone,* which letters were written shortly after the trial of Nuncomar; that it was not the opinion of the inhabitants of Calcutta, natives as well as Europeans, is proved by the addresses† of all the Hindus and Armenians, of all the free merchants, and of the grand jury; of all, in short, except Francis, Clavering, and Monson; and even they refused to recommend the prisoner to mercy, or to interfere in any way to save his life. Either Mr. Macaulay's everybody becomes a nobody, or everybody is an idiot or a biographer except himself.

But let us suppose, for the sake of argument—though my thorough acquaintance with the character of Mr. Hastings will never allow me to admit it as a fact —that the Governor General was indeed the real mover in the business; whom did he move, or could move? not Sir Elijah Impey singly, for that would have been of no use,—not the Court collectively, not the Chief Justice and the three puisne judges in a body, for that would have been alike perilous in the attempt, and impracticable in execution. Hastings, then, could only move Mohunpersand, the Hindu prosecutor; and so soon as the prosecutor brought up the case, the Court could do nothing after trial but proceed to judgment according to the laws of England, which awarded death on the gallows to all felonies, including forgery. Thus, even if the Governor General were the chief mover, the Supreme Court had nothing to do with the movement. The Court had only to try the prisoner brought before them, it mattered not to them how, or by whom. Even if it had been in evidence that Warren Hastings had urged Mohunpersand, the judges could not have proceeded otherwise than they did. If guilt is often screened by a confederacy, it is perhaps, as often denounced by a confederacy.

Though often a fearfully exciting tragedy, the Newgate calendar is not quite such pleasant reading as the Greek tragedians, over which and his articles for the

* See pages 17, 18, of the printed Defence.
† See Appendix, part 2, Nos. 1, 2, 3, 4, 5, of the printed Defence, p. 90, *et sequent.*

Edinburgh Review, Mr. Macaulay is said to have spent most of his time while in India, instead of devoting that time to the public services in which he was ostensibly employed, and for which he was so extravagantly paid out of the public purse; but let Mr. Macaulay take up the Newgate Calendar, the " *Causes Celebres,*" or the " State Trials," and he will find, that the prosecution and conviction of a criminal are often dependent upon charges first laid by a scoundrel, acting upon any principle rather than that of honour and justice. The judge does not investigate the motives of the informer or the prosecutor, nor does the jury: the jury listens to the evidence of the crime, and upon their verdict the judge applies the law. If the *malus animus* of prosecutors and informers had been allowed to stand in bar of legal procedure, the Newgate Calendar would have been but a small book compared to what it is.

CHAPTER IV.

ARREST AND TRIAL OF NUNCOMAR, AND INTERFERENCE OF
THE MAJORITY—NUNCOMAR'S PETITION; CONSULTATIONS
IN COUNCIL UPON IT—EVIDENCE OF MATTHEW YEANDLE,
MR. TOLFREY, AND DR. MURCHISON,* ETC.

IT was on the 6th of March, 1775, that Nuncomar put
his letter of charges against Hastings into the hands of
Francis, or that Francis produced them in the Council
Chamber: it was on the 6th of May, 1775, and not
earlier, that Nuncomar was arrested in consequence of
the party injured by the forgery having reproduced his
charge. Mr. Macaulay says, in his boldly figurative
manner, that Calcutta was astounded by the sudden
news of his arrest. But a rhetorical figure is not a fact;
there is nothing to show that the inhabitants of that
populous city were disturbed or in any way excited by
the news. The Maharajah whom Mr. Macaulay somewhat irreverently styles† "a Brahmin of the Brahmins,"
had been arrested and imprisoned more than once before; his character was infamous, he was detested even
by those who were for the season acting with him in
the hope of sharing the future spoils of the majority;
and among the superior classes, native or European,
there were probably but few who were ignorant of the
desperate game he had been playing throughout the
whole of his iniquitous and changeful life, or who

---

* Kenneth Murchison, Esquire, father of the present Sir Roderick, the
distinguished geologist, and author of " The Geology of Russia in Europe,
and the Ural Mountains." See Mr. Tolfrey's Evidence, Appendix, part 3,
No. 6, p. 198 of the printed Defence.

† In allusion to Philippians, cap. 3, v. 5.

thought his final destiny could terminate otherwise than tragically. Nothing was more familiar to the minds of the natives than rapid rises and sudden downfalls ; and the apathy and fatalism of these people are extreme. Mr. Macaulay is somewhat more correct in describing the manner in which the majority acted after Nuncomar's arrest ; but in no one thing that he touches can he be accurate or sincere. With him the *suppressio veri* takes turn and turn about with the *assertio falsi.* His words are these,—

"The rage of the majority rose to the highest point. They protested against the proceedings of the Supreme Court, and sent several urgent messages to the judges, demanding that Nuncomar should be admitted to bail. The judges returned haughty and resolute answers. All that the Council could do, was to heap honours and emoluments on the family of Nuncomar; and this they did."

Now the "majority" did something more than this : as if to display their contempt for the judges of the Supreme Court, or to influence public opinion by testifying still farther their esteem for the notorious malefactor, they visited Nuncomar in his prison—exhibiting themselves there with pomp and preparation, General Clavering being attended by his aide-de-camp, Captain Thornton. At this last proceeding—of which Mr. Macaulay says nothing—Hastings was exceedingly incensed ; and his wrath must have risen to the highest pitch, when, almost immediately after the occurrence, he thus wrote to his friends at home :

"The visit to Nuncomar when he was to be prosecuted for a conspiracy, and * the elevation of his son when the old gentleman was in jail, and in a fair way to be hanged, are bold expedients. I doubt if the people in England will approve of such barefaced declarations of their connections with such a scoundrel, or of such attempts to impede and frustrate the course of justice."†

Mr. Macaulay, who is "nothing if not" rhetorical, speaking of the reply of the judges to the demand of admitting the prisoner to bail, uses the words "haughty" and "resolute." But why? The answer which the

* Mr. Macaulay, with some flippant remark, ignorantly states, that Mr. Hastings had promoted Goordas.

† Letters to Graham and Macleane, dated May 18, 1775, as given in Mr. Gleig's Memoir.

Court had to return was simply this,—"Forgery is not a bailable offence." This was the voice of the law; there could be no *haughtiness* in it. If the majority repeated their demand with their usual arrogance and presumption; if, as in other cases they menaced the Court, and attempted to overrule it, then, I can well believe, that the rejoinder of the Court would be *"resolute"* enough. My father, for one, had at all times a hearty contempt for bullying and browbeating, and was never the man to be moved from his purpose, or deterred from his duty, by threats of persecution. His was—

> "The virtuous mind, that ever walks attended
> By a strong-siding champion—conscience."

But if bail was denied to Nuncomar, every possible indulgence was allowed to him in his prison. By order of the judges, unusual care was taken to furnish him with the means of performing his ablutions, and other offices of religion, in adherence to the rules of Brahminical life.

I have said that the arrest took place on the 6th of May. There was no hurrying on of the trial. The first session of oyer and terminer held by the Court, commenced in the month of June; *before* that time nothing could be done, and *beyond* that time nothing could be delayed.

A true bill against Nuncomar was found by a grand jury, composed of some of the most respectable and worthy British inhabitants of Calcutta, who, assuredly, would have ignored the bill, if there had been any suspicion of collusion, or any kind of foul play. The bill being duly found by the grand jury, the prisoner was, on the 8th of June, brought before the judges of the Supreme Court, and a jury composed of twelve British subjects inhabiting Calcutta.* Mohunpersand, a native merchant of Calcutta, and the original accuser, made out his case with much clearness, and there was an accumulation of evidence to prove that, nearly six years before, the prisoner had committed forgery on or in a certain bond, with the intention of defrauding the prosecutor

---

* Mr. Macaulay, ever determined to make my father the sole or prominent actor, keeping the three other judges *in the back ground*, as if they had nothing to do with the proceedings, here says,—" Nuncomar was brought before *Sir Elijah Impey*, and a jury composed of Englishmen."

out of a large sum of money. The bond was produced; the seal and signature were sworn to as being false, and the work of Nuncomar. Numerous witnesses deposed not only to this particular act, but to the general character of the prisoner, speaking of the Rajah, as a man who had been repeatedly guilty of *forgery.* Nuncomar had witnesses at hand to swear against nearly everything that the witnesses for the prosecution swore to. The great informer's knowledge and tactics probably did not extend very far beyond this producing of false witnesses, in which he had proved himself a proficient; but he was assisted by counsel—by two English barristers, Messrs. Farrer and Brix—of eminent ability and repute; and so far from being, as some have alleged, unacquainted with the nature of the English laws relating to forgery, and with the dangerous predicament in which he stood, he was very well informed as to both these circumstances, and knew perfectly that life and death depended upon the issue. In fact, as I have already stated, the particular law in question, as well as other criminal laws of England, had been applied in Calcutta, long before the Supreme Court was established, and before the passing of the Regulating Act, which did but republish, confirm, and provide for, the due execution of the Statute of George I., in the 13th year of his reign, A.D. 1726; and the confirmatory Charter of George II., granted in the 26th year of his reign, A.D. 1753; and as far back as 1765, Radachund Mettre, *a Hindu of rank like Nuncomar,* had been condemned to *death* for *forgery;* and though he had received the King's pardon, other natives had been hanged for the same crime, years before the trial and conviction of Nuncomar.

This Rajah was a man of remarkable ability; and, like most of his countrymen, quick in inquiry and retentive of what he learned; his connection with Francis must have familiarized his mind with the provisions of the Regulating Act, and with the unqualified injunctions which the letters patent gave the judges to administer the law in cases of *forgery,* and other felonies, as they were administered in the courts of England. Moreover, during his imprisonment, his counsel—both respectable barristers—had had free access to him, and they were fully competent to acquaint him with the bearing of our law upon his indictment.

Nuncomar was not ignorant of the law, neither he nor his counsel ever thought of disputing or challenging the jurisdiction of the Supreme Court, as was done for him by others, though not until a long time *after he had been hanged*; but the jury first impannelled they *did* challenge, and the privilege being of course allowed, the following jury were ultimately sworn:—

Edward Scott,	John Ferguson,
Robert Macfarlane,	Arthur Adie,
Thomas Smith,	John Collis,
Edward Ellerington,	Samuel Touchett,*
Joseph Bernard Smith,	Edward Satterthwaite
John Robinson,	Charles Weston.

Nuncomar was upheld by the belief that the majority of the Council who had employed him, urged him into conspiracy and dealings with false witnesses; rewarded him, flattered him, honoured him even when lying in jail as a criminal; were not only stronger than the Governor General, but also seemed to be stronger than the law —threatening to step in between him and the execution of the sentence of the Supreme Court. By this fallacious hope was he sustained, from the moment he was carried to prison, down to that in which he ascended the scaffold. Nor were efforts wanting on the part of the majority of the Council to buoy him up in this cruel delusion. Messages were continually sent to him in prison by General Clavering and Colonel Monson— Francis being too cunning to commit himself in this way—and to these messages answers were returned by the Rajah.† On the trial, however, his witnesses were out-numbered by those for the prosecution, among whom were included very many, if not most of the prin-

---

* It is observable that Mr. Samuel Touchett was one of the jury on Nuncomar's trial in 1775. (See Howell's State Trials.) Although in 1780 the petition commonly called Touchett's petition, so named from him, was presented to Parliament, and contained the charges against Sir Elijah Impey; one of its objects being to transmit the power of respiting from the judges to the Government with a clear reference to this case; though the same Mr. Touchett, like the rest of the jury, when strongly urged by Nuncomar's counsel, had refused to apply for a respite on that occasion. See appendix to Report on Touchett's petition, No. 3.

† Affidavit of Matthew Yeandle, the jailer of Calcutta.

cipal native inhabitants of Calcutta. The deed now
produced in Court was taken as a convincing proof of
guilt, and the whole tenor of the man's life corroborated
it. There was no indecent precipitation, or any irregularity whatsoever in the trial : it was slow, circumspect,
and solemn. Even Mr. Macaulay seems to admit as
much as this. He says—"A great quantity of contradictory swearing, and the necessity of having every
word interpreted, protracted the trial to a most unusual
length." Conspirators do not proceed thus. It was not
in this fashion that the infamous Judge Jeffries dealt
with his prisoners, although Mr. Macaulay, with an
absurdity equal to his presumption, has dared to assi-
milate with that execrable monster of injustice my most
upright father!

The Court had no option whether to proceed
or not, unless grounds could be proved for appeal
against its jurisdiction, or for quashing the indictment :
the first was not attempted; the second was, but upon
grounds proved not to be admissible. The cause of
the prisoner was heard as well as that of the prosecutor
—with equal patience and impartiality. Nay, it is the
opinion of all who have carefully perused the trial, and
who are competent to judge in such matters, that great
favour was shown to the prisoner, *particularly by the
direction of the presiding judge.* In the end the jury
returned a plain and unqualified verdict of guilty, without the slightest hint of recommending the prisoner
to mercy. The four judges concurred; and Sir Elijah,
as president and organ of the Court, pronounced sentence of death. During the proceedings he had taken
neither more nor less part than his three brethren:
therefore, if there was guilt in the trial and sentence,
Justices Chambers, and Hyde, Lemaistre, were as guilty *and*
as he. And what can be said of the twelve "good men
and true," who sat as a jury, and returned the verdict of
guilty? Why nothing less than this,—that if there was
a conspiracy—if the Rajah had not a fair trial—they
were as guilty as the four judges sitting on the bench !
Yet, incredible as it may seem, when Sir Elijah Impey
was to be held up as the murderer of Nuncomar, no
breath of censure, no whisper of suspicion was ever
heard against any one but him.

From the Court Nuncomar was remanded to his prison; where he continued to be treated with all tenderness, consistent with safe custody, in his unhappy position.* In 1765, when Radachund Mettre lay under sentence of death for forgery, the principal native inhabitants of Calcutta drew up and signed an earnest petition in his favour; but now no such step was taken by the natives, neither Hindu nor Mohammedan; nor could a single English resident of either party be found to recommend the prisoner to mercy, or to pray for a suspension of his execution—though solicited to the utmost verge of propriety by Mr. Farrer,† his humane and spirited advocate. Not a friend nor relative petitioned for the life of the convict. They could hardly have been withheld by fear of Mr. Hastings; for, though not stronger than the law, Francis, Clavering, and Monson were, at that time, far stronger than the Governor General: the majority in Council were ruling all things with an absolute sway, and they continued so to rule for many months after that period. From *them* the family and friends of Nuncomar had received offices of emolument, together with such honours as such strange statesmen only could confer. To *them*, therefore, they might have reasonably petitioned in behalf of their relative—Mr. Macaulay's "Brahmin of the Brahmins!" Yet they petitioned not. Like Nuncomar himself, they probably rested upon the confident hope that Francis, Clavering, or Monson would prevent his execution. But assuredly it was not for the judges of the Supreme Court to enter into these secret speculations, or to invite petitions from family partisans or friends. The only party or person that petitioned for Nuncomar was Nuncomar himself!

The instances are most rare in which attention is paid to a prayer for mercy put up by a condemned prisoner, at the very last moment, and without any other recommendation; and these must be kept altogether distinct from the present case: for this single, personal,

---

* See official document, No. 18 Appendix, part 5, p. 61, of Sir E. Impey's Defence, where the name of Radachund Mettre appears as sentenced to death for forgery, but pardoned, Feb. 27, 1765.

† Thomas Farrer, Esq., then M.P. for Wareham, gave his evidence from his place in the House of Commons, Feb. 11, 1788. See Appendix, part 3, from p. 105 to 161 of the printed defence.

and tardy petition was never presented to the judges at all. It was *burned by the hands of the common hangman* as a libel on the Supreme Court,—and it was so burned, not by order of the Supreme Court, to whom it was not addressed, and who knew nothing of it until several days after the convicted felon had been hanged ; not on the motion of Hastings, who was afterwards said to have plotted the prisoner's death, and who, at that moment, could carry no measure whatsoever ; but on the motion of Francis, who controlled everything that was done in Council, and who afterwards pretended that he and his colleagues had been extremely anxious to save the Rajah !

"These men," says Mr. Mac Farlane, with perfect truth, and with a mass of evidence to bear him out, "had seized upon all the powers of government; they had repeatedly set the authority of Hastings at defiance, voting another president to fill his chair; they had interfered in matters of far greater import; they had broken treaties and alliances of his making, and had made treaties and compacts of their own; they had declared to his own face, and to the Court of Directors, and to still higher authorities at home, that Hastings was an embezzler, a plunderer, a conspirator, and that they believed him to be capable of the darkest crimes, and Nuncomar wholly innocent of the two charges—of the conspiracy on which he was admitted to bail, and of the forgery for which he was to be hanged; they continued to defy his authority after the event, as before it; and everything goes to prove, that if they had been seriously bent on preserving the old Rajah's life, they might have preserved it. If they had been animated by the generous feelings and the enthusiastic regard for justice which Francis afterwards laid claim to for himself and his colleagues, they would have risked hostile collision, and actual civil war in the streets of Calcutta, rather than have permitted the execution. In a very short time they did risk that extremity. In the present case they seem to have felt that the death of Nuncomar would give them the opportunity of proclaiming to the world—unacquainted with the particulars—that Hastings had precipitated the arrest, trial, and execution of a troublesome witness whose charges he could not answer, in order to terrify other witnesses from appearing against him. And to this account they certainly began to turn the old Rajah as soon as he was dead."*

* Our Indian Empire.

I have stated that Nuncomar's petition was not addressed to the Supreme Court, and that the judges
knew nothing of it until after the prisoner had been
executed, when, of course, it was too late for mercy
from any quarter. The petition was addressed to the
Council, but was not written until the eve of the day
fixed for the execution—so long did the unhappy prisoner's confidence last in his political patrons, the treacherous majority. But that which is strangest of all,
and so startling as to be incredible, if it were not supported by irrefragable evidence—the Rajah's petition
was not *presented* at the Council Board until *eleven days*
after the petitioner had been hanged ! To those who
love to put the worst construction upon whatever they
choose to think mysterious—to those who can scent a
conspiracy wherever there appears to them anything
like a combination of time and circumstances, or a difficulty of explaining, upon just and rational grounds, any
perplexity at a critical moment, in the conduct of public
men—there will be found far better foundation for believing that Francis, Clavering, and Monson, were engaged in a conspiracy to bring the Rajah to the gallows,
than that there was any such plot between Warren
Hastings and Sir Elijah Impey. I must, of necessity,
refer to this part of the subject when I put my father
upon his defence before the House of Commons, and
repeat the words of that defence ; but the present
seems to me the proper place for introducing certain
official documents, without which this dark story cannot be properly understood, and I here introduce them
accordingly.

Extract of Bengal Secret Consultations, August 14, 1775.*

" General Clavering—I beg leave to inform the Board,
that, on the 4th of this month, a person came to my house,
who called himself a servant of Nuncomar, who sent in an
open paper to me : *as I imagined that the paper might contain some request that I should take some steps to intercede
for him, and being resolved not to make any application what-*

---

* Nuncomar was executed on the 5th of August. I shall relate that
execution presently, my immediate object is merely to show that neither
Sir Elijah Impey, nor the other judges, could possibly prevent its taking
place, and that nothing whatever was done by any other party to prevent it.

ever in his favour, I left the paper on my table until the 6th, which was the day after his execution, when I ordered it to be translated by my interpreter. As it appears to me that this paper contains several circumstances which it may be proper for the Court of Directors, and his Majesty's ministers, to be acquainted with, I have brought it with me here, and desire that the Board will instruct me what I have to do with it: the title of it is, 'A Representation from Maharajah Nuncomar to the General and Gentlemen of Council.'

"Mr. Francis—As the General informs the Board, that the paper contains several circumstances which he thinks it may be proper for the Court of Directors, and his Majesty's ministers, to be acquainted with, I would request that he lay it before the Board.

"Mr. Barwell—I really do not understand the tendency of this question, or by what authority the General thinks he may keep back, or bring before the Board a paper addressed to them, or how this address came to be translated for the particular information of the General before it was presented here.* If the General thinks himself authorised to suppress a paper addressed to the gentlemen of Council, he is the only judge of that authority: for my part, I confess myself to be equally astonished at the mysterious air with which this paper is brought before us, and the manner in which it came to the General's possession, as likewise at the particular explanation of every part of it before it was brought to the Board. If the General has a particular commission to retain this paper from the knowledge of those to whom it is addressed, he alone is the proper judge how he ought to act; when the paper comes before me I shall judge of it.

"General Clavering—If Mr. Barwell will be pleased to recur to the introduction of my minute, he will observe that I mentioned having put the paper into the hands of my Persian translator; *consequently could not know the contents of it, or to whom it was addressed, till it was translated.*† I brought

---

* It was General Clavering's bounden duty to have presented such a paper as soon as he had received it. If the Board were not sitting, he ought to have called them together. The paper was presented to him by a servant of Nuncomar, and he knew that Nuncomar was to be hanged the very next morning. There was, therefore, not a moment to lose. He also knew, or as he says, "imagined," that the paper was a petition. He says that he was resolved not to make any application whatever in Nuncomar's favour; but this resolution ought not to have prevented his handing the petition to the gentlemen of the Council to whom it was equally addressed. How could he know that Hastings and Barwell might not be inclined to make some application in favour of the convict? He put it out of their power by keeping the paper!

† Nuncomar's petition was so short, that General Clavering's Persian interpreter, who was always at hand in his house, might have given him

it with me to the Council the first day which they met, after I knew its contents; *but the Board not having gone that day into the secret department, I did not think it proper at that time to introduce it.** Nobody can be answerable for the papers they may receive. All that I can say is, that this paper had *the seal and signature of Rajah Nuncomar* to it; † and I bring it to the Board just in the form I received it, *that is to say, open.*

"COLONEL MONSON—As this paper is said to contain circumstances with which the Court of Directors, and his Majesty's ministers, should be acquainted, I think the General should lay it before the Board.

"THE GOVERNOR GENERAL—I do not understand this mystery. If there can be a doubt whether the paper be not already before the Board, by the terms of the General's first minute upon it, I do myself insist that it be produced, if it be only to give me an opportunity of knowing the contents of an address to the Superior Council of India, excluding the first Member in the title of it, and conferring that title on General Clavering; and I give it as my opinion, that it ought to be produced.

"GENERAL CLAVERING—I am sorry to observe, that the Governor General should have mistaken the title of this address to the Board, by calling it an address to me as Governor General, when the title of it had been so recently mentioned, by my saying it was addressed to the *General,* and *the Gentlemen of Council;* which, in my opinion, does not express, either by words or by inference, that ever that title is such as the Governor General has mentioned. At all events, I am no more answerable for the title of the paper, than I am for its contents.

"THE GOVERNOR GENERAL—I did not say that the

the sense of it in ten minutes. But the General preferred leaving it upon his table "until the 6th, which was the day after the execution," when, according to his own account, he first put it into the hands of his interpreter! In one minute the General might have known from his interpreter, that the petition was not meant for him singly and solely.—See Bengal Secret Consultations, 14th and 16th August, 1775.

* How delicate is the General's attention to official etiquette! In a hundred other instances, he, and Francis, and Monson, set the established rules of the Council-chamber at defiance, and made a secret committee of their own. But if the Board had gone that day into the secret department, what could it have availed Nuncomar, who had been hanged several days before?

† Whatever may have been General Clavering's ignorance of the language of the country, and of the Persian character, he must have known the seal of Nuncomar as soon as the petition was presented, even supposing the Rajah's servant had not given him that explanation, or any information as to the contents of the paper.

address gave the General the title of Governor General, but meant only to imply, that it conferred that title on him, by mentioning him particularly, and the rest of the Council collectively.

"Resolved, that the paper delivered by the servant of Nuncomar to General Clavering, be produced and read.

"The General is accordingly requested to produce it, and it is read.

"N.B. This paper is ordered to be expunged from the records by a resolution of the Board, taken at the subsequent consultation, on the 16th instant."

Extract of Bengal Secret Consultations, the 16th August, 1775.

"The Persian translator sends in a corrected translation of the petition of the late Maharajah Nuncomar, delivered in by General Clavering, and entered in consultation the 14th instant; in which, the Board remark, *that the address is made in the usual form, to the Governor General and Council, and not as was understood from the first translation of it laid before the Board.*

"THE GOVERNOR GENERAL moves—that, as this petition contains expressions reflecting upon the characters of the Chief Justice and judges of the Supreme Court, a copy of it may be sent to them.

"MR. FRANCIS—I think that our sending a copy of the Rajah Nuncomar's address to this Board, to the Chief Justice and the judges, would be giving it much more weight than it deserves. *I consider the insinuations contained in it against them, as wholly unsupported, and of a libellous nature;* and if I am not irregular in this place, I should move, *that orders should be given to the sheriff, to cause the original to be burned publicly, by the hands of the common hangman.*

"MR. BARWELL—I have no objection to the paper being burned by the hands of the common hangman; but I would deliver it to the judges, agreeable to the Governor's proposition.

"COLONEL MONSON—I differ with Mr. Barwell in opinion. *I think this Board cannot communicate the letter to the judges; if they did, I think they might be liable to a prosecution for a libel.** The paper I deem to have a *libellous tendency, and the assertions contained in it are unsupported.* I agree with Mr. Francis in opinion, that the paper should be

* The Act 13 Geo. III. c. 63, sects. 15, 17, prohibits the Court from trying any action of indictment against the Governor General and Councillors for any offence not being treason or felony; and exempts them from arrest and imprisonment. See ante pp. 37, 38.

burned, under the inspection of the sheriff, by the hands of the common hangman.

"GENERAL CLAVERING—I totally disapprove of sending to the judges the paper, agreeably to the Governor General's proposition, because I think it might make the Members of the Board who sent it, *liable to a prosecution ;* and therefore agree with Mr. Francis, that it should be delivered to the sheriff, to be burned by the hands of the common hangman.

"THE GOVERNOR GENERAL—I should have no objection to any act which should publish to the world the sense which this Board entertain of the paper in question; but it does not appear to me that such an effect will be produced by Mr. Francis's motion. The inhabitants of this settlement form but a very small part of that collective body commonly understood by that expression of the world. The petition itself stands upon our records, through which it will find its way to the Court of Directors, to His Majesty's Ministers, and in all probability will become public to the whole people of Britain. I do not, however, object to the motion of its being burned.

"The Board do not agree to the Governor General's motion for sending a copy of the address of Maharajah Nuncomar to the judges; but resolve, that orders be sent to the sheriffs, with the original letter, to cause it to be burned publicly, by the hands of the common hangman, in a proper place for that purpose, on Monday next, declaring it to be a libel.

"MR. FRANCIS—I beg leave to observe, that by the same channel through which the Court of Directors, and His Majesty's Ministers, or the nation, might be informed of the paper in question, *they must also be informed of the reception it had met with, and the sentence passed upon it by this Board; I therefore hope, its being destroyed in the manner proposed, will be sufficient to clear the characters of the judges, so far as they appear to be attacked in that paper ; and, to prevent any possibility of the imputations indirectly thrown on the judges from extending beyond this Board,* I move, that the entry of the address of the Rajah Nuncomar, entered on our proceedings of Monday last, be expunged.

"Agreed, that it be expunged accordingly, and that the translations be destroyed."

And accordingly the paper was burned, under the inspection of Mr. Tolfrey, the substitute of Sheriff Macrabie, who was Francis's brother-in-law.*

* Q. "Was you present when a paper was burned in consequence of an order of the Governor General and Council, of the 16th of August, 1775?"

The whole of that document, as translated into English, will be found in the appendix to the present volume. In this place, I need merely bring under the reader's eye, an abstract of the passages in it, which the Council deemed libellous and unsupported; and of the publication of which, Francis, Clavering, and Monson, expressed so much dread and fear on their own account.

After affirming that he himself was an innocent and an honourable man, and his prosecutor, Mohunpersand, a great scoundrel and liar, Nuncomar complained that many English gentlemen had become his enemies, and joining with "Lord" Impey, *"and the other justices,"* had tried him by the English laws, which were contrary to the customs of his country, in which there was never any such administration of justice before; * and taking the evidence of his enemies in proof of his crime, had condemned him to death: that many principal people of the country, who were acquainted with *his honesty,* had frequently requested of the judges to suspend his execution until the King's pleasure should be known; but this they had refused,† and were unjustly taking away his life.

Although the extracts of the " Bengal Secret Consultations" which I have quoted, and which contain a tale so startling, have been printed and reprinted for more than half-a-century, and are accessible to any inquiring and pains-taking writer, they seem to have been utterly unknown to the *tranchant* Mr. Macaulay, whose sword

---

A. "I received a paper, a small Persian paper, *sealed up,* with instructions from the Governor General and Council, to have it *burned as a libel by the hands of the common hangman.* It was burned by the jailer; there was no common hangman. It was burned *sealed up,* without the contents being disclosed."—*Examination of Mr. Tolfrey at Calcutta*—See Appendix, part 3, No. 7, p. 178, Sir E. Impey's Defence.

" Why," asks Sir Elijah Impey, " this anxiety that the contents of the paper should not be disclosed? Why was it ever brought into the secret department?"—*Notes in Appendix to Speech before the House of Commons.*

* This assertion was palpably false, and the Rajah knew it to be so. He knew that Radachund Mettre had been tried and convicted for forgery in 1765, on the 2 Geo. II. c. 25.

† This is equally false. The judges could not refuse a reprieve which was never asked for; nor could they have granted it had it been asked for, without stating sufficient grounds, as required by the Charter annexed to the Regulating Act. See sec. 20, ante p. 42.

H 2

is not two-edged, and can only cut in one direction; he says not a word about the minutes of Council, nor even about the petition. It would not have suited his line of argument to do so; for the slanderers of my father, in their several minutes, declare, over and over again, that it was libellous in Nuncomar to assert that there was a confederacy against him, and that he had not been fairly tried.

But yet I firmly believe that Mr. Macaulay, who does all he can to consign the memory of an honourable man to eternal infamy, by the mere impulse of false reasoning, never gave himself the trouble to look for the books in which, both the secret consultations, and the abortive petition are contained; and that he is so little read in the large subject which he so daringly presumes to undertake, as not even to have known of the existence of such books,—unless, indeed, he knowingly suppresses their authority: in either case I do not envy him his option between gross ignorance, and deliberate falsehood!

In the charge relating to Nuncomar, as in other charges, he has gathered his materials chiefly from the reports of hostile committees of the House of Commons, which were dictated by Francis, and adopted by Burke, into whose mind Francis had infused his venom; from *Annual Registers,* which were written under the immediate controul of that rash and misguided statesman; from parliamentary speeches, rich in eloquence, but poor in fact; and, most of all, from Mr. James Mill's one-sided and theoretical history of India. Indeed, Mr. Macaulay has, in most cases, done little more than strew the flowers of rhetoric over the dry dull prose of Mr. Mill; he has, in no one particular, endeavoured to trace this un-British historian of British India to his authorities; he has never taken the pains to discover, by reading and research, whether the dicta which Mr. Mill delivers, with so much starch and sententious brevity, be really solemn truths, or falsehoods cloaked in mock solemnity. What confidence, then, is to be reposed in an author of so little research, who, though pretending to write biography and history, is careless of his facts, and only solicitous about his style? Is it to be endured, that a wretched sophist like this, should, with his unhallowed defamation, harrow up the feelings of the living, and desecrate the memory of the dead?

But if Mr. Macaulay has nothing to say touching Nuncomar's petition to the Supreme Council, and the strange method which General Clavering pursued in regard to that petition, he is very eager to show that the Supreme Court, who had received no petition, and who knew of none, ought to have respited the convict. In attacking the reverend biographer of Warren Hastings with his usual virulency, and in dealing out wholesale accusations of ignorance, and negligence, which ill become a writer so negligent of facts, and so ignorant of Indian affairs as he himself is, Mr. Macaulay says,—

" Mr. Gleig is so strangely ignorant as to imagine, that the judges had no further discretion in the case; and, that the power of extending mercy to Nuncomar resided with the Council. He therefore throws on Francis, and Francis's party, the whole blame of what followed"—i.e. the execution of the prisoner.*

Now, in one sense, Mr. Gleig is wrong in assuming that the Court could not respite the prisoner; but in another sense, he is right : the Act and Charter, or letters patent, gave the power of respite not *absolutely*, but *conditionally*.† It required the Court to state the *reason* for granting a respite. Without a reason no respite could be granted. Therefore, all that Mr. Gleig means to assume is, that the judges being unable to find any good reason why the prisoner should be respited, had no option, unless the jury or the Supreme Council had interfered.

---

* " We should have thought," continues the right honourable reviewer, " that a gentleman who has published five or six bulky volumes on Indian affairs, might have taken the trouble to inform himself as to the fundamental principles of the Indian government."

I should have thought that this bitter censor of other men would have taken that trouble,—that he would, at least, have acquainted himself with the meaning of the Regulating Act, the letters patent, constituting the Supreme Court, and the Statutes and Charters of George I., and George II., —*I* should have thought a gentleman sent out to India to compile laws for the country, should have had the habits and accuracy of a lawyer, with such a share of legal knowledge and experience, as to have made it impossible for him to declare that he was no lawyer; *I* should have thought that a Member of Council, after residing some five years in India, would have known something about Indian affairs, and would have left behind him at Calcutta something to tell that he had been there.

† See ante p. 42.

" The Council," says Mr. Macaulay, with far greater
inaccuracy than that which he fancies he has detected in
Mr. Gleig, " *had, at that time, no power to interfere.*"
Not so : for at that time, the Council *had* the power,
and *might have interfered ;* but not only did it *not* interfere, but, through Francis, Clavering, and Monson, *prevented* an interference in favour of the prisoner.   Upon
this point, Mr. Macaulay is pleased to remember, that
Sir Elijah Impey did not stand alone, and that he had
colleagues, for he speaks of " *the judges* " collectively.
Yet, immediately afterwards, as if to retract the concession, he returns to the singular number, and implies a single responsibility in my father.   He says,
" That Impey ought to have respited Nuncomar, we
hold to be perfectly clear."   And again, " a *just* judge
would, beyond all doubt, have reserved the case for the
consideration of the sovereign.   But Impey would not
hear of mercy or delay."   Why this return to the singular number ?   Why Impey alone ?   Could Impey be
an unjust judge, and Chambers, Lemaistre, and Hyde,
be just ones ?   Could Impey, of himself, refuse to hear
of mercy or delay ?   Was he the whole Court ?   Were
his three colleagues absent, or asleep, or deaf, or dead ?
If a petition for a respite had been presented, to whom
would it have been addressed ?   Not to the Chief Justice solely and singly ; but to the Chief Justice, and
judges of the Supreme Court all together ; and if such
petition had ever been sent, all the four judges must
have answered it.   But neither Sir Elijah, nor the other
three judges, ever heard of any petition or application
for mercy or delay, simply because none were ever presented to them.

Even his light dramatic reading might have informed
the right honourable reviewer and essayist, that there
are certain things impossible to *sense*.   Lord Burleigh,
in " The Critic," was a great man, and a keen one, yet
he could not *see* the Spanish fleet because it was " *not
in sight.*"   So neither Sir Elijah Impey, nor any one of
the three puisne judges, could " *hear* " of mercy or delay,
because the words were never uttered.

But, to be serious.   My father in his convincing and
triumphant defence on the Nuncomar charge, before the
House of Commons,—and that defence *was* triumphant,

and *is* convincing to every enlightened and honest mind, albeit Mr. Macaulay knows nothing about it, or rather chooses to suppress any such knowledge,— plainly states, how the Court could have shown no reason—which, by the Charter, they were obliged to do—for respiting the prisoner. That passage I shall hereafter give at full length. Here I would only ask, what was there in the case of Nuncomar, *primâ facie,* to recommend him to the indulgence of the Court as an object for a respite? Was it to be found in his evil reputation, in his universally infamous character, in his malignity, avarice, and disloyalty? Was it to be found in his cheatings, swindlings, forgeries, and false-witnessing? Or in his recent conspiracy against the Governor General? Or in his remoter perfidy which contributed to the horrors of the Black Hole, with the execrable murder of one hundred and twenty-three British subjects?

Let it, too, be noted on the other hand, that many weighty causes suggested themselves for carrying the sentence into execution. There was the prevalence of the crime of forgery among the natives, and the common belief, however erroneous, in those days, that the penal laws might check it; there was the apprehension, lest the natives might understand a respite as tantamount to a reprieve or an acquittal, and so treat it as a mockery or denial of justice; there was the chance, or rather the certainty of the imputation of fear under a threat of rescue; and of weakness and dereliction of duty; nay, of bribery and corruption: for it is a fact, that one of the judges (Lemaistre) was audaciously offered a large sum of money to save the life of Nuncomar.

Either of these conclusions might have stood much in the way of that security and reliance on the newly-established Court, which were essential to its future authority. It could scarcely be expected that a criminal of Nuncomar's rank would be speedily brought up for judgment; and if this conspicuous malefactor were respited or reprieved, how could the extreme penalty of the law be inflicted on a humbler delinquent? If a respite or reprieve had been granted, the ground of attack might have been changed, and Francis, in after years, might have taxed my father with having trafficked in justice.

If, at this crisis, India had been lost by the temerity of Francis and his adherents, instead of being saved, as it was, by the policy of Mr. Hastings, aided by the firmness of the Supreme Court; what then would have been the predicament of my father? Can any reasonable man, with all these facts before him, doubt for a moment, that the loss would have been shifted from the shoulders of the majority of the Council, and the catastrophe imputed partly, if not wholly, to the timidity, or corruption, of Sir Elijah Impey; and that, in 1788, or long before, he would have had to plead at the bar of the Commons, against the reverse of those charges which were then brought against him?

I have said that, from first to last, the hoary sinner Nuncomar, looked to the majority for security. Nor have I hazarded this assertion, as Mr. Macaulay hazards his, for I have evidence taken upon oath to support it. Matthew Yeandle, the jailer at Calcutta, swore,—

"That the said Maharajah Nuncomar *always conceived hopes of being released, even to the day before his execution, when he wrote a letter to the Council for that purpose; and that messages were continually sent to him by General Clavering and Colonel Monson, and answers returned.* And this deponent further said, *That he always understood, both from the said Maharajah Nuncomar and his attendants, that it was from the influence of General Clavering and Colonel Monson that he expected his enlargement."* *

I have likewise said that great kindness and indulgence were exercised towards Nuncomar while lying in prison, and that this was done by order of the Court. For this assertion, too, I have evidence—and, in such a case, the best that could be desired. Matthew Yeandle, keeper of the public jail of Calcutta, makes oath—

"That on the 6th day of May, Maharajah Nuncomar was taken up on a charge of forgery, and *committed by Mr. Justice Lemaistre and Mr. Justice Hyde* to the custody of this deponent. And this deponent further saith, that he quitted his

* This affidavit was sworn at Calcutta, on the 18th of January, 1776. It is to be found in the Appendix to the Report of the Committee of the House of Commons; to whom the petition of John Touchett, and John Irving, was referred. It is also given in the Appendix to my father's defence before the Commons (p. 180), and in several other publications, at *none* of which Mr. Macaulay has ever looked, unless he has wilfully suppressed his knowledge of them *all*.

bedroom in order to accommodate the said Maharajah Nun-comar therewith, and gave up the use of an outer room thereunto adjoining, for the accommodation of the attendants of the said Nuncomar. And this deponent further saith, that *the said rooms are detached from the other part of the jail, and have no communication whatsoever with the felons or debtors therein confined.* And this deponent further saith, that he was present when the said Maharajah was arrested ; and that *the room wherein he was confined is a larger and much better room than that from whence he was taken, and better than any of the rooms in the house of the said Maha-rajah Nuncomar.* And this deponent further saith, that he *received repeated directions from the* CHIEF JUSTICE *to treat the said Nuncomar with all possible tenderness, and to grant him every accommodation and convenience his situation would admit.* And this deponent further saith, that neither before nor after his condemnation, were irons affixed to his feet, and every person who was desirous of seeing him had free access at all times of the day; and that the said Maharajah Nun-comar *was visited during his confinement by Captain Webber, one of the aides-de-camp to General Clavering, and Mr. Ad-dison, secretary to that General, and the two Mr. Fowkes's ; and that Mrs. and Miss Clavering, and Lady Ann Monson, sent their compliments to, and inquired after the said Maha-rajah Nuncomar.*"

During the first days of his captivity, Nuncomar re-fused to take any food in public ; and pretended that he could not, and did not, take food in any other way. This was a stale trick, but for a moment it seems to have deceived the jailer. This deponent said,—

"That he did not see any alteration whatsoever, in his countenance, speech, or appearance, until the evening of the 10th of May,* when the said Maharajah Nuncomar altered the tone of his voice, and spoke so low, that he could scarcely be heard, and seemed so faint, that he could not lift his head from the ground. And this deponent further saith, that the CHIEF JUSTICE sent a physician† that evening to visit the said Maharajah, and sent for him, the deponent. And this deponent further saith, that at the time he was at the house of the Chief Justice, Mr. Justice Lemaistre and Mr. Justice Hyde were there; and this deponent heard the CHIEF JUSTICE desire Mr. Justice Lemaistre (*under whose warrant, and that of Mr. Justice Hyde, the said Nuncomar was con-*

---

* The 10th of May was the fourth day after his arrest.
† Mr. Murchison.

fined) to consent that the said Maharajah might be permitted to go to the outside of the said prison gate. And this deponent further saith, that the said Mr. Justice Lemaistre was very unwilling so to do, and alleged that he considered the conduct of Maharajah Nuncomar merely artifice; and that he thought such order would be illegal, and therefore could not join in it. And this deponent further saith, that he received directions for permitting the said Maharajah Nuncomar to go to the outside of the said prison gates, as he had requested, about ten o'clock of the night of the said 10th of May, and immediately communicated the same to the said Maharajah Nuncomar. And this deponent further saith, that the said Maharajah Nuncomar did not avail himself of such permission until the next day, between the hours of ten and twelve in the forenoon ; and that he walked from his said room to the outside of the said prison, without any assistance, and did not appear any ways exhausted, and had recovered his speech, and talked in the same tone of voice that he usually did. And this deponent further saith, that the said Maharajah Nuncomar was, during the said five days, frequently in private with only his own servants, and had water taken to him, but that he did not see any food conveyed to him. And this deponent further saith, that the usual diet of the said Maharajah Nuncomar was sweetmeats, which might have been easily conveyed to him without the knowledge of this deponent."*

To this I may add the affidavit of Dr. Kenneth Murchison himself.

"This deponent, Kenneth Murchison, surgeon, maketh oath, and saith, that on or about Wednesday, the 10th of May, 1775, Sir Elijah Impey, Knight, requested him, this deponent, to go to the jail in which Maharajah Nuncomar was then confined, and to report to him, the said Sir Elijah, the state and condition of the health of the said Nuncomar ; that in consequence of the said request, he, the said deponent, went to the said jail, where he found the said Nuncomar extended on the ground, in a seemingly weak and helpless condition ; that the said Nuncomar—as the interpreter told this deponent—declared that he had received no manner of sustenance since the Saturday next preceding that day ; and that the said Nuncomar spoke in a low and feeble voice. And this deponent further saith, that he felt the pulse of the said Nuncomar, that his pulse appeared to him not

* Affidavit of Matthew Yeandle. Appendix, part 3, No. 7, of the printed Defence, p. 180, and Appendix No. 2 to the Report of the Committee on Touchett's Petition.

weak, but regular, and not as he should have expected in a man who had fasted so long. And this deponent further saith, that he does not mean to say that he had not fasted that length of time ; but if he had really fasted so long, it was an extraordinary case, and inconsistent with the symptoms which, in the best of his judgment, he believes must have appeared. And this deponent further saith, that on his return to Sir Elijah, he made his report to the effect abovementioned ; and further acquainted the said Sir Elijah, that if, in fact, he had not eat or drank during the time abovementioned, it was necessary he should take sustenance before the next morning."*

Let us now hear the affidavit of the under-sheriff, who performed most of Sheriff Macrabie's duties for him.

"Samuel Tolfrey, of Calcutta, in the kingdom of Bengal, gentleman, maketh oath, that he, this deponent, was under-sheriff of Calcutta aforesaid on the 6th day of May last, and committed Maharajah Nuncomar to the public jail of Calcutta aforesaid, by virtue of a warrant for that purpose, under the hands and seals of Mr. Justice Lemaistre and Mr. Justice Hyde. And this deponent further saith, that on the 10th of the said month of May, he was informed by Matthew Yeandle, keeper of the said jail, that the said Maharajah Nuncomar was expiring, owing to his having refused to take sustenance in the said jail, in consequence of which information, he, this deponent, went to the said jail, and found the said Maharajah Nuncomar extended on the floor; that he was, or pretended to be, unable to lift up his head, and spoke in so faint a voice, that this deponent was under the necessity of kneeling close to the said Maharajah Nuncomar, in order to distinguish what he said. And this deponent further saith, *that he saw the said Maharajah Nuncomar two or three times between the time of his confinement, and the said 10th of May ; and that, till that evening, he was firmly persuaded that the refusal of the said Maharajah Nuncomar, was only a pretence to procure his enlargement. And this deponent further saith, that he verily now believes, that the illness of the said Maharajah Nuncomar, on the said 10th of May, was mostly affected.*"†

After making this affidavit the same witness said,—

"I went with Mr. Jarrett‡ to the house of the Chief

* Affidavit, sworn to at Calcutta, on the 18th of January, 1776. *Ibid.*
† Affidavit of Samuel Tolfrey, the under-sheriff. *Ibid.*
‡ Mr. Jarrett was attorney for the prisoner.

Justice, and represented the weak and dangerous situation the prisoner appeared to be in. *The Chief Justice appeared much distressed at the account, and immediately sent Dr. Murchison to the jail, and sent for the jailer. He also sent for Mr. Justice Lemaistre and Mr. Justice Hyde. It was late at night. They came; and, after some conversation, the particulars of which I do not recollect, the jailer received instructions from the Chief Justice immediately to allow the prisoner to go on the outside of the prison, properly secured, as he had requested.* I do not recollect being present on any other applications made by Mr. Jarrett."

I could produce more evidence of the same sort to prove the great humanity with which the convict was treated in his prison, and the care and anxiety of Sir Elijah in this particular; but I have already produced enough.

There was no indecent hurry in the execution. There was abundance of time allowed for the getting up and presenting of petitions if any party had been disposed to get them up. Twenty days intervened between the prisoner's sentence and his death. He was hanged on the morning of the 5th of August; and the execution passed off not only without any riot or attempt at rescue, but even without any visible excitement among the natives. Of this I have been well assured by many persons who were present or who were in Calcutta on that day; and there is ample testimony, taken upon oath, to prove that the native population regarded the execution with great indifference. But this sober and unexciting truth does not suit Mr. Macaulay, any more than it suited Philip Francis, and the orators he inspired, and the writers he furnished with their data. He and they were determined to make a moving scene. Mr. Macaulay, indeed, surpasses himself in his own particular line, while describing the execution. He says,—

"The excitement among all classes was great. Francis, and Francis's few English adherents, described the Governor General and the Chief Justice as the worst of murderers. Clavering, it was said, swore that, even at the foot of the gallows, Nuncomar should be rescued."

But how did Francis and his adherents describe the three other judges who were as much concerned in the trial as Sir Elijah Impey? And how did they describe that jury of twelve respectable Englishmen who had returned the verdict of guilty, with the full knowledge that such a verdict must be followed by the sentence of death? In reality, neither Francis nor his faction had yet ventured to give any such description of the Governor General and the Chief Justice. Mr. Macaulay *anticipates* their malice and slander. As usual, he is spinning fine phrases without thinking of facts and dates. Francis and his friends allowed many years to pass before they dared to describe Mr. Hastings and Sir Elijah Impey as "the worst of murderers." These odious epithets they never hazarded in *Calcutta*, where they would have been laughed at; but in *England*, where people were unacquainted with the facts, and careless about the veracity of reports. When these expressions began to be uttered, it was in a secret, cautious, and cunning manner; and at first more in the way of insinuation than by direct statement. The rearing of the monstrous fabric of calumny and falsehood occupied the genius of Francis for fourteen long years. When the first foundation stones were laid, it is probable that the architect himself did not know either to what a height he would raise his edifice, or how enduring it would prove; so strictly have both he and Mr. Macaulay—those "great anonymous writers"—observed the rules of their prototype, Don Basile!* He did a little at a time—*parva metu primo*—and then, watching the effects of that little—*mox sese attolit in auras ingrediturque: solo, et caput inter nubila condit.* True, he began very early to make insidious minutes in Council; but those were kept secret; and on the day when Nuncomar was hanged, he would no more have thought of describing the Governor General and Chief Justice as "the worst of murderers," than he would have thought of proclaiming George the Third as a usurper and tyrant in the public places of Calcutta. Even if he had then complained of the execution as harsh, every man might have asked him, Why, then, had he and his majority of Council permitted it? why had they not stayed execution and insisted on a reprieve? Why keep back his petition till after he was hanged, and then order it to be burned as a libel?

* See ante p. 32.

But to return to the last sentence we have quoted—
Where did Mr. Macaulay ever hear or read that
General Clavering swore Nuncomar should be rescued
even at the foot of the gallows? Where did he find
this vow proceeding from a man, who had kept Nuncomar's petition close until several days after the Rajah
was no more, and who had declared before the Council
that he was resolved not to make any application whatever in the Rajah's favour? I have read until my eyes
have been nearly blinded, and I have employed younger
and keener eyes than my own in reading whatever
relates to this case; not merely a few books on one side,
like the right honourable reviewer, but many books,
folios and quartos, pamphlets, and papers, on both sides
of the question, and I have not been able to find, or
to get indicated to me, any passage containing this rash
vow of General Clavering. It may, indeed, be assumed,
that the parliamentary orators and impeachment managers were not very scrupulous as to what they
affirmed; but I cannot find even in their speeches and
reports any allusion to this vow. I and my friends may
have been unfortunate in our research; but I am rather
inclined to believe that this bold allegation proceeds
solely from Mr. Macaulay's own fertile imagination.
In all his articles and essays he seeks to dramatise the
characters he introduces. This is all very well, provided
that truth or verisimilitude be not altogether sacrificed to
theatrical effect. It is, doubtless, an effective style of
writing, and after effect Mr. Macaulay is always aiming.
He especially dramatises the character of Clavering;
and as this gentleman was a soldier and a general,
quick in speech and hot in temper, he is constantly
producing him, in the guise and attitude of

"The Earl of Chatham with his sword drawn,"*

or of those precious conventionalities, the hot old general
officers that figure among the *dramatis personæ* of

---

* " The Earl of Chatham with his sword drawn,
    Stood waiting for Sir Richard Strachan;
    Sir Richard eager to be at 'em,
    Stood waiting for the Earl of Chatham."
  Let me not be thought to trifle with a grave and important subject, if
I treat these exaggerations with contempt. There is no levity in derisive
indignation : *ridentem dicere verum fortius ae melius*—when we have to

Morton, Reynolds, and other playwrights, who had possession of our stage in the earlier part of the present century. Mr. Macaulay, knowing nothing about the petition of Nuncomar, nothing about the minutes of Council, nothing about Clavering's declaration, puts the General into a towering passion, and makes him talk nonsense about the foot of the gallows, because Nuncomar is going to be hanged.

I shall show, in another chapter, the sort of authority Mr. Macaulay has for the incidents he introduces into his terrible and awful description of the scene which followed the execution ; the grief and horror that were on every face ; the cries and contortions of the natives, which appalled the European ministers of justice, without producing the slightest effect on the iron stoicism of the prisoner ; the howl of sorrow and despair that rose from the innumerable spectators as the drop fell ; the hundreds that turned away their faces from the polluting sight, fled with loud wailings towards the Hooghley, and plunged into its holy waters, as if to purify themselves from the guilt of having looked on such a crime, &c. Those who were in Calcutta, saw nothing and heard nothing of the sort. Yet Mr. Macaulay is not without a groundwork, such as it is, for his picture. That ground-work exists in a letter which was never seen or heard of until twelve or thirteen years after the execution ; when it was produced by the enemies of Sir Elijah Impey, to strike the parliament and people of England with horror. That letter purported to have been written on the spot, and at the time of the execution, by Francis's *brother-in-law*, Sheriff Macrabie, but bore internal evidence of having been written, or dictated, or retouched, by Francis's own skilful and experienced hand.

deal with the trickery of a quack, all reasoning is thrown away. Where subtle fallacies require detection, or ungrounded assumptions can be met by demonstrative proof, neither logic nor evidence shall be wanting ; but when Mr. Macaulay presumes, upon his reputation for sophistry, or sarcasm, or even on mere book-learning, and a knack at writing to blind the eyes of plain common sense, he will be disappointed, and find himself, possibly, not invulnerable by weapons like his own, though unenvenomed by fraud, ribaldry, or malevolence, unworthy the education of a scholar and a gentleman. A rhetorician may be exposed by a syllogism ; a false informer by authenticated facts ; but for a vain impostor the best and most cutting punishment is laughter.

I must do Mr. Macaulay the justice to say—*nihil tetigit quod non ornavit*—he has superadded ornaments and flourishes all his own. But pity is it, that his rhetoric should for ever be digging pitfalls for his veracity.

" *Nihil est tam inhumanum, quàm eloquentiam a naturâ ad salutem et conservationem datam, ad bonorum pestem perniciemque convertere.*"—Cicero Offic. 2.

CHAPTER V.

SECRET PROCEEDINGS OF THE MAJORITY IN COUNCIL—THE
JUDGES SEND A COPY OF NUNCOMAR'S TRIAL TO ENGLAND
BY ALEXANDER ELIOT—HASTINGS'S SCHEME OF ADMINIS-
TRATION—SIR ELIJAH IMPEY'S LETTERS ON THE CORRUP-
TION AND VIOLENCE OF THE PROVINCIAL COURTS, ETC.

NUNCOMAR having been hanged, and the despotic majority of Council having done nothing to prevent it, and General Clavering having treated the only petition that was ever presented, in the strange manner which has been related, that majority lost little time in turning the catastrophe to the purposes of their own intrigues and jealousies. Their first steps, as I have hinted in the preceding chapter, were secret and cautious.

The first digging of the mine in which the train was to be laid, and to be crammed with the combustibles of so many years accumulation, was in the secret department of the Council at Calcutta. Not being able to make anything of the conspiracy against the Governor General, after it had been denounced to the Supreme Court, they considered the opportunity very favourable for asserting that the accusers and witnesses against Hastings, were all scared away by the death of the Rajah; although, in fact, they had been put to flight months before that event.

On the 15th of September, one month and ten days after Nuncomar's execution, Clavering, Monson, and Francis, entered a minute to this effect,—

"After the death of Nuncomar, the Governor, we believe, is well assured *that no man, who regards his safety, will venture to stand forth as his accuser.*

I

"On a subject of this delicate nature, it becomes us *to leave every honest man to his own reflection.* It ought to be made known, however, to the English nation, that the forgery of which the Rajah was *accused,** must have been committed several years; that in the interim he had been protected and employed by Mr. Hastings; that his son was appointed to one of the first offices in the Nabob's household, with a salary of one lac of rupees; that the accusation, which ended in his destruction, was not produced till he came forward, and brought a specific charge against the Governor General, of corruption in his office."

Still proceeding *pian piannino,* and eschewing all mention of, or allusion to the judges, the said three Members of Council, entered another minute on the 21st of November, being three months and sixteen days after the execution of Nuncomar.

"It seems probable," says this second minute, " such embezzlements may have been universally practised. In the present circumstances it will be difficult, if not impracticable, to obtain proofs of the facts. The terror impressed upon the minds of the natives, by the execution of Maharajah Nuncomar is not to be effaced ; for *though he suffered for the crime of forgery,* yet the *natives* conceive he was executed for having dared to prefer complaints against the Governor General.

"This idea, *however destitute of foundation,* is prevalent amongst the natives, and will naturally deter them from making discoveries, which may be attended with the same fatal consequences to themselves.

" Punishment is usually intended as an example, to prevent the commission of crimes ; in this instance, we fear, it has served to prevent the discovery of them."

This is a tolerable fair specimen of the Junius style of innuendo. Quite intelligible though very cautious. It is admitted that the Rajah had suffered for the proved crime of forgery, and that the contrary idea is destitute of foundation : no personal opinions are expressed, no European is implied to believe a rumour—in which, in fact, none seem to have believed at that time—and everything is thrown upon the poor ignorant and naturally suspicious natives. But the drift is evident enough.

---

* Accused! why he had been accused, indicted, tried, convicted, and hanged for it,—and all with the *bene placet* of these writers themselves of insidious minutes.

Nuncomar, while living, had utterly failed in proving his charges against Warren Hastings: if the majority had fancied he could ever have made good those charges, they might, and, in all probability would, have kept him alive. But he was dead—and because they had found him useless, they had done nothing to save him—and now they were at liberty, by slow degrees, to make the world believe that many mysteries were buried with him; and that the dread of encountering the like fate prevented other Hindus from coming forward as witnesses against the Governor General. In other words, Francis hoped to make a great deal more of the dead Rajah than he had been able to make of the living one. The device was every way worthy of the craft and malignity of Junius. It was calculated to take with the unreflecting multitude. And so many years afterwards, when it was brought forward as an ostensible charge in parliament, and when Hastings had been removed from power and from the country, how difficult must it have been for him to disprove such an allegation!

By degrees the dark hints of *King Francis** and his majority became bolder, and their insinuations more plain; yet never *in India* did they venture to describe the Governor General and Chief Justice as the murderers of Nuncomar—as Mr. Macaulay makes them appear to do on the day of the execution—nor even covertly did they yet dare to assert that the judges, or any one of them, had murdered the Rajah for accusing Mr. Hastings. They indeed laboured—unhappily, not without success —in propagating unwarranted reports in England, where people were so little qualified to judge of them. Francis — *nequid inausum aut intractatum sclerisve dolive fuisset*—left not a stone unturned, nor an effort untried, to bring down odium both on the personal character and on the government of Hastings, after whose post of pre-eminence he already hungered, with an appetite which never left him; for even in his old age, when he had been long removed from India, and when he had sunk into comparative insignificance at home,† he still aspired to be Governor General of India. When Hastings so emphatically

---

* See ante, p. 64.
† See Lord Brougham's Public Characters.

said " *Francis writes,*" he told nearly the whole history of the man while at Calcutta; except when engaged in certain licentious pursuits, which I shall be forced to allude to in some detail, his keen pen, with its ink of gall, can hardly ever have been out of his hand.

Clavering was no great penman, nor was Monson; but *Junius,* who had made himself what he was by writing—*Junius,* who had obtained ten thousand pounds a-year by libelling—could write for them all; and frequently, as I believe, he wrote what their sense of honour would never have allowed them to approve of, if it had been put under their inspection, or borne their signature, before being sent to England. Not a ship left the Hooghley for the Thames without a ponderous packet from Francis. Much of the matter was circulated among private or literary and political friends of the writer; not a little of it got anonymously into print, while the information derived from it, and the poignant style in which it was written, gave at once matter and inspiration to whole pages, or, at times, whole chapters, of the *Annual Register;* to which, mainly, people at home referred, for their information about India. Moreover, the despatches of the majority to the secret committee of the Court of Directors—in which Hastings had always some bitter enemies, and in which there arose adversaries no less violent against my father, so soon as the Chief Justice and the Court interfered with the high-handed proceedings of the Company's revenue-collectors—teemed with strictures and insinuations against the almost superseded Governor General, and with absolutely sickening encomiums of the wisdom and justice of their own administration. Especial care was however taken, for a time, not to attack the Supreme Court on any vital point. During the year which immediately followed the execution of Nuncomar, and for many years after that event, there was, in these despatches at least, no breath of the mighty scandal. *That* was kept in reserve for future operations. In the meantime, even Francis himself was compelled to admit that the Court was an object of admiration and reverence to the whole Bengal community; and that the judges were officially, as well as personally, popular in Calcutta; and, to such an extraordinary degree, that it looked like-an infatuation in the jaundiced vision of Junius.*

It was with elaborate skill, and wonderful perseverance, in malice and innuendo, that Francis prepared the public mind in England for unjust and injurious impressions of the spirited conduct of the Supreme Court. From 1775 to 1781 he was constantly weaving his dark and complicated web. For the far greater part of this time there was no possible opportunity of answering him, or bringing him to any account for his slanders : they appeared anonymously, or with various fictitious names on the title-pages. To the uninformed public, it seemed to be a war waged by many against the "tyrants of the East ;" but all this time Francis was the sole belligerent ; or, if he did not write every attack with his own hand, he dictated the subject-matter ; or he gave the theme, and infused the spirit of his own malevolence into the breast of some one of the many needy and unscrupulous pamphleteers of that day. Towards the end of the period we have just named, when the scheme for impeaching Warren Hastings was almost matured, and when Francis was, in a measure, compelled to submit to the publication of minutes and other papers, with his name affixed to them, more than one party came boldly forward to meet the insidious charges, and to denounce the evil motives of this friend to humanity, and reformer of abuse ! A spirited sea captain—Captain Joseph Price—who had been taken into employment by Hastings during the wars in India, who had rendered very important services during that momentous struggle, and who had been described by Francis himself, in a minute of Council, as a brave and able officer, drew down upon his head a large share of invective, apparently for no better reason than because he thought Hastings a greater man than Francis. While yet in India, Captain Price learned that Francis had entered something very defamatory of him in the minutes of Council. Forthwith he had a meeting with Mr. Shore,† at that time a friend of Francis, who offered to wait upon the latter for an explanation. Through Shore, Captain Price received Francis's answer,

---

* Francis's Pamphlets.
† Afterwards successively Sir John Shore and Lord Teignmouth.

that the animadversions had been *retracted* on the re
presentations of Hastings and other members of Council. " No such thing," continues the frank sailor;
" they were permitted to be entered up fair on the
Company's records, and three months afterwards were
transmitted to Europe !" The captain, in the interval,
had left India for England. But when he took up the
pen in the course of the year 1781, to refute some of
the accumulated slanders which more particularly regarded himself, the Captain thus expressed his scorn :
" The insidious malice of a man, base enough to assert a
falsity with confidence, but not brave enough to defend
it ; who, when he is taxed on the spot by the person he
injures, retracts his falsehoods, and, when that person
leaves the country, re-asserts them to the Court of
Directors !"* The captain takes a short spirited review
of Francis's character and conduct, speaking of " his
strong bias to inveterate calumny, and of that cowardly
fear of consequences," which made him always proceed
with such cautious circumspection. Captain Price continues thus :—

"This may not be an improper place to inform others, as
well as yourself, how some of your dark proceedings have
come to light.

" Towards the end of the last, and the beginning of the
present year, a number of anonymous pamphlets, under various
denominations, were published on India affairs declared to be
made up of fair and just extracts from the proceedings of the
Governor General and Council of Bengal. . . . . In
these proceedings the most flattering encomiums are lavished
on the abilities, the integrity, and the unwearied application
of Mr. Philip Francis; and the utmost scurrility and unjustifiable abuse vented on the Governor General. . . . But
I found no kind of difficulty in admitting into my mind, that
you might have been the man, who, contrary to your oath,
and, perhaps, to your allegiance, furnished the materials for
the above publication. Your general stamp of character, your
notorious personal enmity to the Governor General, and your
impatient ambition to obtain, what I think you never will be entrusted with—the Government of Bengal—too plainly marked
the man who was capable of ushering into the world, at the expense of a breach of the first moral obligation, productions in-

---

* " A letter from Captain Joseph Price, to Philip Francis, Esq., late a
member of the Supreme Council at Bengal." London, 1781.

famous in the extreme; tending to vilify the character of a man whose abilities you envy, and whose integrity you have not the virtue to imitate. . . . . . I know your abilities and great dexterity in the arrangement of words, for the purpose of making the worse appear the better cause. Much do you owe to the nation, and to the East India Company, as well as to individuals, for the time you have misspent, and the paper you have wasted, in entering up unsupported assertions, mysterious allusions, and barbarous insinuations against the honour of the Company's old servants on the face of their consultations, where they will for ever remain monuments of the disingenuity of your disposition, and the depravity of your heart."

This was certainly strong writing, and the Captain's rhetoric, unlike that of Francis, and his admirer Mr. Macaulay, was supported by *truth*. But what could Captain Price, and one or two other men like him, do against the great Junius, and the formidable combination he headed? That combination against the Governor General and the Chief Justice of India, was the more formidable from the circumstance that Burke, who entered heart and soul into it, united to his eloquence and genius, a thorough conviction that all things in India had been cruelly mismanaged, and that Francis was not a selfish and malignant false witness, but a true and honourable accuser.

Against so many pens and tongues which were now employed all on one side, Captain Price could have no chance of victory. *His* was but a *single* pamphlet,— the name of *their's* was Legion. Besides, Francis had so long had the field to himself, and had so perseveringly and cunningly constructed his works for assault and for defence, that there was no dislodging him by a *coup de main*. The public mind had been abused during six years: it must take at least six or more to disabuse it. People had read only one story, and they had read it so long, and—as they were made to think—upon so many concurrent authorities, that few were disposed to entertain any doubt as to the correctness of their impressions. Francis too, had a face of bronze: instead of being disturbed and abashed by any detection of falsehood in his statements, he only promulgated new fictions with a bolder face. Captain Price said to him,—"Your whole pursuit, sir, has been to assert new falsehoods, and not to lose time in defending old ones." *

Though far from possessing a knowledge of the extent to which the majority of the Council were carrying their defamatory processes, Sir Elijah Impey, a few months after the execution of Nuncomar, had good reasons to suspect that they were remitting to England very unfavourable and incorrect accounts of the whole of that affair. And hereupon, he and his learned brethren of the bench, resolved to transmit by a safe hand, an authenticated copy of the Rajah's trial, &c., and to have the same printed and distributed in England. With such a document before them, it was thought that no enlightened public men, or indeed any one man in his senses, could be duped and excited by such misrepresentations; but, alas, in this expectation the judges were deceived.

Mr. Alexander Eliot, a younger brother of that Sir Gilbert Eliot, who became my father's official accuser, and one of the bitterest of his assailants in parliament, had been living at our house in Calcutta, as a member of the family, being treated by Sir Elijah as a son or younger brother. He was equally dear to Warren Hastings; who not only loved him for his amiable and attaching qualities, but also prized him for his eminent abilities, of which, though young, he had given abundant proof in many difficult transactions. But Eliot was not exclusively the dear friend of the Governor General and Chief Justice: he was cherished and respected by all classes, with the exception of Francis and his faction; and even they never hazarded a censure upon him. There was probably not, in all Calcutta—where all knew him—a single man, European or native, but loved him.

As Alexander Eliot was going to England on affairs of his own, as well as some particular business of the Governor General, and as he had interpreted during the whole of Nuncomar's trial, it was reasonably concluded that he would be the best person to carry that trial, and superintend the printing of it in London.

When, many years after, this question was put to Samuel Tolfrey the under-sheriff of Calcutta—"What

* " A letter from Captain Joseph Price to Philip Francis, Esq.," &c.

was the general character of Mr. Eliot among the gentlemen in Bengal?" Tolfrey replied,—"*One of the highest characters I ever knew a man to possess; and I believe the most deservedly and the most universally given.*"

When he was asked—"From the idea you entertain of the character of Mr. Eliot, do you think that if Mr. Eliot had conceived the execution of Nuncomar was a legal murder, that he would not have broken off all connections with Sir Elijah Impey?"—Tolfrey replied with warmth—"*Certainly; I think Mr. Eliot would not have undertaken to carry the trial home, if he had thought that the Court had acted wrong in the course of the trial; as I understand that the intention of sending it by him, instead of trusting it to any other channel, was, that he who had so complete a knowledge of the business, might clear up any misrepresentation that should be made concerning it.**

Many other witnesses, at different times, and in different places, gave an equally decided testimony to the honour and integrity of Eliot, and to the reasons which pointed him out as the fittest person to be entrusted with the conveyance and publication of the trial. The manuscript copy of that document, was not compiled solely by my father: it was drawn up by Samuel Tolfrey, by the order of all the judges, and with the assistance of three of them. The materials for it consisted of notes taken by the sheriff, and by the under-sheriff; *by the counsel for the prisoner,* and by Mr. Eliot, who had acted as interpreter; by the judges, and by one or two other parties. *All* the judges, at different times, looked over the trial while Tolfrey was writing; when it was finished, it was sent round to the judges; and the authority for publishing it was signed by *all* the judges. I could give other evidence of these facts, but the following will suffice to prove that the account of the trial was to be considered as proceeding from all the judges.

The first is a note addressed to the very respectable man who published the trial.

* Appendix, Part 3, No. 7, to the Speech of Sir Elijah Impey at the bar of the House of Commons, &c."

"*London*, *May* 3, 1776.

"Sir—When I quitted Bengal, Sir Elijah Impey, the Chief Justice of Bengal, authorised me to say, that the trial of Maharajah Nuncomar was drawn up from his and the other judges' notes.   I am, Sir, &c.,

"ALEX. ELIOT.

"To Mr. Cadell, bookseller, Strand."

The next note needs no introduction.

"*Fort William*, *August* 10, 1775.

"Sir—We give you full power and permission to print and publish, if you think proper, the trial of Maharajah Nuncomar, as authentic, from the copy which has been delivered to you.   "We are, Sir,

"Your most humble servants,

"E. IMPEY,
"ROBT. CHAMBERS,
"S. C. LEMAISTRE,
"JOHN HYDE.

"To Alexander Eliot, Esq."

The following is one of my father's letters sent by Alexander Eliot :—

"I take the liberty of introducing Mr. Eliot to you in the character of my friend. You would, no doubt, from your connections, have been otherwise acquainted with him. He is more intimately acquainted with the interest of the Company, the mode of transacting every department of their business, the general policy of the country, and is better informed of the nature of the transactions of the new administration and their disputes, than any man you can converse with. You will be satisfied of this from the first conversation you have with him. He is a man of strict honour, and will not deceive you in any particular. Though he is so young, you will find he has a confirmed judgment; he is looked to as a man of the first abilities in the settlement.

"I possibly may be affected in consequence of the unfortunate divisions, which, I fear, must give the legislature and his Majesty's ministers much trouble; no inconsiderable part of which will, most probably, fall to your share. You will find something must be done, or all the advantages that the nation or the East India Company can expect from this country must, in a very short time, be annihilated. *I trust to our old acquaintance and friendship, that you will endeavour to prevent my character and fortune from suffering from secret insinuations inserted in the public consultations of the Council—*

which the members of it refuse to communicate—or from asser-
tions to my prejudice conveyed by private letters ; for, from
their conduct, though I have given them no cause of just pro-
vocation, I have everything to fear. If there should be occasion, I trust you will order extracts of all such parts of the
consultations, as either respects me or the courts of justice.

" Mr. Eliot will give you full information of what has
passed. Though I feel myself personally much injured, and the
behaviour of the Council with respect to the Court most highly
reprehensible, I have forborne complaining to his Majesty's
ministers, as I know I must thereby add to the embarrassments which I know they must be under from the news they
will receive from India.

" You will see I am popular here. It has not been my own
seeking; for I think it is at least doubtful whether it will serve
or disserve me in England. Every endeavour has been used
by the Council to depreciate the Court. They have rendered
themselves universally odious. They have been the cause of
the addresses to the Court. They [the addresses] were endeavoured to be suppressed; one who refused to sign immediately got a contract; one who persisted in signing has been
turned out of his office.*

By the same ship which carried the high-minded and
true-hearted Eliot, the bearer of as full and authentic
a report of a criminal trial as ever had been sent from
any country, in any time, Sir Elijah wrote to several of
his nearest and most distinguished friends, claiming their
attention to the said trial as soon as it should be printed,
and requesting their candid opinion upon it.

Most of these friends were lawyers, like himself; real
lawyers, who prided themselves in their profession, and
never thought of *denying it*; men, in every way competent to give an authoritative opinion. The means
which, in our times, seem almost to have annihilated
space, and to have brought Bombay, and even Calcutta,
to the vicinity of London, were all unknown in the days
of my father ; and to the tedious intercourse between
England and India, both he and the Governor General
owed many a long season of doubt and anxiety. Twelve
or fourteen months commonly elapsed between the

* Letter from Sir Elijah Impey to Mr. Cornwall, dated Calcutta, August
1775. Mr. Cornwall was at this time a Member of Parliament, celebrated
for his eloquence and political honesty. In a postscript to this letter Sir
Elijah says, that Mr. Cornwall is to show it to Thurlow, Dunning, Lord
Shelburne, Sutton, and Wedderburn.

despatch of a letter and the receipt of an answer to it. The ship which carried Eliot was between six and seven months on its voyage. When he reached London, he lost no time in putting the MS. into the hands of Mr. Cadell, the bookseller. He carefully corrected the press with his own hand; and, when the book was finished, he placed copies of it not only in the hands of Sir Elijah's private friends, but also in the hands of ministers, the Court of Directors, and others. Dunning, by the very first opportunity* which presented itself after he had perused the trial, wrote to his friend, Sir Elijah, to express his entire satisfaction with it. Dunning's eminent qualifications as a lawyer remain undisputed. He was one of the ablest English lawyers of that or any other period. His competency to form a judgment upon the case was accompanied by a moral rectitude, and a natural frankness, which would have deterred him from delivering an opinion which he did not sincerely and thoroughly entertain. In his intercourse with mankind, Dunning's failing was the very opposite of flattery. He was bluff and rough. The opinion he sent to my father was concise. Here are his words:—

" The publication of the trial has been of use, as it has obviated abundance of ridiculous and groundless stories. I see nothing in the proceedings to disapprove of, except that you seem to have wasted more time in the discussion of the privileges of ambassadors than so ridiculous a claim deserved."

If so many of my father's letters and papers had not been unfortunately so scattered, as to be irrecoverably lost, at least to me, I should have been, doubtless, able

---

* Sir Elijah's affectionate brother, Michael Impey, did not wait for the publication of the trial to send his congratulations to Calcutta. Among my family papers I find the following lettter :—

" We are all as much pleased as is possible ; nothing being able to give us more satisfaction than hearing you and my sister are well. Next to this we receive the greatest pleasure in finding, not only by letters from you, but by letters received by many of my friends, how much the people of Calcutta admire your impartial administration of law, shown by their address—which I have read, the trial I am promised—and the great desire they express to have it perpetuated, by placing your portrait in some public place, as a testimony of their approbation, which action of theirs shows the opinion they entertain of your judgment, and the rectitude of your heart. Those people cannot form a greater idea of both than the people do here by their universal applause. Dated Hammersmith, 10th April, 1776.

to produce, under their own hands, similar opinions and attestations from Wedderburn, Wallace, Sutton, and other legal friends. My father always took a just pride in the unanimity of opinion among his best informed friends ; and, in his defence before the Commons, he manfully affirmed that all his professional friends had expressed their approbation of the manner in which the trial of Nuncomar, and all the matters connected with it, had been conducted by the Supreme Court ; and, on the same occasion, and in confirmation of the same opinion, he produced, besides the above quoted letter from Dunning, another from Sir W. Blackstone.

For a long time the publication of the trial stopped the spread of prejudice in that direction. Alexander Eliot returned to Bengal, to renew his close intimacy with the Governor General and the Chief Justice, and to resume those administrative offices for which he was so admirably qualified. His sway over the affections of men, and the proper conduct of public business, became stronger than ever ; and he was in the high road to become at least the second man in India—second only to Hastings— when death removed him from the world, to which he was a bright ornament. He died shortly after in the flower of his age. *Cosa bella mortal passa a non dura.* Hastings erected a monument over his solitary grave, and afterwards wrote a few tender, and not inelegant, verses to his memory.

> " An early death was Eliot's doom;
> I saw his opening virtues bloom,
>   And manly sense unfold,
> Too soon to fade ! I bade the stone
> Record his name, 'mid hordes unknown,
>   Unknowing what it told !"*

Strange was it that Sir Gilbert Eliot, the brother of this gifted and beloved being, should rush into the ring with those who assailed the reputation, and sought the absolute ruin, of his best and dearest friends. So strange, that even the madness of faction, and the temptations of oratory, and the wild excitement of popular

---

* These verses occur in that imitation of Horace's *Otium Divos royat,* to which Mr. Macaulay alludes.

applause, seem scarcely sufficient to account for it. Yet is it no less strange than true. Sir Gilbert Eliot anticipated, and even suggested, most of the topics of Mr. Macaulay's unscrupulous audacity. It was not for any want of exertion on Sir Gilbert's part that my father, the friend of that gentleman's own brother, who never could have held fellowship with a base or vicious mind, was not visited with condign punishment as the legal murderer of Nuncomar!

During the interval over which I have passed, from the execution of the Rajah to the return of Alexander Eliot to Calcutta, Sir Elijah Impey had not been an idle man. He was grieved by the troubles and dissensions he witnessed, and by the insidious attacks of which he saw himself the object; but he did not relax a jot of his energy. Although the Supreme Court occupied much of his time, he prosecuted his study of the Oriental languages, and he assisted the Governor General in drawing up a more fixed scheme, and better rules, for the revenue courts, which the Regulating Act and the Royal Charter had left, to a great degree, independent of the Supreme Court. Hence there arose frequent conflict of authorities. But these revenue courts were radically bad; all proceedings in them were attended with enormous expense; too generally there was the mere show, without any of the reality of justice; and, in many cases, the poor natives felt the expenses to amount to a denial of justice altogether. All parties— the judges of the Supreme Court, the Governor General, and the majority as well as the minority in Council— agreed in declaring that these adaulut courts must be corrected and remodelled. But the said courts had a double function; and although Warren Hastings was willing to deprive them of the faculty of judging in territorial questions, or in mere disputes between one zemindar, or farmer of land, and another, yet neither he, nor the majority hostile to him, felt at all inclined to take the tax and revenue causes out of those adaulut courts. The reason of this was very apparent; the adaulut courts were presided over by the servants of the Company; by Europeans, appointed by the Governor or the majority of Council; and these laymen—for there was not one of them that was a lawyer, or that appears to have had the rudiments of a legal education—were about the least likely men in all Hindustan to be impartial judges between the Calcutta Government and the ryots, or cultivators of the soil, or any direct contributors to the revenue. They were all interested parties. Tax-gatherers themselves, and looking either for honour or promotion, or some other substantial benefit by raising, each in his own district, the amount of revenue, was it to be expected that they should be patient in hearing the reclamations of the natives ? But the native vakeels and banyans, whether Mohammedan or Hindu, employed under these Europeans, were still less capable of patience and impartiality. Their general rule was to work out the wishes of their employers, and to swell the revenue of the district as much as they could ; for they depended upon the immediate chiefs of the district, as those Europeans depended upon the Supreme Council of Calcutta, or upon the Directors in Leadenhall-street; who, at that time, universally measured the value of their servants, whether civil or military, by the amount of money they poured into their coffers. If exceptions might be made to this general rule and practice of the natives employed in the adauluts, it was under influences and impulses by which the sacred cause of justice was assuredly no gainer; they were open to bribes ; they were, as they ever had been, notoriously corrupt. To the poor they were inexorable ; in their eyes the Company, or the Company's revenue-collectors, were always in the right; but when the defendants were wealthy, and willing to use some of their wealth in bribery, they could sometimes see that the Company was clearly in the wrong. It was not on his first arrival at Calcutta, but after he had passed more than five years in the country, that Sir Elijah Impey declared to Lord Rochdale, one of the Secretaries of State, that the corruption and maladministration of the adauluts or country courts of justice, in which the members of the provincial councils presided, were most notorious.* The only appeal from these courts was to the Sudder Dewannee Adaulut, the constitution of which was almost equally vicious, leaving it entirely under the

* MS. Letters, afterwards printed in the Parliamentary Reports.

control of the Governor or Council at Calcutta. The other three judges of the Supreme Court were not less sensible than my father was of the mischievous tendency of the whole of this system. Mr. Justice Chambers was, perhaps, even more active than Sir Elijah, in pointing out the necessity of a sweeping reform ; and in suggesting to the Governor General, and the majority of Council, that both the adauluts and their court of appeal, the Sudder Dewannee Adaulut, ought to be, and must be, made more independent of the government of Calcutta; and that in matters of territorial disputes and of revenue, the government must not be judge and jury in its own cause. Hastings, as I have said, was ready to yield in part; but in what related to taxes, &c., he was not a whit more unwilling to concede than were the majority hostile to him; and, as for THOSE pretended reformers, and friends of suffering humanity, THEY never, in action, forsook the principle, either wholly or in part, that as much money as possible must be extorted, in order to raise the East Indian dividends, or to put an end to the pecuniary embarrassments— mostly created by themselves—in order to prove that *they* had been wise administrators and good stewards to the Company. In a letter to Lawrence Sulivan, Esq., of the 21st of March, 1776, Warren Hastings pointedly declares that some alterations must be made in the prevailing system ; that the powers of the Supreme Court must, in some way, be enlarged ; and that his respected friend, Sir Elijah, had put into legal language, and into the form of an act of parliament, a scheme for the better administration of justice, which he, the Governor General, had drawn up, and sent over to England, to be submitted to his Majesty's Government. In this letter Hastings severely censures the hostile majority for their conduct towards the Supreme Court. He says, not merely that my father, but that all the judges—without whose concurrence Sir Elijah never did anything of any moment—approved of his plan. After this Hastings adds—

" With this preface, I assure you that it is scarcely possible to have acted with more moderation or caution than Sir Elijah has observed in all cases in which the ordinary process of the Supreme Court was likely to affect the collection and management of the public revenue. Indeed, the other judges merit the same testimony in their favour. Had a cordial understanding subsisted between the Court and the Council, much of the inconvenience that has arisen from the writs of the Court would have been avoided, nor would the revenue have been in the least affected by them; but it seems to have been a maxim of the Board to force the Court into extremities, for the sake of finding fault with them. Yet, in many cases, the acts of the Court have been, and must continue to be, the unavoidable cause of embarrassment. This is owing to a defect in its constitution. By the limitation of its powers it must ever remain a doubt what is the extent of them, as every man in the provinces is, in reality, subjected to the authority of the Company. If it was constituted to protect the people from oppression, that design would be entirely frustrated, were the Board at liberty to employ agents who should be exempt from its authority; and you will have seen many instances in the papers which I have sent home of *the most glaring acts of oppression committed by the Board, which would have produced the ruin of the parties over whom they were exercised, but for the protection of the Court.* Great complaints have been made of the zemindars and others, who are not liable to the jurisdiction of the Court by the plain construction of the Act, having been arrested, and some thrown into prison by its warrants. But no attention has been paid to the necessity which there is of bringing the persons who are even excluded by the Act from the jurisdiction of the Court, in the same way before it to establish their exemption.* They may plead to its jurisdiction, and obtain their discharge; but, till this is done, I cannot see how it is possible to make the distinction; for, if every man who declared himself to be no British subject, nor employed by any, was, in virtue of his own declaration, to be exempted from their authority, all men would make the plea. Their right to this exemption must be tried to be known, and they must be compelled to appear, or give bail for their appearance, that it may be tried.†

* The majority of Council were ever ready to tell the zemindars and others, that, by the Regulating Act, and by the Charter and Letters Patent, they were altogether exempt from the jurisdiction of the Supreme Court, and not bound in any way to attend to its writs or summonses. Unhappily, Mr. Hastings was afterwards brought to alter the opinions expressed in this letter to Sulivan; and hence arose the only serious difference with my father. This took place in 1779, during the Governor General's frail and ephemeral coalition with Mr. Francis.

† Yet, subsequently, it was made a charge of tyranny and oppression on the part of the Supreme Court that they compelled this appearance, and arrested the refractory zemindars; and the Governor General, as if forgetful of what he had here written to Sulivan, not only joined for a

" *The truth is, that a thing done by halves is worse than if it were not done at all.   The powers of the Supreme Court must be universal, or it would be better to repeal them altogether. . . . .* I hope that my plan will be found to provide the most effectual relief against all the imperfections of the Act as it now stands.   On the one hand, it proposes to give to the Supreme Court an unlimited—but not exclusive—authority over all; and, on the other, it provides for the administration of justice in all cases to which its jurisdiction cannot conveniently extend, without the danger of a competition with it.   In this coalition of the British judicature with the Dewannee, the latter will obtain more steady and confirmed authority than it has yet ever possessed; and, being opened to the daily inspection and controul of the judges—of the Supreme Court—the Dewannee courts will acquire a more regular and legal form than they could have, if left to themselves.   But I trust the design will best speak for itself, for it has at least the merit of simplicity and precision.   One only alteration has been made in it in the draft which Sir Elijah is making for me.   The superintendent of the Court, called Adaulut Dewannee Zillajaut, who was proposed to be a member of the Provincial Council,* as is now the case, holding that office by rotation, is now proposed to be an independent officer—I mean, independent of the Provincial Council—and to be removable only for misconduct, or by voluntary resignation; and he is to be the judge of all causes that do not immediately regard the revenue—as disputes between farmers, and other proprietors or agents of the collections—which are left to the Provincial Councils.

" *Mem.*—The superintendent at present holds his office in monthly rotation.   My plan lengthened it to a year.   Mr. Chambers, on the same grounds, suggested the propriety of making it perpetual, and to be held by a person, not a member of the Provincial Council, which I immediately adopted, the Chief Justice concurring in the same opinion."†

This plan was never carried into effect.   So indolent, or so occupied with other difficult business, was the government of Lord North, that the plan seems scarcely to have been taken into consideration.   The Premier

---

season in that loud outcry, but also resorted to acts of violence against the Supreme Court, or against those who were executing its writs !

* That is to say, a servant of the Company, appointed by the Calcutta government, in whose causes he was to act as judge !

† See Letter in Memoirs of the Right Hon. Warren Hastings, by the Rev. G. R. Gleig.

was charged, apparently upon good grounds, of being no friend of the Governor General, but of being very anxious to conciliate General Clavering,* whose parliamentary influence was very considerable, and of the greater importance from the strength and talent of the opposition, and the still declining popularity of Lord North's administration. But no public man in those days, unless he were a Director, or in some way connected with the Company, would devote an hour's attention to the affairs of India. In vain my father wrote, letter upon letter, to Thurlow, for assistance and advice; that eminent lawyer, who was already beginning to open to himself the way to the woolsack, returned no answer to these letters, although some of them contained appeals to the memory of by-gone times and early associations, which must have touched a heart not hardened and absorbed by ambition and political intrigue.

Such, however, was the calm enduring nature of my father's affection, that I never heard him speak harshly, or even warmly, of Thurlow's long neglect of him : but *I* am not restrained by the same feeling; Thurlow was not *my* early friend and most frequent associate; and what Sir Elijah Impey never said, *I* may say without indecorum. Yet, will I not say more than this, that his disregard of an absent friend, if simply considered in a personal point of view, was neither kind nor generous, but, if referred to public principle, obviously unjust. It was out of the defeat, or rather the non-execution of Mr. Hastings's plan of law reform, which we have just heard him describing in his own words, that arose, some four years after, that business of the Sudder Dewannee Adaulut, which Mr. Mill, and Mr. Mill's follower and refiner, Mr. Macaulay, have placed at the head of Sir Elijah Impey's judicial offences; making it, in atrocity, second only to the execution of Nuncomar, and, in the baseness of its alleged motives, worse even than that monstrous act of criminality, as by them misstated or misunderstood. I shall come closer to that question very soon; meanwhile pursuing the narrative form, as that likely to be most intelligible and most fair, I pro-

* Else why was General Clavering decorated with the red ribbon, and Hastings left without any honorary distinction ?

ceed to place events in something like their chronological order.

As the plan of the Governor General was consigned to ministerial oblivion ; as the jurisdiction of the Supreme Court was not made universal, in compliance with Hastings's desire ; as tax-gatherers, and provincial councils, were left to try revenue cases, and were encouraged not only to plead an exemption from the jurisdiction of the Supreme Court, but also to bid defiance to the authority of that Court, it could not, by any possibility, happen otherwise, than that flagrant acts of injustice should continue to be perpetrated upon the poor ryots, and that angry altercations, and still more violent collisions, should take place between the adauluts and the Supreme Court.   Mr. Macaulay, in relating these violent dissensions—as in nearly every other instance—looks nowhere for his facts but in the grossly prejudiced and coldly pragmatical pages of Mr. Mill.   In fact, he does nothing more than bestow the graces of eloquence upon another man's hard, angular, and lapidary style.   Mill never resided in India; he was a clerk in Leadenhall Street, and wrote like one.   His decorator, Mr. Macaulay, smoked his hookah some five years in Bengal, and, moreover, writes well.   To that right honourable gentleman's pithy points, and figurative declamation, I have nothing critically to object, except that there is always too much of them, and that their effect is ruined by excess— μέλιτος τὸ πλέον.   But are facts to be made subordinate to grandiloquence ?   Shall fine words be allowed to stand in lieu of truth ?   Are we to admire an assassin because he commits his deed with a keen and polished weapon ?   After admitting that the authors of the Regulating Act " had established two independent powers, the one judicial, the other political," and, "with a carelessness scandalously common in English legislation, had omitted to define the limits of either," Mr. Macaulay, by a conclusion most illogically at variance with his premises, throws the whole blame of the disputes thus confessedly resulting from imperfect legislation, not on the legislature itself; not partly on the Council, and partly on the Court ; nor even on the errors, if errors there were, but on the wilful misconstruction of " THE JUDGES" ALONE.

" The judges," he says, "took advantage of the indistinctness, and attempted to draw to themselves supreme authority, not only within Calcutta, but through the whole of the great territory subject to the presidency of Fort William."

Leaving entirely out of view the sufferings of the poor ryots or *tax-payers*, he lavishes all his sympathy upon the tax-*gatherers*. The poor were avowedly protected and benefitted by the Supreme Court, and regarded its establishment as a blessing; the revenue officers, the provincial councils, and their native agents, who had so long been judges in their own cause, cursed the Court, and, no doubt, occasionally felt the vengeance of its laws. Mr. Macaulay pities the oppressors, not the oppressed. By his account, not the judges, but the collectors, were the patrons of the natives! *Itaque nunc Siculorum Marcelli non sunt patroni; Verres in eorum locum substitutus est.* Yet, if he had read the Regulating Act and Charter, and the parliamentary debates which preceded the passing of that Act, he would have found that its primary intention was to erect a court of law, which should be strong enough to stand between the fiscal rapacity of the Company's agents and the feebleness of her subjects, Mohammedan or Hindu.

" Arrest on mesne process," he continues, " was the first step in most civil proceedings; and, to a native of rank, arrest was not merely a restraint, but a foul personal indignity. Oaths were required in every stage of every suit; and the feeling of a Quaker about an oath is hardly stronger than that of a respectable native. That the apartments of a woman of quality should be entered by strange men, or that her face should be seen by them, are, in the East, intolerable outrages—outrages which are more dreaded than death, and which can be expiated only by the shedding of blood. To these outrages the most distinguished families of Bengal, Bahar, and Orissa, were now exposed."

All this is sheer exaggeration; or, if not so, was the Supreme Court answerable for the misconduct of its officers, or to be deterred from its duty to its clients by the avarice of a contumacious collector, or the evasions of a fraudulent vakeel? As well might one argue that the High Court of Queen's Bench should be restrained from issuing its writs for fear of their being improperly executed or illegally opposed! In another place, Mr.

Macaulay, separating my father from the other judges, and holding him up singly to the abhorrence of mankind, calls the people who executed the writs of the Supreme Court, " Impey's alguazils;" and then bemoans the outrages which, he says, these men committed upon the native great men, whom, for the effect's sake, he compares to English bishops put in the stocks, &c. &c. Now, in sober truth, these native great men never exposed themselves to the possibility of being thus treated; and, if they were ever caned or pilloried, it was by proxy, and in the persons of their vakeels; a case not uncommon among themselves, and held to be perfectly lawful. If a rajah or zemindar refused to pay a tax, or was behind hand in his rent, his vakeel was sent for, and well thrashed, and the vakeel retaliated upon the poor ryots. These processes are universal in all Oriental despotisms. And these, in British India, were some of the abuses which the Supreme Court undertook to correct. The judges considered themselves bound to protect the poorer classes; but the collectors of the revenue were not so scrupulous. Most of the latter class, as I have said, were European magistrates in the provincial adaulots. These gentlemen, who never appeared themselves, found it to their advantage to employ native agents; who, being armed with their authority, cared not how much they flogged and plundered the ryots, so long as the revenue was collected. The zemindars, or large farmers, did the same with those who farmed lands under them.

The ryots could do nothing against these strong men, except in getting their case made known to the Supreme Court; but that Court issued its writs, and not unfrequently brought the oppressors up to Calcutta, or fined and imprisoned them if refractory. The sheriffs, under-sheriffs, and sheriffs' officers, may, or may not, have proceeded harshly upon some occasions; but if they so acted, it was contrary to the instructions and intentions of the judges. It was, however, high time to prove that there was a law stronger than these strong revenue agents; that there was a law before whose majesty all ranks should be equalled, and all privileges and exemptions cease. It especially concerned the newly-instituted Court, to convince the ryots that the law was the poor man's friend and defender.   Mr. Macaulay thrusts himself into zenanas, among Begums and their attendants, who were now and then troubled because they considered their house as an asylum for delinquents ; when he ought rather to have entered the hut of the poor taxpayer and cultivator of the soil.   If, in the perfumed air, and among the jewels and radiant muslins of the one, the name of the Supreme Court was a name of fear, that name was heard with very different emotions in the other.   In the lowly bungalo, women and children blessed the judges, whom Mr. Macaulay condemns; and cursed the oppressors and spoilers, whom he commiserates.   In one of his private letters, written at the time, my father says—" We are making these vultures of the East disgorge their prey"—meaning those English and native revenue collectors, who hitherto had been judges in their own causes.   It was upon this, and it was for this—exclusively and solely for this—that the cry was raised by the servants of the Company, that the Court prevented the collection of the revenue ; that its jurisdiction must consequently be limited ; or, that fortunes must cease to be made in India, and the affairs of the Company go to irretrievable ruin.

In an unhappy hour Hastings lent an ear to this cry. Proclamations were issued by the Council to the natives to resist the officers of the Court. The sheriff, in attempting to execute the writs, came into conflict with the military force of the Government. Now, no doubt, many outrages were committed on both sides ; and for these outrages the Court, or rather the Chief Justice, was made responsible !   In England, on such an occasion, the case would be reversed.   The reason is plain enough.   *Here* the sheriff raises his *posse comitatus ;* if that is insufficient, he applies to the Home Secretary, the Secretary to the Commander-in-Chief, who sends out a squadron of horse-guards, and the business is settled ; for, happily, none of these functionaries are at all concerned in the collection of the revenue, or in any way opposed to the courts of law ; but, on the contrary, obliged to support the warrants of her Majesty's justices.   In India, on the contrary, at that time, from the Governor General down to the lowest Company's servant, native or European, all were not only responsible to the Directors at home, but personally interested, in every province, for their share of the collection, either in the way of commission or salary.   The Supreme Court became unpopular for a time in Calcutta, not because it oppressed the people, but because it was obnoxious to the tyrannous greed of their rulers.   The sentiment expressed by my father, that "these vultures of the East" must be made to disgorge their prey, was not calculated to conciliate the friendship of the Company's tax-gatherers. But Mr. Macaulay again pities the oppressors, and not the oppressed.   He sheds rhetorical tears over the presumed and fanciful sufferings of native zemindars, who farmed and extorted the Company's revenue; but for the native ryots, who paid and smarted under the payment of it, he has no compassion.   It would not be easy, even in all his flashy articles for magazines, or reviews, or in the three collective volumes of "Essays, Historical and Critical,"—which essays are but reprints of his *Edinburgh Review* papers—to select a passage more abounding in false feeling, rhodomontade, and nonsense, than the following :—

" A reign of terror began—of terror heightened by mystery; for even that which was endured was less horrible than that which was anticipated.   No man knew what was next to be expected from this strange tribunal.   It came from beyond the black water, as the people of India, with mysterious horror, call the sea.*   It consisted of judges, not one of whom spoke

---

* Mr. Macaulay, who is always so ready to censure others for not knowing the languages of the country, is said to know himself little or nothing of the dialects of the East.   The life he led at Calcutta —writing Edinburgh Reviews, &c.—was not likely to render him familiar with Bengalee or Hindustanee.   He makes a fine sentence with his " black water," " people of India," " mysterious horror," &c., yet I may be allowed to doubt whether he ever heard any of the people of Bengal speak with horror of the sea, or call it the black water.   Indeed, it seems to me pretty evident, that the right honourable reviewer has borrowed the picturesque compound " black water," and the " mysterious horror," from the story of Cheetoo, the Pindarree robber-chief, as told by the late Sir John Malcolm, with much more simplicity and effect than Mr. Macaulay will ever attain to.

" When Cheetoo, the Pindarree chief, was flying in hopeless misery from the English, he was often advised by his followers to surrender to their mercy.   He was possessed, however, by the dreadful idea, that they would transport him beyond the seas, and this was more hideous to him than death.   These followers, who all, one after another, came in and obtained pardon, related, that during their captain's short and miserable

the language, or was familiar with the usages of the millions over whom they claimed boundless authority. Its records were kept in unknown characters; its sentences were pro- nounced in unknown sounds.* It had already collected round itself an army of the worst part of the native population— informers, and false witnesses, and common barrators, and agents of chicane; and, above all, a banditti of bailiffs' followers, compared with whom, the retainers of the worst English spunging-houses, in the worst times, might be considered as upright and tender-hearted. Numbers of natives, highly con- sidered among their countrymen, were seized, hurried up to Calcutta, flung into the common jail—not for any crime even imputed—not for any debt that had been proved—but merely as a precaution till their cause should come to trial. There were instances in which men of the most venerable dignity, persecuted without a cause by extortioners, died of rage and shame, in the gripe of the vile alguazils of Impey. The harems of noble Mahommedans—sanctuaries respected in the East by governments which respected nothing else—were burst open by gangs of bailiffs."

Now, this modern " Don Basile" found the raw mate- rials for these finely-wove sentences in his great text- book, " Mill's British India." Mr. Mill found the statements in letters written or dictated by Francis, in parliamentary harangues, and in *ex-parte* evidence, which amounted to no evidence at all ; and he set them down in his book without examining them, and, in some instances, without understanding them. Mr. Macaulay took them all from Mr. Mill, merely breaking them up into short, pithy sentences, and furbishing them up with his peculiar varnish. It mattered not to him that this reign of terror was a mere fable. He looked not to discover what were really the feelings with which the Supreme Court was regarded by the people of India, for whose protection it had been called into existence. He takes no pains to ascertain the truth of the fact,

sleep, he used continually to murmur, ' Kala panee! Kala panee ! '— The black water ! O, the black water ! "—*Account of Malwa.*

In Central India, in the regions remote from all sight of the ocean, the natives, indeed, call the sea the black water, and have a terrible idea of it, and of the countries beyond it. But Mr. Macaulay was never in Cen- tral India to hear the sea so called by the people of India ; and the people of Bengal, who, for the most part, are familiar with the sight of the ocean, do not, as I believe, call it by any such name, or regard it with any such terror or " mysterious horror."

* He forgets the sworn interpreters of the Supreme Court.

whether the judges were ignorant of the languages and usages of the country or not.   He knows nothing of my father's laborious study of the languages, the laws, and customs of the country; nothing of what was done by his colleagues, who certainly had a better notion of the duties on which they were employed, than to consume their time in writing periodical pamphlets.   He never examined whether that army of informers, and false witnesses, and agents of chicane, were called to their standard by the Supreme Court, or whether they were ever countenanced by it, or whether the severity of that Court was not, for the most part, directed against those evil classes of men.   I believe that such men existed; I believe that the Supreme Court may often have been obliged to listen to their evidence.   But the Court could not choose.   A false witness must be proved to be such before his evidence can be rejected.   Is not the most upright judge, the most impartial jury, frequently obliged to give ear to informers, false witnesses, barrators, and agents of chicane?   But, because such men are constantly appearing in our English courts, are we to say that our judges collect or suborn them?   We have Mr. Macaulay's own word for it, that the people of the East are vindictive, venal, subservient, and monstrously addicted to bearing false witness against their neighbours.   Very probably no single cause could be tried by the Supreme Court of Calcutta without eliciting perjury and false evidence.   But are the crimes of the witnesses to be imputed to the judges?   Was it otherwise in the Mayor's Court, and in the other Company's courts which existed before my father went to India?   Is it otherwise, now that my father has been almost forty years in his grave, and that more than half a century has elapsed since his first presiding over the Supreme Court?   Let Mr. Macaulay ask living judges, who have presided over the courts of Calcutta, Bombay, or Madras, or the barristers and attornies who have practised in those courts.   There are many such gentlemen now in England; but as the right honourable reviewer, late member of Council, and ex-Secretary-at-war, has scornfully denied his being a lawyer, it is possible that he may affect to despise the society and conversation of men eminently learned in the law, and justly glorying in their honourable profession.

The translator of the code of Gentoo laws,* had never studied for the English bar, but he was well acquainted with the native laws, and the character of the people. I knew him well. He was a most ingenious and indefatigable man; a fine classical scholar, as well as a great modern linguist,—a quick and accurate observer. He tells us, that he once heard at the Supreme Court at Calcutta, a man, not an idiot, swear upon a trial, that he was no kind of relation to his own brother, who was then in the Court, and who had constantly supported him from his infancy.†

As for Mr. Macaulay's alliterative " banditti of bailiff's followers," they ought, perhaps, rather to be looked for among those men who hounded out and ran down the natives for revenue, than among the retainers of the Supreme Court, who frequently interrupted their chase. Models of virtue, humanity, and honour, are scarcely to be looked for among jailers, bailiffs, and bailiff's followers; but wherever there is a court of law there must be some such officials: but who ever yet dreamed of making a Chief Justice answerable for the violence committed by a bailiff? And why are these banditti of bailiff's followers converted all at once into " the vile alguazils of Impey"? Partly, perhaps, because Mr. Macaulay would display his powers of illustration by leaping from an Italian figure into a Spanish trope; but more, I fancy, because he would make the careless reader believe, through a mere flourish of the pen, that all the sheriff's officers and bailiffs through the wide limits of Bengal, Bahar, and Orissa, were especially the retainers of my father, who had no more to do with their appointment, than had the other three judges; or, peradventure, the Supreme Council itself: for its members were too greedy of patronage and power not to thrust their own dependants even into the precincts of the Court.‡ There were other noblemen in Seville besides Count Almaviva; but when " Don Basile" wished to defame that one Count, he no doubt forgot all others for the time. So does Mr. Macaulay with my father, and the other members of the Supreme Court. Yet, whether this lively writer

---

* The late distinguished Nathaniel Brassey Halhed, Esq.
† See Preface to Halhed's Compilation of the Code of Gentoo Laws.
‡ Namely, by means of their Advocate General, Sir John Day, and their Company's standing barrister, Mr. George Boughton Rouse.

chooses to call them *banditti,* in the Italian fashion, or
alguazils, in the Spanish, men who think more of facts
than of words, will believe, that the sheriff of Calcutta,
and his under-sheriff, had far more to do in their
appointment, not only than any judge of the Supreme
Court singly, but than all the Court collectively. I can
well fancy that bailiff's followers in India, being exclusively, or very nearly so, natives, were a good deal
worse than bailiff's men in England. The judges
could hardly go forth with them as a colonel with his
regiment, or a captain with his troop. Mr. Macaulay
would make his readers believe they went plundering
and breaking into harems with them; that they went
forth on all occasions with the banditti, or alguazils, in
the fashion of Swift's attornies,—

> " Thorough town and thorough village,
>   All to plunder, all to pillage."

But, in fact, the judges could only give out their writs
that they might be executed according to the forms of
law. In two instances, and no more, the one at Dacca,
the other at Cossijurah, both within the jurisdiction of
the Court, disturbances took place in consequence of the
opposition of Government to the writs of the Court. At
the former place it has been asserted that the sheriff's
officers were guilty of some violence which may possibly
have invaded the precincts of the harem,—no doubt
an unpardonable offence in the eyes of Hindus and
Mohammedans. The charge in the latter instance, is
best answered by a reference to the cause of Cassinaut
Baboo *versus* the Rajah of Cossijurah, which was tried
in the Supreme Court in 1779. It is much too long
to be quoted, but will be found in a letter dated
the 12th of March, 1780, from Sir Elijah Impey to
Lord Weymouth, in the Reports of the Committees of
the House of Commons, pp. 367—374 of vol. 5. I
may also refer to another letter, dated the 26th of the
same month, p.p. 182—187, which recites the circumstances of another cause, in which the judges checked
the tyranny and oppression of the Company's provincial
councils, or adauluts. From these two letters—though
printed in the reports for the purpose of collecting evidence against Sir Elijah,—might be collected

matter sufficient for his defence in all that relates to the jurisdiction of the Court; but then they must be taken in conjunction with his own explanations, and coupled with vouchers and affidavits for every fact. These vouchers were mostly enclosed in long letters, at different times, to the Earl of Rochford, from 1775 to 1779, and in subsequent despatches to Viscount Weymouth, up to the period of Sir Elijah Impey's return to England, in 1783. Many other causes are included in the same long correspondence, but as these two causes furnish the matter collected as specially applicable to Sir Elijah, they are sufficient to refer to.* An attentive and impartial examination of those pages, might, without going any farther, have enabled the reviewer to arrive at conclusions very different from those which he has drawn; but if he had coupled with them the voluminous records preserved at the India House, the registers kept by the Company's solicitor at Draper's Hall, and the minutes of the Privy Council,—if he had consulted these with one tithe of the labour I have applied to this investigation, the reviewer might have found himself in a better condition to sit in judgment upon so complicated a question as that upon which he has undertaken to pronounce. But the man who declares Sir Elijah Impey a judicial delinquent, without reading his triumphant defence on the Nuncomar charge, was but little likely to go with any research into a charge of incomparably less importance. Sterne's critic merely looked at his stop-watch, and Jedediah Buxton counted the words and syllables without bestowing a thought on the matter of Garrick's recitation. This Edinburgh critic merely attends to the roundings of his periods, and looks into nothing but the unsifted husks of Mr. Mill's history.

Of those numbers of natives highly considered among their countrymen, who were seized and flung into the common jail of Calcutta, without any crime and without any debt, I can find nowhere any trace; none in my father's correspondence, private or public; none in Hastings's copious letters; none in any official or other

* See Report from the Committee on Touchett's Petition: I. General Appendix, with references, from No. 7 to No. 39; II. Patna Appendix, from No. 1 to No. 22; III. Dacca Appendix, from No. 1 to No. 12; IV. Cossijurah Appendix, from No. 1 to No. 27.

report. The great natives, as I have said, suffered through their vakeels. Some of these vakeels may have enjoyed the consideration of a portion of their countrymen, and may have been put, for a season, under arrest for resisting the authority of the Court, or for refusing to make restitution of the spoil unjustly wrung from the poor ryots. Their sufferings—which, in most cases, were mere temporary inconveniences—may touch the tender heart of one who has such a sympathy for tax-gatherers as Mr. Macaulay exhibits; but what could the Court do but proceed against them according to law? It was in these classes, that existed the extortioners whom Mr. Macaulay dreams about. The Supreme Court was not a court of revenue—there were no extortioners presiding *there*,—it was a court *to put down* extortioners, and its activity in this respect, won for it the gratitude of the poor and the hatred of their oppressors.

The Calcutta government quarrelled with the Supreme Court, because the judges would not allow the extortioners to be at all times judges in their own causes. Sir Elijah Impey wrote to the Secretary of State,—

"It is with the deepest concern that the sense of my duty, and the desire of the other judges, call upon me to declare to your Lordship that, after four years' experience, it is our unanimous opinion that the corruption, depravity, avarice, rapacity, and despotic principles, to which British subjects long resident in this country have been naturalized from early youth, and which they have been taught by constant examples, and in which they have been strengthened by old habits, are so universal, and the distinctions drawn by the most moderate of them, between themselves and the natives, are so strong, and so injurious to the latter, that the adopting the measure proposed would be of the worst consequence to this country.

"To submit the causes of the injured to the determination of their oppressors, would not only add insult to injury, but would authorise the guilty to give, by the forms of justice, both indemnity and legal sanction to their mutual crimes. To suffer these British inhabitants to determine on the jurisdiction of our Court, would be to annihilate it."*

The right honourable reviewer is fond of parallels, and comparisons, and similitudes, of all kinds, however

* Letter to Lord Weymouth, dated the 26th of March, 1779.

far-fetched, but most of all he fancies such as seem to be historical. Let me, then, ask him a question or two in this way :—If he had been living in the rapacious days of Henry VII.—not as a law-maker or cabinet minister, but as a modest, plain, honest burgher—does he conceive that he would have shed many tears upon hearing that Empson and Dudley were flung into Newgate, or the Fleet Prison ; or does he think that there was much weeping among the citizens of London, when Henry VIII. put those two extortioners to death upon Tower Hill ? I must dismiss these remarks on my last extract from Mr. Macaulay's libel by adding, that his story about the men of the most venerable dignity that died of rage and shame at being put under arrest, must be classed with that other fiction of General Clavering's oath to rescue Nuncomar, though at the foot of the gallows. There is as much discoverable foundation for the one tale as for the other : both are oratorical flourishes, and nothing more. Rousseau, one of the greatest of masters himself, always doubted the truth of a story that was too pointedly and finely told. "Alas !" said he, "I know by experience how much of the true is sacrificed by professed writers to the rhetorical." *

But if Mr. Macaulay had not been of the numerous herd of those "who think too little, and who talk too much ;" if he had read before he began to write, discharging his mind, at the same time, of prejudice and party malice, he would have found truly touching pictures of oppression, and stories, both terrible and pathetic, in which the judges of the Supreme Court boldly stood forward as the defenders of the oppressed, and punished those who had been protected by the Company's courts, and the native agents of those adauluts. I will give the right honourable essayist and reviewer a story or two, upon which his rhetorical powers might have been fairly exercised, prefacing them, as my father did, with a few more remarks on the violence and corruption of those courts. Sir Elijah wrote to the Secretary of State :—

" We are likewise unanimous in our opinion, that the representations made in England of the frauds, cruelties, and ex-

* Rousseau's Confessions.

tortions committed by British subjects, or by persons deriving power and influence from them and the Company, were by no means exaggerated; but, on the contrary, that there exist at present numberless sources of fraud and rapine totally unheard of there [*i. e.* in England], and more especially in the provincial councils, which act as adauluts or courts of civil jurisdiction, and in the Board of Commerce, at Calcutta, composed of senior servants of the Company. The first [the provincial councils or adauluts] have been so perverted in the execution, as to be now the greatest engines of oppression which the miserable inhabitants of this country labour under. In some of them, as we have been credibly informed, and of which we entertain no doubt, the administration of justice has been let to hire to dewans and banyans of those gentlemen, whose duty it was to preside in those courts, and those to whom it was let out were left to indemnify themselves by what they could extract from the suitors. In others, the forms and terrors of justice have been held forth merely to give colour and force to rapine and extortion. Of two most notorious instances of the latter we have had an opportunity of taking judicial notice, without the least impeachment of the authorities of those courts, to which, while they are suffered to exist, we think ourselves bound to allow all the rights, privileges, and immunities, which were intended to protect more upright judicatories.

"One of the causes I allude to was tried on the 29th March, 1777, in which Bebee Sukeen was plaintiff, and Anderan Mullick defendant.

" The plaintiff was a widow of opulence, family, and virtue. A charge, without the least colour of truth, was forged against her, for having had and murdered a bastard child. This was done for the purpose of giving a pretence for putting a guard over her house, and treating her with inhuman severity, by the authority of the provincial council [or adaulut] *and this was done till a large sum of money was extorted from her.* The plaintiff recovered damages to the amount of 33,575 Patna Sonaut rupees. This action was against a black agent. Other actions were about to be commenced against *British subjects,* who were suspected to have partaken of the money extorted from the widow, but who thought—as we have been informed—that it was more proper to make a compromise than to stand a trial.

"The other cause was tried in November last. In that Nanderah Begum was plaintiff, and Bahadre Beg, and other officers attending the provincial council at Patna, were defendants. In that cause, it appeared that the plaintiff, widow of an Omrah of the empire, to whom her husband had, by deeds executed in his lifetime, given personal effects to the value of some lacs of rupees, and considerable landed property, was, under pretence that the deeds had been forged—though proof was made to the contrary—plundered and stripped of the whole estate, turned out, without bed or covering, into the public streets, compelled to take refuge in a monument inhabited by fakeers, and to depend on their charity for subsistence. She was then pursued by a guard of sepoys, who had orders not to suffer any sustenance to be conveyed to her, and who executed their orders so rigorously for three days, that during that period she subsisted only on rice and flat cakes, which the fakeers found means to convey through common drains or chinks in the wall of the ruinous room which they had assigned her for an asylum. The insults offered to her were carried to such lengths, that her attendants called upon her to escape from them by putting an end to her life; which fatal purpose she was on the point of executing with a poignard, which she had secreted for that purpose, when a timely relaxation of an intended indignity happily prevented this enormous injury from ending most tragically. This action was likewise brought against black agents, whom the Council at Patna had, contrary to their original institution, empowered to hear and determine a petition, in which there was no allegation whatever of any forgery. Judgment was for the plaintiff, with three lacs of rupees damages;* and actions have been, or will be, commenced against the Patna Council, for the severities exercised on the lady at the monument, by their express order, to which the defendants in this action before us did not appear to be parties."†

In these two tales Mr. Macaulay might have found all the materials for a truly pathetic and dramatic narrative : ladies of rank—and one of them of the very highest rank short of royalty—defenceless widows, merciless sepoys, compassionate fakeers, a pagoda, a foul and ruinous chamber, famine, a threatened rape, and a meditated suicide. But, as he found no allusion to these two tragical stories in Mr. Mill's book, he says, and, very probably, knows nothing about them : or, had they come to his knowledge, I must suppose that he would have suppressed them ; for they go not to support, but to destroy his conclusions against Sir Elijah

---

* This was the sentence against which the Court granted an appeal in 1779, and which was dismissed by the King in Council, 1789.

† Letter to Lord Weymouth, dated 26th March, 1779.

Impey and the Supreme Court. If the case had told *against* them, who can doubt that it would have been made the most of to their prejudice?

The interested servants of the Company, or—which is the same thing—the venal agents of those Company's servants, might complain, murmur, and storm; but the business of the Court kept steadily on the increase. The judges could do nothing to force that business; but the Council of government could, and actually did, much to check it, by leading the people of Bengal to believe that the Court was not strong enough to protect them; and that, by appealing to the Court, they must excite the displeasure of the government. The poor natives were but too easily intimidated; for it was no new thing in India, for the will of a prince, or the arm of his tax-gatherer, to overpower the law. At home, the Court of Directors, who generally held those measures the most legal which realised the most money, grew very sensitive and apprehensive about their dividends. They had not properly studied the apologue of the goose which laid golden eggs. Their alarms were aggravated by the correspondence of Francis; who, at one and the same time, attacked the judges and the Governor General. In a letter to Alexander Eliot, who was still in England, Sir Elijah Impey says,—

" The last accounts received from England, in Maclean's letters, are so alarming, from the turn affairs have taken, both with regard to Mr. Hastings and the Court, that I am sure it requires greater exertions than we can expect from our friends to prevent a disastrous conclusion. I am perfectly satisfied I need not call upon you at this crisis, and that you have already done what is in your power. Maclean says that the powers exercised by the Court are universally condemned; that the Directors tremble for the revenues; that if Indian affairs were brought before parliament the judges would meet no quarter; that attempts have been made to prejudice Lord Mansfield against them; and that he fears friendships will give way to politics. . . . . . I do positively assert, that no power whatsoever has been assumed by the Court which would really affect the revenues. Doctrines, indeed, have been flung out by some friends of ours, which, if carried into execution, would, I think, have prejudiced them to a high degree; but I have effectually counteracted them in every instance. In this I have been assisted by Mr. Justice Chambers. I tell you I could not do without him. A warm friend of ours* has such very high notions of the liberty and general protection from the laws of England, in all revenue cases, that I found it absolutely necessary to oppose him. This has been done without breaking in upon the harmony that existed among us. I am bound to do justice to the support Chambers has given me. Indeed, without it, the country might actually have been in that confusion which it is endeavoured to persuade the ministry and directors has taken place. Private attacks upon me, to prejudice me with Lord Mansfield, are made.† I have not the honour to be personally known to his lordship, but by pleading before him in Banco, where I do not know "he had reason to be prejudiced in my favour." If prejudices *against* me have taken place, I can only appeal to the faithful representations of those on the spot, who are intimately acquainted with my conduct and motives. I have written a very hasty letter to the Lord Chancellor,‡ a copy of which I enclose to you. This I must desire you to show to the friends to whom I desired my former papers to be communicated, and, if you think it right, to Lord Mansfield, in whose opinion, as you have frequently heard me say, it would give me great pain to stand ill, not only from interested views, but from the high idea I have formed of his character."§

At every step my father corresponded with eminent crown lawyers and ministers at home, explaining the motives of his conduct without reserve, and in the clearest manner. At this time his expressions were sufficiently warm, but it was only in cases of injustice, extortion, or oppression. He writes to Lord Chancellor Bathurst thus, for example :—

"I much fear the frequency of my letters may be troublesome to you. But as the ship which will convey this, will carry an appeal in the case of Commaul *versus* Goring and others, in which the evidence has run to an enormous length ; I could not resist the impulse of my desire to stand exculpated before your Lordship for the introduction of much matter, neither, in my opinion, relevant to the cause, nor admissible as proofs. I laboured as much as I could at the trial to prevent it, but the zeal of my brother Lemaistre forced it on

---

* Mr. Justice Hyde.

† Here we begin to trace the deep laid plot of Mr. Francis to make it appear that Lord Mansfield had declared an opinion adverse to Sir Elijah's conduct.

‡ Bathurst.

§ MS. Letter, dated Calcutta, 19th Sept., 1776.

the cause by long examinations, which took up the greatest part ot the time which was spent in it.

" The Court is increasing daily in business. We are beginning to make the vultures of Bengal to disgorge their prey. Causes kept back by the timidity of the natives—which had been much increased by assurances from those who should have supported the Court, that the foundation of it was unstable, and would be destroyed; and, therefore, that they—the poor natives—could receive no permanent protection from it—are now bringing forward by them; and I am convinced we shall, in a great measure, give redress for past injuries, and, by the frequency of our judgments, strike sufficient awe to prevent great enormities in future.

" *The institution of the new office for receiving and examining petitions of the natives, and for prosecuting the suits of the poor gràtis, has, and will continue to be, greatly conducive to those important objects.* We have, in two causes tried at the sittings which I am now attending, had proofs of *extortion and cruelties,* equal, at least, to any that have appeared in print in Europe. The salt contractors have, in those two instances, been principal actors.

" A melancholy accident has happened here, which, I fear, has been occasioned by this new institution. Mr. William Chambers is the examiner of petitions. He had a principal servant, in this country called a dewan, of uncorrupted integrity, and who had been very diligent in assisting the poor petitioners, some of whom complained of great injuries, and had very high demands. Sums of money had been offered to this faithful servant, which he had rejected. Last Saturday se'nnight he was murdered in his bed, by a man who, a few days before, offered him his services to play on the sittar, a musical instrument resembling a guitar. There were gold ornaments on the hands and neck of the deceased, and plate and other valuables were in his room at the time. As none of them were taken away, and the assassin had been with him but a few days; and, as there had been no quarrel, or assignable cause whatsoever, for the perpetration of so horrid a deed, there is the greatest occasion to suspect that he was hired by some person likely to be affected by the new institution. We have not yet been able to find any clue to discover either the murderer, or the motive of the murder."*

As this faithful man was in the service of Mr. William Chambers ; and as Mr. Macaulay holds all the servants,

* MS. Letter, dated Court-house, Calcutta, 1st April, 1777.

not only of the judges, but of the sheriffs, to be my father's chosen creatures, that right honourable libeller would, no doubt, have considered the murdered man as one of "*the alguazils of Impey.*" But, if anything is capable of proof, it is this : Mr. Macaulay is entirely ignorant of the subject he discusses, and neither knows why, nor among whom, the Supreme Court was unpopular. He follows Mr. Mill, and Mr. Mill was just as uninformed as Mr. Macaulay : and thus is history written !

At nearly the same time as the date of the foregoing letter to Lord Chancellor Bathurst, I find my father writing a very long and confidential despatch to Thurlow. This despatch, like so many others, opens with the expression of a modest doubt, lest Thurlow might be wearied by the frequency and length of his letters ; but it shows throughout how many were the difficulties of his situation, and how eager his desire to shape his conduct by the strictest rules of law and equity ; to avoid all usurpation of authority, or extension of jurisdiction. In this letter he complains of Justice Hyde, whose temper and manners occasionally disturbed the unanimity of the Court; and whose views, as to the extent of its powers, ran into extremes, which it may be necessary to notice hereafter.

Giving him every credit as an upright judge, he, nevertheless, informs his correspondent, that Hyde had just claimed, for the Supreme Court, *the full right to judge in causes of arrears of revenue claimed by the Company.* My father, on the contrary, considered that these causes must continue to be judged by the Company's courts, called dewannee adauluts, and that the Supreme Court could do nothing more than prevent extortion or violence, having neither the faculty nor the time to judge of the revenue arrears. " It is absolutely impossible," he says, " that, with human powers, we could, in the modes by which we must proceed, determine one-hundredth part of these causes ; and, to me, the question seems reducible to this ; whether the revenues shall, or shall not, be collected ? I do not say the present mode is unexceptionable ; there are evils which I wish the legislature would remedy."

But the home legislature was too busy to apply any

remedy to these errors ; and, upon the remedial changes suggested by Warren Hastings, a tremendous quarrel broke out in the Supreme Council.

It was long before this time that my father and his colleagues became fully sensible of the humiliating effects of those parts of the Regulating Act, which left their salaries to be paid by the East India Company ; that is to say, by the very party whose money-claims, and other pretensions, they were so frequently called upon to oppose. For the annual saving of a few thousands, his Majesty's Government had put his Majesty's judges in this false position. Even before the Company began "to tremble for their revenues," or to apprehend that they would be lessened by the strictly impartial administration of justice at Calcutta, the Court of Directors, not only departing from the liberality of British merchants, but forgetful even of the principle of common honesty, behaved to the Supreme Court like mere stock-jobbers, or exchange brokers, nicely calculating all the changes and variations of the money-market; which, to the uninitiated, and those who are employed in higher avocations, must ever remain a source of perplexity and disadvantage. I find the judges accordingly complaining, more than once, of this unexpected treatment ; whereupon Sir Elijah Impey, in behalf of himself and his brethren, wrote in the following straightforward manner to the Secretary of State :—

" The salaries of the Judges of the Supreme Court of Judicature being, by Act of Parliament, estimated in pounds sterling, here has been some difference as to the mode of payment, which has caused a correspondence between the Governor General, the Directors, and the Judges; and, as we have ever thought it improper to correspond with the Directors, without acquainting his Majesty's ministers with the contents of our letters, I have the honour of laying before you the several papers that have passed between them and us, hoping your lordship will think our demands and proposals reasonable, and trusting we shall have the assistance of Government to procure for us our just rights in an amicable manner."*

These differences were settled at last, though not much either to the honour or contentment of the Company ; but it was lamentable that they should ever have

* MS. Letter, dated 19th Sept., 1776.

been allowed to arise. My father always considered this dependency of the judges for their salaries on the Company, as one of the greatest blemishes of the Regulating Act; alike degrading to the bench, and tending to litigation and ill-will. This is a view of the subject so obviously just, that it needs no illustration; and I now haste to other matters of greater interest and importance.

CHAPTER VI.

CONTINUED OPPOSITION OF THE MAJORITY IN COUNCIL—
DEATH OF MONSON—MR. WHELER APPOINTED GOVERNOR
GENERAL—DISPUTE BETWEEN HASTINGS AND CLAVERING
—DEATH OF CLAVERING—PROCEEDINGS OF THE COURT
OPPOSED BY THE COUNCIL—TRIAL OF FRANCIS.

THE opposition against the Governor General, by the majority in Council, of which Philip Francis was the head and front, had never ceased for a day ; while the weakness and distraction it produced became, every moment, more and more alarming from the serious turn which matters were taking in our American colonies ; from the great probability of France drawing her sword on the side of the insurgents ; from the presence of a hostile fleet on the coast of Coromandel; and from intrigues by French agents in almost every native court. Hastings, like a great statesman, foresaw all that would happen, and applied all his energies to prepare for the struggle; for he was well aware that it was one which must involve a question of no less importance than this, " Whether France or England should hold dominion of the East ?" But he was thwarted at every step by the majority of the Council. They proceeded to condemn, and then to counteract, his newly-adopted system of revenue and finance; which, though not free from faults, was better than any that had preceded it, and far superior to that which they would have substituted in its place. As they could conciliate the Court of Directors only by raising the amount of remittances to England, they were pitiless towards the tax-paying population, and the most exacting and clamorous of creditors towards those subsidiary princes, who were in a state of utter dependence on the Company. In the act of tearing to pieces the treaties which Hastings had made with those princes, they exacted from them more than the price they were to pay for advantages which Hastings had promised them, and which the majority had annulled. And while they were grinding both prince and people, and everywhere diffusing alarm—while they were assuring the Directors, in Leadenhall-street, that they were swelling their revenues—they wrote to his Majesty's ministers, as well as to their own factious correspondents, that the people of India were crushed and tortured by the encroachments of the Supreme Court, and that the whole empire was put in jeopardy by the inordinate ambition of the Governor General. But it was chiefly by means of the letters—the treacherous, backbiting innuendos of Francis—that all manner of false impressions were created in England.

Hastings was no less diligent in sending home complaints and representations on his part; and these were now more frequently addressed to the Prime Minister than to the Court of Directors, of whose opinion and approbation he was long distrustful, as he well might be, after having seen with what ease they could condemn in one despatch, what they had applauded in another, and with what rapidity they could change their plans. Still, as the sworn servant of the Company, the Governor General could not enter into a scheme upon which General Clavering is said to have embarked.

" The fact is," says Colonel Maclean, writing from London, under the date of the 25th of June, 1776, "a plan is formed for reducing the Company to the simple transactions of commerce, and for taking possession of all its territorial rights and acquisitions; and General Clavering has undertaken the execution of this plan. The King is bigoted to him, and will not hear of anything that thwarts him. And it seems nothing short of your disgrace will satisfy his friends. Unless you and your friends are given up to his vengeance, he will return in the first ship, *et magna res manebit infecta.*"*

* Letter to Hastings, as given by Mr. Gleig, vol. II., pp. 48—70.

General Clavering's parliamentary connections were very powerful; and, in the present embarrassing state of affairs, it was a point of vital importance with Lord North to ensure their support. The Prime Minister himself, though confessedly an amiable and good-natured man, had some prejudice, and, perhaps, some political jealousy, against Hastings. I would not speak so confidently of the feeling of his Majesty, George III.; but I conceive it to be very apparent, that the Premier really wished and intended to place General Clavering at the head of affairs in India. When, on the 15th of December, 1775, a meeting was held at the India House, to debate the question, whether an address should not be sent up to the Crown, for the immediate removal of Hastings and Barwell, Lord North's friends voted for that address. The measure was, however, rejected by a considerable majority; and this decision, which left the great mind of Warren Hastings at liberty to act for the welfare of India, gave great chagrin to the minister, who was losing America. Still the Governor General persevered in addressing Lord North and his colleagues; still he continued to represent that his arms were tied, and that the greater part of public business at Calcutta was at a stand-still; that the judges of the Supreme Court were insulted and outraged by the majority of the Council, and were only hindered from coming to an open rupture by his endeavours, and their own regard to public order.*

The judges were not always on the side of the Governor General; being guided, not by passion, caprice, or partiality, nor even by the conviction that, in the main, Hastings was in the right; but by the letter, or the spirit *of the English law*, which they were bound to administer. In the course of these never-ending quarrels, they, more than once, delivered opinions directly adverse to the Governor General, and favourable to Francis, Clavering, and Monson. If, at the time, this was resented by Hastings, he afterwards approved or acquiesced in it. He confessed that Sir Elijah Impey, the calmest and firmest of the Court, had saved him from the commission of grievous errors—had preserved

* Hastings's Correspondence, as given by Gleig.

his honour, if not his life. This Mr. Macaulay inter-
prets into an allusion to Nuncomar's execution ; a more
candid critic, or a better informed historian, would have
referred it to the interposition of the judges in the
quarrel between Hastings and Clavering, which we are
now approaching, but must not anticipate.

While the war in the Council-chamber was at its
height, Colonel Monson fell sick, and was obliged to
absent himself. In the letter to his brother Michael,
dated the 10th of September, 1776, from which I have
already quoted, Sir Elijah says,—

" Colonel Monson is very ill; most people think he will
not be able to return to business, or even to live in this
country. . . . The dissensions in Council still subsist,
but they are quieter on account of the absence of one of the
majority, which has given Mr. Hastings an opportunity of
showing his moderation."

But moderation was of no avail with men whose
passions, schemes, and ambition, were immoderate.

On the 25th of September, fifteen days after my
father's confidential letter to his brother, the majority
was reduced to an equality in number with its opponents, by the death of Colonel Monson. Thus, there
remained only two on either side, but the casting vote
of the Governor General gave him the superiority. On
the very next day after Monson's death he accordingly
writes thus :—

" It has restored me the constitutional authority of my
station; but, without absolute necessity, I shall not think it
proper to use it with that effect which I should give it were
I sure of support from home. . . . . . . Thus
circumstanced, it is my wish to let the affairs of this government remain in their present channels, and to avoid alterations which, in the course of a few months, may possibly
be subject to new changes, and introduce weakness and
distraction into the state."

And again, in a letter written on the same day, to
John Graham, Esq., he continues thus to declare his
intentions :—

" If a friend of Clavering's is sent out to reinforce his
party, I must, in that case, either quit the field, or resolve to
remain, and have a new warfare, perhaps more violent than
the last, to encounter. The first is a wretched expedient,

which I will never submit to. Having gone through two
years of persecution, I am determined now, that no authority
less than the King's express act, shall remove me, or death.
. . . . .   I have already drawn the line of my conduct,
with the concurrent opinion and advice of Mr. Barwell and
Sir E. Impey, and have written to Lord North, to inform
him of it."*

Being unable to defer the great question of the new
settlement of the revenue, &c., the Governor General
very soon used his re-acquired authority with boldness
and effect, deciding all measures connected with that
pressing question by his casting vote, and leaving Clavering and Francis, even as they and Monson had recently left him and Barwell, to protest and declaim.
But those two members of Council bore the hardships
of this, their new situation, with incomparably less
equanimity than Hastings and Barwell had borne their
two years' inefficiency. Yet, it appears, that the Governor General acted according to that moderate rule,
which he had explained to Lord North, and, with greater
freedom of detail, to a private friend in England, as
partially above quoted.

But Hastings and Barwell could have no chance of
carrying out the new revenue settlement, without first
re-modelling all the provincial councils, which, during
their late predominance, Francis, Clavering, and Monson, had filled with their own relatives, friends, or de-
pendents, who had long since declared themselves the
mortal enemies of the Governor General, and would
now have done all in their power to render his designs
abortive. During two years the tripartite majority,
whereof

    " What seem'd its head
    The likeness of a kingly crown had on"—

had appointed to all places of emolument or power. To
lose this immense patronage, to see their appointments
made void, and their cousins, or creatures, removed,
was gall and wormwood to the two surviving sections
of the King, Francis and Clavering. The General fell
sick, " being covered with boils," as Mr. Hastings re-

* For the remainder of these letters, see Mr. Gleig's Memoirs, vol. II.,
beginning at p. 108. I extract no more than is necessary to the thread
of my narrative.

lated to his correspondent, Graham, in the foregoing letter. The constitution of Francis was of sterner stuff, and a palliative was applied to his ill temper, by an offer from Hastings, to allow him "a fair share of the patronage." This offer induced him to give a momentary assent to the new settlement. But the dark author of the letters of Junius was never steady to any engagement, but continually changing aspect and demeanour, like the perplexing spectrum in Lord Byron's witty, but indecorous poem:*

> "Now it wax'd little, then, again, grew bigger,
> With now an air of gloom or savage mirth;
> But as you gaz'd upon its features, they
> Changed every instant—to *what*, none could say."

But to some points Francis was steady enough; steady in revenge, steady in pursuing every object of his spite, steady in his love of power, as well as in his love of money. There is, therefore, one inaccuracy in the following account of him, as given at this moment, by the great man whose life he embittered :—

"Francis," said Hastings, to his and my father's friend, Alexander Eliot, "you will perceive, has promised, in one minute, to give his support to it—the new settlement—though he says he disapproves of the principles on which it is founded ; yet, in another minute, in reply to mine, thanking him for that assistance, he retracts that promise. The movements of that man of levity are difficult to foresee, or comprehend. His interest is the only steady principle in his composition, and it operates in him as powerfully as in any man I ever knew; yet, even this cannot always concentrate him, but, by fits, he flies from off it."†

At this moment, not only Sir Elijah Impey, but also Mr. Justice Chambers, made some slight efforts with ministers, and their friends in England, to be admitted into the Supreme Council. All the judges had long conceived that at least one of their body ought to be a member of that Council, where many questions were decided which involved points of law ; and, in the decision of which, the want of legal knowledge had often been apparent. My father's proceedings in this matter

---

* The Vision of Judgment. Few can regret more than I that the late excellent and revered Southey should have provoked this malicious piece of wit, by an injudicious application of his powers to an unworthy topic.

† Letter, dated 23rd November, 1776, as given by Mr. Gleig.

were marked by the mildness and modesty that belonged to his character. About a month after Colonel Monson's death, he thus wrote to Thurlow, beginning with a melancholy, but marked remonstrance, against his habitual neglect.

" Dear Thurlow,—You must excuse me for my complaints of not having heard from you, though I have written to you from every stage on my voyage, and almost by every ship, since my arrival in India. The transactions here, the turn India matters have taken in England, and the pushes made against me by General Clavering, all add to my anxiety. . .

" I now feel a degree of absurdity in showing a wish to be appointed of the Council, well knowing I must be obliged to my friends, if I so far withstand the attacks made upon me, as to keep the ground I now possess. I, therefore, did not drop a hint of this in my last. Since that I have received a letter from the Lord Chancellor [Bathurst] dated the 7th of April [1776] full of terms of approbation, kindness, and friendship, which have given me the courage to make the proposition. Chambers is employing himself on the same object; and, though I could not help having some awkward sensations if he was put over my head, yet, if I should not succeed, I am far from wishing him ill success. Some time or other the inconvenience of not having a member of the Court a member of the Council will be seriously felt. Misapprehensions, misrepresentations, and jealousies, which could be easily cleared up, as they arise, with immediate explanations, do, will, and must, ferment into animosities and enmities.

" Your partiality to me I have experienced; and, though your silence has alarmed me, I still cannot believe that it is altered. If my interest is not contrary to the inclination of Government, and their general plan, I still hope you will endeavour to promote my wish. It may be strongly biassed, yet I really think that it is necessary, for the tranquillity of the settlement, and the uniting the powers of Government in this country, that one judge of the Court should be admitted into the Council."

" Whether you laugh or frown at this application I cannot guess; and whether you think it proper to assist me in it or not, I shall always acknowledge myself under obligations to you.   Yours, most sincerely and affectionately,

E. I.*

* MS. Letter to Thurlow, dated Calcutta, 20th October, 1776.

When Mr. Macaulay was legislating,* or pretending to legislate in India—without being a lawyer—he was allowed a seat in the Council. Such a seat was never granted either to my father or to Sir Robert Chambers. Lord North, in all probability, never once gave the subject a serious thought; and I am afraid that the bustling, ambitious, and aspiring Thurlow, did little to promote the desire of his absent friends. He was already, and had for some years been Attorney General; he had attracted the particular notice of George III., by the zeal and energy with which he had supported the policy of Lord North's government respecting America; and the great seal, which he actually obtained in the summer of 1778, through the resignation of Lord Bathurst, seemed even now to be within his grasp. In the month of March, or April, 1777, before which my father's letter could hardly have reached him, Thurlow, his colleagues, and party, were involved in tremendous troubles by the ill-success of the wretchedly conducted war in the American colonies, and by the increasing power of the opposition in either House of Parliament. Canada had been invaded by the republicans; General Howe compelled by Washington to evacuate Boston. The Earl of Chatham in the Lords, and Burke in the Commons, were denouncing the whole war as hopeless and ruinous. Ministers had not time to bestow a thought upon India, or on any person connected with that portion of the British Empire.

Both the Governor General, and the Chief Justice, were exposed to the enmity of some of the authorities in Leadenhall Street; whose enmity was embittered by a knowledge of their corresponding with his Majesty's Ministers. Upon ex-parte evidence, the Court of Directors wrote a strong reprimand to Hastings, accusing him of having usurped an undue authority since the death of Monson.

A considerable time before that event, when Monson was well or active, and Hastings almost overwhelmed by the majority of Council, he, in a moment of despondence, had announced to his friends, Graham and Maclean, that he thought seriously of resigning.

* Under Act 3 & 4 William IV.

Colonel Maclean, after keeping this letter by him for several months, showed it to the chairman, and deputy-chairman, and another director in the India House; and upon their report, the resignation was hurriedly, yet formally, accepted, and a successor to Hastings was chosen in the person of Mr. Wheler. Further, the Court of Directors resolved that General Clavering, as senior Member of the Council, should occupy the chair at Calcutta till Mr. Wheler arrived. Mr. Wheler was accordingly presented to the King, and accepted as the future Governor General.

The news of these proceedings reached Calcutta on the 19th of June : they were brought, in what Hastings calls " a mysterious packet ; " and as soon as this packet was opened, everything was thrown into fresh confusion. Hastings declared that the Court of Directors could not accept what he had never given ; that his letter about resigning had been revoked by a subsequent letter ; that Colonel Maclean had no authority to publish a letter written in the confidence of friendship, and expressive merely of the mortified feelings of the moment ; that nothing in that letter amounted to a tender of his resignation, and that, even if it had, it was annulled by a second, written not many weeks after, and strongly declaring his intention to remain at his post, lest British India should be ruined and lost, by the levity, incapacity, ignorance, and rashness, of Francis and his confederates.

He refused, therefore, to submit to General Clavering's taking the chair, and summoned the Council to assemble under his own presidency as before. On the other hand, Clavering insisted on his right, and summoned the Council in his own name. Barwell attended the summons of Hastings, Francis that of Clavering ; and thus, there were in Calcutta two councils, each claiming the supreme authority. General Clavering and Francis met at the usual Council-table ; Hastings and Barwell at the Board of Revenue. The General immediately proceeded to take the oaths as Governor General, *ad interim*, and to deliberate and preside. Hastings requested the judges of the Supreme Court to attend him at the Revenue-board, to give him their opinion. The judges met immediately, but to no purpose ; for

General Clavering had got possession of all the despatches from Europe, and refused not only to deliver
them up to Hastings, but also to show them to the
judges. Hastings assured the judges, in writing, that
if, upon inspection of the said despatches from Europe,
they should find any act of his from which his resignation could be deduced, he would immediately vacate
the chair. Clavering and Francis then condescended
to enclose *copies* of *some* of the despatches, upon which,
they said, their claims were indubitably and immovably
grounded. They did not offer to abide by the decision
of the judges, but they agreed to suspend the execution
of their orders as a Council, till the judges should have
given their opinion.

In the meanwhile, Clavering demanded the keys of the
fort and treasury, and wrote a letter to the commandant of the fort, requiring his obedience ; and Hastings,
equally active and far more self-possessed, clenched
the keys with a firmer grasp, sent opposite orders to
the commandant, and showed himself fully determined
to meet force by force. The sword of civil war seemed
half unsheathed. But the military man, Clavering,
cooled at the sight of this unexpected boldness in the
civilian; and, unquestionably, had it come to an issue,
the vast majority of the army in India would have
stood by their experienced Governor, rather than by
their untried Commander-in-Chief.

The judges were unanimously of opinion, that it
would be illegal in General Clavering to assume the
chair, or otherwise persevere in his course. Thus
baffled, the confederates wrote a letter to the judges,
acquiescing in their judgment. Francis, however,
showing his pride and malignity, seceded from the
Council re-assembled under the presidency of Hastings,
and would not apologize for his absence.

With this decided majority, that is to say, himself
with his casting vote, and Mr. Barwell, against the
General, Hastings now carried a resolution that
Clavering, by taking the oath as Governor General,
and by his violent proceedings, had vacated his seat as
senior Member of the Council, and could no longer sit
at the board in any capacity. But here the judges,
with Sir Elijah at their head, refused to go along with

him, and Hastings, who took a different reading of the law, was in his turn compelled to yield.*

This is one of many examples which might be adduced of my father's perfect impartiality, and independence on the friendship of Hastings.

The hostile parties now consented to refer their several claims to England for decision; and, in the meantime, to leave everything at Calcutta as it stood before the arrival of the " mysterious packet."

My father's letters to Thurlow, Dunning, and other friends, closely agree with the preceding narrative of events, nor does there appear ever to have been any difference of opinion as to the facts here stated; Mr. Macaulay alone, whether ignorantly or maliciously, slurs over the decision of the judges, and hints that the Court was partial.

In his letter to Thurlow, of the 29th of June, 1777—the same date as that of Hastings to Lord North—my father puts in a strong light the impetuous and unconstitutional behaviour of Clavering. His words are these :—

" On the day after the arrival of the ' mysterious packet,' General Clavering sent a letter by his military secretary, demanding the keys of the fort and treasury, by virtue of the authority devolved on him as Governor General. He ordered the secretary of both departments — viz., the general department, and that of the revenue—to issue a summons, in his name, as Governor General, to Mr. Barwell and Mr. Francis, to meet in Council. The secretary of the general department obeyed, and issued the summons accordingly, in consequence of which, Mr. Francis attended, and the General and he held a Council, at which the General took his oaths, as Governor General, assumed the chair, and presided, and came to several resolutions to proclaim the change of government. At the same time Mr. Hastings, who had not yet received the General's letters, was at the Revenue-board, the place where, in the routine of business, the Council was to be held, for which the secretary of that department had, some days before, issued a summons in the name of Mr. Hastings, as Governor General. Mr. Barwell, who had received his summons to attend the General's Council, came to

* Letters from Warren Hastings to Mr. Sykes and Lord North, both dated the 29th of June, 1777, as given by Mr. Gleig. Abstract of the proceedings as given by Mr. Mac Farlane in " Our Indian Empire."

the Revenue-board, produced it; and, about the same time, Mr. Hastings received the General's letter. They answered by requiring the General to attend the Board, and declaring their ignorance of the power of Governor General having devolved on him. Mr. Hastings and Mr. Barwell immediately wrote to Colonel Morgan, the commandant of the fort, and Colonel Muir, the commandant of Barrickpoor—16 miles from hence—acquainting them with the General's claim, and ordering them to obey no orders but from the Board. Colonel Morgan instantly shut the fort, and returned for answer, that he would obey no orders but from the Board. Colonel Muir returned the same answer. At the same time they sent the orders to the commandants, they addressed a letter to me, to assemble the judges, to assist with their advice, which was immediately followed by one desiring us to assemble at the Revenue-board. We went accordingly. Mr. Hastings there repeated to us what had happened. . . . He then desired our opinions, whether the powers of Governor General were actually vested in the General, and whether the proceedings were regular; saying that, if we thought that the powers of the Governor General were vested in the General, he would immediately acquiesce in that opinion, and retire to a private station. We told him the two questions must depend on the first; and that, not having the papers, we had not the proper materials to judge. We proposed that he should demand the papers, or copies of them; he said they had been demanded, and refused. Mr. Barwell said he would go to the General's meeting and demand them, as a member of the Council. He went, and on his return, reported, that the papers were in possession of the General, who would not deliver them, but told him he might hear them read, and required him to take his seat at that Board. We then proposed that a message should be sent to Mr. Auriol, desiring him to acquaint the General that the judges were assembled, and with the questions which had been referred to them. We said, if the papers were then refused, and he would state their contents in writing, to the best of his recollection, we would advise him, to the best of our abilities, with this reservation, ' if the facts were accurately stated.' This message produced an answer from Mr. Auriol, that the General was preparing a letter to the judges, requesting us to appoint a time to receive the papers, and to consider them, and give our opinions in the absence of both parties. We appointed six o'clock in the evening, at my house.

" In the evening the General's secretary attended, with a

letter from the General and Mr. Francis, informing us they
had suspended their resolutions, desiring our opinions, and
enclosing the papers, Nos. 1, 2, 3, 4, 5, 6, 7.   Mr. Hastings
and Mr. Barwell sent their proceedings of that day, together
with a clause of 13 Geo. III., and the commission granted
by the Company to Mr. Hastings to be Governor General,
and to command the garrison, &c.   The evening was now far
spent, and, about four o'clock in the morning, we delivered
to the gentlemen attending on both sides, letters directed to
the several gentlemen, declaring our opinions, that the powers
were not actually vested in the General.   At noon, we received a letter from the General and Mr. Francis, informing
us that they acquiesced in our opinions.   Mr. Hastings and
Mr. Barwell kept up the Council at the Revenue-board by
adjournment to the 23rd, when they resolved that General
Clavering had vacated his offices of senior Councillor, and
Commander-in-Chief.   On the evening of this day, I received
a letter from General Clavering and Mr. Francis, inclosing a
minute which they had entered on the consultations, which
set forth the reasons for what they did on the 19th.   At five
in the morning of the 24th, I received another letter from the
General and Mr. Francis, with a letter from Mr. Sumner,
informing them of the resolutions of the 23rd, about the
General's offices, and desiring the judges to point out a
means of redressing the grievances which the General complained of.   The judges met at ten that morning at my
house.   I was desired to go to Calcutta to endeavour to
reconcile matters, which I did, having seen Mr. Hastings,
Mr. Barwell, and Mr. Francis, then in Council.   Mr. Hastings
and Mr. Barwell agreed to follow the advice of the judges.
The judges, on my return to them, agreed on a letter in which
they said they could not be of opinion that the Governor
General's Council, could, by their own authority, declare
vacant the seat of any Member of their Board ; and advising
them to recede from such resolutions as prevented the General
from the free exercise of his offices, and that neither party
should act on their claims, but reserve them for decision in
England.   The acquiescence of Mr. Hastings and Mr. Barwell
was in two hours afterwards signified to us by a letter from
them.   The General and Mr. Francis thanked us in the same
manner for our attention to their application.   The next day
they all met in Council, the General re-assuming his seat as
senior councillor;   and everything at present is calm.   They
agreed at this last meeting to send the proceedings on both
sides to the Court of Directors.   I have apprehensions from
some passages in the General's and Mr. Francis's minutes—
though I am almost afraid to attribute conduct so illiberal to

them, when they well know the very disinterested part I have
taken in this business—that, even in this affair, they will
arraign my conduct in England. Perhaps Mr. Hastings may
have more reason to complain of me, which, however, he no
way does. Last night the General came to me alone, to return me thanks, and to enter into confidential discourse, and
remained with me three hours. The General still insists that
he is by right Governor General. . . Though I love and
revere Mr. Hastings, as I find that the Administration have
made their final option, and that General Clavering is to be supported, I will not by advice or otherwise thwart the measures
of Government. Even should the government here be flung
into the hands of Clavering, I will really and truly support
his administration as far as I legally may, as much as if it
were in other hands; but from what has already passed in
England, and from the minute of the 23rd of June, I much
fear his intrigues, and that notwithstanding his professions to
me here, his intentions are hostile to me. . . . . Mr.
J. Stewart writes me the subject of a conversation you held
with him. I am much obliged for the kindness to me with
which you expressed yourself; but, to a mind agitated as mine
has been, you have no idea of the consolation it would be to
see it expressed under your hand by letter." *

Several important changes were now made among
the agents and residents at the native courts: Mr.
Middleton was again sent to reside at the court of the
Nabob of Oude, and Mr. Bristow who had been nominated by the majority, was recalled; Mr. Francis Fowke,
son of that Mr. Joseph Fowke who had been tried for
a conspiracy against the Governor General, was removed
from Benares, and other alterations were made in favour
of Hastings's friends, evidently to the great satisfaction
of the nabobs and people of India. Colonel Monson's
place in the Council was soon after occupied by
Mr. Wheler; who, although nominated as Governor
General, consented to fill a subordinate post. The
new Member of Council generally, but not invariably,
voted with Francis and Clavering, against Hastings
and Barwell; but before this party could recover the
ascendancy, it was broken up, or reduced to a minority,
by the death of General Clavering. The General died
about two months after his desperate effort to dispossess
Mr. Hastings as Governor General.

* Letter to Thurlow. In MS. letters from India, in my possession.

On the 30th of August, of this same turbulent year, 1777, my father wrote triplicate letters, as was frequently his custom, to his three principal correspondents, Sutton, Dunning, and Thurlow. Of these triplicates, I find the rough draft usually inscribed " *mutatis mutandis.*"

To Dunning he said :—

" I send you this to acquaint you with the death of Sir John Clavering, who died yesterday of a bloody flux, which he had on him for little more than a week. . . . This event, by removing the favourite object of Government, may give a turn to Mr. Hastings's affairs in England, and make even the King's Ministers desirous of his remaining in India. Perhaps it may give an opening to my friends to procure a seat for me in Council. . . . I most sincerely think, that the Chief Justice's having a place in Council will contribute much to the strengh, ease, and harmony, of the Council and Court. If there is any way in which you can assist me, I am sure I need not solicit you.''

The letter to Thurlow was to the same purport, and nearly in the same words; but enclosed in it were two other letters, one to Lord North, and one to Lord Weymouth, which Thurlow, the Attorney General, was to forward, if he saw nothing objectionable in them. In that addressed to Lord North, Sir Elijah said :—

" As by this event—the death of Clavering—there will be a vacancy in the Council, I have taken the liberty of submitting to your Lordship, the propriety of the Chief Justice having a seat at that Board. I do this with the strongest sense of the rectitude of my own intentions, and of my attachment to his Majesty, and the nation's interest.''

The letter to Lord Weymouth was of the same tenor. The very same day my father also wrote to Lord Chancellor Bathurst. In this last letter, the following passage may be worth notice :—

" Sir John Clavering was taken ill about a fortnight ago, returning home from a visit at my house. He died, and was buried yesterday.''

By the same conveyance he addressed his brother, telling him, that he had made a fresh application for a seat in the Council, but that he was not at all sanguine in his expectations. Except from his brother, and Dunning, it appears he received no answer to any of these letters.* The ship which sailed from Calcutta at the beginning of September, probably did not reach England until the end of January,—perhaps not until the end of February, 1778.

On the 2nd of June, of that year, Lord Bathurst, who had appointed my father, ceased to be Chancellor, and the seals were transferred to Thurlow; a change in the home Government by no means favourable to any of the judges in India.

Death had thus removed, in rapid succession, two Members of the Supreme Council. Before the death either of Monson or of Clavering, the health of Sir Elijah Impey, and of more than one of the puisne judges, had been seriously affected. My father had undergone a sharp illness. He attributed the disorder solely to excess of mental labour, and considered that the climate of India had not had much to do with it. At least so he wrote to his brother, whose alarms appear to have been excited by some unfounded reports of his death about this time :—

" I have indeed had some very slight disorders, which must fairly be attributed to fatigue, and not to the climate, but they have long since vanished, and as I take great care to spare myself, never sitting in Court after one at noon, I have no reason to expect their return. If increase in bulk, hearty appetite, and sound sleep, indicate health, I have the strongest pretensions to it. I use exercise, which is esteemed absolutely necessary here. You will hardly credit, what nevertheless is actually fact, I mount my horse every morning, without fail, at five o'clock, I dine at one, sup at half-past nine, and go to bed at eleven. This is not the general mode of living in the settlement, hours being very late and irregular : but I intend to live for my friends and family, and will not, even by the stream of custom, be driven from my purpose."

Francis had outlived his two original colleagues, but continued, nevertheless, to exercise a considerable controul, by means of his ascendancy over the mind of Mr. Wheler; not sufficient, however, to counteract

---

* Throughout the MSS. in my possession, there are evident traces of uninterrupted intercourse between my father and some of his correspondents, particularly Dunning ; but their letters, except in a few instances, appear to have been either carelessly preserved, or to have fallen into hands, from which I have vainly endeavoured to redeem them.

Hastings with his casting vote, and the steady adherence of Barwell.

Some time elapsed before Clavering's vacancy was filled; and, during that interval, the Governor General assumed the real direction of affairs. On the 22nd of November, 1777, Hastings wrote to a private friend :—

"The death of Sir John Clavering has produced a state of quiet in our councils, which I shall endeavour to preserve during the remainder of the time which may be allotted to me. The interests of the Company will benefit by it; that is to say, they will not suffer, as they have done, by the effects of a divided administration."

This quiet in the Councils of Calcutta happened at a very opportune and critical moment. When Clavering died, danger was approaching on all sides. The vaccillating policy so long pursued by the majority of the Council, had alarmed or alienated the friends, and emboldened the enemies of British India. Most of the Mahratta chiefs were looking forward to war and plunder; complicated intrigues, plots and combinations, were forming at Poonah; a French ship had put into one of the Mahratta ports, a French agent was reported to be resident at Poonah, and there exercising a predominant influence over the savage mind of Hyder Ali. Rumours were everywhere spread by Frenchmen, or their secret agents, that the English monarchy was falling to decay; that her fleets and armies had been defeated, that she had lost America, and must soon lose all that she possessed in India. It was not alone the great body of natives that was affected by these reports —they spread discouragement and alarm among the officers and servants of the Company, and over every British subject in Hindustan. A commercial as well as bodily panic ensued in Calcutta. Every Englishman who had money hastened to remit it home by the first available transport, considering all property as insecure in India. These fears increased the danger, by lessening the means of Government to meet it. The empire which he and the great Lord Clive had erected was tottering on the very edge of a precipice, when Hastings, enabled by the circumstances here narrated, and with a brave disregard of responsibility, seized the powers of which he ought not to have been deprived for a single day.

Animated by his spirit, and directed by his genius, the English officers in India proved themselves worthy of contesting so glorious a dominion. Marches of a wonderful length, campaigns of an unprecedented extent and complication were undertaken, and conducted to their close with gallantry and success. Goddard, Popham, Bruce, and other officers of the Company, who now first made their names known to the world, performed prodigies of valour; and the veteran, Sir Eyre Coote, who had fought with Clive at Plassey, now surpassed his former exploits.

It is not in my province to relate how our Indian armies, thus put in motion by their immortal Governor General, triumphed over the most formidable confederacy which England has ever witnessed in the East— over Hyder Ali, the Mahrattas, the Dutch, and their French allies! The brilliant story has been recently told with what I consider sufficient accuracy, and an adequate feeling of national renown. The whole conduct of the war depended on the Governor General, his energetic loyalty, and fertility of resource. At nearly every move, Francis and his adherents condemned these plans, and suggested others which would have been ruinous indeed. But, luckily, Francis could now only figure in protests and misrepresentations. Clive himself had never acted with more determination or intrepidity than Hastings at this momentous crisis.

If, in achieving this great delivery, under circumstances of nearly every possible difficulty, discouragement, and obstruction, our distinguished Indian statesman did occasionally resort to measures which might not be perfectly justifiable at a time less critical than that in which he was called upon to act, a large allowance must be made for every imputed irregularity. Had he failed to do that which he did, India must have been abandoned like America. Nay, if Francis had been enabled to defeat the brilliant efforts of Warren Hastings, India would have been lost long before the American colonies. About the last public act performed in India by the author of Junius, was his opposition to the splendid campaign of Major Popham, which shook the power of the Mahrattas in the very heart of their own territory. Harassed by his incessant cavils, and eager to have a united administration at so portentous a moment, Hastings, in an unhappy hour, tried once more to effect a reconciliation with Mr. Francis. The Governor General, as the event proved, could scarcely have committed a greater mistake. The temper of Francis was uncontrollable; his mind open to no conviction. On Hastings's side there existed many justifiable suspicions and antipathies which could hardly be removed by any compromise : Francis had offered him insults difficult to be forgiven by any man, unless on a death-bed. Hastings always attributed the far greater part of the agony of mind he had endured, to the "incendiary impressions" of the ex-clerk of the War Office ; and he had reason to apprehend, or proofs sufficient to know for a certainty, that, while listening to overtures of accommodation in India, Francis was defaming him, worse than ever, by his correspondence in England, and was seeking to estrange his best friends in India. He had said on one occasion,—

" Francis is the vilest fetcher and carrier of tales to set friends, and even the most intimate friends, at variance, of any man I ever knew. Even the apparent levity of his ordinary behaviour is but a cloak to deception."*

The hollow compact was, however, made towards the close of the year 1779 ; Francis promising to cease or moderate his opposition, and Hastings agreeing to concede a larger share in the distribution of place and profit to his opponent. The Governor General knew the *soi-disant* patriotic member of Council too well to have expected, for a single moment, that Francis was to be swayed by any other motives than those of his own interest and ambition. The hollow truce had scarcely been concluded, ere the virulent spirit of Junius drove Hastings into a quarrel with my father and the other judges. He filled the ear of the Governor General with tales against the Supreme Court, and he procured more than one order for preventing execution of the writs issued by the Court. He raised and encouraged doubts among the natives, touching the jurisdiction of the Court and its extent ; and he twisted the defective Regulating Act and Charter as he chose. In vain my

* Letter to Sullivan, as given by Mr. Gleig.

father had written volumes of letters to procure from his Majesty's Government some clearer definitions : in vain had he suggested many capital amendments to that Act and Charter : he and his brethren were left to abide the perilous issue of their own unassisted construction.

To support the authority of the Court, as they understood it, and to carry into execution the laws of England which they were sent out to administer, Sir Elijah Impey and his assessors were unanimously resolute. They, however, did nothing of the least moment without reporting their proceedings to the Secretary of State; and everything they did, was either tacitly or expressly approved by his Majesty's Government.

It was still in decisions on proceedings connected with the collection of the revenue, that differences of opinion arose between the Supreme Court and the Supreme Council of Calcutta; or rather between the judges and Hastings, Francis, and Wheler; for Mr. Barwell was always either neutral in these quarrels, or decidedly in favour of the judges; nor was it until Barwell's departure for England that matters were driven to extremity. In a country like India, neither sheriff's officers, nor sheriff himself, could often execute a writ without being attended by some armed force. By order of Council, this force was, more than once, refused to the sheriff; and, on other occasions, sepoys were sent, not to strengthen the sheriff's officers, but to rescue prisoners out of their hands. If a native had been arrested, the cry was set up that the jurisdiction of the Court did not reach him; if an Englishman had been seized, no matter how contumacious, his cause was espoused in Council, and by all the interested servants of the Company. In one of his letters to Lord Weymouth, Sir Elijah says,—

"So little conversant are the English here with justice, that every cause decided against a British subject creates a personal enmity to the judge."

Mr. Macaulay speaks as if these quarrels of the Council with the Court, arose solely out of oppressions tyrannically exercised by the judges against natives of rank and consequence. Far different was the case.

The "Board of Commerce," composed entirely of servants of the Company, exercised very important judicial

functions, and claimed an extensive jurisdiction.   Their
proceedings frequently attracted the notice of the Chief
Justice and other judges of the Supreme Court.   In
that very full and explanatory letter to the Secretary of
State, from which I have already made many quotations,
he says,—

"The corruption of the members of the Board of Commerce
is matter of public conversation; and it is without doubt, that
the most gross frauds, in relation to the sales and contracts
which the Company entrusted to them, were formed into a
regular system, very early after their institution, and have
been uniformly practised ever since.   We are convinced that
a bill of discovery, with proper interrogatories pointed to this
charge, and brought against the members of that board, and
their black agents, would furnish matter to prove that they
had great reason to wish for the non-existence of our Court."

This my father proceeds to exemplify, at a length
which it is important not to abridge.

"The minds of two gentlemen had been much inflamed
against the Court, on account of the unsuccessful issue of two
causes in which they had been defendants.   An action had
been brought against Mr. Cottrell, who is a member of the
Board of Commerce, and keeper of a warehouse belonging to
the Company, for an assault and battery upon Jugamohun
Shaw, an opulent Hindu merchant, who had purchased copper
at the Company's sales.   He, thinking the copper he had
bought was short in weight, applied to Mr. Cottrell to have
it reweighed.   This so much incensed that gentleman, that,
without further provocation, besides treating the merchant
with other indignities, he struck him with his cane, and
turned him out of the warehouse.   For this injury, the Court
assessed damages, in November last, at 1000 sicca rupees,
which we estimate to be equal to £100.   From Mr. Cottrell,
we conceive, the Board of Commerce, and from them, the
other Company's servants' dependants, caught the flame.

"An ejectment had been brought against Lieutenant-Colonel
Henry Watson, for part of the land on which he proposes to
make docks.   It appeared on evidence, that this land had
been forcibly taken by the then government from the lessors
of the plaintiff, without pretending any right to it; that they
had received no recompense for it either from the Colonel or
the Company.   The cause was tried on the 6th of February
last.   The Court, after having in vain endeavoured to prevail
on the defendant to accept a compromise, which was offered
by the injured party, and which appeared to be very reason-

able, found itself under the necessity to give judgment for the plaintiff, which the judges expressed great reluctance in doing, on account of the expenses the Colonel had been at in his works, and the supposed utility of them. From that moment the Colonel became an enemy of the Court.

"From the warmth of this gentleman, and his great assiduity and perseverance, we are able to account for the zeal with which the military have prosecuted this business."

Many other causes might be cited in which the decisions of the Court were given in favour of otherwise helpless natives against the powerful servants of the Company. Others again might be quoted in which no native was concerned, but in which plaintiff and defendant were alike Europeans, and servants of the Company.

Of this latter class, the most conspicuous cause of all, was one in which Philip Francis, Esq., Member of the Supreme Council, was *defendant*. And from the conduct of Sir Elijah Impey on that occasion, may be, in great measure, deduced the persevering and implacable hatred of the author of Junius. As the friend of Mr. Hastings, I believe he always disliked my father; that he wrote and spoke against him to public men both in England and at Calcutta is well known; but until the Court sentenced him to pay rather heavy damages in an action for criminal conversation, which I shall presently quote, he continued to frequent the house, and to profess *in public* a great respect for the character of the Chief Justice. When Samuel Tolfrey, one of the witnesses examined in Sir Elijah's Defence in 1788, was asked " whether there had been any coolness observable between Sir Elijah Impey and Mr. Francis, after, or in consequence of, the trial and execution of Nuncomar?" that gentleman deposed upon oath that " there had been none; but that a coolness began to appear after the *crim. con.* trial, in which a verdict had been given against Mr. Francis."

The author of Junius, to many other unamiable qualities, added that of being vain of his reputation as an *homme aux bonnes fortunes*. This formed a conspicuous part of that levity for which Hastings scorned the man. The ex-clerk of the War Office, was eager to figure as the gallant gay Lothario of Calcutta, if not

in circles nearer home. In some quarters these pretensions only made him ridiculous ; but in others,
they gave disgust and pain. I believe also, that,
in more than one instance, the malevolence of Francis,
if not first awakened, was increased by the checks
his vanity received from women of virtue and piety. So
little was my father given to scandal of any kind, so
averse was he to dwell upon the failings even of the
enemy who had most defamed him, that I do not remember to have once heard him relate the circumstances of the trial, nor do I find a single allusion, in
his papers, to the cause of Le Grand *versus* Francis, to
which I allude, and which produced so great a sensation in Calcutta at the time.

I extract the following account of the trial, from a
volume of my friend, the late eminent civilian John
Nicholls, Esq., who had ample and authentic sources of
information on the subject. Mr. Nicholls introduces this
account in his comments upon the impeachment of
Mr. Hastings, and the parliamentary proceedings
against my father, which he mainly imputes to the
ill will of Francis :—

" Mr. Francis was a man of considerable abilities. He was
a very superior classical scholar ; and he was capable of
laborious application. Strong resentment was a leading feature in his character. I have heard him avow this sentiment
more openly and more explicitly than I ever heard any other
man avow it in the whole course of my life. I have heard
him publicly say in the House of Commons, ' Sir Elijah
Impey is not fit to sit in judgment on any matter where I am
interested, nor am I fit to sit in judgment on him.' A relation of the ground of this ill-will may be amusing.
Mrs. Le Grand, the wife of a gentleman in the civil service in
Bengal, was admired for her beauty, for the sweetness of her
temper, and for her fascinating accomplishments. She attracted the attention of Mr. Francis. This gentleman, by
means of a rope-ladder, got into her apartment in the night.
After he had remained there about three quarters of an hour,
there was an alarm ; and Mr. Francis came down from the
lady's apartment by the rope-ladder, at the foot of which he
was seized by Mr. Le Grand's servants. An action was
brought by Mr. Le Grand against Mr. Francis, in the Supreme Court of Justice in Calcutta. The judges in that
Court assess the damages in civil actions, without the inter-

vention of a jury. The gentlemen who at that time filled this situation, were Sir Elijah Impey, Chief Justice, Sir Robert Chambers, and Mr. Justice Hyde. I was intimate with the first and the third from early life, having lived with them on the western circuit. On the trial of this cause, Sir Robert Chambers thought, that as no criminality had been proved, no damages should be given. But he afterwards proposed to give thirty thousand rupees, which are worth about three thousand pounds sterling. Mr. Justice Hyde was for giving a hundred thousand rupees. I believe, that Mr. Justice Hyde was as upright a judge as ever sat on any bench; but he had an implacable hatred to those who indulged in the crime imputed to Mr. Francis. Sir Elijah Impey was of opinion, that although no criminal intercourse had been proved, yet that the wrong done by Mr. Francis to Mr. Le Grand, in entering his wife's apartment in the night, and thereby destroying her reputation, ought to be compensated with liberal damages. He thought that the sum of thirty thousand rupees, proposed by Sir Robert Chambers, too small ; and that proposed by Mr. Hyde, of a hundred thousand, too large. He therefore suggested a middle course, of fifty thousand rupees. This proposal was acquiesced in by his two colleagues. When Sir Elijah Impey was delivering the judgment of the Court, my late friend, Mr. Justice Hyde, could not conceal his eager zeal on the subject; and when Sir Elijah named the sum of fifty thousand rupees, Mr. Justice Hyde, to the great amusement of the bystanders, called out, ' Siccas, brother Impey ! ' which are worth eleven per cent. more than the current rupees. Perhaps this story may not be thought worthy of relation; but it gave occasion to that animosity, which Mr. Francis publicly avowed against Sir Elijah Impey; and the criminal charge, afterwards brought against him in the House of Commons, was the offspring of that animosity. 1 will follow up this anecdote by mentioning the consequences of the action brought by Mr. Le Grand. The lady was divorced : she was obliged to throw herself under the protection of Mr. Francis for subsistence. After a short time she left him, and went to England. In London, she fell into the company of M. Talleyrand Perigord. Captivated by her charms, he prevailed on her to accompany him to Paris, where he married her; and thus the insult which this lady received from Mr. Francis, and the loss of reputation, which was, perhaps unjustly, the consequence of that insult, eventually elevated her to the rank of Princess of Benevento.

" As I took part in the defence of Mr. Hastings on the two charges which I have mentioned, and was known to interest

myself much in the welfare of Sir Elijah Impey, I speak with
some reluctance of Mr. Francis; but the impeachment of
Mr. Hastings, and the accusation of Sir Elijah Impey, both
originated with him." *

* " Recollections and Reflections, Personal and Political, as connected
with Public Affairs, during the Reign of George III.   By John Nicholls,
Esq., Member of the House of Commons in the fifteenth, sixteenth, and
eighteenth Parliaments of Great Britain."   2 Vols. 8vo.   London, 1822.

CHAPTER VII.

————

THE vacant seat in Council was given, not to the Chief
Justice, Sir Elijah Impey, nor to Mr. Justice Chambers—
who had also endeavoured to obtain it—but to General
Sir Eyre Coote, Commander-in-Chief of the forces in
India. This veteran was quite competent to make a
proper distinction between the ability and genius of the
Governor General, and the vain pretensions and audacity of that jarring member of his Council, whom, nevertheless, he was now attempting to conciliate, at no small
hazard of the public service, and at the certain sacrifice
of private friendship and personal interest. Coote saw
that the schemes of Warren Hastings, which he was carrying out as well as old age and infirmity would allow,
were saving and enlarging our Indian empire, which
the counter-projects of Francis must have involved in
shame and confusion for a time, if not in ultimate ruin.
Without pledging himself in all cases, but reserving to
himself the same freedom of judgment which Sir Elijah
Impey had always exercised in the same civil feuds, Sir
Eyre Coote generally, and upon conviction, voted at
the Council board with Warren Hastings. But his
duties as Commander-in-Chief kept him almost continually in the field, and at the distance of many hundred

miles from Calcutta. In his absence, Francis, by his influence over Mr. Wheler, though he could not entirely annul, could often invalidate that of Hastings and his firm confederate Mr. Barwell; and Barwell, now weary of the struggle, was anxious to vacate his seat and return to England. Francis, too, had been talking of returning home, but if Hastings had believed in the existence of any such intention, it is obvious that he would never have entered into that ill-advised compact—that *" malè sarta gratia"*—with Francis, which interrupted, for a brief space, his long established, and eventually inseparable union with the Chief Justice.

Upon discovering that he could not overrule the new Commander-in-Chief and Member of Council, as he had done General Clavering and Colonel Monson, and that all his artifices to command a majority produced no effect, the baffled agitator lost all his confidence and singular prestige.

" Francis," writes Hastings to Sulivan, "is miserable, and is weak enough to declare it in a manner much resembling the impatience of a passionate woman, whose hands are held to prevent her from doing mischief. He vows he will go home in November, but I do not believe that his resolution is so fixed as he pretends."

The vow was made when Sir Eyre Coote was at Calcutta, and sitting in Council. When the Commander-in-Chief was far away, contending with Hyder Ali and the French, there was a noticeable revival of the spirit of Francis, and with it the opportunity of doing mischief, by embarrassing the Governor General. Hastings, therefore, thought it necessary to conciliate him, and few means were so likely to tend to that effect as hostile proceedings against the Supreme Court, and a breach in the forty years' unanimity of two most honourably connected friends. Among all the sacrifices of feeling and principle which Warren Hastings, in the midst of many arduous struggles for the preservation of a mighty empire, conceived himself obliged to make, I count this not the least : but though I approach the subject with great reluctance, and with a determination not to expatiate upon it—for it is one from which my father, in after times, most scrupulously abstained—yet that the sacrifice was made I am compelled by verity to acknowledge and to lament.

Petitions reflecting on the judges of the Supreme Court were set on foot; one to be presented to the Court itself, another to be sent to England, and laid before Parliament. The signatures of the Governor General's aid-de-camps and most confidential servants were set to these petitions, as if to prove that Hastings had entirely set himself against the Chief Justice and his brethren. My father remonstrated, and endeavoured to show that an open collision between the Supreme Council and the Supreme Court must be attended with the most lamentable consequences. Hastings had recourse to general professions and protestations; but the actual hostilities were carried on with greater heat than ever; and, in various other cases, the authority of the Court was notoriously defied, its judges loaded with abuse, and its servants maltreated in the provinces. Upon this Sir Elijah did that which he had never failed to do: he wrote a calm account of the transactions to his Majesty's government, and his legal friends in England. In a letter to Thurlow—now Lord Chancellor—dated January 11, 1780, he said,—

"The process of the court has been opposed by force. . . A capias was issued by Mr. Justice Hyde in August last, against Rajah Soondenarain, zemindar of Cossijurah, within the district of Midnapore, in the province of Bengal, on an affidavit that the notice on which the cause of action arose had been executed in Calcutta, and that the defendant was employed by the Company in the collection of the revenues due and payable to the Company. The Sheriff returned *non est inventus* to the writ. The cause was duly proceeded in under the Charter. Affidavits were filed for the purpose of obtaining the sequestration. I had been so ill in October and November, that I was obliged to be absent from the Court. The Sheriff having received information from his officer, who had got possession of some land and other effects under the sequestration, that the markets or bazaars were prevented from supplying him with necessaries, that the country had been alarmed, that a number of armed people were assembled, that he considered himself (being afraid to go out) as a prisoner on the premises, and every moment expected to be dispossessed, applied to Mr. Justice Hyde for advice what he should do. Justice Hyde referred him to me. I told the Sheriff that, as no actual violence had been committed against the officer, and as the complaint consisted more in apprehensions of what would be done than what had actually been done, I thought it would be premature for the Court to interpose—even if an affidavit of the facts had been laid before it, which, from the situation of the officer, it was impossible to procure. I advised him to send such a *civil* force to protect his officer as he thought would be sufficient; and, with them, a letter to the chief of Midnapoor, inclosing a copy of the last clause of the Charter, and in consequence of it requiring his assistance, and desiring him to send some person with the Sheriff's officers to be witnesses that they did *no more than their duty.* Such a letter was sent, but no answer returned to it. The reinforcement went to the Sheriff's officer, but they found the officer removed from the sequestration by a company of sepoys under the command of a Lieutenant Bomford, and under the direction of a civil servant [of the Company] named Swainston, who had made the officer a prisoner, seized all his papers and the inventory he had made of the effects sequestrated, and afterwards seized, imprisoned, and disarmed, all that had come to his assistance, forced them on board boats, and then set them at liberty in the town of Calcutta. The secretary of the Revenue Council wrote to the Sheriff that some arms had been seized, and offered to restore them. This happened in November last.

" Notwithstanding the whole of this was done by order of the Governor General and Council, it was but last week that the Governor General mentioned the matter to me. He came to my house and told me he had been long uneasy lest a circumstance which had happened relative to the zemindar of Cossijurah should disturb our private friendship. He then complained that an armed force had marched through the country to execute the process of the Court, which was a thing not to be endured; and that if zemindars were to be subjected to process of the Court, *the revenue must receive great detriment.* I assured him that actions proceeding from sentiments of duty, however contrary to those I might entertain, should never operate upon me in prejudice of my private friendship. I represented to him the subjection in which the Court would be to the Council if the Council assumed to themselves to determine on the jurisdiction of the Court, and the dangerous consequences of defendants not subjecting the question of jurisdiction to the judgment of the Court—resisting the compulsory process by force, and being supported in it by that power of government which ought to enforce obedience to its orders; that, if the Sheriff was resisted by force, he had no other means but force to effectuate the commands which he received; and that it seemed to be extraordinary to complain of that force which resistance had made necessary. He complained that application had not been made to the Council for assistance. I told him that it had been made to the chief of the district; and that, if he promised me assistance should be given on requisition, I would undertake that no other force should be made use of but what should be borrowed from his Government. He declined making me such promise, but insisted on the defendant not being an object of the jurisdiction, and that the affidavit was not sufficient to ground the process on. I said I could not submit the execution of the process to the determination of the Council on the point of jurisdiction, or propriety of the affidavit. I again required to know whether the Council would assist in the execution of our warrants, writs, &c., to which he would give me no answer. I told him I was alarmed at the confusion which an open resistance to the Court from the Council would create in this country, and the effects which it might have at home; I told him that I had been informed that the resident at Midnapore, Mr. Swainston, had been with the sepoys, and that they acted under his orders; that I expected the business would be moved in the term which was to commence in a few days; that the authority of the Court must be vindicated; and if the facts were made out, the necessary consequence would be the commitment of Mr. Swainston; that it would be very disagreeable to me to be driven to such extremities, but that I was resolved at all events to do my duty, if it became necessary; that I was still in hopes some temper might be found; that if the defendant would still plead, I would do all that lay in my power to prevent any prosecution being carried on, and that I did not doubt I should be able to effect it; that if the defendant was not, as he said, an object of the jurisdiction, no prejudice could arise to him from pleading; for that he would then have judgment in his favour, and would be no more molested. He seemed much moved with what I said; but told me he could not give me any answer then, though it was what he much wished; that he saw all the consequences, but could do nothing without consulting Mr. Barwell; that he would talk to him and give me an answer in a few days; that he much feared the consequences of the Government retracting what they had done would be worse than their persisting. Some days afterwards, when on a visit to him, I again mentioned the subject. He said he was not prepared with his answer. The term began on Friday, the 7th instant. I was informed that the motions for the contempt would be made on Monday. I therefore, on Sunday noon, wrote to the Governor a letter, of which D is a copy, and received his answer E. I waited at home for him on the Monday till I was obliged to go to Court (and I am so punctual to my time that it is well known at what hour I go there) without seeing him, and I have not heard from him since, which, I suppose, is the mode in which he means to let me know there is to be no accommodation. The illness of the Sheriff has prevented the motions being made, but I am in daily expectation of them.

"What I allude to in my letter, with regard to passages in former conversations, which might make a favourable impression on him, had no reference to the late conversations here related, but to former declarations from him to me, that during his government no act hostile to the Court should be done, and that rather than commit himself to a contest with the Court, he would leave his government."

Sir Elijah goes on to tell the Lord Chancellor that a paper in the Persian language, which extravagantly exalted the dignity and power of the Company, and derogated alike from those of his Majesty and his Judges, had been circulated without any previous knowledge of the Court; and that the said Persian paper implied that the writs of the Court were to be resisted by force. My father further adds,—

"Surely, for the peace of the country, and to prevent bloodshed, the Court ought to have received some notice of the intended opposition, that we might have deliberated whether under the force put on us, and on account of the disgrace the Court must incur, and the disturbances likely to ensue, we would not surcease the execution of duties in cases where the Governor General and Council avowed they would arm the defendants to resist our authority with open force.

"If they were of opinion that the Court was acting against law, and that this was the proper mode of preventing it, surely they should have apprized us of it. But as I am of opinion that there can be no possible means of our knowing whether we have jurisdiction over defendants but by their submitting the question to be tried ; and as I think the Court, not the Council, and still less the parties accused, competent to decide that question: having, as is done in all cases, obtained an affidavit from the plaintiff that the defendant is an object of the jurisdiction, and stating the facts by which he becomes so, I shall not hesitate to grant process. I will, to the utmost of my power, by legal means vindicate the authority given by his Majesty to the Court, as long as he shall think proper that the powers of it shall exist ; and, as far as in me lies, will not suffer it to be diminished by any authority less than that from which it was derived. If I am obliged to submit to force, it shall not be until every effort has been exerted to prevent it.

"If we submit, from that moment our jurisdiction is limited to Calcutta, and our authority but feeble there. A court of justice, in the ordinary exercise of its civil functions, considered as hostile by the government of the country in which it resides, deriving its authority from powers scarcely recognized by that government, and opposed, instead of supported, by its secret influence and open force, is in a situation, to which perhaps no other was ever exposed, except the Supreme Court at Fort William in Bengal.

"Depend upon it, my dear Lord, the opposition to the Court in this point, as well as in many others, does not arise from any zeal for the revenues, or any affection for the natives.

"The protection of zemindars—who are almost universally collectors of revenue—is a most fruitful source both of power and of wealth. They are most admirable intermediate agents to execute all acts of despotism ; and the protection from debts, or compulsion to pay them, is seldom procured without a pecuniary compensation. Of large sums of money paid on both accounts, I believe there can be not the least doubt, though the proofs might be very difficult.

"In the present case, it is currently reported, that the zemindar of Cossijurah has paid 75,000 rupees for the protection which he has received. The money is said to be paid to Mr. Pearse, uncle of Mr. Barnet, chief of Midnapoor ; I will not vouch for the truth; but believe the report is not without some grounds. A gentleman had so little idea of the impropriety of such a transaction, that he acquainted me that a native of this country had a demand against a zemindar for a very large sum of money lent; and that he had not interest enough with the Council to procure it, and was ready to give him five anas in the rupee, if he could prevail with the Council to suffer him to enforce payment. And the gentleman had folly and assurance enough to desire me, on account of the profit he was to receive, to use my influence with the Governor for the recovery of the debt.

"To the zemindar himself, and to the revenues, if the Governor General and Council wish justice to be done, it must be indifferent where their debts are recoverable. All who know how business is conducted in these provinces, must know that the parties never attend to it themselves; they attend by vakeels or agents; if not, they must attend on account of revenues in Calcutta; and, from the intricacies, delays, and exactions which they perpetually experience, must be in continual attendance; but *personal attendance* is dispensed with. It is notorious that they are imprisoned and flogged, and otherwise punished by their representatives the vakeels.

"There is but one thing which embarrasses me in enforcing our process: for I should have, no doubt, to punish any native for contempt in resisting the authority of the Court, as I think that power incidental; for, without it, we could not exercise our functions.   But should a native, or any other person, not subject to our jurisdiction, stay a sheriff's officer, or any one assisting him, in executing the orders of the Court, I do not see that the Court can have any possible authority to punish *him* for it; and it would be in vain to expect justice, in such an instance, from courts under the influence and absolute direction of the Company's servants.

"If my word is to be taken—and I speak from positive knowledge and experience,—I do aver that, except in the Supreme Court, no justice, civil or criminal, is fairly and uncorruptly administered, throughout the provinces.   The Act of Parliament, which made some impression when it was a new thing, is almost become obsolete; and, with such lights as you are likely to receive from those who are, or have been, connected with the Company, I think I may prophecy the English legislature will never be able to apply remedies to the numerous evils which are bringing this country to hasty ruin.

"It is impossible, without having been on the spot, to know the nature and different sources of corruption.   Those who have been deep in it, are too much interested to reveal them; and those who have not, make it a point of honour of doing nothing which may be what they call an injury to the service. . . . . . .

"I shall undoubtedly keep my word with Mr. Hastings, and even go beyond it with regard to our private friendship; for though I cannot, with all prejudices in favour of him, be induced to think that he is now acting on sentiments of duty; yet I revere him for many noble qualities, and believe him, when he tells me *he is not left to himself in this business.* At the same time, after the frankness and openness with which I have treated every subject relative to the powers of the Court, and the claims of the Governor General and Council; the ready attention I have given to his remonstrances to accommodate our proceedings to the practices of the provincial council, the general care and support I have uniformly afforded to his government, and, after the positive promises I have repeatedly received from him of private confidence, and that no acts should proceed from him hostile to the Court,— I must confess, I think I am not without reason to complain that a paper * of so much consequence to the power of the Court, should, by his authority, be circulated through the country, and,—without any previous communication with me, —that he had issued orders to resist the Court by military force, and that he now refuses to discuss with me such points as portend a difference between the Court and the Council.

"I write now, or rather dictate, without time to revise. .

"It is most probable, as what has been done has been long and secretly preconcerted, that an account of this transaction, with such glosses as the Governor and Council are able to give it, may have been transmitted to England by an earlier ship. I shall not fail, if I have opportunities, to acquaint you with further particulars as they arise: and when the business is terminated, shall trouble you with the whole, and perhaps an enclosure to his Majesty's Secretary of State, to be delivered, or not, as your Lordship may deem proper . . . . . .

"With the warmest attachment,

"I am, my dear Lord, &c. &c.

"*Fort William, January* 11, 1780.

"P.S. I have not time to write to my friend Dunning. If your Lordship sees no impropriety in it, may I beg you to communicate this to him ?"†

This letter to the Lord Chancellor was composed in a great hurry, and in a very agitated state of mind ; for, although upheld by a sense of duty, my father's affectionate nature could not but be touched to the quick, by this seemingly irreconcileable quarrel with so old and intimate a friend. I believe that, even when most excited, his sentiment towards the Governor General was far more nearly akin to sorrow than to anger ; in other respects, Coleridge's well-known lines are but too applicable to the case :—

> "Alas ! they had been friends in youth;
> But whispering tongues can poison truth;
> And constancy lives in realms above;
> And life is thorny; and youth is vain;
> And to be wroth with one we love,
> Doth work like madness in the brain."

Yet this letter to the Chancellor, however calculated to excite emotion similar to that which it expresses, nevertheless conveys a much clearer and juster notion of the

* The Persian Manifesto.
† MS. in my possession.

grounds of quarrel between the Council of government and the Supreme Court, than can be collected either from the insipidity of Mr. Mill, or the ornamented falsifications of Mr. Macaulay. It will also serve to prove the real motives which afterwards prompted Mr. Hastings to offer, and Sir Elijah Impey to accept, the presidency of the Sudder Dewanee Adaulut,—a complicated subject, of which the right honourable essayist seems not to possess the slightest knowledge ; albeit he pronounces upon it in so summary a manner, as to induce some careless readers to believe that he really knows something about the matter. To those, however, whose opinion is of greater value, it must appear, that subjects of this delicate nature—involving the cause of historical truth no less than personal honour—merit an investigation of deeper research and better temper than such writers as Messrs. Mill and Macaulay are either disposed or qualified to bestow upon them. I shall therefore go on to develope the true nature of this business, with a patience and fidelity more adequate to its importance, though at the hazard of some fatigue.

The dangerous and unbecoming conflict between the judges and the Council went on apace. It continued until there no longer remained a rational or dispassionate man in India, but became alarmed at its progress. Supported by a conscientious principle, my father would have died in that breach, rather than have forsaken his duty as a judge and president of the Court. Not all the zemindars, sepoys, chiefs of factories, and revenue officers, in Bengal ; nor all the native and British troops now spread far and wide over the provinces subject to its jurisdiction, could have wrung from him the sacrifice of so indisputable a right. Of this, Hastings was made sensible at last; and for this— when his temporary excitement had subsided—the Governor General loved, honoured, and esteemed the Chief Justice, even more than he had respected him before : for, when once convinced, he was far too generous and just not to acknowledge and atone for every wrong. Several times, indeed, it appears that Hastings would fain have put an end to this contention ; his own correspondence shows how greatly he was grieved at its continuance ; and—though somewhat more tardily—how much he doubted whether he had been always in the right; but Francis occupied his ear, and was ever ready with some argument of expediency, or some mis-statement of facts, to exasperate or misguide his better judgment, against the counsels of a truer friend.

Besides his great anxiety to neutralize the opposition of Francis in the Council, while the war was yet pending, with all the collective forces of Hyder Ali and his allies, Hastings had, at this most critical juncture, the strongest motives for gratifying all the superior servants of the Company, of whom not a few were but too much disposed to thwart his plans, and to misrepresent his policy.

Now, these selfish agents of the Company, being the very "vultures" attacked by the Supreme Court, could not have been more effectually propitiated than by taking part with them against that Court.

In discussing a case of such delicacy, where it may well be supposed my feelings as a son and as a friend are almost equally affected, I may surely be allowed a moment's pause, ere I presume so much as to hold the scales, far less to decide the balance. For Warren Hastings I would even here make that allowance which I claim for him on less questionable occasions. His predominant object was that of a disinterested politician —to save India, at whatever private cost. My father's was equally unselfish, nor less patriotic: but he pretended to no politics. Bred a lawyer, and appointed a judge, he was resolved to uphold the law. Yet would he fain, if possible, have reconciled his charter of justice to the exigency of the times. If these were made irreconcileable by the legislature itself, could he adjust them? If he remonstrated with the Government at home, and with the authorities abroad, without prevailing with either, was he to be blamed for the result? Was he not rather to be extolled, if, nevertheless, he persevered in his public duty at the expense of an unappreciable private loss? I am no man's idolator, and though on this side idolatry I reverence no two men more, I can form as impartial an estimate on the respective characters of the Governor General and the Chief Justice, as if the one had not been my father, and the other my friend " *Fortunati ambo !*" The first will descend to posterity as a heroic statesman, the latter as a righteous and uncompromising judge.

That they were not exempt from the frailties of humanity, nor gifted with supernatural intuition, I am not so weak as to deny. They may possibly both at times have been unduly impressed with the relative importance of their own peculiar objects; but that those objects, either when coincident or disagreeing with each other, were therefore of necessity base, dishonest, criminal, or corrupt, is a deduction as illogical as unfair; and it will require a much more powerful reasoner than Mr. Macaulay, to establish a conclusion so absurd, as that the same man could have been at once partial and impartial, servile and independent, a firm opponent and yet a mercenary tool.

Be it admitted, then, that the Governor General's primary object was to save British India ; and that, in the unprecedented difficulties in which he was placed, among other expedients, he grasped at one of the most likely means to promote that end : and none was more likely, however irregularly brought about, than unanimity among the Company's servants.

The contrary humour in certain of these servants had often deranged some of his best schemes; as any reader will perceive, if he attentively studies the history of the war, from its commencement in the year 1777, to its conclusion in 1782. But greatly, also, did the tyranny, corruption, extortion, and rapacity, of some of these same Company's servants, thwart the high-minded Governor General, and commit the great cause for which he was nobly contending. These were the abuses which the Supreme Court attempted to correct; but Hastings, though he owned the motive, was, for a time, persuaded to resist the interference ; the rather, perhaps, as during that long and arduous war, he found himself grow poorer and poorer, while these money-making Council-men and collectors were growing richer and more influential every day.

In discharge of their duty, on the other hand, Sir Elijah Impey and the other judges continued to issue process. Undeterred by the threats, or by the actually perpetrated violence of the Council, chiefs of districts, and military men, they sent forth their writs whenever and whithersoever the law of England prescribed.

The Governor General published a proclamation authorising disobedience to the process of the Court; and supported it by an armed force. The Chief Justice, insisting upon his chartered right, issued warrants for apprehending the soldiers who acted under the direction of the Council, and arrested them in the very heart of their camp; attempts were even made to put this process in execution in the highest quarters, civil as well as military.*

At the beginning of the month of March, the Governor General and the Members of Council were severally served by theCourt with summonses, on a plea of trespass. Mr. Barwell appeared to action, but the rest refused. The judges endeavoured to show that there could be no degradation in making appearance, and that the highest in dignity, no less than the lowest, were bound to respect his Majesty's Court of Justice. This reasoning had no effect; and Hastings, as well as Francis his new ally, continued to disobey, and both were clearly in contempt of Court.

In consequence of these events, my father suffered no less in personal feeling, than in the interests of his family : so long as he had been on friendly terms with the Governor General, he had looked forward with no unreasonable expectation of some share of that patronage, which has always been bestowed upon men of eminent station. He had consequently been recommended, about this time, to procure a writership for one of his sons,† a youth of great promise, who, under the guardianship of his uncle, with the especial superintendence of Dunning, had already distinguished himself at Westminster, and at Tiverton School. But under the present circumstances, Sir Elijah displayed his usual spirit of independence, by declining to ask the slightest

* See First Report from the Select Committee of the House of Commons, appointed to take into consideration the State of the Administration of Justice in the Provinces of Bengal, Bahar, and Orissa. Printed in the year 1782.

† My brother, the late Archibald Impey, Esq., well known at the English bar, and afterwards as Counsel to the East India Company, and latterly as Commissioner of the Court of Bankruptcy.

favour of any one connected with the East India Company.

On the 12th of March, 1780, he wrote thus to his brother :—

"The unfortunate turn that things have taken here makes it totally impossible for me to be of any assistance to him, except he was to come out in the service of the Company; for the Governor General and Council, without any provocation whatsoever, have committed public hostilities to the Court. I can do nothing for him myself, and am in no situation to ask anything of any member of this government. . . . . . The contention which I am now involved in, the particulars of which you may learn from Mr. Dunning, or Sir Richard Sutton, for I have not time to give you the detail, makes my remaining extremely disagreeable to me, but both my private fortune and public duty require it."

In this confidential letter, which of course was never meant for publication, Sir Elijah relates in the simplest terms, an anecdote which does honour to his humanity and munificence.

A young cadet, who was merely known to him through a letter of introduction from no very intimate friend in England, had fallen mortally wounded in a duel, near his residence. He caused the young man to be brought into his house, where he died ; and after his death, he discharged a debt which he owed to some native schroff, or banker.

In writing another explanatory letter to Dunning, on the 2nd of March, about seven weeks after the date of that long narrative addressed to Thurlow, from which I have given such copious extracts, Sir Elijah thought himself under the necessity of resorting to a precaution which was altogether unusual with him. It is thus explained in the opening paragraph of the letter itself :—

"You will receive a large packet, and a long letter, by the Swallow packet, which brings this ; they are in the hands of the chief mate, Mr. Tomkyns. I am in that situation as not to think it prudent to trust any papers of business in the packet made up *by the Company's servants.*"

Opening his heart to Dunning more freely than he could with Thurlow, he gave a detail of his many wrongs and sufferings since the commencement of this quarrel between the Court and Council, solemnly declaring to the man from whom he concealed nothing, that he had only endeavoured to do his duty, and that the violence all proceeded from the other side.

His words to Dunning are these :—

"The public outrages committed against the Court, have been without any provocation. The power which is exerted against me would not have existed in the hands in which it is, if I had not myself helped to keep it there, and it was used against me at the time when, to all appearance, I was living in the utmost confidence and familiarity with the possessor of it."

He goes on to complain, like the frank, straightforward man he was, of the temporising policy of his friend :—

"I was," he says, "a guest in his house, when he meditated these hostilities, without my receiving the least intimation of his discontent with the Court. I only learnt it by the military force of the Company being used to oppose the process of the Court in the ordinary course of justice.

"This has hurt me much more than any anxiety which I felt during all the time that I knew Clavering was endeavouring to ruin me in England. . . . . . *No situation can possibly be more irksome. I have scarcely a social comfort beyond my own family: the flattering expectation of credit and reputation, from the happiness I was bestowing on this country, and the benefits I thought would from thence have been derived to my own, totally blasted, and my private fortune and public duty compelling me to remain where I must waste my life in perpetual vexation and ineffectual struggle.*"

It is at the time when my father was almost sinking under the weight of these oppressions, that he is represented by Mr. Macaulay as an imperious tyrant, exulting in his success, and taking advantage of the powers given him by a defective Act of Parliament, to cripple the hands of government, and disturb the internal tranquillity of British India! But did it never strike this clumsy logician, that here, as in other instances, he is detecting his own preceding fallacies? If Sir Elijah Impey had sold his conscience, or bartered his independence to Mr. Hastings; if, in the case of Nuncomar, there had been any truth in that atrocious libel—every allusion to which, while it blots my page, will justify the bitterness of its invective,—if that charge were not utterly and scandalously false, how could my father ever after have ventured to oppose his alleged accomplice? How could he have resisted Hastings in his attempt to banish Clavering from his seat in Council? Or how could he afterwards have stood forward, boldly and fearlessly—as Mr. Macaulay is obliged to allow—in defence of the dignity of his Court? Would he have dared to drive such a man, possessed of such a secret, to the verge of fury and desperation?

Though born, and living at Calcutta, I was but an infant at the time; but I know from other sources, besides the touching letters which are now before me, the anguish of mind, most acutely felt, though manfully endured by my father at this painful crisis; nor am I ashamed or afraid to confess, that the confidential papers, thus, for the first time, forced by public slander into public notice, have caused in my own breast a feeling of unmitigated wrath and defiance.

While the disputes between the Court and Council were still raging, but before they had reached their climax, Mr. North Naylor, a gentleman employed by the Governor General and Council as attorney to the Company, was attached by the Supreme Court for contempt; and, on his refusal to answer interrogatories, committed to prison. The committal took place on the 1st of March, and his release on the 16th of the same month. He was in his usual state of health when committed; he was equally so when released; and in the same health he continued for some months after. But he then fell ill of one of those diseases of the climate, to which men of delicate constitutions, or careless in their way of living, are very obnoxious. He was, and had been ever since his arrival in India, the friend of Sir Elijah Impey, to whom he had been recommended as one of the *protégés* of Dunning, and was the dearer to him on that account.* Private friendships and par-

* Mr. North Naylor was son of the Rev. Thomas Naylor, of Ashburton, in the county of Devon. John Dunning—as many an anecdote reminds us—was a Devonshire man, with strong local attachments. He was a native of Ashburton, and when raised to the peerage in the spring of 1782, took the title of Baron Ashburton of Ashburton, in the county of Devon. Naylor was not the only Devonshire man he recommended to the patronage of his friend in India.

tialities of course could not influence the Court in the discharge of its duties ; but Naylor's imprisonment, in which my father took no active part, did not for a single moment interrupt the good feeling which existed between him and the Company's attorney.   My father watched over him in his sickness, and grieved for his decease.   In a letter written between the 2nd and 10th of August, my father says to Dunning :—

"All your young men are well except Naylor ; who, in truth, has hardly ever been quite well since he has been in this country, for any length of time together.   Lately he went to a place called Biercaul with a party for the benefit of the sea air.   He profited much by it, but on his return up the river to Calcutta, he caught what is here called an Ingelee fever, from the name of a swampy, unhealthy, noxious country, which he passed.   It was intermittent, with most violent paroxysms ;   one of the most dangerous disorders in this country, when caught at the season of the year in which it attacked him, the middle of June, at the commencement of the rains.   He recovered from that, and went up the river to confirm his health by change of air, continued well till about ten days ago, when he returned to Calcutta with a violent disorder in his bowels, which has turned out a confirmed dysentery.   From the debility and exhausted state to which his habitual illness and late severe fever reduced him, there can be, on this new attack, but small chance of his recovery; and he proceeds so rapidly to his dissolution, that I fear I shall not be able to despatch this without my apprehensions for him being fatally realized. *I have a great love and esteem for him.*   He is an excellent young man, and has given me, *since the scrape he got into* [the attachment and committal by the Court], *most convincing proofs of his attachment to me.* On account of his health, I have suspended giving any judgment on the attachment by the Court.   I see him myself every morning, and my cousin Fraser goes to him every evening.   No man can be taken more care of."

In a subsequent letter to the same common friend, dated the 19th of August, he thus announces his death :—

"What I so much dreaded has happened. My poor Naylor is no more.   He expired early this morning.   He has left one daughter by his deceased wife.   I inclose you his will, and an estimate of his estate drawn up by his most intimate friend, Mr. Joseph Cator, one of the guardians of his child

and executor of his will.* The dear child will be very amply
provided for; as, besides what Naylor has left her, Mr. Cator,
who had always undertaken to educate and provide for her,
had, with uncommon generosity, settled £5000 upon her before poor Naylor's death."

The young lady, Miss Harriet Naylor, whom I well
remember as a most amiable and interesting orphan,
though living till the day of her marriage in her
guardian's house, was always treated by my parents with
the same tenderness as if she had been a daughter of
their own. The playmate of their children, and one of
the most frequent of their guests, she looked up to them,
and regarded us, next to the family at Beckenham, as
her dearest friends. That lamented lady is no more ;
but the sons of Joseph Cator—than whom there needs
no more honourable witnesses—live to attest the truth,
or at least the tradition of those facts ; and yet—can it
be believed?—between malice and ignorance, efforts have
been made to represent Sir Elijah Impey as the perse-
cutor of North Naylor ! The atrocious attempt was not
begun until Francis returned to England, and Naylor
had been two years in his distant grave. It was then
that, instigated by Francis and his willing dupes, Sir
Gilbert Eliot, as in the case of his brother Alexander's
death, took advantage of Naylor's decease, to prefer
those charges against my father, which, had they been
living, both would have repelled with astonishment and
disgust, as equally monstrous and absurd.

Such is the real history of the Select Committee of
the Commons having inserted in their first report of
1782, that " *Naylor's death had been, in all probability,
hastened, if not caused, by his sufferings under confinement ;* " then, grossly misrepresenting the facts of the
case, they described his imprisonment as having been
rigorous, and *upwards of a month* in duration, and
affirmed that he had died " *soon after his release upon
bail.*"†

When foul insinuations and direct falsehoods like

* Naylor's will, a copy of which is among my father's papers, bears date,
the 10th of August, 1780, only nine days before his death. Appended to
the will, was a very confidential letter from Mr. Cator to Sir Elijah, which
is also in the same collection of MSS. in my possession.
† See Report of the said Committee, p. 48.

these could be admitted into parliamentary reports, and published to the nation, six years before the threatened impeachment of Sir Elijah Impey, we need not be much astonished at the accumulated falsehoods which found their way into those charges, when the fury of impeachment was at its height; when the Governor General and the Chief Justice were considered by the managers to be inseparably implicated, and both alike discredited, ruined, and helpless victims.

I have advisedly abstained from any strictures, beyond the few words in my preface, on the gross ignorance, and shameful neglect of documentary evidence, displayed by the Company's clerk and historian, Mr. Thornton; but here I think it is imperative on me to expose one glaring instance of that writer's ignorance and temerity.

Mr. Thornton, whose general style is as unornamental and dull as any business letter of the Court of Directors, becomes flighty and rhetorical wherever he finds Mr. Macaulay is so; and, in narrating the history of Sir Elijah's administration of justice in India, his thoughts and phraseology are little else than an imitation, as far as in him lies, of those exhibited in the *Edinburgh Review*, by his great paragon Mr. Macaulay. But, as if resolved to have one topic all to himself, or as if to give proof that he too could be figurative for the nonce; or, perhaps, to make a vain show of research and familiarity with a subject which even Mr. Macaulay has not ventured to revive; Mr. Thornton makes a solemn stand on this allegation: and boldly advancing beyond the mere insinuations of the Committee's first Report, he directly charges my father with extra-judicial tyranny and oppression in the committal of Mr. Naylor.* It is too painful to soil these pages with the revolting nonsense alluded to; but to refute the despicable remnant of this story, if it has not been sufficiently refuted above, I need merely say, that Sir Elijah Impey was not in Court—was not in Calcutta—was not within many miles of that presidency during the greatest part of these proceedings.

On the 1st of March North Naylor was committed to

* See "History of the British Empire in India." By Edward Thornton, Esq., vol. II., p. 145.

prison at Calcutta, on the 16th he was set at liberty.
From the 6th of July, 1778, to the 15th of March, in
the following year, my father was with his family at
Chittagong,* above 316 miles north-west from Calcutta.
He was in ill-health, and my mother brought to bed at
that place, which will account for so long an absence;
and during those seven months, Mr. Justice Hyde presided in the Supreme Court. It was Hyde, therefore, and
not the Chief Justice, who committed Naylor to prison.
If any harsh words were used, they are doubtless to
be regretted. That Hyde might have used them I
will not dispute; but my father was distinguished
through life for the suavity of his temper; and had he
been present, instead of far away, such words would
never have been uttered by him. He who never resorted to unbecoming language against the most worthless criminal ever brought to the bar, could never have
employed it against a man he loved and esteemed, and
whose offence amounted to nothing more than too implicit obedience to his employers.

I have now done with Mr. Thornton. But if
the Honourable East India Company must needs
keep a historian, as the vender of patent razor strops
kept a poet, surely it will behove them to look out for
a writer of more accuracy and judgment.

The decided conduct of the Supreme Court in attaching and imprisoning Mr. Naylor, did not work any
change in the resolute hostility of the Council. Looking up to Hastings as to a sovereign prince, and
believing that the Court must succumb to his authority,
the timid natives almost entirely ceased making any
further application for the Court's protection. Many
of them indeed—including not a few who had benefitted in person and in fortune by the courage of the
judges, and the protection of English law—were induced
to sign a petition against the Supreme Court.

But Hastings, whatever was the recklessness of his
new ally, was far from being at ease, or satisfied with
his own ascendancy. He had contemned, and for a
time effectually annulled a power delegated by the
Crown, and he doubted whether he could answer for it

* Chittagong, the same as Islamabad. See Major Rennell's "Description of the Roads in Bengal and Bahar, &c."

before his King and country. He therefore very prudently applied for, and obtained, an act of indemnity against so questionable a measure; and besides this—though impelled by the most exalted and best-intentioned motives—he saw that the event was throwing nearly the whole of British India into a lamentable state of uncertainty and confusion. Various schemes were either suggested to him, or originated in the resources of his own fertile mind, to avert the catastrophe. At one time the project was started, and strongly advocated for trying all civil—including revenue causes—like criminal causes of action, by jury.

But the jurymen were all to be British subjects and *servants of the Company*—military officers, writers, revenue collectors, and the like. This would have made the monstrosity complete, for one and the same party would then have been plaintiff, witness, judge, and jury, in the same cause! "Who," exclaims Sir Elijah in one of his letters, "who ever heard of trying a thief by a jury of highwaymen?" But the whole scheme, with its inevitable tendency to increase the power and tyranny of the Company's servants over the natives, was luminously exposed by the Chief Justice to the Lord Chancellor, to Dunning, Sutton, and others, as well in India as in England. Neither the Regulating Act, nor the Charter, gave the Council liberty to adopt any such excessive change.

The Company's advocate,* and such other lawyers as were at Calcutta, and dependent on the Governor General and Council, demurred, and shook their heads at this preposterous expedient. Even Francis was compelled to give it up as impracticable, and highly dangerous to *himself*. Still, the government felt that matters could not remain as they were, but that something must be done to restore a semblance of justice, and an appearance of harmony between the two conflicting authorities.

At last, after a variety of opinions, the Council came to these conclusions:—"That the provincial dewannee adauluts should be re-organized; that the natives who sat in them, should be all turned out, and their places filled by *junior* servants of the Company:" that is, by

* Sir John Day.

young and inexperienced writers, whose interests, both official and personal, would thus necessarily be thrown into the balance of justice against the natives. And these remodelled courts were to be independent of the Supreme Court at Calcutta; and if the natives were to be allowed any appeal, that appeal was to be made, not to his Majesty's judges, but to the Governor General and Council.

The star of Hastings must have been eclipsed by the intervention of Francis when it underwent this disastrous change. But Hastings repeatedly declared in private, "that he was impelled by others : that he was not a free agent." These very expressions occur in more than one of my father's letters written at the time.

Mr. Barwell continued to be strongly opposed to all these projects; declaring that it was, and ever had been, his opinion, that the Council or government had not, nor ought to have, anything to do with the ordinary administration of justice; and that no real exercise of legal power in India, resided anywhere except in the Supreme Court.

After the words I have cited, my father added the following in a narrative too long to transcribe :—

"Mr. Barwell said, if he was called on in England, he should give the same opinion. This is not the only conversation in which Mr. Barwell has said the same thing; he has constantly held this language from the first establishment of the Court. I have experienced so much candour, openness, and sincerity from that gentleman, that there is not a man existing on whose word I can more confidently rely; I know him to be possessed of that manly honour which renders him incapable of professing sentiments he does not really entertain; of disavowing any part he has taken, or even of submitting to an explanation, except for the purpose of not being misunderstood by those for whom he entertains a regard."

But the proposed measure was carried and adopted, not on the 11th of April, as stated by Mr. Mill, but on the 28th of March.* On the last-named day,—

* Here the error of a few days is not perhaps of much importance, historically or otherwise; but gross errors of date, which really are of importance, occur in Mr. Mill's "History of British India;" and as this writer made pretensions to great correctness, and has found admirers who mistake dullness for accuracy, his chronological slips ought to be pointed out. Mill is even guilty of an error in the date of Colonel Monson's death,—

"The Governor General and Council established another plan for the administration of justice throughout the provinces; by which they ordained that there should continue to be courts of civil judicature in each of the grand divisions therein mentioned; and that over each of these courts, *a Company's covenanted servant* should preside under the title of *Superintendent of the Dewannee Adaulut*, and his jurisdiction was to be independent of the provincial councils; that the provincial councils should try and determine all revenue causes; and that the Superintendent of the Dewannee Adaulut should try and determine all other civil causes. They also established various other regulations. By these regulations an appeal was given, in certain cases, from the Dewannee Adaulut to the Governor General and Council, in the Court of Sudder Dewannee Adaulut."*

By these regulations, which it took some time to carry into effect, the revenue causes were to be separated from the other causes, but the judgment and decision of both were to be left solely to the covenanted servants of the Company.

Now, the great mass of the civil causes to be tried in the country arose out of the revenue claims of the Company; and were, by their very nature, inseparable from revenue causes. Two results were inevitable : I. The natives found that both the provincial councils and the new dewannee adauluts held it their primary duty to increase the amount of money paid by their several districts into the Calcutta treasury : II. The members of the provincial councils, and the superintendents of the dewannee adauluts, found that they could rarely, if ever, agree where the jurisdiction of the one court ended, and where that of the other began. There was no separating the inseparable. Neither the members of the provincial councils, old or new, nor the junior servants of the Company appointed to preside over the adauluts, were men that had received a legal education—some of them had received but little education of any kind.

a very important event, attended by immediate consequences. Monson died on the 25th of September ; Mill says, " early in November, 1776, Colonel Monson died." I could, but I need not, multiply examples of this kind.

* Appendix No. 3, to First Report from the Select Committee appointed to take into consideration the state of the Administration of Justice, A.D. 1782.

This doubly confounded the confusion; this of itself made the quarrels between the two bodies more irregular, violent, and illogical, than they otherwise might have been; but even if the two separate offices had been filled by the very ablest lawyers in Great Britain, the disputes about respective authority and jurisdiction could never have been set at rest, for they were inherent in the act of Council of the 28th of March.

This new conflict, to which not a single allusion is made by Mr. Macaulay, or by any of the defamers from whom he takes his cue, soon embarrassed the Governor General and Council quite as much as their disputes with the Supreme Court. It became ultimately, and not long after, the main cause which induced Hastings to appoint the Chief Justice President of the Court of Appeal or Sudder Dewannee Adaulut. This, as I shall show in the next chapter, was strongly avowed by Hastings himself, and accordingly entered upon the minutes of Council.

On the 16th of August, after he had had time to watch the operation of this divided authority, Sir Elijah Impey wrote to the Lord Chancellor :—

" The corruption and mal-administration in the adauluts, or country courts of justice, in which the members of the provincial councils presided, was so notorious, that when the resolution was taken to oppose the legal functions of the Supreme Court, it was thought necessary at least to preserve some appearance of having justice administered in the provinces.

" The Government, therefore, abolished the old adauluts, and erected new ones; over each of which is placed one of the junior servants of the Company as judge, who is (which was never exacted before of any judge of an adaulut) to take an oath to administer justice impartially, and not to accept bribes. The gentlemen appointed are . . . ."

Here the Chief Justice enumerates the names of no less than six gentlemen, affixing the dates, and place of each appointment. These names, for obvious reasons, I shall not repeat. He then continues,—

" Each of these, except the two last, decides, not only on more property than the Supreme Court, but, I am inclined to think, than all the Courts in Westminster Hall put together. Though the provisional councils had complained of the adauluts, as parts of their offices which were burthensome, responsible, and unprofitable, and professed to wish to be discharged of them, on the separation of them from the councils, there was almost a mutiny among them.

" Mr. Morse, one of the advocates of the Supreme Court, had applied to the members of the Council and obtained a promise of being appointed a judge to one of these courts; but when it was known to the Company's servants, it raised so general a clamour, that the promise was not adhered to.

" It would naturally be imagined, as these judges are selected not from the *senior* servants of the Company, that they were persons who had distinguished themselves by their abilities or integrity. But none of them, except, perhaps, Mr. Campbell, are eminent for any particular qualifications for their offices, either by knowledge of jurisprudence or the languages of the country. One of them, Mr. *****, is of the meanest capacity, totally illiterate in his own, and ignorant of any Eastern language, and one of the most expensive, dissipated men in the country. I doubt whether he is of age.

" Another, Mr. **** ****, considered the salary of the office, viz., 1200 sicca rupees per month, so little worth his consideration, if restrained from other emoluments, and had so little idea of any other moral restraint from corruption than the oath, that he hesitated some time whether he would submit to the test.

" There has not been the least intimation, public or private, of these innovations in the country courts to me, and I believe there has been none to the other judges.

" The Sudder Adaulut, or Court of Appeal, which had been discontinued ever since the appointment of the Governor General and Council, was at the same time revived, but has not yet sat. Causes of consequence involving rights to zemindars, &c., are not, as formerly, determined there; but by the Board at large, simply on the report of an English gentleman called Keeper of the Khalsa [Exchequer] Records, without any evidence coming before the members of the Council."

In the same letter to the Lord Chancellor—of which nearly a counterpart was written to Dunning, in order to be shown to Sir Richard Sutton and other common friends—my father thus dwelt upon the condition to which the Supreme Court had been reduced.

" Although our process beyond Calcutta has been almost universally disobeyed, the sheriff's officers abused, and in some cases the plaintiffs imprisoned,* yet the orders of the Governor General and Council have spread such terror, that but one application has been made to the Court in consequence of these outrages. . . . . . . This will prove the truth of my assertion, that the natives have been given to understand that the powers of the Court had been, by the authority of Government, restrained to the town of Calcutta. Beyond it, in fact, they are annihilated, though the jurisdiction of the Court be ever so clear. The business of the town merely, will not furnish subsistence to the advocates, attorneys, and officers of the Court.

"A clerk of the Quarter Sessions having been removed from his office without cause, sued for the salary which had been fixed to his office, and enjoyed by his successor, and was successful. Since which, the Governor General and Council have absolutely refused to hold quarter sessions; and *from that time the town has been without constables or other peace-officer than the Sheriff.*†

Also in this same letter to the Chancellor, Sir Elijah alluded to the harsh and unjust manner in which he and his brother judges were treated in money matters ; to the serious shocks which his health had sustained, and to his earnest desire to be provided for anywhere in England, or even in Ireland. The extracts will show how little my father had gained, in a pecuniary sense, by five years' residence, and five years' trouble and vexation in India.

" It is now two years since the Company have allowed bills to be drawn on them; and when they do, I am not by any means certain that the judges will be indulged with any share of them by the Council here. I understand that the Directors make considerable profits in England by granting to old Indians at home remittances for money here. I feel the not procuring the Company's bills very severely, for I know of no means of remittance, except by sending specie, which I shall not be able to do, after payment of insurance and freight, at a smaller loss than 25 per cent.

" This you will think very heavy to me, when I assure you, though I live with the greatest attention to economy, which is sharpened by my wish to return to my family and friends, so many contingents, expenses from sickness and other causes,

---

* This is " *a reign of terror*" not mentioned by Mr. Macaulay or by Mr. Mill.

† From the original draft, in my father's hand, in my possession.

continually arise, that I have not been able to lay up more than £3000 in any year. When, indeed, and how, we shall have our salaries paid here I cannot tell: they are at present in arrears, and when we apply for payment to the treasurer, the answer is, there is no money in the treasury. . . . .

" My health, I thank God, is at present better than it has been for some time past; but, as I am subject once or twice a year to violent attacks of the cholera morbus, here called the *mort de chien*, and to other disorders in my bowels, and to a nervous affection which seized me about two years ago, and nearly deprived me of the use of my right arm,* leaving a numbness in my fingers and hands, which has rather increased this summer; I cannot but consider my health as pre-carious.

" As I should not, except under the most urgent necessity, desert my post, without express license from England, it would be a great relief to me, if I could be indulged—should my constitution absolutely require to be recruited by my native air—with leave to absent myself from it, till restored; or for such limited time as should be thought reasonable to try the experiment. . . . . But my finances are such, that I must run all risks rather than resign my office. Should what I request be not thought unreasonable, though it is a delicate subject to mention, I must beg leave to suggest to you the expediency of the appointment of an efficient judge as successor to Lemaistre, for the transacting the ordinary business of the Court. I do not again trouble you with solicitations for a seat in Council. If you think it advisable, I have before said enough of it; if you do not, too much. All that I will add on that head is, that notwithstanding what has passed, and though I do not think I have been treated as I deserved, yet Mr. Hastings and I continue on good terms, and I esteem him so much the properest man to hold the office of Governor General, that I should give him my most hearty support, as, indeed, I should think it my duty to do, to any other person, whom his Majesty should think worthy to be honoured with so high a trust.

"After all, I should think myself much happier to obtain an office in England or Ireland, which would furnish me with a competent livelihood, than to enjoy much greater emolu-ments in this country."

In going to India, my father had anticipated a diffi-cult and laborious career, but one which would be

* Of this last symptom my father had frequent returns during the re-mainder of his life.

benficial to that country and to England, and honourable to himself.   He grieved for the overthrow of these
expectations, and doubly felt the indignities offered to
himself as a faithful servant of the Crown, and a zealous
lover of his country.   In a narrative of events which he
drew up at this time, he says,—

"Many circumstances combine to render the contentions I
am now involved in particularly disagreeable; it proceeds
from a quarter, from whence I think it should not have come;
*the benefits which I was conscious of having diffused in this
country, and flattered myself with the hope of deriving to my
own, are at one stroke annihilated ; the King's power is insulted in my hands ; I personally incur in the public eye
degradation almost to contempt. . . . .*
"*The suffering the territorial acquisitions to remain in the
Company, and the clear right of the Crown to them to be considered as equivocal, creates in the Company, who must know
the weakness of its title, a perpetual jealousy of every act of
sovereignty exercised by the King, and a desire to thwart it.*
Too impotent to enforce obedience to its orders, when the will
or interest of their servants are opposed to them, it is still
strong enough, with their hearty concurrence—which it is
always sure to have in every measure which increases their
power, or promises them immunity—to resist his Majesty's
authority, and almost to keep back his Royal name from
public notice.
"It is a settled principle in this government, to enforce
nothing which cannot be done by its own authority.   To call
in the aid of a court of justice is considered as showing imbe-
cility, and a confession that its authority does not extend to
the case.   Hence—though Calcutta is, for convenience, order,
and health, the worst regulated, and most in want of police, of
any civilized town in the known world, but *one* bye-law has
been tendered to the Court by the Council, and that forced
from them under very particular circumstances.   Every other
regulation that has been made for the town has been by edict
of the Council, and not by any ordinance authorised by Act of
Parliament."*

In the same narrative, Sir Elijah states the frequency
and impunity with which the Act 13 George III., had
been evaded or set at defiance, the continuance of
forbidden monopolies, and the perseverance of the Com-

* From the original MS. in my possession.

pany's servants in private trading in spite of the Act.
[Among these private traders and speculators were, at
different times, several Members of the Supreme Council,
and in this number, Philip Francis was particularly
accused of trading in company with his brother-in-law
Macrabie.] My father dwells at most length upon
the opium monopoly.

" Opium, notwithstanding the Company's orders, still
continues a monopoly. It was granted to Mr. John Mackenzie, who having been an ensign on the Bombay establishment, and secretary to the late General Wedderburn, by the
means of the present Attorney General, was appointed by the
Company a factor here: and soon after his arrival, in consequence of the recommendations he brought out with him, was
put into a very lucrative office—that of customs-master.—
The profits from this monopoly are immense. They have
been extorted not only by compelling the cultivators of poppy
to sell it to the monopolist at the price fixed by him, and by
imprisonment and corporal punishment to prevent the disposal
of it to others, but by forcing, by the same means, those whose
lands are not employed in that culture, to convert it to the
raising of poppy only. The opium grows chiefly in Bahar.
No private force would be sufficient to these ends. By some
agreement with Mackenzie, the chief and provincial council at
Patna, who are in possession of full powers over the province,
became the monopolists and sole traders in opium. Mr. Kerr,
a surgeon, who had some dealings in that commodity, and was
obstructed by the Patna council, made his complaints to the
Governor General and Council, but could not prevail on them
to interfere; he then commenced a *qui-tam* action against
certain members of that council, for trading contrary to the
statute. But either fearing to incur the odious name of
informer, or having compromised the matter, he has not gone
on with the suit. This is the only essay to a prosecution on
the Act since the erection of the Court. But I do not remember, out of the different suits ordered by the Directors,
that one has been commenced. Of this I am sure: none
have been prosecuted with effect. And whilst the King's
authority remains secondary in India to that of the Company,
and no stronger controul is exerted over its servants, than can
be felt from the impotent hands of despised Directors, I may
take upon me to predict, not only that no public suits will be
instituted by Government, but private prosecutions on the
Act will be so discountenanced, that few will have resolution
enough to engage in them.   .   .   .   .

" My attention has been always anxiously directed to support the authority of Government, and to facilitate the collections of the revenue; and though patronage, influence, and arbitrary will, may have met with some small check, the legal and avowed powers of the state have received no diminution from the Court. They might have acquired strength, if the administrators of it would have condescended to make use of the King's authority in his Court of law.

" *I can recollect no example in history, of any court but this, which has been erected by an authority different from that which has been in the possession of the executive power of the country in which it was established, and which the executive power undermined by its own secret influence, and opposed by its open hostility.*"

Without being anything of a lawyer, that ex-lawgiver for India, Mr. Macaulay, may surely comprehend the difficulties of a situation like this. I am no lawyer myself, and regret it, though I have no cause to blush at disclaiming a knowledge to which I never pretended ; but it has been my happiness and pride to associate and converse with many able and virtuous men of that profession, who have bestowed no slight attention upon this subject, and are in every way competent to give a sound and unprejudiced opinion upon it. By their testimony, living as well as dead—if not sufficiently guided by my own common sense and honest investigation—I am justified, as far as I have yet gone, in these conclusions :—

I. That the primary establishment of a Supreme Court of Justice in a province, where hitherto there had scarcely been any laws recognisable by a mixed population, except the will of a commercial company and its agents, was in its nature of the highest consequence ; and, in its various and complicated details, one of exceeding difficulty to conduct.

II. That to compile rules and regulations for such a court, invested with wide and ample powers, to check the most inveterate and crying abuses, to protect and conciliate natives accustomed to none but the most mistaken notions of jurisprudence, to put down the tyranny of their foreign rulers, and to uphold the authority to which both were amenable—required not only an enlightened study and capacious mind, but one which came armed, moreover, with every constitutional support.

III. That far from receiving that support, the Court itself, thus newly organised, and exposed to every vulgar prejudice, had, besides, from its very beginning, to struggle with every possible obstruction from those quarters where it was, by right, entitled to all assistance.

IV. That in spite of their accumulated labours, perplexities, and wrongs, the Chief Justice and Assessors of the Supreme Court—embarrassed by the ambiguity of their Act and Charter, discountenanced and neglected by the ministers at home, and opposed with open violence by the provincial government—did, nevertheless, all they could, by legitimate means, to maintain the dignity and efficacy of their commission.

I have arrived at these conclusions by advancing no speculative theory, but by deductions drawn from premises which rest upon substantial and well authenticated facts.

Whatever may be the effects, or no effects, produced by this documental record on the minds of men resolutely bent on slander, and pre-determined to shut their eyes to all evidence, I cannot but believe that the dispassionate reader, after an attentive perusal of this Chapter, will widely differ in his estimation of those which Mr. Macaulay has taken upon trust from Mr. Mill, and Mr. Mill from the impression made by Mr. Francis, respecting the judicial administration of Sir Elijah Impey, and the jurisdiction and authority claimed by the Supreme Court. Upon this subject I shall myself say no more. There is a letter to Sir Richard Sutton, in which my father reasoned on the point of law as to the refusal of the Governor General and Council to put in appearance when summoned by the Court, and in which he demonstrated that his proceedings thereupon were strictly conformable to English law, and to the Regulating Act and Charter. That letter is too long to be quoted here, and has not sufficiently a documental character to be inserted in my Appendix. But, by the time this volume is published, it will be lodged, with the rest of Sir Elijah's papers, in the Library of the British Museum, where any inquirer may consult it.

With this additional reference, I persuade myself that sufficient argument will have been used, and sufficient vouchers produced, to explain and verify this portion of my narrative.

CHAPTER VIII.

COALITION OF FRANCIS AND HASTINGS—THE QUARREL
AND DUEL—EXTENSION OF POWERS OF THE SUDDER
DEWANNEE ADAULUT—SIR ELIJAH IMPEY ACCEPTS THE
PRESIDENCY—FRANCIS RETURNS TO ENGLAND, ETC.

SIR ELIJAH IMPEY clearly foresaw that the compact
between Hastings and Francis would not be binding;
and, that their sudden political friendship would be
succeeded by an exasperated enmity. He knew the
rectitude of his misguided friend too well, to believe
that he could persevere for any length of time in a
wrong course; and he had too long experienced the
faithlessness of his unprincipled enemy, to expect that
he would ever adopt a more honourable one.

No great man was ever yet without a sense of proper
pride; and the pride of Warren Hastings was daily
wounded by the concessions he found himself obliged to
make to his former adversary, and by the arrogance with
which they were exacted. He had not forgotten the days
of Clavering and Monson, when Francis had declared
—" We three are king :" he recognised a revival of the
same haughty tone, and was not disposed to crown his
colleague anew, or to elevate him into a dictator.

For proofs of the galled and irritated state of the
great Governor General's mind at this period, I need
only refer to his own letters, as published by Mr. Gleig,
whose record will retain a permanent and substantial
value, when the baseless fabric of his reviewer shall
have sunk into oblivion.

P

On the 5th of May, 1780, my father wrote to his friend and physician, Dr. Fleming, who was then in the camp, with the army of Sir Eyre Coote :—

"I have been made a sacrifice to new connections. *But however close the present union may be between Mr. Hastings and Mr. Francis, I believe you will join with me in thinking that it cannot be durable.* . . . . But though the treatment I have received is not what I had reason to expect, I am resolved not to act as adversary to him [Hastings] in any respect, but in the cases in which he has or shall make it necessary to me so to do for self-defence."

It should be stated in fairness, that Mr. Barwell's great anxiety to quit the Council and return to England, had had much to do in forcing upon Mr. Hastings this incompatible league and alliance. At the united prayer of the Governor General and Chief Justice, Barwell had repeatedly deferred his departure; but he had not ceased to represent that he must be gone as soon as he possibly could. At last, at the end of March of this year, 1780, seeing that the coalition was formed, and hoping that it would act well, or that Francis would at least be true to the more important parts of his engagement, Barwell sailed for England. Hastings had soon cause to regret his departure. My father had his misgivings from the first. In a letter to Dunning, dated the 18th of August, 1780,—the very day on which the duel was fought between Hastings and Francis,—he said,—

"Mr. Barwell left this country on the strongest assurances that Mr. Francis would coincide with Mr. Hastings, *or he would never have gone.*"

There was never any sincere *coincidence*, except when the Member of Council carried the Governor General along with him into extremities against the Supreme Court. To divide two such friends as the Governor General and the Chief Justice, was an enjoyment suited to the malignant nature of Francis.

The ship in which Barwell embarked had scarcely descended the Hooghley, ere the quarrel between the Council and Court rose to its highest pitch. Every overture for reconciliation was argued down by Francis, or through his agency counteracted and annulled. One unalterable condition of his alliance was, that there should be disunion—for enmity he could never effect—between the former friends. Hastings must either feel the piercing thorn of Francis for ever in his side, or altogether renounce his legal monitor, and the cause of justice legally constituted in India.

But when the Member of Council attempted to make usurpations upon the authority of the Governor General, in matters wherein the Supreme Court was not concerned, and when he again began to thwart the policy, and to disturb the arrangements under which the war was so successfully proceeding * on the side of Bombay, Poona, and Surat; when disgrace upon disgrace was everywhere falling upon our flag in the western world, to be redeemed only by our triumphs in the east; then it was, that, after fruitless representations and remonstrances, the spirit of Warren Hastings rose superior to the base mind which had held it too long in thraldom.

As early as the month of June, he accused Francis of duplicity; by the beginning of July, he complained to friends at home of his seeking to break the compact; and before the end of that month, he found that the renewal of his opposition had renewed alike every former difficulty,—exposing him to the hazard of open ignominy, derision, and defeat. " I am not Governor," wrote Hastings in the bitterness of his soul, "all the powers I possess are those of preventing the rule from falling into worse hands than my own." †

A flagrant breach of the contract on the part of Francis brought matters at last to a crisis. On the 14th of August, 1780, Hastings, in answering a minute of Council, declared :—

" *I do not trust to Mr. Francis's promises of candour, convinced that he is incapable of it. I judge of his public conduct by his private, which I have found to be void of truth and honour. . . . .*"

" Judging it unbecoming," writes Hastings to a friend, " to surprise him with a minute at the Council-table, or to send it first to the secretary, I enclosed it in a note to him that evening. The next day, after Council, he desired me to

---

* Under General Goddard and Captain Popham.
† Letter to Mr. Sulivan, as given by Mr. Gleig.

withdraw with him into a private apartment of the Council house, where, taking out of his pocket a paper, he read from it a challenge in terms. I accepted it, the time and place of meeting were fixed before we parted, and on the morning of the Thursday following, between the hours of five and six, we met." *

If the shot of Francis had proved fatal to Hastings, two things, in all probability, would have happened :—

I. Francis, for a brief space of time, would have succeeded—as, being the challenger, he seems to have contemplated—to all the rank, power, and patronage, of Governor General.

II. British India would have been as utterly lost as the thirteen provinces of America !

But, happily, there was no sacrifice of life, and it was not Hastings, but Francis, that was wounded. " Unprotected by the impenetrable mist" that then hung over him as the author of the Letters of Junius,† the Member of Council was not invulnerable to his adversary's ball. They had both fired nearly at the same moment. Francis fell, and was conveyed to a house in the neighbourhood ; but in two hours it was ascertained that his life was in no danger.

Writing on the day of the event, my father gives the following account of it :—

" This morning Mr. Hastings and Mr. Francis fought with pistols. They both fired at the same time; Mr. Francis's ball missed, but that of Mr. Hastings pierced the right side of Mr. Francis, but was prevented by a rib, which turned the ball, from entering the thorax. It went obliquely upwards, passed the back-bone without injuring it, and was extracted about an inch on the left side of it. The wound is of no consequence, and he is in no danger. Mr. Francis had departed from his engagements with Mr. Hastings, and a minute from him accusing Francis of breach of the faith and honour which he had pledged, provoked the challenge from Francis, which ended in this duel. *Shall we have no end put to the distractions of this Government?* . . . . Sir Eyre Coote, who has been absent from the Presidency for nine or ten months, is returning, with intentions amicable to Mr. Hastings. Mr. Francis and Mr. Wheler form a majority now,

---

* Letter from Hastings, dated the 30th of August, as given by Mr. Gleig.
† C. Mac Farlane. " Our Indian Empire."

and next week the balance will be turned on the other side."*

Four days after writing this, Sir Elijah said in a postscript to a duplicate of this letter to Dunning :—

"*Mr. Hastings and I, notwithstanding what has passed, are on good terms.* It is in vain to think of a real reconciliation between Mr. Hastings and Mr. Francis. Mr. Francis, since the duel, has, by a formal message, refused to admit a visit from Mr. Hastings; and, by the same, declared that he would not meet him but in Council. This, he said, proceeded not from *resentment,* but *what he esteemed propriety.*† Whoever is Governor General, be it Mr. Hastings, or any other person, he ought to have his hands strengthened both with new powers and determined friends in Council. Nothing but vigorous and uniform measures, can give a chance of propping this tottering empire even for a few years longer.

" Hyder Ali has entered the Carnatic, laying all waste with fire and sword. He is in the neighbourhood of Madras: the garden-houses are deserted, and the people all in the utmost consternation.

" *Our salaries were paid yesterday.*"

This last underlined sentence is full of much significance ; for it shows that immediately after this duel, and final rupture with Francis, the Governor General held up the olive branch to the judges of the Supreme Court, whose pecuniary claims had been purposely kept in arrears for many months, evidently at the instigation of Francis. Sir Eyre Coote returned, took his seat in Council, and forwarded this reconciliation. Excuses, expressed chiefly by an altered demeanour, and in deeds rather than words, were offered to the Chief Justice for the insults to which he had been exposed. It was confessed that the newly-remodelled provincial councils and adauluts had ended in a complete failure ; and it was intimated that some important change must take place—some decisive measure be taken to restore harmony to the country, and justice to its native population.

---

* Letter to Dunning, dated the 18th of August. On the 20th of August, my father wrote an account of the duel to his brother, in very nearly the same words.

† I believe there were few persons at Calcutta that did not smile at Francis's new-found sense of propriety, or that were unaware of his implacable resentments.

On the 29th of September—just six weeks after the duel—the Governor General entered this minute in Council :—

"The institution of the new courts of dewannee adaulut *has already given occasion to very troublesome and alarming competitions between them and the provincial councils*, and too much waste of time at this Board. These, however, manifest the necessity of giving more than an ordinary attention to these courts in the infancy of their establishment, that they may neither pervert the purposes, nor exceed the limits of their jurisdiction, nor suffer encroachments upon it.

"To effect these points, would require such a laborious and almost unremitted application, that, however urgent or important they may appear, I should dread to bring them before the consultation of the Board; unless I could propose some expedient for that end, that should not add to the weight of business with which it is already overcharged.

"That which I have to offer, will, I hope, prove rather a diminution of it. By the constitution of the dewannee courts, they are all made amenable to a superior court, called the Sudder Dewannee Adaulut, which has been commonly, but erroneously, understood to be simply a court of appeal. Its province is, and necessarily must be, more extensive. It is not only to receive appeals from the decree of the inferior courts, in all causes exceeding a certain amount; but to receive and revise all the proceedings of the inferior courts, to attend to their conduct, to remedy their defects, and generally, to form such new regulations and checks, as experience shall prove to be necessary to the purpose of their institution. Hitherto the Board has reserved this office to itself, but has not yet entered into the execution of it, nor, I will venture to pronounce, will it ever with effect, though half of its time were devoted to this single department. Yet, without both the support and controul of some powerful authority held over them, it is impossible for the courts to subsist ; but they must either sink into contempt, or be converted into the instruments of oppression.

"This authority, I repeat, *the Board is incapable of exercising ;* and if delegated to any body of men, or to any individual agents, not possessing in themselves *some weight independent of mere official power*, it will prove little more effectual. The only mode which I can devise to substitute for it, is included in the following motions, which I now submit, on the reasons premised, to the consideration of the Board :—

"That the Chief Justice be requested to accept of the charge and superintendency of the office of Sudder Dewannee

Adaulut, under its present regulations, *and such other as the Board shall think proper to add to them, or to substitute in their stead ;* and that on his acceptance of it, he be appointed to it, and styled the Judge of the Sudder Dewannee Adaulut.

" I shall beg leave to add a few words in support of this proposition on different grounds. I am well aware that the choice which I have made for so important an office, and one which will minutely and nearly overlook every rank of the civil service, will subject me to much popular prejudice, as its real tendency will be misunderstood by many, misrepresented by more, and perhaps dreaded by a few.

" *I shall patiently submit to the consequences, because I am conscious of the rectitude of* my intentions, and certain that the event will justify me, and prove, that in whatever light it may be superficially viewed, I shall be found to have studied the true interests of the service, and contributed the most effectually to its credit.

" The want of legal powers, except such as were implied in very doubtful constructions of the Act of Parliament, and the hazards to which the superiors of the dewannee courts are exposed in their own persons, from the exercise of their functions, has been the cause of their remissness, and equally of the disregard which has been in many instances shown to their authority; they will be enabled to act with confidence; nor will any man dare to contest their right of acting, when their proceedings are held under the sanction and immediate patronage of the first member of the Supreme Court, and with his participation in the instances of such as are brought in appeal before him, and regulated by his instructions.

" They very much require an instructor, and no one will doubt the superior qualifications of the Chief Justice for such a duty.

" It will be the means of lessening the distance between the Board and the Supreme Court, which has perhaps been, more than the undefined powers assumed to each, the cause of the want of that accommodating temper, which ought to have influenced their intercourse with each other.

" The contest in which we have been unfortunately engaged with the Court, bore at one time so alarming a tendency, that I believe *every Member of the Board foreboded the most dangerous consequences to the peace and resources of this government from them.* They are at present composed; but we cannot be certain that the calm will last beyond the actual vacation, since the same grounds and materials of disunion subsist, and the revival of it, *at a time like this,* added to our other troubles, *might, if carried to extremities, prove fatal.*

" The proposition which I have submitted to the Board may,

nor have I a doubt that it will, prove an instrument of conciliation with the Court; and it will preclude the necessity of
assuming a jurisdiction over persons, exempted by our construction of the Act of Parliament from it; it will facilitate,
and give vigour to the course of justice; it will lessen the
cares of the Board, and add to their leisure for occupations
more urgent, and better suited to the genius and principles of
government; nor will it be any accession of power to the Court,
where that portion of authority which is proposed to be given,
is given only to a single man of the Court, and may be revoked
whenever the Board shall think it proper to resume it."

On the 24th of October, there was another consultation in Council, nearly a month having been allowed
for deliberation on the question, whether Sir Elijah
Impey should or should not be president of the Sudder
Dewannee Adaulut. Sir Eyre Coote, modestly professing a soldier's ignorance of the law, supported the Governor General, wishing the experiment to be tried, but
reserving to himself the right of voting against it, if hereafter he should find that it proved detrimental either to
the government or to the community. He said in his
minute of consultation, that this, his assent, was " for
the *trial of an expedient* which might be attended with
favourable consequences, and *not for its absolute establishment.*"

Now it seems to me, that this brave and unpretending
veteran, explained the nature of the arrangement far
better than any of those who professed a clearer insight
into the subject. It was experimental,—it was *the trial
of a provisional means,** resorted to under most difficult
and embarrassing circumstances, and at a moment of
great danger; it was never intended as an absolute or
permanent establishment, either by the Governor
General, the Chief Justice, or the puisne judges, who
approved of the arrangement—as they expressed it—
" *pro tempore.*"

Mr. Wheler, who, it will be remembered, had been
appointed in England to succeed Mr. Hastings as Governor General, on the mistaken supposition that he
had resigned, but who had afterwards accepted the seat

---

* As I shall presently show, in his own words, Hastings himself emphatically declared that it was a temporary remedy, adopted through the
urgency of the case.

in Council vacated by the death of Colonel Monson—had usually, but not always, voted in opposition to the Governor General. He adhered to the same course in this instance; and acting, no doubt, as he ever had done, upon fair and honourable principles, now entered a very long minute against the proposition. He expressed, nevertheless, great deference and respect for the character and learning of the Chief Justice; but still thought that the expedient proposed by Mr. Hastings did not fall within the scope of the Regulating Act, and doubted whether the Governor and Council could legally grant the appointment. He also thought that the proposed measure would be injurious to the power and splendour of the Governor and Council. "Such an influence," said he, "possessed by the Chief Justice of the Supreme Court, *might too much hide the government from the eye of the natives.*" He accordingly suggested various other expedients: "1. That the Council, reserving to itself the right of hearing all appeals, should introduce into the court of appeals *the Company's own chief law officer*, the Advocate General, Sir John Day; who, if a judge of appeals should be created, had the most natural right to it. 2. That the Supreme Court, and Governor General and Council, might sit together as a court of appeals. 3. That one of the inferior judges might advantageously be substituted for the Chief Justice. 4. That, what would be better still, the judges should sit in rotation."

Mr. Wheler did not explain why it would have been more consistent with the Regulation Act to confer the appointment on Sir John Day than on Sir Elijah Impey. They were both officers appointed by the Crown: Sir John had been very jealous of his privileges and precedence in that capacity, over all the Company's servants. This had not prevented him, however, from having already accepted an increase of salary by a grant from the Council, for which he lay under a censure of Parliament at that moment. He had also much obstructed the business of the Supreme Court, though he did not go all the lengths of his employers. As little did Mr. Wheler make it appear why an inferior judge would have been more eligible in conformity with the Regulating Act; or what advantages would have been

gained by the judges sitting in rotation; or what purpose could have been answered by the Supreme Court
and Supreme Council sitting together, except to introduce upon the bench itself those unbecoming disputes
which it was the very object of the new Sudder
Dewannee Adaulut to set at rest. I venture upon
these comments only to explain the reason of my dis-
sent from Mr. Wheler's suggestions, as far as relates to
their practical operation; not as implying, in the remotest degree, any question as to their motive. Mr.
Wheler and my father, though differing sometimes
widely in their opinion of men and measures, always
expressed the highest esteem for each other, and never
ceased to live in harmony together.

Francis entered a minute still longer, and more wordy,
than that of Wheler. He, too, but with none of his
colleague's sincerity, professed great deference to the
character and learning of the Chief Justice. As all
present in Council, and every European in Calcutta,
knew the circumstances of his *crim. con.* trial, and the
undisguised hatred he had ever since borne to Sir Elijah
Impey, the author of Junius was very emphatic on this
point, as those are always apt to be who are conscious
that their assertions must be disbelieved. He entered
thus into his long minute:

"I hope it is unnecessary for me to say, that no idea of
personal disrespect to the Chief Justice, can be intended by
anything I shall offer on the public question before me; if
any expression that may appear to have such a tendency,
should escape me, *I disclaim it.*"

Long before this Francis had secretly represented, to
his correspondents in England, the Chief Justice as the
judicial murderer of Nuncomar; and within a few
months, being himself then in England, he was spreading that abominable calumny now openly, now clandestinely, by word of mouth and in printed pamphlets. No
new light could have broke in upon him. He knew everything connected with the Nuncomar case as far back as
the year 1775—he never pretended to have made any
after discoveries—yet at the close of 1780, he could declare, under his own hand, that he had no disrespect to
the Chief Justice! Is it not almost incredible that any

faith should ever have been given to the testimony of such a man?

With equal consistency, and in no less pointed terms, Mr. Francis revived the recollection of the late violent contest between the Supreme Court and Council, touching the jurisdiction of the Court, and then added—

"The Chief Justice cannot be supposed to have changed the opinions which he has at all times so steadily maintained; and those opinions would lead him to submit to the jurisdiction in many instances in which the Council, upon *their* principles, would resist it. Thus the Council, by making the Chief Justice Judge of the Sudder Dewannee Adaulut, would *put into the power of the very man with whom they have been contending, to give up what they hitherto insisted on as their essential rights.*"*

Notwithstanding this opposition to the motion of Mr. Hastings, but with the approval of Sir Eyre Coote, it was resolved on the same day—the 24th of October—"That the Chief Justice should be requested to accept of the charge and superintendence of the Sudder Dewannee Adaulut, under its present regulations, and *such other as the Board shall think proper to add to them, or to substitute in their stead;*† and that on his acceptance of it, he be appointed to it, and styled the Judge of the Sudder Dewannee Adaulut."‡ On the very next day, *before anything had been settled as to salary or emoluments,* Sir Elijah Impey accepted the charge and superintendency of the office; expressing to the Governor General and Council his sense of the honour conferred upon him by the trust confided to his care. He manifested also great readiness to devote his vacant time to the service of the public.||

* The arrangement did, in matters of appeal and revision, give this power to the Chief Justice; and hence arose that tranquillity which Mr. Macaulay can attribute only to the effects of a "bribe" given to a British judge in the shape of a paid place; a place, be it remembered, of most difficult and laborious occupation.

† Many alterations and reforms were contemplated in the provincial councils and adauluts, and were carried into effect by Hastings shortly after the departure of Francis. Men of better education and better morals were put into the adaulut courts; and the worst of the functionaries left in those courts were kept in awe by the knowledge that appeals lay with the Chief Justice, and by the certainty that he would sharply revise their proceedings.

‡ Extract from Bengal Consultations in East India House.

|| See his letter as printed in the First Report of the Select Committee.

Immediately after this adjustment, Francis, who had talked of returning to England, prepared for the voyage, calculating that he could now carry with him the means of ruining, or at least of procuring the recall* of Sir Elijah Impey. On the 12th of November, before the Governor and Council made the tender of the salary and allowance, the Chief Justice wrote to his brother—

"Since my last, Mr. Francis has declared his resolution of vacating his seat in Council. He proceeds to Europe on board the *Fox*, Captain Blackburn, who will sail either the latter end of this or the beginning of next month. This, I apprehend, will create an opening for the new arrangements of Mr. Hastings's government; the first symptom of which is, that, notwithstanding the disagreeable contests, during which I have made it my duty to support the independence of the Supreme Court against the aggression of Government, the Governor and Council have solicited me to accept the superintendency of the native courts of justice, and to preside in the tribunal of dernier appeal called the Sudder Dewannee Adaulut. Such a trust, reposed in me under circumstances which bear the strongest testimony of my having acted, though in a manner adverse to them, yet under a sense of public duty, cannot but be flattering to me. This new office must be attended with *much additional labour;* yet, in the hope that I may be able to convert these courts, which, from *ignorance and corruption,* have hitherto been a *curse,* into a *blessing,* I have resolved to accept it. *No pecuniary satisfaction has been offered or even mentioned to me, but I do not imagine it is intended that my trouble is to go unrecompenced.*"†

On the 22nd of December, a month and ten days after the date of the preceding letter, the Board of Council at Calcutta, resumed the consideration of the Governor General's minute proposing the salary and

---

* This he contrived by means of Mr. Burke's ascendancy over the mind of Lord Rockingham, during his lordship's last short administration, in 1782. The Earl of Shelburne, on the resignation of Lord North, having been called upon to arrange the new cabinet, had placed the Marquis at the head of it, and retained for himself the office of First Secretary for the Southern Department, where, shortly after, yielding to the preponderance of the Rockingham party—among other measures which he did not approve—nevertheless consented, by an official letter, which I shall hereafter quote, to the recall of Sir Elijah Impey, upon the sole charge of accepting this appointment.

† MS. Family Letters.

allowance to the Chief Justice, and agreed to the proposition that it should take place from the date of his appointment; and the Court of Directors were advised of the appointment.*

In the meanwhile Francis had left India, having sailed in the *Fox* on the 3rd of December. His departure contributed most materially to that peace and unanimity, the cause of which is so grossly misrepresented by Mr. Macaulay, but of which the real enjoyment was an inappreciable benefit, as well to the natives of India, as to the Europeans, who either ruled or resided in the settlement, and were amenable to its laws. It was to obtain this blessed end, not for the base love of lucre, which has been imputed to him, that my father was induced to accept a new and toilsome office, at a time when his health was much shattered, and required rest instead of an increase of labour. On the 27th of January, 1781, he wrote to Barwell—

"The Sudder Dewannee Adaulut is placed under my management. *It will be no agreeable thing to me,* but as it was the Governor's act, I am contented.

"The resignation of Francis, and the inability of Wheler, make me think it is barely possible, if my friends would exert themselves, that I might now be put in Council. This has been suggested to me. You, who are on the spot, will know the feasability of it."

Sir Elijah incurred great labour, and not a little expense, in drawing up rules and regulations for this Sudder Dewannee Adaulut. His disorders were seriously aggravated by this increase of toil. But he soon doubted the propriety of taking any pay or allowance whatsoever, without the previous consent of his Majesty's Government, which had appointed him Chief Justice of the Supreme Court; and on the 4th of July, 1781, many months before he could by any possibility know how successfully Francis was blackening his character in England, for accepting the new office, my father addressed a letter to the Board, informing them, " *that he should decline appropriating to himself any part of the salary annexed to the office of Judge of the Sudder Dewannee Adaulut, till the pleasure of the Lord Chan-*

* Extract from Bengal Consultations in the East India House.

*cellor should be known.** Sir Elijah Impey did more for
nothing, than Mr. Macaulay has since done for the
enormous sum of money which was paid to him during
his residence in India.

Accompanying this letter to the Council, there was
the fruit of many month's hard labour, in the shape of
a code, which Sir Elijah had compiled, of rules, orders,
and regulations, for the Sudder Dewannee Adaulut, &c.

Of this code, the Board expressed their warm and
entire approbation :—

"We cannot," they said, "testify in too strong terms our
sense of the trouble you have taken, and the ability with
which you have executed and compiled this laborious work,
which we have ordered to be made public as soon as copies
can be printed, both in its present form, and in the languages
of the country; it being our desire to render them of public
and permanent utility, not doubting that they will be pro-
ductive of the most salutary effects to the inhabitants of these
provinces, by the introduction of a uniform administration of
justice, and by facilitating its process."

With respect to his scruples about accepting the
salary as Judge of the Sudder Dewannee Adaulut, they
said,—

"We can offer no opinion upon that resolution, which appears to have proceeded from a delicacy of which you yourself
can be the only proper judge. But we must express our
regret that you should have thought it necessary to prescribe
to yourself this forbearance, because the labour and importance
of the office which you have accepted from us would most
certainly entitle any person who possessed it to an adequate
recompense, and must, in our estimation, be considered as
more especially your due, from the very qualifications which
are immediately connected with the only circumstance that
could have given occasion to your doubts of the propriety of
receiving it."

Sir Elijah's doubts, however, were not removed by
this letter; and he not only refused to accept the salary
offered to him, but he kept a regular account of the
fees paid into the Court during the very short time that
he presided over it, in order that such monies might be
paid into the treasury of Calcutta. And, that these

* Extract from Bengal Consultations, in the East India House.

monies were so paid, I have a most authentic and official evidence, which I shall presently produce.

My father's preparatory labours were long and arduous; but he did not preside over the actual business of this new court longer than six months, during which time, the receipt of fees and other payments amounted only to £2548 14s. 8d., or thereabout.* Some men may have an alacrity in sinking into infamy and acquiring wealth; but it would have been difficult for any man, even if he had put all these proceeds into his pocket, instead of paying them into the treasury as Sir Elijah did, to have grown "infamous and rich" upon them: yet these are Mr. Macaulay's words. During my researches in the East India House, I discovered the following letter and official account, which seem to me so important and conclusive, that I prefer placing them under the reader's eye in the body of my book, to throwing them into the appendix.

Extract from Bengal Revenue Consultations, November 15th, 1782.

To the Honourable the Governor General and Council, &c. &c., in their Revenue Department.

Honourable Sir and Sirs,

I have the honour to transmit to the Governor General and Council, a true copy of the accounts made out by the accountant and treasurer of the Sudder Dewannee Adaulut, of all sums of money, as well received from the Mofussil dewannee adauluts, as in the Sudder Dewannee Adaulut, on account of deposits during the months of April, May, June, July, August, and September, 1782, which said copy is signed by the accountant and treasurer, and countersigned by the Judge of the Sudder Dewannee Adaulut; and likewise my reports for the months of April, May, June, July, August, and September, 1782, verifying from what judges of Mofussil dewannee adauluts I have, during that period, received, as well the accounts of the sums of money required to be transmitted from them to the Sudder Dewannee Adaulut, and also the other accounts, papers, transcripts, proceedings, and records, required to be transmitted by the courts of Mofussil dewannee adauluts; and when I have not received the same, ascertaining from whom I have not received the same; and where I have received part, ascertaining what part I have not received,

* I have taken the current rupee at 2s.

together with the names of the defaulters in that behalf, ac
cording to the eighty-ninth and ninetieth articles of the regulations for the administration of justice in the courts of Mofussil
dewannee adaulut, and in the Sudder Dewannee Adaulut,
passed in Council on the 5th of July, 1781, which said copy
and report are hereunto annexed.

I have the honour to be,
(Signed)   E. IMPEY.

Fort William, October 25, 1782.

An account of the sums of money received from the Mofussil Dewannee Adauluts, as in Sudder Dewannee Adaulut,
on account of deposits during the months April, May, June,
July, August, and September, 1782.

Received of Mr. William Johnson, Re- gister of the Sudder Dewannee Adau- lut, on account of deposits, from the 1st of April to the 30th of September, 1782 .... Sicca Rupees	10695	13	0	12407	3	0
Received of Mr. John Champain, Judge of the Mofussil Dewannee Adaulut, at Derbungah, on account of deposits, during the months April, May, June, 1782......................	1517	14	3	1760	12	0
Received of Mr. Richard Goodlad, Judge of the Mofussil Dewannee Adaulut, at Rungpore, on account of deposits, from the 1st of April to the 30th of Sep- tember, 1782	180	9	9	209	8	3
Received of Mr. John Addison, Judge of the Mofussil Dewannee Adaulut, at Nattore, on account of deposits, during the months April, May, June, 1782	723	8	11	839	5	2
Received from Mr. Alexander Duncan- son, Judge of the Mofussil Dewannee Adaulut, at Dacca, on account of deposits, April, May, June, 1782. ..	35	1	8	40	11	9
Received also of Mr. Alexander Duncan- son, Judge of the Mofussil Dewannee Adaulut, at Dacca, during the months July, August, and September, 1782..	119	11	3	138	13	6
Received of Mr. Edward Otto Ives, Judge of the Mofussil Dewannee Adaulut, at Moorshedabad, on ac- count of deposits, during the months April, May, June, 1782	1402	6	11	1626	13	2
Received also of Mr. Edward Otto Ives, Judge of the Mofussil Dewannee Adaulut, at Moorshedabad, during the months July, August, September, 1782	675	7	2	783	8	3

Brought forward........	17806	11	5			
Received of Mr. Lawrence Mercer, Judge of the Mofussil Dewannee Adaulut, at Rajehaut,* on account of deposits, during the months of April, May, June, 1782	101	1	1	117	3	7
N.B. An account of sums of money received from the following Mofussil Dewannee Adauluts, omitted to be sent to the Sudder Dewannee Adaulut in time to be inserted in the former account.						
Received of Mr Shearman Bird, Judge of the Mofussil Dewannee Adaulut, at Midnapore, on account of deposits, from the 1st of December, 1781, to the 30th† of February, 1782................	634	0	0	735	7	0
Received of Mr. Alexander Duncanson, Judge of the Mofussil Dewannee Adaulut, at Dacca. from the 1st of October, to the 30th of December, 1781	43	3	0	50	1	9
Received also of Mr. Alexander Duncanson, Judge of the Mofussil Dewannee Adaulut, at Dacca, from the 1st of January to the 31st of March, 1782	7	3	0	8	5	3
Received of Mr. John Addison, Judge of the Mofussil Dewannee Adaulut, at Nattore, on account of deposits, from the 1st of January to the 31st of March, 1782 ..	61	7	1	71	4	4
Received of Mr. Hugh Austin, Judge of the Mofussil Dewannee Adaulut, at Burdwan, on account of deposits, from the 1st of January to the 31st of March, 1782 ..	1180	7	5	1369	5	2
Received of Mr. Benjamin Grindall, Judge of the Mofussil Dewannee Adaulut, at Janjepore, on account of deposits, from the 1st of January to the 31st of March, 1782	1402	7	8	1626	14	0
Received of Mr. Thomas Law, Judge of the Mofussil Dewannee Adaulut, at Patna, on account of deposits, from October, 1781, to March, 1782	3335	3	0	3702	0	11

Current Rupees 25487 5 1

(Signed)   E. IMPEY,
EDM. MORRIS, *Treasurer and Accountant.*

* Quære Rajemal.
† This and one or two other trifling discrepancies occur in the document; in consequence of which I returned it to the East India House, to be compared with the original, and I have received the following obliging communication from T. L. Peacock, Esq.:—

"Dear Sir,—The paper has been compared with the original, and is correctly copied; it will not, therefore, be right to alter it. It is a manifest clerical error.   "I remain, &c., &c.,

"T. L. PEACOCK."

An account of the sums of money received from the Mofussil Dewannee Adauluts, on account of fines, during the months of April, May, June, July, August, and September, 1782.

Received of Mr. John Champain, Judge of the Mofussil Dewannee Adaulut, at Durbungah, for the months of April, May, and June, 1782, the sum of Sicca Rupees	10	0	0	11 9 9
Received of Mr. Edward Otto Ives, Judge of the Mofussil Dewannee Adaulut, at Moorshedabad, during the months of April, May, June, July, and August, 1782, the sum of......	106	15	3	124 1 3

Current Rupees 135 11 0

(Signed)   E. IMPEY,
EDM. MORRIS,
Treasurer and Accountant.

Mr. Macaulay might have found these documents where I found them; but he preferred the easier process of defamation; and without any research, or any knowledge at all of the subject, he declared that my father had grown "infamous and rich," by his acceptance of the presidency of the Sudder Dewannee Adaulut. Sir Elijah was never a rich man; and if he was infamous, then is virtue infamous, honour infamous, and an immaculate conscience as black as Tophet.

Surely, nothing looks less like selling his conscience for an additional salary than the conduct of the Chief Justice throughout this business; nor does it seem as if it had ever entered into the mind of the Chief Justice, who must be supposed to have been well acquainted with the scope of the Charter and Regulating Act, under which he acted, that there was any illegality in his accepting the presidency of this remodelled court. His only doubt was touching the *emoluments;* and therefore he determined not to accept of a single rupee until his scruples were removed by the highest legal authority, and until the Government at home, and Court of Directors, should confirm the appointment and the offer of the salary. And yet, as he afterwards showed, there were *precedents for his accepting the* *additional salary* without any delay or scruple whatever.*

If the Governor General could have bought and the Chief Justice could have sold a conscience, then Mr. Hastings must have had the power, within himself, of paying the price, and Sir Elijah Impey must have been satisfied to take it at his hands; but the Governor General had no such power, and the Chief Justice would take nothing without the consent of His Majesty's Government, and the approval of the Lord Chancellor of England,—things not to be obtained clandestinely, and not likely to be demanded openly by a man conscious of being engaged in a nefarious compact. Sir Elijah wrote upon the subject not only to the Lord Chancellor, but also to the Attorney General and other eminent lawyers. It has been seen how frankly he mentioned the matter to his honest right-minded brother; and he wrote with equal frankness to his best and most virtuous friends in England,— to men who would have shrunk from any illegal and dishonourable action, and from the perpetrator of it.

Mr. Francis, who first raised the outcry, knew perfectly well that my father had accepted the onerous office *without any salary.* He was himself present when the proposal was carried to appoint the Chief Justice to be Judge of the Sudder Dewannee Adaulut. The word *salary* was not then mentioned. Francis, as I have shown, sailed from Calcutta on the 3rd of December. Now, it was not until the 22nd of December, that the Board of Council definitely and unanimously resolved, that a salary and allowance should be attached to the new office. On the same day, they advised the Court of Directors of the appointment. Francis, being on the high seas, could not know what passed at Calcutta on the 22nd of December. Allowing about six months for the voyage, he did not reach England till till June, 1781. But it has been shown that, as early as the 8th of August following, it was known at Cal-

* The amount of the proposed salary has been variously stated. Some have carried it to as high a figure as £8000 per annum. On the minutes of the Revenue-council, and in Sir Elijah Impey's correspondence, it is specified at £5000 per annum ; but as Sir Elijah never received it, or any part of it, the difference is of no consequence.

cutta, that he had already accused Sir Elijah of having accepted the office *with the salary.*

It would appear then, first, that he had accused him of what he knew to be untrue; and secondly, that he had accused him *before he left India,* which of course could only have been done by letter. Now, in the library of the British Museum, there is an anonymous pamphlet, published by Debret, in 1781, entitled, "Extract of an Original Letter from Calcutta, relative to the Administration of Justice by Sir Elijah Impey." The Introduction states, that "it was written *by a gentleman in Bengal to a person of station in England,* and received in October, 1781." On the title page is a quotation from Tacitus—"*Ut antehac flagitio nunc legibus laboratur.*" On the fly leaf is a manuscript note, signifying that the pamphlet was written by Sir Philip Francis; and, indeed, the style and tenour of the composition, the coincidence of dates, and the classical malignity of the motto, all bear the strongest evidence of the fact. And it seems equally probable, that "*the gentleman of station in England*" was no other than Mr. Burke : for all his biographers agree that he corresponded with Francis while in India ;* and it is too well known how completely that gentleman had gained the ear of the Committee to require any farther proof by whom and in what manner their report was influenced.

By these clandestine means, not only the Select Committee, which began to sit in 1781, and of which Mr. Burke was a member, but the Court of Directors also, were misled into the belief that the Chief Justice had accepted the office *with the salary;* so that when they applied to counsel for their opinion, two out of the four —Mr. Mansfield and Mr. Rouse—were adverse to the appointment, though not on legal grounds ; while Sir James Wallace the Attorney General, and Mr. Dunning, who had both been better informed, were of a different opinion : and the Chancellor, Thurlow, to whom Sir Elijah had likewise written, warmly defended him in the House of Lords.

This subject will be made still more clear in a subse-

* It has since transpired through a recent publication of "Burke's Correspondence," that their acquaintance began as early as 1773. See p. 25 of this volume.

quent chapter. Upon the minor charges against my father, I shall say but little : his very prosecutors seem to have been ashamed of them. The crushing weight of scandal lies in the Nuncomar charge, which, if substantiated, would have made him a judicial murderer; and in this Sudder Dewannee Adaulut charge, which, had it been proved, would have made him the meanest of mankind,—a trafficking judge, a lawgiver capable of selling his soul and conscience for gold! But the first was disproved, and the last not so much as even brought forward after all.

CHAPTER IX.

THE climate of Bengal proved fatal to two out of the
four judges of the Supreme Court. The amiable and
accomplished Sir William Jones, who so efficiently
supported and continued the efforts of Hastings to encourage and promote the study of the Oriental languages, antiquities, laws, and customs, was appointed
to fill the vacancy of Mr. Justice Lemaistre, who died
in 1778-9. Upon his arrival at Calcutta, Sir William
became intimately acquainted with Sir Elijah Impey, to
whom he was the bearer of letters from several common
friends. Among these letters there was one from Lord
Ashburton—Dunning. Sir William was also the
bearer of a letter from Lord Shelburne, his patron, to
Mr. Hastings.

As Sir William did not arrive in India until late in
the year 1783, and as Sir Elijah quitted the country at
the close of that year, their personal intercourse was of
short duration : but, while it lasted, it was of the most
intimate and friendly kind ; and when Sir William was
removed by death in India, and his widow returned to
this country, the intimacy between Lady Jones and our
family was renewed.

If Sir William Jones had entertained those notions
on the two cases, of Nuncomar and the Sudder De-

wannee Adaulut, which were afterwards promulgated
by my father's enemies, could this intimacy and friendship have ever existed? Sir William Jones was an
honourable man, an upright judge, and the declared
foe of everything which bore the name and character of
faction. He had lived in the closest intimacy with Burke,
but when—after his arrival in India—Burke, stimulated
by the malice of Francis, and carried away by his own
impetuosity, declared open war not only against Hastings, and all the friends of Hastings, but also against
every man that was neutral in the quarrel, or that required evidence before he would commit himself to an
opinion on the case, Sir William met him with a bold and
spirited remonstrance. He loved Burke, and he owed
him obligations; but he could not, in his conscience,
submit to the vassalage which Burke required of him.
The following letter is honourable to the judge, and
contains matter characteristic of the orator and statesman. It will enable the reader to judge to what an
extent the passions of Burke were enflamed.

" *Garden House, near Calcutta,*
" *April* 13, 1784.

"To Edmund Burke, Esq.

"My dear friend, &c.,

"   .   .   .   . You have declared, I find, that if you hear
of my *siding* with Hastings, you will do everything you can
to get me recalled. What! if you *hear* it only! without examination, without evidence! Ought you not rather, as a
friend, who, whilst you reproved me for my ardour of temper,
have often praised me for integrity and disinterestedness, to
reject any such information with disdain, as improbable and
defamatory? Ought you not to know from your long experience of my principles, that whilst I am a judge, I would
rather perish than *side* with any man? The Charter of
Justice, indeed, and I am sorry for it, makes me *multilateral;*
it gives me an *equity* side; a *law* side; an *ecclesiastical* side;
and, worst of all, in the case of ordinances and regulations,
a *legislative* side; but I neither have, nor will have, nor
should any power or allurement give me, a *political* side. As
to Hastings, I am pleased with his conversation, as a man of
taste, and a friend to letters; but, whether his public conduct be wise or foolish, I shall not, in my present station,
examine, and if I shall live to mention it after examination in
the House of Commons, I shall speak of it as it deserves, with-

out extenuation, if it be reprehensible, and without fear of any man, if I think it laudable." *

This is just what my father did, both before the Commons, and in the House of Lords; these are precisely the sentiments he always expressed; and it was in this spirit that he said, in reference to the party distractions in India, " *The judges, of course, are of no party.*" The Charter of Justice also made my father *multilateral*, without making him a partisan, or giving him " a *political* side ; " and yet, without any examination into circumstances, without any evidence, he was accused by the vehement, impetuous Burke, of *siding* with Hastings; he, also, because Burke had *heard* certain clandestine and unauthenticated reports, was not only threatened, like Sir William Jones, but was actually recalled; and was, after his recall, subjected to the worst species of persecution that could beset any man in a free and civilized country. And simply upon the void evidence of Burke's parliamentary speeches, and the speeches and impeachment-articles of men who acted with him, and under him, historians, reviewers, and essayists, have held up Sir Elijah Impey to the abhorrence of the world.

With a confident hope that every candid and intelligent reader will be sensible of all the bearings of Sir William Jones's remarkable letter, I pass to other events which were antecedent to the date of that letter.

I must again disclaim any intention of dwelling upon the complicated political history of India, during the last few years of Mr. Hastings's administration. It is

---

* Correspondence of the Right Honourable Edmund Burke, between the year 1744, and the period of his decease in 1797. Edited by Charles William, Earl Fitzwilliam, and Lieutenant General Sir Richard Bourke, K.C.B. In four volumes. London : 1844. Vol. III., p. 30.

Mr. Nicholls, in his " Recollections," gives a parallel case to this. " I put," says he, " this question to him—i. e. to Burke—' Can you prove that Mr. Hastings ever derived any advantage to himself from that misconduct which you impute to him ? ' He acknowledged ' that he could not.' . . . . . . Before the charges were laid on the table, I had a second conversation with Mr. Burke on the subject. When he found that I persevered in my opinion, he told me, ' that in that case, I must relinquish the friendship of the Duke of Portland.' I replied, ' that would give me pain ; but I would rather relinquish the Duke of Portland's friendship than support an impeachment which I did not approve.' We parted, and our intercourse was terminated." Vol. 1, pp. 293–4.

very generally known that those were years of unprecedented difficulties and alarms, and that the ability of
no great statesman was ever more severely put to the
test than was that of the truly great, though not always
faultless, Governor General. The expenses of the war
were tremendous, and were left to fall almost entirely
upon the treasury of Calcutta. Thus Hastings was
obliged to raise money in every way he could. No
doubt he occasionally went beyond the line of strict
justice; but the whole country was *in statu belli*, and the
point at issue was, whether England should be dispossessed by the French, or retain her Indian empire. Some
of the native princes, who owed their political existence
to the power of English arms, and who were entirely
dependent upon the government of Calcutta, were known
to possess hidden treasures of immense amount. In
some cases these princes were nothing but tributaries to
the ~~country~~, and were bound to aid in the support of
that power to which they owed their musnuds. Many
contributions seem to have been paid with tolerably
good will; but, in some instances, they were refused
or delayed, on the plea of poverty. Cheyte Sing,
the Rajah of Benares, who had owed his rank
and half his possessions to the English, broke
several promises and engagements he had made
with the Calcutta Council. The Governor General,
who saw his resources exhausted at a moment when
money and troops were most wanted, resolved to bring
this rajah to account. For this purpose he quitted Calcutta to proceed to Benares. So little did he anticipate
danger, or the possibility of resistance, that he took
with him little more than the body-guard which attended him on ordinary occasions. He even conducted
Mrs. Hastings with him up the country as far as
Monghire. Arriving at Benares on the 14th of August,
1781, Hastings sent to Cheyte Sing a long paper.
The Rajah replied in an evasive and arrogant tone;
and upon this he was arrested in his own palace
at an early hour of the following morning. The
arrest led to a popular insurrection, in which much
blood was shed, and from the fury of which the
Governor General himself escaped with extreme dif-
difficulty. The Rajah went into the country and raised

troops to fight against the English; the Governor
General withdrew to the strong hill fortress of Chunar.*
Troops were marched rapidly to the support of Hastings;
and before the 21st of September, Cheyte Sing was
beaten at all points, and an end put to the insurrection.
Hastings seated upon the vacant musnud a young
nephew of Cheyte Sing, and took the entire jurisdiction
and management of Benares into his own hands. By
this revolution, a prospective addition of about £200,000
per annum was made to the revenues of the Company;
but the Governor General could not find the store of
ready money he so much needed; the flying Rajah
having carried off his hidden treasures with him.
Asoff-ul-Dowla, Nabob of Oude, stood indebted, on
the Company's books, in nearly one million and a-half
sterling. Like the Rajah of Benares, he was entirely
dependent on the Company, and on the protection of
their troops against the plundering Mahrattas and
Rohillas, as well as his own turbulent subjects.
The Nabob had been repeatedly warned that money
must be forthcoming. He was journeying between
Lucknow and Benares, to meet the Governor General,
when he received accounts of the insurrection. He did
not retrace his steps, as might have been expected, but
continued his journey to Chunar. In that fortress,
while 30,000 insurgents were gathering round him,
Hastings calmly negotiated with the Nabob. Asoff-
ul-Dowla protested that he had no treasure to bestow,
but that two ladies in his dominions had far more
money than they ought in justice to have retained.
These two Begums were, one the mother of the late

---

* It was on this occasion that the rabble of Benares reviled Mr.
Hastings in these doggrel rhymes :—
> " Hatee pur houda! ghora pur zeen,
>   Juldee jao, julde jao, Warren Hasteen! "
Which may be translated—
> Horse, elephant, houda, set off at full swing,
>   Run away, ride away, Warren Hasting.
And it is to these self-same rhymes that Mr. Macaulay alludes, when he
talks of " a jingling ballad about the fleet horses and richly-caparisoned
elephants of Sahib Warren Hostein," with which nurses sing their children
to sleep, as if they were sung to the *praise of*, instead of in *triumph over*
their enemy! This is, doubtless, a trifle; but it is by trifles, no less than
matters of consequence, that the inaccuracies of a writer like Mr. Macaulay, are often liable to detection.

Nabob, Sujah Dowla, the other his wife, and the parent of the reigning Nabob. It was said that great doubts might be entertained as to the validity of Sujah Dowla's testamentary bequests; that the will under which the Begums claimed, had never been produced; and that the deceased Nabob could not lawfully alienate the treasure and territory or jaghires of the state, which of right belonged to his successor. It was agreed between Asoff-ul-Dowla and Hastings, that the two Begums should be dispossessed of a great portion of their immense estates, and that the Nabob should have and hold these jaghires; that the Begums' hidden treasures should be seized, and the money paid over to the Company in partial or entire discharge of the debt which the Nabob owed to the Company. It was pleaded, in justification of this seizure, that the two Begums had promoted insurrection in Oude, and had encouraged the partizans of Cheyte Sing, immediately after the outbreak at Benares. This much at least appears to be certain, that there had been commotions in Oude, and that detachments of the Company's troops had been attacked by the retainers of the Begums. There were Englishmen, as well as Indians, who swore to the facts, that the Begums, or their agents, were privy to the Rajah's plans, and had sent Cheyte Sing assistance as soon as he began to collect an army to wage war upon the Company. The insurrection at Benares happened on the 16th of August; the treaty of Chunar was signed on the 19th of September. The Nabob of Oude undertook to obtain possession of the jaghires for himself, and of the money for Hastings. He returned to Lucknow, and from that city he went to Fyzabad, the residence of the Begums. Those two ladies were very tenacious of their money. The hidden treasure was not to be found. Severe and unjustifiable measures were resorted to, *not by Hastings, but the Nabob*, to extract a confession; and, by slow degrees, money was extorted from two eunuchs of the household, to the amount of about £500,000. As this fell far short of the estimated amount, other acts of severity were practised, which I do not mean to justify; but abundant evidence has been adduced to prove how much they have been exaggerated. I shall add one more proof. In 1803, Lord Valentia found at Lucknow, well, fat, and enormously rich, Almas Ali Khan, on whose sufferings Burke had been so pathetic. After all the cruel plunderings he was said to have undergone, this eunuch was supposed to be worth half a million sterling. He was upwards of eighty, six feet high, and stout in proportion; he had been an active and intriguing courtier, he was now almost in dotage, and the Nabob was eagerly looking after his inheritance. He had been notorious for the rigour with which he had extorted taxes, when he administered Oude. The younger of the two Begums was also alive and hearty and—*very rich.** The money obtained was immediately applied by Hastings to the support of the ruinous war in the Carnatic; to the operations on the side of Bombay, and in subsidies to keep the Mahrattas quiet. But for the money obtained at Fyzabad, India must have been lost.

These pecuniary exactions were continued through many months, and the most violent of them had not been resorted to at the time when Sir Elijah Impey, at the request of the Governor General, received the depositions which were given in to verify and support a narrative of the insurrection which Hastings drew up with his own hand at Benares. Situated as my father was, and being where he was at the time, it was impossible for him to refuse taking these depositions; and he took them in a regular manner, as they would have been taken by any lawyer, and as they might have been taken by any reputable party, acting as an *amicus curiæ* on the occasion. Yet this was included, by parliamentary orators, among my father's crimes; this was the theme upon which Sheridan exhausted his ribaldry and abuse—and it is of this that Mr. Macaulay says,—

" But we must not forget to do justice to Sir Elijah Impey's conduct on this occasion. It was not, indeed, easy for him to intrude himself into a business so entirely alien from all his official duties. But there was something inexpressibly alluring, we must suppose, in the peculiar rankness of the infamy which was then to be got at Lucknow. He hurried thither as fast as relays of palankin-bearers could carry him. A crowd of people came before him with affidavits against the Begums, ready drawn in their hands. Those affidavits he did

* See Lord Valentia's Travels.

not read. The greater part, indeed, he could not read; for they were in Persian and Hindostanee, and no interpreter was employed. He administered the oath to the deponents, with all possible expedition; and asked not a single question, not even whether they had perused the statements to which they swore. This work performed, he got again into his palankin, and posted back to Calcutta, to be in time for the opening of term. The cause was one which, by his own confession, lay altogether out of his jurisdiction. Under the Charter of Justice, he had no more right to inquire into crimes committed in Oude, than the Lord President of the Court of Session of Scotland to hold an assize at Exeter. He had no right to try the Begums, nor did he pretend to try them. With what object, then, did he undertake so long a journey? Evidently in order that he might give, in an irregular manner, that sanction which in a regular manner he could not give, to the crimes of those who had recently hired him; and in order that a confused mass of testimony which he did not sift, which he did not even read, might acquire an authority not properly belonging to it, from the signature of the highest judicial functionary in India."

There is not a word in this false and flippant passage but can be confuted. Sir Elijah Impey made no hurried journey from Calcutta. He was travelling up the country, with the intention of going, at least, as far as Benares, when he received Hastings's request that he would take the depositions. As the insurrection had been so easily subdued, and as perfect tranquility had been restored, to the infinite satisfaction of the great body of the quiet, industrious population, there was no great danger in the journey. Sir Elijah was accompanied by his lady and the usual train of slow-moving Indian servants. He took with him his confidential moonshee, or interpreter, Gunsian Dass; although, as far as he himself was concerned, he stood in no need of any interpreter.* There was no racing in palankins, there was no hurry of any kind.

My father and mother, with their numerous attendants, proceeded by water up the Ganges, as far as that

---

* Gunsian Dass was one of the most faithful and affectionate of Indians. He became a sincere and intelligent convert to Christianity. My father, after his recall, obtained a small pension for him, and corresponded with him with that kindness and regard which he paid to every deserving man that had ever been in his service. Among the relics I possess of this good Indian, is a well-used English prayer-book.

mode of travelling was convenient and direct; and after quitting the river, they proceeded by slow stages towards Benares.   At Monghire they joined Mrs. Hastings, who had suffered agonies of alarm on account of the Benares insurrection, and the imminent danger to which the Governor General had been at one time exposed.   This journey had been projected by my father, not only before the insurrection had broke out, but even long before Hastings reached Benares to call Cheyte Sing to account.

Sir Elijah quitted Calcutta at the end of the month of July; and the events at Benares had not taken place till the 16th of August.   On the 3rd of August, Sir Elijah was at Daudpour,* whence he wrote to the Governor General.   On the 12th of August, being then, as the head of his letter intimates, " on the way to Benares," Hastings wrote to my father, begging him to send him his route, and the dates of his proposed visit to each English station, in order that he might be received with every mark of respect and attention.   In this letter, Hastings ingeniously instructed my father how to keep his pinnace, on the Ganges, cool, by means of a canvass awning, and a little mechanical arrangement; which, to make it clearer to his conception, he accompanied with a slight pen-and-ink sketch.   The whole of this affectionate letter shows the mind of the writer to have been perfectly at ease.   He complains of the bad conduct of the Rajah of Benares, but anticipates no resistance, and no difficulty whatever in dealing with him.   It should appear, that at this moment, it was not even certain that Sir Elijah would go so far up the country as Benares.   The following passage from Hastings's letter, will sufficiently demonstrate how slowly my father was travelling.

" I wish you to see Benares, and shall be glad to see you there: but you must regulate your visit thither by my return to it, of which I will give you timely notice—a precaution perhaps not necessary—as my motions are likely to be rapid, and as you are likely to meet with many stops in your way. . . . . I am well, and wish *you* were as well."

* Daudpour is about six miles beyond Plassey, on the road by Monghire, from Calcutta to Patna.   See Rennell's map.

In fact, Sir Elijah, on quitting Calcutta, had proposed to inspect the different local courts that were subject to the Sudder Dewannee Adaulut; and the tour was undertaken partly for recreation and health, and partly for business. And now, may I not ask, what becomes of Mr. Macaulay's hurried and unconsidered assertion, that Sir Elijah Impey " *hurried* " to Lucknow, "as fast as relays of palankin-bearers could carry him "? Or how can we estimate the implication of that writer, that Sir Elijah's journey had no other object than that of taking the depositions at Lucknow, "in an irregular manner," &c.? When the insurgents had driven the Governor General from Benares to the rock of Chunar, and when his life was in peril, he wrote a hasty note, in pencil, to the Chief Justice. The purport of it was, to request him to urge on the marching of troops to Chunar, where, for some time, the Governor General was left with only fifty men; Sir Elijah did urge on the troops, and promoted, by other measures, the relief of Mr. Hastings from his perilous situation. My father and mother remained some time at Monghire, with Mrs. Hastings, whose health had been seriously affected by her anxiety of mind.

On the 1st of October, the Governor General wrote from Benares to the Chief Justice, to thank him and his lady for their kind attention to Mrs. Hastings.

" She will entertain you," said this letter, " with the history of our late successes. . . . . . I see no possibility of future danger. I have written that I should desire Mrs. Hastings to proceed to this place; and in that case, I shall still *hope* that you and Lady Impey will be of the party." *

It should appear from these words, that even now Hastings had some doubts whether my father would go on as far as Benares. These doubts, however, must have been removed in the course of a week or two, for on the 15th of October, I find the Governor General— still at Benares—writing to Lady Impey :—

"I, with the greatest pleasure, contemplate your near approach to this place, but cannot suffer you to reach it without giving you that assurance, and expressing the impatience with which I look for your arrival, and have already begun to

* MS. letter in my possession.

compute the distance which I hope is daily lessening between us. Allow me, my dear madam, at the same time to thank you, which I do most heartily, for your kind attention to Mrs. Hastings. I shall reckon it amongst the most fortunate incidents of my life, that on such an occasion, she had the comfort and support of such society as that of your ladyship and my friend Sir Elijah.

"I shall have the pleasure of meeting you between this and Buxar, and hope that the novelty of this scene, and the beauty and fine air of Chunar, will repay you for all the troubles and fatigues of your journey. The escort of tents will set off from hence either to-morrow or next day, and will be on the shore opposite to Buxar, by the 21st."

It was not until the 25th or 26th of October, more than two months after the insurrection at Benares, that Sir Elijah Impey and his lady arrived at the latter city. The overland journey from India to England is now commonly performed in much less time than they had occupied in travelling from Calcutta to Benares.*

After spending some time at Benares, Sir Elijah, who had the curiosity of a traveller to gratify, readily agreed to go on from Bahar into Oude, in order to receive the written affidavits which Hastings was collecting to corroborate his long narrative of the transactions at Benares, and in Oude. Sir Elijah did not pretend to go as a judge, or even as a magistrate—his jurisdiction could in no case extend beyond Bahar; but merely to verify Mr. Hastings's narrative by written depositions to facts relating to the insurrections at Benares, and to the troubles excited by the agents of the Begums. And he determined to proceed, at the Governor General's request, not to hold an assize of oyer and terminer, to try, hear, and decide, upon any case, civil or criminal,—not to advance any pretence whatever of exercising jurisdiction over the province which had been the seat of the transactions; but simply and solely to act as *amicus curiæ*, and for the specific purpose of collecting affidavits which Hastings had prepared in his own justification. Whether true or false, this narrative had nothing to do with the punishment which had been inflicted upon Cheyte Sing and the Begums; it was

* The distance from Calcutta to Benares, by Monghire, is computed by Rennell at 565 miles and 6 furlongs.

merely meant to prove to the Council at Calcutta, to the Court of Directors, and to the Government at home, that there had been a formidable insurrection at Benares, and troubles in Oude.

The Governor General's letters show that all the service he expected from the Chief Justice was, that he would take the affidavits, which Sir Elijah or any other man assuredly could take, without any breach of law. My father, in effect, did no more than this; and yet, for this, he is compared to the Lord President of the Court of Sessions in Scotland holding an assize at Exeter! It is true that the Chief Justice of the Court at Calcutta had no more right to try the Begums, or any other criminals at Lucknow, or at Fyzabad, than the Lord President of the Scotch Sessions had to open an assize in Devonshire; but there was nothing to hinder either the one or the other, if called upon so to do, from justifying the acts of an official man by taking affidavits. The Lord High Chancellor, or the Lord Chief Justice of England, might have done all that the Chief Justice of Bengal did, without degradation of his office; for he would have acted not in his judicial, but in his private character; and in his private character, there was nothing in law, there was nothing in equity, to prohibit the little that was done by my father at Lucknow. Any private gentleman might have taken the affidavits. It was not necessary that he should be a lawyer. The captain of a man-of-war, nay, even the commander of a merchant ship, is not unfrequently called upon, in foreign and remote countries, to receive affidavits affecting the interests or the characters of British subjects settled in those countries. The insurrection at Benares had been of too formidable a nature to allow any man in British India to doubt of its existence; it was not for Sir Elijah to decide whether it had, or had not, been provoked by Hastings, in his eagerness to get money to carry on the war, and to preserve our Indian Empire; he could no more sit in judgment upon Hastings, than upon Cheyte Sing and the Begums; but it is clear, from his declarations upon oath, that he had been induced to believe, that Cheyte Sing's revolt was pre-concerted, and that the Begums favoured it by means of their agents.   But while at Lucknow, my father was not called upon either to investigate the facts, or to deliver any opinion on them. He had nothing to do there but to receive the affidavits, nor did the Governor General ever expect more from him.

Parliamentary rhetoric may deal in achronisms, but history ought not. It was made to appear in the oration of Sheridan—and the same is implied by Mr. Macaulay's *Historical Essay*—that there was the closest connection between Sir Elijah's journey to Lucknow, and the treatment of the Begums and their household : but these extremities were not resorted to by the Nabob of Oude until months after the return of the Chief Justice to Calcutta; nor does my father appear to have known anything about those transactions, until they were revealed, and monstrously exaggerated, in Hastings's impeachment and trial. In the course of that trial—on the 6th of May, 1788—my father, who voluntarily appeared before the Lords, declared upon oath,—

" That his journey to Lucknow in 1781, was merely, and for no other purpose, but to authenticate the 'Narrative' of Mr. Hastings. He himself had recommended that measure then, and avowed it now, as a method of establishing the ground upon which Mr. Hastings had acted, and for verifying the statements he had made in that narrative; that he did not consider those affidavits as affording grounds for seizing the treasure, or for resuming the jaghires of the Begums; nor did he, as a private individual, affix in his own mind any motive beyond that of authenticating the Benares narrative; that he was not acquainted in detail with the contents of those affidavits, neither did he then, nor should he now, acknowledge *that* to be necessary."

During this part of his evidence, Sir Elijah, alluding to some insinuations which were audibly cast upon his testimony from the managers' box, said,—

" My Lords, I trust it is understood that I stand here as a voluntary witness. I am upon oath. I speak to the best of my recollection; and I have a character to support. That character the honourable manager shall not invade by any indirect insinuation. Your lordships will bear me out when I submit, that were it my intention, I might justly hesitate to answer many of these questions pending the inquiries re-lative to myself in another place. But all hesitation I disdain. I will speak freely and fairly, because I have nothing to conceal; but with submission to your lordships, I will not passively allow words to be put into my mouth which I have never uttered, or conceived in my thoughts."

To this the lords nodded their assent. Sir Elijah Impey then deposed, that the confederation of the Begums with Cheyte Sing, was as notorious as that of the Jacobites with the Pretender, in 1745; but that the insurrection had been since subdued, and the country which he had traversed, reduced to a peaceable state; that his own retinue was not warlike—not numerous; he travelled leisurely, with a moonshee, a surgeon, and two or three hircars : that Mr. Hastings's situation, at that time, was peculiar, and called for peculiar assistance : that he considered it his duty to offer him all the assistance in his power, for the preservation of India, at that critical period. Here Mr. Burke burst out into this ironical rhapsody,—

" O ! miserable state of the Indian Empire ! O ! abandoned fortune of the Governor ! O ! fallen pride of England, when no assistance could be found but that of Sir Elijah Impey ! a man providentially sent to act in an extrajudicial capacity, in districts to which his jurisdiction did not extend ! . . . . ."

"After some pause, Sir Elijah continued to state ' that though indeed his sojourn at Lucknow was in no official capacity, yet he was aware that his character in the country— and, might he presume to add, some reputation as a lawyer, not unacquainted with the law of nations—gave that authority which would have been wanting had they been irregularly sworn before persons unacquainted with the forms to be observed in such a process; that in Mr. Hastings's position, at that moment, opposed by the rest of the Council, abandoned by his own agents, and acting on his own responsibility, he considered him entitled to all the support he could afford, and that that support was not illegal, though extra-judicial. He admitted that he neither had, nor pretended to have, any legal jurisdiction in that district; yet, in a situation which involved a question of international law, he considered his conduct to be justified by the highest legal authorities.' "

On cross-examination by Mr. Plumer, it was proved that the affidavits were taken with no " *indecent haste*," —that Hyder Beg, a mussulman of rank, was not the only native of high credit who had deposed to the con-

spiracy of the Begums with Cheyte Sing—that several
Europeans of station in the Company's service had
sworn to the same fact; among whom were Colonel
Hannay and Captain Wade; the latter having made
affidavit, that had he been asked by any indifferent
person, then resident in the province, whether there had
been a rebellion in Oude, he should have "thought the
question put in jest." In conclusion, Sir Elijah used
words to this effect:

"My Lords, it has been objected to me that I deviated
from my official character, in taking these affidavits; that, in
doing so, I acted as the secretary, or as some have more
coarsely expressed it, as the *tool* of Mr. Hastings. I did so:
and I am yet to learn that official men are restricted, by the
exact line of their peculiar functions, from doing essential,
though extraordinary service, to the State.* The reverse I
acknowledge to have been ever my practice and opinion. I
trust, therefore, that upon examination it will be found, not
only in this instance, but in many more, that I have stepped out
of the ordinary course, to perform a public benefit, and I contend, that herein I have not only done my duty, but more
than, by mere prescription, was required of me. The minutes
of the East India Company, both abroad and at home—the
testimony of various inhabitants of India—native and European—the recollection of many witnesses examined this
day—the very reports of two committees which have collected evidence against me—and above all, the evidence of
my own conscience, bear witness for me, that I have never
been wanting in the service of my country. I have gone
forth when health, ease, and personal security might have
prompted me to stay behind. I have advised, when I might
have coldly spared my counsel. I have made peace when
I might like others, have fomented discord; and when, either
by standing aloof, or leaning to the stronger side, I might
have earned a guilty gain or worthless popularity. But I
thank God, that the memory of these things raises no blush
upon my face, nor compunction at my heart. What I did
then I am free to acknowledge now."*

To make use of a familiar illustration, I may here
mention, that a master in Chancery, though quietly
seated in his chamber at leisure for any investigation,

* See Topham's Trial of Hastings, where the honest reporter adds—
"At the close of business, several of their lordships discoursed with the
witness; but they never after troubled him to appear before them."

and transacting business in all due form and regularity, is never expected to be acquainted in detail with the contents of affidavits sworn before him. Nor in other cases is it considered necessary for those before whom affidavits are made, to examine into their allegations; it is sufficient if they are regularly sworn: and that the affidavits presented at Lucknow were regularly sworn, was in evidence on Hastings's trial. The affidavits may, or may not, have been collected in a hurry by Hastings and his friends; but with this the Chief Justice had nothing to do; and as more than two months had elapsed between the insurrection at Benares and the arrival of the Chief Justice at Lucknow, and as Hastings was never taken by surprise, but always methodical, it is presumable that the affidavits had not been collected in a hurry. It has been imputed to my father, not merely as an irregularity, but as a crime, that he did not read the affidavits; but I trust it has been shown that there was not even so much as irregularity in his not reading them. It has been said by Mr. Macaulay that he could not read them, if he had wished, as they were in Persian and Hindustanee, and as no interpreter was employed. Sir Elijah's moonshee, or interpreter, was with him during the whole time, and the Chief Justice himself was an excellent Persian and Arabic scholar, and spoke fluently the Bengalee, if not the Hindustanee dialect.

This is the single instance in which Mr. Macaulay, in republishing his review as an essay, acknowledges that he may have been detected in an error by Mr. Mac Farlane. He concludes that Mr. Mac Farlane must have had private sources of information. This is true; but Mr. Mac Farlane also derived the fact that Sir Elijah Impey was well acquainted with Persian and Bengalee, from public documents, which were as open to Mr. Macaulay as to himself, and which Mr. Macaulay ought to have read, before asserting, in his trenchant manner, that Sir Elijah was ignorant of the official language of the country, and of Hindustanee. Mr. Bogle, the gentleman who had travelled into Bootan, and as respectable and as trustworthy a witness as any one of the hundreds who were examined in the whole course of these India proceedings, affirmed that Sir Elijah spoke both Bengalee and Persian with considerable fluency; and other evidence to the same effect, will be found in every printed account of Hastings's trial. If Mr. Macaulay had chosen to examine things not quite so public, but still very accessible—the "Bengal Consultations" in the India House—he would have discovered that Sir Elijah knew the Persian language. Mr. Macaulay sneers at an author far better informed than himself for having mentioned the Bengalee language; which he says, in his smart manner, is of no more use in Oude, than Portuguese is in Switzerland. This last assertion, will hardly stand the test of truth; since the Hindustanee, which is spoken in Oude, and a great many other parts of India; and the Bengalee, which is spoken in the lower provinces, are cognate dialects. But there is reservation and suppression, unfairness or ignorance, in the sentence which conveys this sneer. The mass of the affidavits that were not in English were in Persian; and, therefore, a knowledge of Persian was quite enough to have enabled the Chief Justice to read most of the affidavits given in at Lucknow, if he had thought it necessary so to do. I have been favoured with a communication, confirmatory of this assertion, by a gentleman high in the Company's civil service, who was attached to the political department in the Governor General's office at Calcutta, in Lord Wellesley's time, who afterwards held a very responsible situation under the Marquis of Hastings, and was associated with the Hon. Henry Wellesley, now Lord Cowley, in a commission to settle the territory ceded by the Nabob vizier to the British Government in 1805-6. He acted on that occasion as *interpreter* to the commissioners for enclosing the northern district of the province of Oude, and was long resident at Lucknow for that purpose. A more competent authority upon the point in question could hardly be found. This gentleman says :—" In *verbal* negotiations, sometimes the Hindustanee, and sometimes the Persian, is used, at the option of the parties. Nobles and learned men prefer the latter. The poorer and uneducated classes use the Hindustanee from necessity. It is difficult to write or decipher the Hindustanee, which is in what is called the Nagree character; *nor is it ever done,* except on very rare occasions. But whatever is spoken in Hindustanee in courts of justice, or the like, is instantly *translated* and recorded in the *Persian* language and character. When I was interpreter for the enclosing commission in the upper provinces, the commissioners for settling Cuttack met Lord Hastings at Lucknow, and all their *personal* intercourse was carried on in Hindustanee with the chiefs, rajahs, &c. But, on the other hand, all matters of *Record* and written correspondence were conducted in the *Persian* language."

But, as Sir Elijah himself avowed, he did not read the affidavits, and never considered that he was bound to read them, this dispute about his philological attainments is of little consequence, except as showing the unvarying spirit of ignorance and unfairness with which all parts of his conduct have been held up to obloquy. The Persian is the diplomatic, official, and documental language of all Hindustan ; and, as was proved, and particularly pointed out by Lord Thurlow, and by the Bishop of Rochester (Dr. Horsley), on Mr. Hastings's trial, the greatest part of the affidavits were in Persian and in English. These affidavits, moreover, bore the signatures of the most respectable men, both native and European, in that province ; including the names of several English officers who were in the service of the Nabob of Oude ; and who, like the natives, deposed that the whole country had been in a state of revolt, and that the insurgent Cheyte Sing had been supplied with funds by the Begums.

After the business of the affidavits was finished, the Chief Justice returned to Calcutta with his wife and attendants, travelling leisurely, though not quite so slowly, as he had done from that capital to Lucknow. He was thanked by the members of the Supreme Council, and by nearly every Englishman in Calcutta, for the trouble he had incurred. And so far were the members of Council from expressing any disapprobation of what Hastings had done at Lucknow, at Benares, or at Chunar, that they drew up and presented to him a warm congratulatory address. Hastings gave a duplicate of this flattering paper to my father, who carefully preserved it among his other vouchers. Perhaps more

has been said than was requisite to meet an accusation
so essentially frivolous. It appears, indeed, to have been
originally advanced for no other purpose than to multiply the articles of impeachment moved by Sir Gilbert
Elliot ;* and it is worthy of observation, that the hostile
committee of the Commons resorted to the same expedient, in swelling the charge relative to the extension,
as it is called, of the Court's jurisdiction, into three articles instead of one, viz. "the Patna," "the Cossijurah,"
and " the Extension of Jurisdiction charges ;" the latter
clearly comprehending within itself the two former
articles.

* Throughout Chap. V. for " Eliot" read " Elliot."

CHAPTER X.

MR. FRANCIS arrived in England in the summer of 1781.
From that period the hostilities against the Governor
General, and against the Chief Justice, who has ever
been most unfairly and absurdly coupled with him, were
carried on with far greater heat, and with more intensity
of purpose than ever. Political circumstances soon
occurred which gave an all-commanding power to Mr.
Burke, who had been long the distant acquaintance and
correspondent, but was now the close associate of Philip
Francis. These attacks had been prepared by an insidious communication which Francis had carried on,
during his residence in India, with various political
allies, and principally with Edmund Burke, through
the medium of his relative, William Burke, who had resided in India most part of the time employed in these
transactions.

I have cursorily stated in a preceding page, that these
gentlemen had been acquainted with each other before
Mr. Francis left England for the east : the fact is corroborated by some recently published correspondence of
the great parliamentary orator. On Wednesday, the
29th of October, 1773, Burke, writing from Beaconsfield to the Marquess of Rockingham, says,—

"Francis will be here, by appointment, to-day. I shall
wait no longer than his return, which will be to-morrow,
Thursday morning, when I hope to receive your Lordship's

commands at Grosvenor Square. I find that this Mr. Francis is entirely in the interests of Lord Clive." *

The man, thus thought to have been so entirely in the interests of the great Clive, whose services were rewarded in England by defamation, and threats of impeachment, had now returned home, nearly eight years after this visit at Beaconsfield, with the fixed determination to bring about the impeachment of the equally great, and no less injured Warren Hastings ! To this end, he united himself most intimately with Burke, whose passions had already been inflamed against the Governor General, and whose grand object at this time was, to annihilate the political existence of the East India Company, and to transfer its immense patronage to that home Government, in which, through the Rockingham party, Mr. Francis had every prospect of soon obtaining an eminent place. By that interest he shortly after obtained a seat in Parliament ; where, first as member and prompter of the Committee which drew up the report, and afterwards as witness in Sir Gilbert Elliot's accusation, he gave evidence against my father in his place in the House of Commons.

Francis, though professing an exclusive adherence to Burke and Fox, courted both sides of the incongruous coalition ministry. He endeavoured to ingratiate himself with Lord North, by means of his lordship's secretary, Mr. Brummell;† he beset Lord North's house, and would have crawled up its back stairs; but he found no opening there. The following private letter was written by Mr. Barwell shortly after his return to England, and addressed to Mr. Hastings in Calcutta.

"Ormond Street, Feb. 1, 1782.

" It is with pleasure I inform you that Francis daily loses ground. The petulance and captiousness of his character have totally sunk him in the opinion of the Directors, and his manners have caused that disgust which breaks forth into reproach whenever his name is mentioned. Your friend, Mr. Sullivan, has, with infinite ability, defeated him in his attempt on the direction, and his impatience under it has com-

* Correspondence of the Right Honourable Edmund Burke, between the year 1744, and the period of his decease, in 1797. Edited by Charles William, Earl Fitzwilliam, and Lieut. General Sir Richard Bourke, K.C.B. In four volumes. London : 1844. Vol. I. p. 446.
† Father of the late Beau Brummell.

pleted the business. Just after Francis's arrival, he gave out how well he had been received, and how much distinguished by Lord North. Within six weeks of the promulgation of this puff, I had the satisfaction of detecting him; for upon questioning Mr. Brummell, his lordship's secretary, he laughed, and observed, Mr. Francis had been at Bushy once, and from that period to this had never repeated his visit to Lord North. Lord Mansfield positively declined his first visit, and I do not find that any one of the King's Ministers hold any intercourse with him. Thus circumstanced, he no longer exults, but, chagrined and mortified, complains in bitterness of spirit, and prophecies the loss of India under any government but his own. For God's sake keep on good terms with Impey. I fear much his appointment will be abolished, and that the abolition may be followed by some very disagreeable and harsh measure. I cannot, however, adopt the opinion that they will be able to effect his removal. I have written to him pretty much at large upon this point, and refer you to him. Intelligence from your government of the good that has resulted from placing Impey at the head of the dewannee courts has been of more service to you in the public opinion than anything your friends can urge in vindication, without such avowedly good and solid grounds. It is fit that you should both know your friends as well as those who by proper explanations my be conciliated to your interests. My old acquaintance, the Archbishop of York (Markham), called upon me two days ago with a letter from his son : regarded as a composition, it was elegant ; as the effusion of a heart overflowing with gratitude and honest indignation, matchless. The old man was in rapture, and dwelt upon it with that sedate dignity which marks his character and commands respect. Barber is a warm friend, Pechell and Calliaud merit a diamond statue from you both. Boughton Rous is shuffling, and worth nought. Macpherson Fingall ought to be cultivated. Harrison and old Savage, Directors, may be all you wish by a polite letter. Secretary Robinson is open to conviction. Thurlow, Dunning, Dempster, I need hardly mention as fast friends, and powerful supporters of Sir Elijah Impey. I have thus grouped a number of men who are, have been, or may be useful to you and to our mutual friend.

"I remain,

"Most affectionately and sincerely,

"RICHARD BARWELL."*

* I gladly take this opportunity of acknowledging my obligation to the executors and representatives of Mrs. Hastings, in allowing me to copy this letter from the original, which is preserved among the papers in their

To the great orator and statesman, with whom he became thus closely connected, I impute no unworthy motive; but I believe Mr. Burke to have been inspired with a more than ordinary love of power and influence ; to have been resolutely bent on the subversion of the Company's Charter, and to have conscientiously believed that the native population of India would be better governed by his Majesty's Ministers than by an association of merchants and shareholders. It was, therefore, in conformity with his views, or, as a modification of his plan, that, in 1783, about two years after the return of Francis, that Mr. Fox's India Bill was brought before Parliament. That unfortunate bill, indeed, although it bore the name of Fox, was well known to have been almost entirely the production of Edmund Burke, not unassisted, as, I believe, by Philip Francis. In addition to the personal hatred which he bore to Hastings and my father, the prompter and promoter of all these movements was impelled, by the ambitious hope, if not of immediately succeeding Mr. Hastings in his post, of becoming, sooner or later, Governor General of India.   From the Company he had little to expect ; but, should his political friends secure themselves in the Cabinet, he speculated, perhaps not altogether unfeasibly, on a chance of that promotion. This was no transient scheme, or short-lived expectation. May it not even have entered into the heart of Francis, when he fought the duel in 1780 ? Will it not be remembered that Francis was the challenger on that occasion ? That he was then senior Member of Council ? and that, had Mr. Hastings fallen, the survivor, Mr. Francis, for a season, at least, would have occupied the post to which he so ardently aspired ?   That catastrophe, most happily, never took place, and Fox's India Bill was overthrown ; and not only overthrown,—politically speaking, no less fortunately,—but so universally reprobated, that it ruined and broke up the coalition.

Yet Francis was far from abandoning his lofty pretensions.   The hope of becoming Governor Ge-

possession at Daylesford House. It has never been published before, but was returned to the family by Mr. Gleig, who has omitted it in his Memoir, probably because he considered it unnecessary to his subject. To mine it is essential.

neral deluded him almost to the last of his political career.*

I have already noticed the activity with which the English press, at this epoch, laboured under the auspices of a domineering party. Immediately after the return of Francis from India, there was a fresh issue of pamphlets, levelled at almost every proceeding which had taken place in India during the political and legal administration of Mr. Hastings and my father. I have already mentioned the anonymous pamphlet in the library of the British Museum, entitled, " Extract of an original Letter from Calcutta, relative to the Administration of Justice by Sir Elijah Impey. London : Printed for Debret, 1781." The introduction states that the letter was not intended for publication ; but that it *would be injurious to suppress it at a time " when the administration of justice in Bengal is coming under the review of Parliament."* The letter itself is dated December 1st, 1780, and professes to be written by "a perfectly impartial writer." At page 12 of this pamphlet I find these words :—

" The legal murder of Nuncomar, as it is pointedly called by the great and good Lord Mansfield, showed every person in Bengal what he was to expect."

The whole pamphlet, like many others which followed it, is a laboured calumny upon the character and judicial conduct of Sir Elijah Impey ; and written, though with great plausibility, without any attention to truth, or even decency. It was precisely such a letter as Junius might have written for the *Public Advertiser*. At the conclusion is the following postscript :—

" In looking over what I have written, I find I have been more severe on the judges than I intended. Whatever may be thought by passionate men, or said by others, it is not true that there is no mixture of good in the character of these gentlemen. The Chief Justice is, undoubtedly, a man of ability. He is punctual in his attendance in the court, and despatches the common business with great readiness. Mr.

* See "Lord Brougham's Sketches of Statesmen of the time of George III."

Hyde is slow and formal, but it is thought he does not mean to do wrong; and he is suspected of no other bias on his judgment than what naturally arises from real prejudices, and very real obstinacy. Sir Robert Chambers is thought to have more learning, and better intentions, though less vigour than the Chief Justice."

All this ostentatious display of candour, coupled with the author's concealment of his name, the description of himself and his correspondent, the classical malignity of the motto, the coincidence of the date with Mr. Francis's departure from India, conspire to fix the authorship upon him.

The probability is as great that the *"person of station,"* to whom the letter is addressed, was no other that Mr. Burke; as it seems to have furnished the great orator, among many other unwarrantable expressions, with that to which he gave utterance on Mr. Hasting's trial, on the 27th of April, 1788, and for which he incurred the censure of the House of Commons, six days after, on a motion made by the Marquis of Graham, and carried by a majority of more than two to one, the numbers being 135 to 66. The same words had been traced by my father in his defence, two months before, to this book and another I shall presently quote, and for those words the publisher, Debret, was prosecuted by the Attorney General in the same year.

This virulent pamphlet was soon followed by others in the same spirit. In the course of 1782, the year after Francis's return, there appeared a work in two octavo volumes, entitled, " Travels in Europe, Asia, and Africa: describing Characters, Customs, Manners, Laws, and Productions of Nature and Art : containing various remarks on the Political Interests of Great Britain, and delineating in particular a New System for the Government and Improvement of the British Settlements in the East Indies: begun in the year 1777 and finished in 1781." Like the letter attributed to Sheriff Macrabie, Francis's brother-in-law—of which much has already been said, and more will be said hereafter—this book of Travels, in the form of letters, bears internal evidence of having been, if not written, at least revised and augmented by Francis himself, though it passed under the name of Macintosh.

"The name of Macintosh," says the author of "Our Indian Empire," "is clearly a *nom de guerre*. If such an individual had existed, and if he had been capable of writing so well, without assistance, he would have been heard of again; and he could scarcely have failed, in that day, when good writers were far from numerous, of attaining to celebrity. No such Macintosh was ever heard of after the publication of the book. The writer of that book shuns all the subjects in which Philip Francis was awkwardly implicated during his residence at Calcutta; for example, he says not a syllable about Monsieur and Madame Le Grand, and the crim. con. trial, at which Sir Elijah Impey presided—and he dwells most emphatically upon all those subjects and projects which Francis held to be honourable to himself, as member of the Council, and opponent of Hastings; he applauds all those individuals who took part with Francis, and he condemns, with all the virulence of Junius, those who took part with Hastings. His attack on the Chief Justice is more guarded; and it is worthy of remark, that, though he gives the name in full length of Sir Robert Chambers, and the initials of the two other judges, and of many other functionaries, he gives neither the name, nor so much as the initials, of Sir Elijah Impey. The whole story of the trial and execution of Nuncomar is related very briefly. This looks like the performance of a man who was laying a foundation for future calumnies. Instead of the elaborate account of the execution contained in Macrabie's letter, we have here but one short sentence:—'He [Nuncomar] was found guilty, condemned to be hanged, and was publicly executed, within a few paces of Fort William, to the utter astonishment and terror of all Hindostan!' Short as the account is, it contains, nevertheless, the germ of nearly every slander and misstatement that was afterwards introduced into Sir Gilbert Elliot's speech, and the charges against Sir Elijah Impey. Yet this account makes two of the judges as guilty as the Chief Justice, and exonerates only Sir Robert Chambers in the affair of Nuncomar. It says, 'All the bench, except Sir Robert Chambers, declared that he was amenable to that law.'

"But Sir Robert Chambers, as we have said—and, as it is proved, by abundant evidence—never doubted that the Rajah was amenable to the law of England; never did anything more than offer a suggestion that he should be tried under the statute of Queen Elizabeth, which was milder, indeed, but which was clearly repealed and obsolete. Chambers concurred in the sentence which Impey pronounced, merely as the organ of the Court. If, therefore, there was guilt or error, it was incurred by all the bench, and by Chambers, just as much as by Impey."

There was, indeed, no exception to be made in favour of Sir Robert Chambers with respect to the trial and condemnation of the Rajah, although, as the reader will remember, Chambers would have dealt more leniently with the purse of Francis on his trial for criminal conversation ; and it has always appeared to me, that it was for this consideration, and, perhaps, also to avoid the charge of an indiscriminate severity, that Francis always spoke of Sir Robert Chambers with palpable partiality. It seems that " Macintosh's Travels," as the work was called, obtained a wide circulation ; and, for a time, considerably biassed the public mind. This impression being once created, no efforts were spared by Francis and his party to confirm and deepen it. Hastings had many enemies at the East India House ; and my father but few personal and influential friends in Parliament. With Leadenhall Street he had no connection whatever.

Between the appearance of Francis's pamphlet, in 1781, and of the so-called " Macintosh's Travels," dated the following year, the question of Sir Elijah Impey's acceptance of the Sudder Dewannee Adaulut,* which he and the Governor General had frankly and openly announced, was brought under discussion by the Court of Directors. They had, at first, expressed their unqualified approbation of the measure ; that is to say, so long as they understood the appointment to have been accepted—as it had been—*without the salary.* But at the close of 1781, six months after the return of Francis from the East, taking umbrage at *his* report of the acceptance of a salary, the Directors resorted to legal advice. The counsel they consulted were Dunning, Wallace, and James, afterwards Sir James Mansfield, to whom they applied, through Mr. Smith, the chairman of their select committee, in the following form :—

" The Court of Directors request that you will consider

---

* I write these words as they are usually spelt in Parliamentary reports ; but the right orthography, according to Sir William Jones, is Sedr Diwanei Adálet, which means the Supreme Court of Civil Judicature annexed to the *office of Divan.* See " Correspondence of the Right Honourable Edmund Burke." Vol. II., p. 458.

the Act of Parliament of the 13th of George III., cap. 6$\frac{3}{4}$, 63
and the several minutes and arguments of the Governor General and Council upon the occasion of appointing the Chief
Justice to be Judge of the Court of Sudder Dewanny
Adawlut, and, upon the whole, to advise them.

"Question. Whether the appointment of the Chief Justice to be Judge of the Sudder Dewanny Adawlut, and giving
him a salary to that office, besides the salary he is entitled to
as Chief Justice, was illegal, either as being contrary to the
said Act of 13 George III., cap. 6$\frac{3}{4}$, or incompatible with his 63
duty as Chief Justice of the Supreme Court? and whether
he may be continued Judge of the Sudder Dewanny Adawlut,
consistent with the Act of 21 George III., cap. 70, sec. 21?"

To this the three eminent lawyers replied:

"Answer. The appointment of the Chief Justice to the
office of Judge of the Sudder Dewanny Adawlut, and giving
him a salary, besides what he is entitled to as Chief Justice,
does not appear to us to be illegal, either as being contrary
to the 13th George III., or incompatible with his duty as
Chief Justice. Nor do we see anything in the Act 21 George
III. which affects this question.

"(Signed)   "J. Dunning.
"Jas. Wallace.
"Jas. Mansfield.

"Lincoln's-inn, 19th Dec., 1781."*

Mr. Mansfield, three days after he had subscribed to
this opinion, retracts it in the following note, addressed
to the Chairman of the Select Committee :—

"The Solicitor General presents his compliments to Mr.
Smith, and having considered farther the question relating to
the late appointment of Sir Elijah Impey since he subscribed
the opinion upon it, he encloses to Mr. Smith his present
ideas upon the subject, which he wishes to be laid before
those to whom his former opinion is communicated.

"Since I gave my opinion on the question relating to the
appointment of Sir Elijah Impey to the office of the Judge
of the Sudder Dewanny Adawlut, great doubts have occurred
to me on the question; and, although there is no particular
provision in the statute of the 13th George III., cap. 63,
which seems to have been intended to prohibit any of the
judges of the Supreme Court from accepting such an office,
yet it is by no means clear to me, that the acceptance of such

---

* Extract from the first Report of the Select Committee on the Administration of Justice in India.

an office, *with a salary, or other profit annexed to it,* is not forbidden and rendered illegal by that law. The great object of that law was to erect a court which might more effectually control the British subjects within its jurisdiction than any former judicature had done. The judges who composed it were to be named by the King, and their salaries are fixed by the statute. They do not, in any respect, depend on the India Company, except that the Company are to pay the salaries. To give effect to the Court of Judicature, it seems to be necessary that the judges should be, as far as possible, independent of the servants of the Company. I therefore doubt, whether the acceptance of such an office, *with a salary,* especially to be held at the pleasure of the Governor and Council, be not contrary to the spirit and principle intention of the statute. If it be so, it may, perhaps, not be thought a great stretch of construction to consider the acceptance of the office, *with the salary,* as forbidden by that part of the 23rd section which prohibits the judges to accept any reward, &c. But my doubts would have been the same from the general principle and object of the statute, if the words of that section could not be supposed to extend to this case. I have not been able to get the better of these doubts, although I have been very desirous of doing it, from the great respect I have for the opinions of those gentlemen with whom I lately concurred, and whose judgment ought to have had much more weight and authority than mine.

" J. MANSFIELD.

" Temple, Dec. 22, 1781.*"

Mr. Rous, the Company's standing counsel, also objected to the appointment, *with the salary,* on the plea, however, not of law, but of mere expediency. Like Mr. Mansfield, Mr. Rous had been led to believe that Sir Elijah had not only accepted the salary, but had received it together with other emoluments. Francis, who best knew the contrary, inculcated this belief, not only among lawyers and directors, but also in Parliament, and in general society. Yet the Court of Directors had broadly asserted, in a " memorandum," registered and preserved among their numerous " Bengal Consultations," in Leadenhall Street, that—

" It could hardly have been expected that the Chief Justice should give up his few hours of relaxation, and enter on a fresh scene of labour and perplexity without compensation.

---

* Idem.

The offer of a salary was at once a necessary and a judicious sacrifice; but the property of the Company has by no means been wantonly lavished. £8,000 bore no proportion to the sums which must eventually be saved. Perhaps they were ten times the amount; *and of this salary we are yet to learn that a single shilling has ever been received, though the appointment was passed* in Council in October, 1780. . . . Whatever plan might be adopted for the better arrangement of the judicial office in Bengal, it may be affirmed, that considerable advantage will still be derived from the professional assistance afforded by the Chief Justice to the Sudder Dewannee Adaulut. *His regulations and instructions (for he has already proposed many) will probably continue the standard of practice; his decisions will be firm precedents for future judges, and his example stamp respectability on the office. No weak, indolent, or undignified character, will readily find admission into the vacant seat of Sir Elijah Impey.*"*

It appears likely, notwithstanding the efforts made by the enemies of the Governor General and the Chief Justice, that the Court of Directors would have continued to act in conformity with the opinions here expressed, if Lord North's administration had continued to exist, or if Mr. Burke and his friends had not come into office. But the miserable termination of the American war, by Lord Cornwallis's surrender, at York Town, caused the overthrow of that administration, on the 19th of March, 1782. Then followed the last short ministry of the Marquess of Rockingham; which, at the desire of his Majesty, George III., was arranged by the Earl of Shelburne. In this disunited cabinet Mr. Burke not only obtained a seat, but through his unbounded influence over the mind of the Marquess, became, in a manner, the master of his noble patron, and the sub-Prime Minister of England.

To him especially was committed, as if by the tacit consent of both sections of the new administration, the whole control and management of Indian affairs; and, to this preponderance of the Rockingham over the Shelburne party, at that juncture, I attribute the

* Extract from MSS. in the Clerk's Office, in the India House, entituled " Miscellaneous," p. 533, B. 447. "Memorandum on the Judicial Establishment of India, vindicatory of Mr. Hastings and Sir Elijah Impey."

recall of my father from Calcutta. In this business
the Court of Directors, of course, had not been consulted ; and, therefore, had not much to do, beyond
giving some colour to its equity, by yielding to the
false impressions made upon their minds, in opposition
to their former resolution, relative to the Sudder
Dewannee Adaulut. But this was not the first time
that the Directors of the Honourable East India
Company had exhibited a want of steadiness in their
opinion of men and measures. A few weeks *before*
the resignation of Lord North, they negatived a motion
for removing Sir Elijah Impey from the office of Judge
of their Adaulut. A few weeks *after* the formation of
the Rockingham and Shelburne Administration, they
did the very opposite to this, voting, on the 30th of
April, that the Governor General should be written to,
and the Chief Justice removed from the said office on
the receipt of their letter.*

This decision only went to deprive my father of the
laborious and *unpaid* presidency of their court of appeal, which was a relief, rather than a deprivation.
But Mr. Burke, who had, by this time, deeply imbibed
all the prejudices of his informer, was not disposed to
rest satisfied with this simple measure. Francis had
openly declared, as well in India, as in England, that
he would bring about my father's recall ; and, to this
object, he and his party applied themselves with the
greatest ardour and activity.

On the 3rd of May, 1782, three days after the vote
of the Court of Directors, an address to the King was
carried in the House of Commons, for the immediate
recall of Sir Elijah Impey, to answer the charge " of
having accepted an office not agreeable to the true intent and meaning of the Act 13 George III." On the
24th of June following, notice of motion was given
in the House of Commons, for a *censure* upon Mr.
Chambers, for having accepted the office of Company's
Chief Justice at Chinsurah. But General Smith, who
had given notice of 'this motion, thought proper to
postpone it until the next session. The next session

* See " Bengal Consultations" in the India House, and the " First
Report of Select Committee" in Parliamentary Reports.

came, and was allowed to elapse without any such motion being made; and thus Mr. Justice Chambers was not even so much as censured, though the Chief Justice was recalled. This cannot but appear strange, until accounted for; and the solution of the mystery is this : General Richard Smith had, in the interim, become not only the political friend and ally of Francis, but chairman of the committees of the House of Commons, which drew up the charges of accusation against Sir Elijah Impey.

A large salary, variously stated from £3,000 to £5,000 per annum, was attached to the office which Chambers accepted from the Company ; and afterwards, upon resigning this Chinsurah judgeship, he accepted the superintendence of the police, with another salary, which he enjoyed so long as he remained in India. Mr. Justice Hyde, another of my father's assessors, was allowed to unite to his office of puisne judge in the Supreme Court that of another judgeship, and to receive another salary from the Company. Yet, as far as I have been able to discover, after the faint attempt to obtain the vote of censure upon Justice Chambers in the House of Commons, neither their conduct nor their motives were ever publicly called in question ; and far—very far—be it from me to question them ! They were both able and upright men, fully borne out by the Act, to accept from the India Company an adequate remuneration for the additional offices of *" real business"* which they had undertaken, and had every right to undertake.

Two months and five days elapsed ere the Secretary of State wrote—reluctantly, as I may presume—his letter of recall to my father. But great political changes had occurred during that interval. At the time when his lordship's letter was indited, the Earl of Shelburne had virtually become Prime Minister ; for the Marquess of Rockingham, the late nominal head of the Government, died just one week before the date of the letter of recall, viz., on the 1st of July, 1782. Lord Shelburne, notwithstanding the opposition of the Rockinghamites, with Mr. Burke at their head, almost immediately succeeded him ; but, in the meantime, being thwarted and embarrassed in all his measures, by that fierce faction,

he could no longer command a majority in the House
of Commons, especially upon Indian affairs. His lordship, therefore, about seven days before he was declared
First Lord of the Treasury, in his official capacity as
Secretary of State, set his hand to the letter which
recalled my father from Bengal. Many months, however, before Sir Elijah Impey could reach England, the
violent party which procured the address against him,
had first displaced the Earl of Shelburne, and afterwards caused the coalition of Lord North and Mr. Fox.
Full half a year before my father's arrival, this most
unpopular coalition had been defeated in its turn, and
was succeeded by the first administration of Mr. Pitt.
The immediate cause of the dissolution and disgrace of
the coalition ministry was, as I have stated, that India
Bill, which bore the name of Fox, but which, there is
now good reason to believe, was almost entirely the
composition of Edmund Burke. Thus, before they began
the patriotic work of ruining others, these great orators
—for who will deny them that praise?—these mighty
champions had been themselves signally vanquished on
the hot and perilous field of Indian politics. Is it,
then, too much to surmise, that the recollection of that
defeat and humiliation may, possibly, have tended to
exasperate them against the Governor General and
Chief Justice? Yet, surely, such a lesson might have
taught them somewhat more forbearance.

After the formation of Mr. Pitt's first ministry,
much as they disagreed in other matters, the remnant
of this Rockingham party continued united upon the
great question of India. Closely leagued and banded
together against the great Governor General, they little
regarded the wisdom, determination, and unflinching
courage—they valued not the amazing fertility of resources, without which no British empire in the East
would have been left to debate upon. Still less, perhaps, did they give credit to that judicial knowledge,
steadiness, and impartiality, divested of which, the
most flourishing state sinks into a lawless anarchy.
Thus combined, they succeeded in effecting the impeachment, and almost total ruin, of Mr. Hastings; but
they utterly failed, as will presently be seen, in carrying the impeachment of Sir Elijah Impey. They per-

secuted both, but could convict neither. Hastings was *acquitted;* my father *was never impeached.* Yet, never was so much Parliamentary talent, so much eloquence, so much perseverance, united in one effort, and directed against two more innocent and comparatively helpless men.

And yet, of the more elevated and high-minded actors in this conspiracy, I must not be understood to complain with equal bitterness. One of them, indeed, it may be thought presumption in me to criticise at all; but I do no more than echo the opinion now almost universal, when, allowing for his liability to prejudice, I would fain acknowledge Mr. Burke to have been a conscientious as well as an able statesman, a writer, and a declamer, no less impressed with the truth of what he uttered, than he impressed others by means of the liveliness of his fancy, and the depth of his erudition. Many of his colleagues may have been alike sincere. Most of them were men of rare talent and acquirement. But of Mr. Francis, whatever may have been his abilities, I cannot speak in milder terms than, that he was treacherous, uncandid, cruel, and unchristian. Ever concentrating within himself the venom of his own Junius, he crept, like the poisoner in the tragedy, to whomsoever of them he found slumbering—

"And in the porches of his ear he pour'd
The leperous distilment;"

and there it rankled, working the eager temperament of Burke into a phrenzy—festering at the heart of Fox —or flowing with noisome eloquence from the lips of Sheridan. Francis, I venture to add, was the archfiend who *became " a lying spirit " in the mouths of them all.*

CHAPTER XI.

BEFORE the letter from the Court of Directors to the
Governor General, ordering him to remove Sir Elijah
Impey from the Sudder Dewannee Adaulut, reached
Calcutta, news had arrived there that Mr. Francis,
having obtained entire possession of the ear of Edmund
Burke, was making a great stir in Parliament relative
to my father's appointment to that office.

On the 8th of August, the said letter from the Directors not having yet arrived, Sir Elijah addressed the
Governor General and Council, informing them, that
he had learned, from report, that that gentleman had
accused him, before a committee of the House of Commons, of an offence against the Regulating Act, by
having accepted, as a *compromise* with the Governor
General, the office of Judge of the Sudder Dewannee
Adaulut, *with a large salary*. In this letter to the Governor and Council, my father said—

" The acceptance of the salary, and not the office, I suppose to be charged as the crime. The Governor General and
Council are individually subjected to the same restrictions
with regard to emoluments, in the same clause of the Act,
and by the same words as the judges, yet two of the councillors (General Clavering and Colonel Monson), within a year

after the Act passed, and before they proceeded to Bengal, were appointed openly, by the East India Company, Commanders of the Forces in India, with considerable salaries. I could not imagine, after an office with a salary had been thus accepted by gentlemen, under the same restrictions as I am, with the knowledge of the King's Ministers, of the Parliament, and of the whole nation, that the acceptance of an office, with great trust and real business, could be deemed illegal in me; for I cannot conceive, if the statute prohibits a councillor from accepting an office with emoluments, that the appointment having been made publicly and notoriously, could alter the essence of the fact itself, and except it out of the law, though, as this passed not only without censure, but with the full acquiescence of his Majesty's Ministers, it was surely reasonable to infer that it was never esteemed to be within the Act. But, though I never entertained an idea of its being an offence against the Act, I *had scruples,* from other motives, against applying the salary to my own use, until the whole circumstances of the business should be perfectly known in England by those whose esteem for my character and conduct I was anxious to preserve, and by whose judgment I was resolved to be guided as to the *propriety* of retaining the emoluments of the office. With this resolve I apprised you by a letter dated the 4th of July, 1781. . . .
On the same principle, I had, *long before that letter to you,* and immediately after my acceptance *unconditionally,* in October, 1780, and *long before any salary had been proposed to be annexed to it,* informed the Lord High Chancellor of the appointment. Some time in January, 1781, it was communicated to me, by your secretary, that you had been pleased to annex a salary to the office. Of my resolution not to apply the salary to my own use, if it should be thought improper, I informed the Lord High Chancellor, and his Majesty's Attorney General, by letters, dated in April, 1781; and having, for that purpose, procured copies from your offices, of all your proceedings relative, as well to the provincial as to the Sudder Dewannee Adaulut, I forwarded them in the same letters to England. . . . . I wrote on the same subject to many of my friends. To his Majesty's Secretaries of State I did not write, because, as the whole of your proceedings must be transmitted to one of them, those among the rest *must have come officially before them,* and could not escape their notice, if they had given occasion for censure or doubt respecting the propriety of it. Now, as your proceedings in the course of this business would necessarily be subjected, not only to the East India Company, but to his Majesty's Ministers; and, as I had disclosed the whole to the

Lord Chancellor and his Majesty's Attorney-General, and, as the duties of the office were publicly performed, I must have known that this transaction could not possibly be kept a secret; from hence I trust a fair deduction may be made, that at least I did nothing that was criminal or clandestine.   Sir Robert Chambers having accepted from your honourable board the office of Chief Justice of Chinsurah, *with a salary annexed thereto*, will sufficiently evince that his opinion did not differ from mine with regard to the legality of the act. How far public utility weighed with me when I took charge of the office may be difficult of positive proof, as the chief evidence of it must rest in my own breast.   I will not, therefore, offer my own averments and assurances on the subject, as I cannot expect them to meet with the general credit which I am conscious they deserve.   I shall, for similar reasons, decline to say anything myself of the utility of the office, choosing rather to leave it to the attestation of others, and to the known effects of the appointment.   For, whether my having regulated the office, and discharged its duties, have or have not been attended with labour to myself, and good to the country, your honourable board have now full experience to determine, and to your candour I refer it for an impartial representation at home.

" If by *compromise* with the Governor General be meant any agreement, expressed or implied, of any kind whatsoever, that I should at all relax in any matter which had been, or was likely to be, contested between the Governor General and Council and the Supreme Court—which is the only sense I can put upon the word—I do most positively and solemnly deny the charge, and beg leave to refer to the recollection of the Governor General, whether I did not, in the course of conversations, when he talked of the expedience of the office being placed in my hands, explain to him that it was not to be expected *that my holding the office should, in the least, vary my conduct with regard to the differences of opinion entertained by the Governor General and Council and the Court ;* and whether he did not declare that no such thing was expected, and *expressed some dissatisfaction, that I had thought it necessary to use a caution of that nature.*   And to the judges I appeal, whether, in every case wherein such differences of opinion were involved, I have not, *since the appointment*, persisted in the same uniform language and conduct which I held *before the appointment*.   I had, indeed, both before and after, as soon as the subjects of the differences had been referred to England, as far as I could, consistently with what I thought the duties of my office of Chief Justice, to the utmost of my power, endeavoured to prevent all questions which might either revive the old, or furnish new matter of contention between the Governor General and Council and the Court, from coming to a public decision, that everything might remain in quiet, and with as little ferment as possible, till a remedy from home should be applied to the evil. But as this was the rule of my conduct, *as well before as since* the appointment, I can hardly think *this* is intended to be referred to by the pretended compromise."*

To this manly letter the Supreme Council returned a spirited answer. Hastings, as Governor General, and, as the only remaining member of the Board who created the office in the Sudder Dewannee Adaulut, averring, that if anything had been done therein contrary to the spirit and intention of the Regulating Act, he (Hastings) had unintentionally and unwillingly erred. The other members of the Board acquiesced in the prayer that Sir Elijah Impey would continue to discharge the duties of the office, being "fully satisfied, that whatever objections or doubts may have accrued relative to the legality or propriety of the appointment, are all superseded by its public utility." The letter inserted in the minutes of Council proceeds thus :—

" Speaking in the name of all, we have only to say, that we never wish to avoid censure where a measure of unprovided necessity secures the public tranquillity and advantage, *and where no hidden purposes could possibly have been intended.* The great object for the Company and the State was to preserve the judicial peace of these provinces, with as little deviation as possible from the constitutional law of the parent state, or from the local and original laws of this country. In your appointment to the Sudder Dewannee Adaulut this object has been attained beyond expectation, and the native subject has been supported in his rights and privileges amidst the jarring conflicts of opposite systems of jurisdiction; the inferior ministers of these opposite systems have been restrained, contrary to the opinion of some of the members of this government, from committing oppressions which they knew would find an ultimate appeal to one and the same judge. . . . . We have pointedly referred the Court of Directors to the code of regulations which you have established for the administration of the Sudder Dewannee Adaulut, and to the letters which have passed between us on this subject. It is on these only that the Court of Directors

* "Bengal Consultations" in India House.

can form their judgment of the alleged *compromise*, and we refer them to the Governor General's express minute on the subject."

In this minute Hastings most solemnly declared that he could never have dared to talk to Sir Elijah Impey of a *compromise* ; that, knowing him, as he did, there was no possibility of his entertaining a base suspicion of his character; and that his real motive, and all his motives for recommending that the office and the salary should be conferred on him, were contained in· the public reasons in which he supported the recommendation.   Hastings drew a startling picture—and one no less true than startling—of the miserable looseness, obscurity, and deficiency of the Regulating Act, which threw doubts on the legality of all the adauluts, which made men shrink from an undefined responsibility, and which defined nothing clearly.   He bore testimony to the courage and decision with which the Chief Justice had acted, and to the great public benefit derived from him to the inhabitants of the provinces.   That court of appeal had, under Sir Elijah Impey, become a blessing to the country, and a credit to the Government.

" I have had the satisfaction," said Hastings, "of hearing many who had laboured to dissuade me from proposing it, and who had dreaded the worst evils from it, avow their error, and attest the public benefits derived from it."

On the 15th of November, 1782, Sir Elijah Impey wrote another letter to the Governor General and Council.

" I thank you," said he, "for the testimony you give me of my conduct in the office of Judge of the Sudder Dewannee Adaulut, and, as public utility, at a particular crisis, induced me to accept it, I am much flattered, that, in your opinion, the objects of the appointment have been obtained, and now surrender, with great pleasure, into your hands, an office which I accepted with diffidence and anxiety, and which nothing, under the great responsibility with which I foresaw it would load me, but public motives, could have prevailed on me to undertake."

My father proceeded to state, that, during the time which had intervened between his last letter and their answer—the answer of the Council had been delayed "by the long illness of the Governor General and another member of the Board"—he had kept the Sudder Dewannee Court open by adjournments, but had decided no cause since the 14th of August. He then submitted that, as they had determined to exercise themselves the office transferred to them, whether it would not be proper for them to revise all the proceedings had in the Sudder Dewannee Adaulut, in order to reverse them or confirm them at their discretion. He modestly referred to the vast labours which he had undertaken, and offered to continue his advice and assistance to the Council which was now to regulate those courts of law. Lastly, my father said,

" Besides the regulations which I had compiled for the administration of justice in the adauluts, I had nearly finished a complete set of forms for every process, rule, order, entry, decree, execution, and full records, to be used as precedents in those courts. They now remain in the possession of Mr. Wilkins,* and I purposed to have them printed in an appendix to the Persian translation of the regulations. If completed, I apprehend they might tend much to the ease, accuracy, and uniformity of proceedings, and to the despatch of business."†

During the progress of all this laborious work, the Chief Justice had to attend to the increasing business of the Supreme Court; that increase of business being principally owing to the confidence of the natives in the purity of the judges, and the impartiality of the Court. The labour, as I have already said, aggravated by the enervating climate, had altogether been so severe, as to effect my father's health to such a degree, that, though he lived above thirty years after, I do not hesitate to trace the symptoms of his last illness to the effects of this mental application.

On the 16th of November, 1782, the day after writing the letter from which I have last quoted, Sir Elijah formally surrendered the charge of the Sudder

---

* Mr. Wilkins, afterwards Sir Charles, was at that time interpreter to the Council. He was celebrated for his knowledge of the Sanscrit language; and, on his return from India, became Persian translator to the Company, and was succeeded in that office by Nathaniel Brassey Halhed, Esq., the compiler of the Code of Gentoo laws, &c.

† Bengal Consultations.

Dewannee Adaulut; presenting, at the same time, a true copy of the accounts, made out by the accountant and treasurer of that court, during the very short time that it had been in actual operation under his presidency. That document has been given at full length in a preceding chapter. No farther comment is requisite; but I may, perhaps, be allowed, once more, to remind the reader, that the total receipts amounted to little more than £2,548, and that, of that sum, every rupee was paid into the Calcutta treasury.

On the 27th of January, 1783, more than two months after he had resigned the Sudder Dewannee Adaulut, Sir Elijah Impey received the letter of recall, which had been written by Lord Shelburne, on the 8th of July, 1782, pursuant to the vote and address of the House of Commons on the 3rd of May. The following is his Lordship's letter :—

" Whitehall, 8th July, 1782.

" Sir—I have the honour to transmit to you an address, laid before his Majesty, in consequence of a vote of the House of Commons, on the 3rd of May last, for the purpose of your recall. I am, in consequence thereof, to signify his Majesty's command, that you should take the earliest opportunity, consistent with the necessary arrangements of your affairs, to return to this kingdom, *for the purpose of answering to the charge specified* in the said address.

"I have the honour to be, &c. &c.,

"(Signed)   "SHELBURNE.

" To the Honourable Sir Elijah Impey,
Knight, &c. &c."

This letter clearly proves that Sir Elijah Impey was recalled to answer *one specific charge, and no more.* It is, therefore, of the highest importance, as affording documental evidence, to verify the statement which Sir Elijah made, six years afterwards, at the bar of the House of Commons, namely—that, though he was at that time accused of *six* separate articles of impeachment—beginning with the exaggerated Nuncomar charge—he was recalled to answer *only one,* and that one relating to facts which had occurred more than five years after the trial and execution of that notorious criminal, with which it had been attempted, nevertheless, by implication, to connect the cause of my father's recall, although he had been permitted, during those five years, to preside over the Supreme Court of Judicature in Bengal!

A proof, not altogether insignificant, of the manner in which public business was then transacted, is to be found in the fact that, though the official letter states the fact of having transmitted " the address," &c., no copy of that address was sent. Two days after the receipt of the noble secretary's letter, it was answered thus :—

" Fort William, Bengal,
" 29th January, 1783.

" My Lord,

" On the 27th instant I had the honour of receiving your Lordship's letter of the 8th of July last, signifying to me his Majesty's commands that I should take the earliest opportunity, consistent with the necessary arrangements of my affairs, to return to England, to answer a charge contained in an address of the House of Commons, which had been laid before his Majesty, in consequence of a vote of that house of the 3rd of May last, for the purpose of my recall.

" The votes of the 3rd of May were enclosed in the letter; but the address, though mentioned to have been transmitted, was not.

" I most humbly request your Lordship to assure his Majesty that I am deeply affected with gratitude for the great lenity with which he has been pleased to lay his commands upon me, and that I will not abuse his gracious indulgence by any unnecessary delay in the execution of them.

" But, besides the necessary arrangement of my affairs, the present state of the Bay of Bengal, since M. Suffrein has been master of it, is such as to render it extremely hazardous; and the distress I should suffer in leaving behind me my wife, who expects to be brought to bed in June, will, I hope, plead my excuse, if my departure from hence be protracted longer than it is my earnest wish to effect it.

" My anxiety in the meantime, lest I should appear remiss in paying that prompt obedience to his Majesty's commands, to which I am equally urged by duty and inclination, is the only apology I can make for taking the liberty of troubling your Lordship with this detail of my private and domestic concerns.

" This delay is exceedingly embarrassing to me, as every

hour I remain under a censure of the House of Commons unanswered, cannot but be highly painful to my feelings, aggravated as they are, under all circumstances, by any longer residence in this country.

" I have the honour to be,
" Your Lordship's most obedient,
" And very humble servant,
" E. IMPEY."

The cause of the delay continued : our national fleets were engaged elsewhere; and, for many months, the French remained masters of the Bay of Bengal; so that no British ship could safely leave the Hooghley for Europe. In a duplicate of his letter of the 29th of January, forwarded on the 11th of March following, Sir Elijah acknowledged having received the duplicate of Lord Shelburne's letter of recall, and took occasion to insert these words in the paragraph relative to the state of the Bay of Bengal since M. Suffrein had taken his station there, and since the absence of Sir Edward Hughes, who was employed, with his squadron, on the coast of Malabar :—

" The Hawke, East Indiaman, which brought your Lordship's letter, was chased into shoal water, near Sangur Island, at the entrance of the river, by two of the enemy's ships of war."

My father was thus compelled to remain, under no very enviable circumstances, for about nine months longer, in Calcutta, in order to escape capture by the enemy. In the meantime Admiral Sir Edward Hughes returned to his station in the Hooghley river. This was not till the accomplishment of Mr. Hastings's successful enterprise, in which our fleet had so bravely co-operated, and which ended in the final overthrow of Hyder Ali in the Carnatic.

On the 3rd of December, 1783, Sir Elijah embarked with his family on board the *Worcester*, after an absence of no less than nine years and eight months from his native country. His departure from Calcutta was witnessed with regret not only by his brethren on the bench, and by the Governor General and Council, but by all classes of the community, native and European, free merchants as well as the stipendiary servants of the Company. By his firmness, impartiality, and courage, as a judge, Calcutta had been tranquilized when a civil war seemed all but inevitable; the distractions in the government had been composed, powerful criminals had been brought to justice, the weak had been protected against the strong, the tax-payers against the extortions of the iron-handed collector. As a private individual he had spent his money freely in the country; exercising a liberal hospitality, assisting the suffering poor, and contributing with great generosity to every fund intended for the improvement of their condition. My father never resided for any length of time in any one place without making himself beloved in the neighbourhood. Among the natives of Calcutta and its vicinity, where he spent so many of the prime years of his life, he was exceedingly popular; nor had the pleasant recollection of him faded away many years after his departure.

In public addresses, and in other less ceremonious forms, Sir Elijah brought away with him many testimonials of regard and affection, and left behind him more than one memorial, publicly voted, to preserve the remembrance of his fame and person among the wealthier inhabitants of Bengal. When my eldest surviving brother, now Rear Admiral in Her Majesty's service, made his first voyage to Calcutta, in the same ship and with the same captain who brought my father home, he was treated by people of all ranks with the marked respect due to the son of a dignified and distinguished man. And in my own recollection, and that of my youngest brother, who for twenty years resided in India, there have lived, and are still living, many old and valuable servants of the Company, who began their career in India but a few years before or after Sir Elijah's retirement, who have been known to declare, that they never heard his name mentioned at Calcutta, or up the country, without some expression of reverence or esteem.

Yet Mr. Macaulay, persevering in his mis-statements to the last, sends my father on his homeward voyage, with the remark that he was " stripped of that robe which has never since the revolution been disgraced so foully as by him."

T

Thus it is, that the fame and fortune of public men are too often sacrificed to the prejudice of some prevailing faction,—while their errors are exaggerated, their merits overlooked, their services vilified and unrequited. Nor is it enough to have passed alive through this fiery ordeal of persecution; but even their memory must endure a second tyranny; a tyranny which despoils the good man of his fairest monument, and his descendants of their best inheritance—an honest name; a tyranny which, raking up the ashes of an extinguished party, lights up the evil passions of another generation, and scatters its firebrands into the " valley of the shadow of death ! "

At my time of life, and with the principles which were inculcated in my youth, by a virtuous and accomplished father, in conformity with which I have endeavoured to act, no provocation short of that which I have received, could have dragged me into the field of controversy, or impelled me to the utterance of any offensive personality. Sixty-six years and more have I lived, in peace and charity with mankind; and if now I have become a controversialist, it is for the first time; if now I seek publicity, it is with reluctance, and from no presumption; if now I have betrayed any heat, the flame has been kindled by reverence for the best of fathers, and by indignation at the insolence of his defamer. And here I bid farewell to Mr. Macaulay, I trust for ever, leaving him to reflect upon the plain truths, and irrefragable documents now laid before him, and to settle with his own heart and conscience whether he ought not to retract his calumnies as publicly as *he has promulgated them.* But the right honourable reviewer is a classical scholar, and will comprehend how I am warned by Cicero, not to expect much, or, indeed, anything, from such an adversary, in the way of candid confession, or ingenuous reparation.

Plerique errare malunt, eamque sententiam, quam adamaverunt, pugnacissimè defendere, quàm, sine pertinaciâ, quod constantissimè dicatur, exquirere.

CHAPTER XII.

─────

THE *Worcester*, in which Sir Elijah Impey embarked
with his family and suite, had sprung a leak, and very
narrowly escaped shipwreck off St. Helena.   Her Captain—Cook—had died on board during the passage;
and the first mate, a young and inexperienced officer,
had so completely lost his reckoning, as to come close
upon the Island without being aware of it : the leaky
vessel was with some difficulty saved from running upon
a lee shore.   We landed however in safety, and were
hospitably entertained by the Governor of the Island.
    The *Dutton*, East Indiaman, making the homeward
voyage, reached St. Helena nearly at the time of our
landing.   The *Dutton* had for some years been the
favourite India passage-ship; her commander, Captain
James West, had the just reputation of being a first-
rate mariner, a well-informed, and thoroughly practical
man of business, and in every way worthy of confidential intimacy.   My father, sharing in the general
preference, resolved to re-embark not in the *Worcester*,
but in the *Dutton*.   This proved to be in all respects
a very fortunate decision.   The remainder of the voyage
was pleasant, and unattended by any danger. It was, of
course, my first sea voyage.   I was then about four

years old, and can distinctly recollect some few "portents
of my travel's history." The ordinary business aboard;
the occasional bustle; the hailing of a vessel; or capture of a shark; and, above all, the sensation so likely
to strike a child, on being surrounded by a world of
waters, seem to have rooted themselves in my memory.
But I can also well remember how soon my father contracted a friendship for the captain, and how great a
favourite he was with all the officers, sailors, and passengers on board. To what a degree a long sea voyage
and close confinement on ship-board are a test of
good temper, has passed into a proverb. This mutual
good feeling, so accidentally begun, terminated in
a friendship for life, between my father and Mr. West.
After the sea service, in which he made a handsome
fortune, that gentleman was happily prevailed on to become the constant inmate of our family. This continued until the year 1801, when he married. As a
man of business, he rendered many services to my
father, and after my father's death, to his children.
He was one of the executors to his will, in which trust
he was associated with Mr. Hastings, and Charles
Litchfield, Esq., the late eminent barrister and solicitor
to the Treasury. In mentioning facts like these, I may
surely be excused, not only by my desire to bestow this
grateful tribute on the memory of a friend, long since
deceased, but likewise, by my anxiety to enable the
reader more clearly to appreciate my father's real character—his lasting friendships—his amiable and strongly
attaching qualities.

The voyage from St. Helena must have been drawing
towards its close, when I witnessed a little domestic
scene on board the *Dutton*, which is embalmed in my
memory as one of my first and tenderest recollections.
On a calm evening, the ship was under easy sail,
and my father standing on the deck, surrounded by
his wife and three children, with our ayas, or Indian
nurses. There, on the deck of the old *Dutton*, I
well remember his playfully describing to us the new
scenes to which we were about to be introduced, the
new brothers and sisters, uncle and aunt, and governess,
with whom we were shortly to be made acquainted;
and well do I recall to my mind the transition from

playfulness to gravity, which passed over his features, when, changing his tone, he began thus early to instil into our minds, the duty we were bound to pay to those several relations.

We landed in England in the month of June, 1784.* John Dunning, Lord Ashburton, was in his grave, with nothing left of him but his fame as a lawyer, and the great wealth and honours he had acquired in his professional and parliamentary career; but Sutton, Thurlow, James Mansfield, Lloyd Kenyon, his early fellow-traveller, Alexander Popham, and many other professional friends, were alive to welcome my father to his native land : and heartily did they welcome him. Three years of incessant calumny had not cooled these friendships, or taught the earliest associates of Sir Elijah Impey, to look upon him otherwise than as an honourable, humane, and a firm and upright judge. Most of them grieved, indeed, that he should ever have gone to India : all rejoiced to see him return in good health and buoyant spirits. Rest, and the long sea voyage, had recruited the one, nor could slander, defamation, and all the strategies of political faction, long disturb the other.

Our first residence was in Grosvenor Street. The house, furniture, and establishment of servants, had all been procured beforehand, by the care and consideration of his friends—the noble and well-natured family of Bathurst. His Lordship, then ex-Chancellor,

---

* Of the precise day, and point of landing, I can give no account, nor of any farther incidents of the voyage, beyond what I am able to glean from an old and mutilated memorandum book, which contains the following entries,—

"Friday, Feb. 27, took soundings at 80 fathoms; saw a sail, supposed to be French.

"Monday, March 1, doubled the Cape of Good Hope.

"Monday 15, came to anchor at St. Helena.

"Tuesday 16, went ashore, was met by Mr. Corneille, the Governor, Major Greene, the Deputy Governor, Mr. Wrangham, Mr. Bassett, and the Council; dined with the Governor; lodged with Mr. Stroud, the Surgeon.

"Tuesday 22, agreed with Captain West, of the *Dutton*, for the passage of myself and family, my cousin Fraser, and Dr. Campbell, for £1,000.

"Wednesday, April 7, off Ascension.

"Saturday 10, about seven in the evening crossed the Line.

Thus ends this imperfect log; and though my father is known to have kept a journal in his pocket-books for many years, I must here lament that none were preserved by his executors.

having rightly estimated my father's character and abilities, while practising as a barrister, had obtained for him his Indian promotion, had signed his appointment, and it was now through the same kind and continued regard for Sir Elijah, that the noble members of that family had condescended even to the recommendation and transfer of more than one domestic, from their own establishment to ours. Well, and pleasantly, do I remember the excellent English nurse, who passed from the Countess's service to ours : where she, and her daughter after her, remained, beloved and cherished, till they severally died.

Although recalled *"for the purpose of answering to the charge specified,"* namely, the charge of having accepted the presidency of the Sudder Dewannee Adaulut,—and upon no other charge, either specified or implied,—yet was my father, on his arrival in England, never, after all, called upon to answer to that charge. Four years passed away before any parliamentary measures were resorted to against him. His calumniators, however, had not been altogether idle : by tongue and by the peh, by secret committees and the public press, they had, meanwhile, kept up their insidious attack ; but hitherto they were not able to arrange their parliamentary crusade. For years of this time his Majesty's government left the post of Chief Justice of Calcutta unfilled, in the hope, or at least in the contemplation of Sir Elijah's return to India.

It is not surprising that, disgusted at the treatment he had received, alarmed at the implacable spirit which was manifesting itself against Hastings, and at the unscrupulous resolution of the faction to couple his name and his actions with those of the Governor General— in spite of truth—in spite of glaring facts—in spite of accumulated and still accumulating evidence—it is not, I say, surprising that he should have turned his eyes for ever from the East. Besides these considerations, my father had a young and numerous family to educate; with whom, and with the tenderest and most exemplary of wives, he preferred living in retirement upon the moderate fortune which he had partly inherited, and partly saved, during ten years spent in an uneasy and laborious life abroad. No wonder if, with his dear-bought experience, he had had enough of India! "*Sat Trojæ Priamoque datum.*"

Mr. Hastings, too, having seen the war in India brought to a glorious termination; having seen that vast and greatly-increased empire put in a condition of safety; having witnessed the full and perfect triumph of his policy; Mr. Hastings, too, resigned. He arrived at London in June, 1785,—one year after my father. Their friendship and intimacy were of course renewed: but, meanwhile, a still closer and more frequent intercourse had been formed between Burke and Francis; who, upon the return of the ex-Governor General, now more vigorously pushed forward the impeachment. They had made it a party business, and were enlisting Mr. Fox, then the leader of the opposition, Sheridan the ornamental orator of that party, Mr. Windham, Sir Gilbert Elliot, Sir John Anstruther, Mr. Grey, afterwards Earl Grey, and, in short, all the conspicuous Whigs then in Parliament. It appears that, at first, Burke levelled his artillery only against Hastings, whom he was accustomed to call "the Great Delinquent;" and that he was induced, by the personal animosity of Francis, to take Sir Elijah within the range of his battery. Burke, who had certainly bestowed infinite study upon Indian affairs, confessed, more than once, that they were so complicated, as to be scarcely intelligible, except to those who had long lived in India; and well knowing the prevailing indolence, the besetting sins of Fox, Sheridan, and others of his political friends, he doubted whether they would ever make themselves acquainted with any part of that difficult subject.* With the aid of Francis he undertook the task of instruction; and the whole host of orators, from Charles Fox to Sir Gilbert Elliot, became his disciples. Yet, after all, an avowal was wrung from Burke himself, that only Mr. Hastings, and his Indian friends, could be said fully to comprehend Indian matters.

In the early stages of the crusade, Fox seems to have

---

* On this point see several letters published by Mr. Prior in his excellent life of Burke; and other letters in the "Correspondence" edited by Earl Fitzwilliam and Sir Richard Bourke.

been too conscientious not to hesitate and hang back upon a road so foreign to him, and of which he could see no end. For this backwardness, however, he soon made ample amends, by his constitutional heat and characteristic energy. But that both Burke and Francis found it difficult in the onset to enlist their recruit, and that Fox suggested the safer course, not to charge what they were unable to prove, plainly appears from the letters to which I refer.

Their more unscrupulous manager thought it strange, after all that had passed between them, how Fox, or any one else, could hesitate to rely implicitly upon the faith of himself and Mr. Francis.* Burke endeavoured, likewise, to show that a parliamentry impeachment was not, in its nature, within the ordinary scope of law.† To remove the scruples of Mr. Fox, he was carried down to Beaconsfield by Francis; and Francis afterwards appears to have been the *mezzano* between Burke and Fox, until the latter was fully indoctrinated, and induced to act, in perfect conformity with the will of Edmund Burke. If the reader will turn to Mr. Moore's life of Sheridan, he will see how that brilliant dramatic and political speechmaker was prepared for the part he was to enact in the great tragi-comedy. He scarcely knew more of India and its concerns, than of the geographical divisions and polity of the moon; and he was far too idle and profligate to toil over dry books and voluminous reports. It suited him rather to be lectured, *vivâ voce*, by his preceptors; or, at most, to skim the surface of some few convenient abstracts, which they threw upon his desk, and out of which he spun his flimsey web of oratory and stage effect.

Soon as it was resolved to make a party measure of the impeachment, and to couple the Chief Justice with the Governor General, every Whig, who would not join in the cry, was scouted and run down as a renegade; and even the Ministry itself was tampered with, by means of intimidation, and through the medium of their jealousy of power. To this end, Mr. Burke entered

* Letter from Burke to Francis, dated Beaconsfield, Dec. 10, 1785, in Correspondence of the Right Hon. Edmund Burke, edited by Earl Fitzwilliam, and Sir Richard Bourke. Vol. III. p. 38.
† Ibid.

into a correspondence with Pitt's colleague and bosom friend, Henry Dundas, who had lately been remunerated, for his share in the new India Bill, by the post of President of the Board of Controul, and who was said to be easily alarmed by the pretensions of any rival in that extensive field of patronage.   I cannot positively affirm that Mr. Burke induced Dundas to believe that there existed a wish or intention, in the highest quarter, to place Mr. Hastings at the head of all Indian affairs; such intrigues were doubtless better suited to the spirit of Mr. Francis: but that the report was spread is certain; and it seemed to be verified by the marked distinction with which his Majesty George III. had received the late Governor General, in spite of the heavy accusations which had been heaped upon him.   Be this as it may, there is good proof that Burke attempted to excite a jealousy against Hastings in the breast of Dundas, and through Dundas in the Prime Minister himself.   When the parliamentary proceedings against Hastings and my father were in full progress, but while Mr. Pitt appears still to have been wavering as to what part he should take, Mr. Burke, in a letter dated March 25, 1787, wrote to tell Dundas that unless Mr. Pitt joined in crushing " the Indian faction," he would be crushed by them.

" But," he continued, " I think it, in a manner, impossible that all this should not be felt by you and Mr. Pitt.   I shall, therefore, only take leave to add, that, if ever there was a common national cause totally separated from party, it is this. A body of men in close connection of common guilt, and common apprehension of danger, with a strong and just confidence of future power if they escape, with a degree of wealth and influence, which, perhaps, even yourself have not calculated at anything like its just rate, is not forming, but actually formed, in this country :—*This body is under Mr. Hastings, as an Indian leader, and will have, very soon, if it has not already, an English political leader too.   This body, if they should now obtain a triumph, will be too strong for your ministry, or for any ministry.*   I go further, and assert, without the least shadow of hesitation, that it will turn out too strong for any description of merely natural interest that exists, or, on any probable speculation, can exist in our times. Nothing can rescue the country out of their hands, *but our vigourous use of the present fortunate moment,* which, if once lost, is never to be recovered, for breaking up this corrupt combination, by effectually crushing the leader and principal members of the corps. *The triumph of that faction will not be over us, who are not the keepers of the parliamentary force, but over you ; and it is not you who will govern them, but they who will tyrannize over you, and over the nation along with you.* You have vindictive people to deal with, and you have gone too far to be forgiven. I do not know whether, setting aside the justice and honour of the nation, deeply involved in this business, you will think the political hints I have given you to be of importance. *You, who hold power, and are likely to hold it, are much more concerned in that question than I am, or can be.*" *

Between the recall of my father, and the resignation of Mr. Hastings, many important changes had been made in our legislation for India; changes by which the British Government acknowledged the defects of the previous Acts, under which the Governor General and Chief Justice had been so long compelled to labour.

On the 13th of August, 1784, Mr. Pitt's celebrated India Bill, passed into law. It gave a salutary check to the Court of Directors, who had too often governed a mighty empire on mere commercial principles. It instituted the Board of Controul, by which the government of India may be said to have been managed ever since. I do not feel myself called upon to examine, still less to criticise this Bill, farther than in allusion to the difficulty of legislating for this vast and anomalous *imperium in imperio,* and to the hard and trying condition of all public men in India, who were bound to shape their conduct according to the English Acts of Parliament. It may, however, be allowed me to remind the reader, that even Mr. Pitt's great India Bill, upon which far more attention had been bestowed, than upon any similar previous enactment, was not in existence two years, before it was found necessary to explain and amend it by *three* subsequent bills ; successively introduced by the Prime Minister himself.

Francis, who had been returned to Parliament for the Borough of Yarmouth, in the Isle of Wight, devoted all the eloquence and talent he was master of, to

---

* Correspondence of the Right Honourable Edmund Burke, &c., edited by Earl Fitzwilliam, and Sir Richard Bourke. Vol. III. p. 48—52.

the office of accuser. As there is accumulative treason, so there is accumulative scandal. Having laid a broad basis for his defamation by means of the press, of private correspondence, and conversation, he now built up his pile with a more daring and rapid hand. Errors were now magnified into crimes, and offences, at which he had before only hinted, were now broadly charged upon Mr. Hastings and my father. The same care has ever been taken to connect them, where there had never been any connection at all. Rather than trust to my own feelings in this part of my subject, I will use the words of another writer.

"That *tender-hearted* man, Philip Francis, was the chief source of information to the opposition and prosecution, in all matters concerning the Governor General's dealings with the native princes, rajahs, and begums; and a source which had been flowing in full torrent ever since the return of the ex-Member of the Supreme Council of Calcutta to England, with the wound received at Hastings's hand fresh on his body, and a thousand animosities, personal and political, rankling in his mind. Burke's spirit was indisputably high and noble; but he must have been blinded by his enthusiasm in what he considered the greatest cause in which he was ever engaged, before he could accept, without doubt or softening, the evidence of a man like Francis, in such a case. But, that he and his party did so, is even more notorious than the fact that the ex-Member of the Council—who, by means never explained,* had accumulated in six years, and had brought home, a great deal more money than the Governor General,—possessed the most vindictive and blackest heart of any public man of that day. Francis, himself, afterwards declared, from his seat in the House of Commons, that he 'supplied the information,' that he 'furnished the materials,' that he 'prompted the prosecution!' . . . .

"The venom which had been spread in former days, when Francis was Junius, and a poor clerk in the War Office, over the Duke of Grafton, the Duke of Bedford, Sir William Draper, the great Lord Mansfield, and the King, was now all concen-

* The means were never explained by Francis himself; but they were thus explained by others:—Francis, contrary to the letter and whole spirit of the prohibitory clauses in the Regulating Act, and in contempt of his own oath of office, had trafficked in opium, and other commodities, by means of his brother-in-law, Mr. Sheriff Macrabie. His pay of £10,000 a year, for six years, could never have enabled Francis to bring home the very great fortune which he brought.

trated upon Hastings and Impey. The ex-Member of Council at Calcutta, was impelled by ambition and revenge, two of the strongest of human passions, and both of them more violent and intense in the heart of Francis, than they are usually found to be in human nature. . . . . . .

" How the demoniacal passion of revenge was excited against Hastings, has been sufficiently shown. Sir Elijah Impey, as Chief Judge, had several times curbed the fiery spirit of the Member and leader of Council, and upset his daring projects. That Impey had been the schoolfellow and early friend of Hastings, was, by itself, enough to make him odious in the eyes of Francis; but, in addition to all these grounds for hostility, there was this memorable circumstance,—*Philip Francis, during his residence in Calcutta, had made himself amenable to a civil prosecution, and it had been the duty of Sir Elijah Impey to pronounce sentence upon him, inflicting heavy damages.*" *

Thus was it, that long before he was called to any account himself, my father heard his name linked with that of Hastings in nearly every oration delivered in Parliament, on the affairs of India, by Francis, Burke, Fox, Sheridan, or any other member of that party.

It was on the 4th of April, 1787, that Burke, in his place, charged Warren Hastings with high crimes and misdemeanours, and delivered nine of his articles of charge. This was the beginning of the impeachment proceedings, which lasted altogether ten years. Among these nine first charges, was included the one relating to the trial and execution of Nuncomar ; and, in supporting this charge against Mr. Hastings, nearly every possible scandal or falsehood was heaped upon Sir Elijah Impey. Yet, many more anxious months passed ere my father could publicly reply to the horrible accusation ; and, during the whole of that interval, the unfavourable impression on the mind of the public was artfully deepened by my father's persecutors.

On the 30th of May the King prorogued Parliament. Sir Gilbert Elliot's motion for the impeachment of Sir Elijah, was therefore put off until the next session.

A few days before the Christmas holidays—on the 12th of December, 1787—Sir Gilbert presented to the House six articles of charge of various high crimes and

* Our Indian Empire. Vol. I. p. 422.

misdemeanours against Sir Elijah Impey,* late Chief
Justice of Bengal, &c. Sir Gilbert, who was closely
linked with Burke and Fox, and who was one of the
most approved orators of the House of Commons,
delivered a very long and impressive speech, in which he
professed to describe Sir Elijah's legal career, from his
first arrival at Calcutta, down to his recall on the resolution of the House, provoked by his having accepted
the Presidency of the Sudder Dewannee Adaulut from
Hastings—an original complaint, which occupied but a
very small part of the present oration—the chief objects
now proposed by Sir Gilbert being to couple the Chief
Justice with the Governor General, in the alleged
iniquity of the execution of Nuncomar, and of the
transactions which had taken place at Benares and in
Oude. The greatest stress of all was laid upon the
case of the Rajah; and Sir Gilbert roundly and repeatedly declared, that he had been murdered not by
the four judges collectively, but by Sir Elijah alone, in
order to screen the Governor General. Nothing can
be more clear than the source from which the orator
had derived his statements. Sir Gilbert did little more
than repeat and embellish the materials which had been
furnished by Francis.

Twelve years had now elapsed since Nuncomar's
death, yet hitherto nothing had been heard of that *pathetic* letter which gave the minute account of the Rajah's
execution. This letter, which was made to pass as the
production of Francis's brother-in-law, Macrabie, Sheriff of Calcutta at the time of that event, was now produced for *the first time*, and read to the excited House
by Sir Gilbert Elliot. But where had this epistle been
concealed for twelve long years? Was it not, to say
the least of it, more than suspicious, that a violent prejudice against my father had been inculcated in the
mind of a man so closely connected with Francis? But
I will venture even to affirm, that the letter was never
written by the Sheriff of Calcutta. Macrabie was a
very successful trader on his own account, and a no less

* Though my father had been above three years in England, his Indian
appointment had not yet been filled up; nor was it until the 10th of
November, of this present year, that he had acquainted the Court of
Directors that his Majesty *had been pleased to accept his resignation.*

skilful agent for his brother-in-law in his secret and
illicit contracts for opium, but was never believed to
have given any proof of literary acquirements. This
letter, on the other hand, was very ably written; as a
piece of fiction it may be called admirable; nor am I
singular in asserting that it bears internal evidence of
having been composed or retouched by the author of the
Letters of Junius. In this opinion, I believe that
every candid reader will concur, who will carefully
examine the style and consider the circumstances
and the *time* in which it was *first* produced. Such
a reader need scarcely be reminded of the book of
"Travels," which had been published some five years
before Sir Gilbert Elliot delivered his speech against my
father. In that book, little more was said of the execution
of Nuncomar than that he was hanged; but in this famous letter the minutest details were given of his last
moments, a most vivid and startling picture was drawn
of the closing scene, and the astounding effects which it
produced on the native population. Sir Gilbert Elliot's
rhetoric was founded solely on this *questionable* letter.
His speech appeared in the Annual Register, published
in 1788; and in the Appendix to that same volume of
the Register, the world saw *for the first time* the letter
attributed to Sheriff Macrabie. It was there stated to
have been written immediately after the execution of
the convict; but no attempt was made to explain where
so interesting a document had been sleeping for twelve
long years. If there had been any fairness in the report
of proceedings published in the Annual Register, Sir
Elijah Impey's triumphant defence would have appeared
in the same volume; but this did not suit the views of the
party who wrote for or controlled that partial publication.
The letter thus assumed to be authentic, thus unques-
tioned, thus uncriticised, was put upon record, and made
accessible to all readers in a highly popular work; and,
in the course of the fifty-eight years which have since
elapsed, many are the hearts that it has wrung, and not
few the pens it has misguided. Writers and compilers
have been duped by its speciousness, and have not
paused to inquire into its authenticity. Yet, in sober
truth, the particulars it narrates are either directly con-
tradicted by contemporary accounts upon legal evidence

or found to be utterly inconsistent with the moral history of India, and the character, condition, and habits of the natives.

" If," says Mr. Mac Farlane, "what is very doubtful, as well as what is absolutely false, be deducted from this pathetic narrative, very little that is either pathetic or picturesque will remain to adorn the tale. It is not true that Nuncomar was ignorant of the predicament in which he stood; it is not true that natives had never been executed for the crime of forgery; it is not true that the mode of executing by hanging was so peculiarly awful and horrible in the eyes of the Hindus, for hanging had been a not uncommon mode of putting criminals to death among the Hindus themselves; it is not true that the life of a Brahmin was regarded as sacred by the Hindus, let his crime be what it might, for Brahmins had been repeatedly executed by sentence of native courts ; it is not true that Nuncomar was the head of the Hindu race and religion, or that his death excited among the Hindus the same feeling that a devout *Catholic in the dark ages would have felt* at seeing *a prelate of the highest dignity* sent to the gallows by a secular tribunal. If any such feeling had existed, the Hindus of Calcutta, who were very numerous (and in many instances exceedingly well informed that the majority of the Council— Francis, Clavering, and Monson—were at the moment more powerful than Hastings), would have signed a petition, as they had done in the case of Radachund Mettre, who was, like Nuncomar, both an Hindu and a Brahmin. Nuncomar may have been of the highest caste, *and ' a Brahmin of the Brahmins ;'* but men with these hereditary advantages or qualities neither were, nor are, secured against misfortune, poverty, obscurity, contempt ; and then, as now, many Hindus of the highest caste occupied the lowest posts in society, filled the most menial offices, and lived and died in obscurity. When Nuncomar possessed wealth and political power, he was highly considered; but the consideration of his countrymen ended with his wealth and power. When one of the best informed and most respectable witnesses * upon Hasting's trial, was asked whether the Rajah Nuncomar was not a very considerable person among the Hindus, he replied that he had been so at one time, but that he had ceased to be so long before his arrest. There is nothing at all uncommon in Nuncomar having displayed in prison, or on the scaffold, the composure and resignation which have been ascribed to him; but it is very doubtful, whether there were any of those ' *howlings and lamentations of the poor*

* Major Rennell, the distinguished Eastern geographer, &c.

wretched people, taking their last leave of him,' which rend
the heart in Sir Gilbert Elliot's speech, and in the letter
attributed to Sheriff Macrable; and it is very doubtful indeed
whether, at the moment the drop fell, the Hindus set up a
universal yell, and with piercing cries of horror and dismay,
betook themselves to flight, running, many of them, as far as
the Ganges, and plunging into that holy stream, as if to wash
away the pollution they had contracted in viewing such a
spectacle.''

I have been assured, not merely by my father and
Mr. Hastings, but by other persons who were in Calcutta on the day of the execution, that the scene excited
very little interest among the Hindus, and that the
rest of the natives witnessed it with quiet indifference, or
the more openly expressed opinion, that the Rajah,
" *the worst man in India*," met with the fate he had
long merited.

Sir Gilbert Elliot proceeded to demonstrate that there
was   no   greater   delinquent—Hastings   always   excepted—than the late Chief Justice. He energetically
called upon the gentlemen of the law, to which body
he himself had once belonged, to throw off from the
nation, and from their profession, the guilt of an individual lawyer, by bringing him to punishment for
crimes which had been committed in the name of the
law. The articles of charge which he moved to be read,
related—

I. To the trial and execution of Nuncomar.

II. To the conduct of Sir Elijah in a cause called the Patna
cause.

III. To extension of jurisdiction, illegally and oppressively,
beyond the intention of the Act and Charter.

IV. To the Cossijurah cause, in which the extension of
jurisdiction had been carried out with peculiar violence.

V. To the acceptance of the office of Judge of the Sudder
Dewannee Adaulut, which was affirmed to be contrary to law,
and not only repugnant to the spirit of the Act and Charter,
but fundamentally subversive of all its material purposes.

VI. To the conduct of Sir Elijah in Oude and Benares,
where, it was declared, the Chief Justice became the agent
and tool of Hastings.

The charges being received, and laid upon the table,
were, upon a motion, read by the clerk, *pro formâ;* after
which, Sir Gilbert moved that they should be at once

referred to a committee. This precipitation was objected to by Mr. Pitt, who suggested that the charges ought, in the first place, to be printed, and then referred, not to a select committee, but to a committee of the whole House. This mode of proceeding was adopted; and the 4th of February, 1788, was fixed for the Committee to sit.

CHAPTER XIII.

SIR ELIJAH IMPEY'S TRIUMPHANT DEFENCE ON THE NUN-
COMAR CHARGE.

On the appointed day—the 4th of February, 1788—
before the Committee proceeded to business, a petition
was presented from Sir Elijah Impey, praying to be
heard in answer to the charges, before the House proceeded any further. The prayer being granted, he was
called to the bar. He was attended by his counsel, the
Attorney,* and Solicitor General,† and assisted by his
son, my late brother Archibald Elijah, then a very
young student-at-law, who excited much interest in the
House, by the clear and intelligent manner in which he
read, and handed to his father, the several affidavits and
other vouchers called for in the course of the defence.
This defence was not read, but *orally* delivered.‡ Sir
Elijah began his address to the Chairman of the Committee, in these words :—

"Sir,—Having observed with great concern from the votes
of this House, that an honourable Member had presented
articles of charge of high crimes and misdemeanours against
me, I esteemed it a due attention to the House, as well as

* Sir Richard Pepper Arden, afterwards Lord Alvanley, and Chief
Justice of the Common Pleas.
† Sir Archibald Macdonald, afterwards Chief Baron of the Exchequer.
‡ Much to the dissatisfaction of his accusers. They had witnessed the
disadvantage under which Mr. Hastings had recently laboured from the
fatiguing process of *reading*, and had calculated upon a repetition of
the same effect. They were besides disappointed, when, calling for a copy
of Sir Elijah Impey's speech, they were told that none existed, which they
might otherwise have turned to his disadvantage.

justice to myself, to endeavour to obviate, as early as possible, that matter; which, from the articles having been referred to a committee of the whole House, I apprehended had already subjected me in some measure to its censure ; and was in hopes, by the assistance of a Member of this House, who had taken the pains of making himself master of the facts which have given rise to the accusation, to have disclosed the nature of the defence which I could make to it ; by which it would demonstratively appear, that there was no probable ground that the articles could be finally supported, and therefore that the House would not think it consistent with its dignity, wisdom, and justice, to proceed further upon them. The sudden indisposition of that gentleman* having rendered his attendance in his place impossible, I despaired of having the real merits of my case—which has been strangely misrepresented, and, I had reason to think, almost universally misunderstood—made intelligible, unless I was permitted to lay it before the House; I, therefore, though unprepared for the occasion, presented a petition that I may do it myself. I now return my thanks for the indulgence granted me thus to obtrude myself on your attention, and request that it may be further extended to me for the haste of the occasion, which will necessarily oblige me to make my address in a cruder manner than my respect for this Assembly would otherwise have allowed. But before I enter into it, I beg leave to state some particular difficulties, which I am laid under by the former proceedings of this House, and by the specific cause assigned for my recall.''

Sir Elijah then represented that he had been recalled upon one charge, and was now accused on five other charges. He said that the whole matter of the four first articles had been collected from evidence which had been drawn up by Committees of the House, the last of which sat in 1781 ; that this evidence had been fully discussed, had been the subject of an Act of Parliament, and yet had furnished no charges against him at the time. He continued :—

" On the 27th of January, 1783, I received a letter from the Earl of Shelburne, dated the 8th of July, 1782, which conveyed his Majesty's commands to me to return to this kingdom for the purpose of answering a charge *specified* in an address which had been laid before his Majesty, in consequence of a vote of the 3rd of May, 1782. That vote related

---

* Sir Richard Sutton, Bart., Member for Boroughbridge.

only *to the acceptance of an office not agreeable to the true intent and meaning of the Act* 13 *George III.** As the cause assigned for my recall was *subsequent* to all the transactions which have furnished matter for these charges, I entertained no idea that anything *within the knowledge of the House, prior* to the cause which had been selected as a charge against me, would be objected to me. In this opinion I was confirmed by the letters of my private friends ; and I was thereby induced to esteem his Lordship's letter, so particularising the charge, to be *a specific notice* of the whole evidence which I was to bring with me for my defence. I could not suspect when the *acceptance of an office* had appeared the most proper subject for prosecution, that an accusation *for so foul an offence* as that contained in the first article, could have been omitted. Under these impressions, though I collected all possible materials to defend myself against the charge of which I had notice, I did not bring any with me for the defence of those acts, which, knowing them to be legal, and done in the necessary and conscientious discharge of my duty, *I had no reason* to think could ever have been imputed to me as criminal, and for which *I had reason* to think all intention of arraigning either me, or the other judges, after the fullest consideration, had been totally abandoned. Had notice been given me, even after my arrival, or *within two years* of it, that these charges would have been preferred against me, I should have had full time to procure authentic vouchers and records for my judicial conduct, and witnesses to such other matters as could not be proved by written evidence. Thus misled by appearances, I am called to answer those charges without any evidence but that which I may be able to extract from the very materials which have been compiled against me, and from some few papers, which I have casually, not purposely, brought with me."

---

* This letter has been already quoted, but, like other matter, it is necessary to recite it.

" Whitehall, July 8, 1782.

" Sir,—I have the honour to transmit to you an address laid before his Majesty, in consequence of a vote of the House of Commons on the 3rd of May last, for the purpose of your recall. I am, in consequence thereof, to signify to you his Majesty's commands, that you should take the earliest opportunity, consistent with the necessary arrangements of your affairs, to return home to this kingdom, for the purpose of answering to the charge *specified* in the said address.

" I have the honour to be, with the greatest esteem,
" Sir,
" Your most obedient humble Servant,
" (Signed)   SHELBURNE.
" Sir Elijah Impey, Knight, &c. &c."

After having read and commented at some length on the strictures made by the Committee on the body of evidence attempted to be applied to the four first charges, he remarked :—

" These strictures contain as strong objections as can be made to any evidence adduced to support a *criminal charge ;* and as the Committee has not pointed out what particular facts are proved by competent evidence, and what by evidence liable to the objections they have stated, it will be difficult either for this House or any party accused on it, to discover whether the whole, or any of the facts stated, have been so proved that they ought to be credited *in a judicial proceeding.* I request I may not be understood by this observation to take any objection to the propriety of the evidence *for the purpose for which it was collected*—REFORM—but to the application of it to a purpose foreign to that for which it was collected—A CRIMINAL CHARGE. It is stated as ' a body of facts *to serve as a foundation of provisions, and to enable the House to determine on the fitness of the application of the laws of England to Bengal, and to decide on the extent of the jurisdiction of the Supreme Court, for the purpose of superseding or contracting it.'* This was the professed object of the inquiry. Though the representations of the East India Company, or of the Government in Bengal, might be admitted on their credit alone, without any investigation, as sufficient for the object of REFORM, yet I submit that those representations, or such parts of the evidence as are liable to these objections of the Committee, cannot legally be applied to substantiate A CRIMINAL CHARGE, *even if collected for that purpose.*"

It had been urged that the first article relating to Nuncomar's execution, was supported by the general sense of mankind; but he observed that, before the sense of mankind in general could be admitted, it would be just to examine *by what means* it had been acquired. If it was found to be the opinion of the public, founded on an impartial statement of the facts, on ample discussion of the argument on both sides, on a full investigation of the proceedings, its authority was irresistible, and in that case it might be truly said that *vox populi est vox Dei.* But, if partial representations had been laid before the public ; if one side of the question only had been stated ; if no inquiry had been made into the facts ; if it turned out that the public had been abused and misled ; then the public opinion would be of no value ; and to give weight to it would be to deliver up the lives, properties, and fame of the best men to the rage of partisans and the virulence of libellers,—the base and mercenary instruments of every malignant and unprincipled faction.

" It is now twelve years," said he, " since this nation has been deluded by false and perpetual informations, that the Supreme Court of Judicature had most absurdly, cruelly, and without authority, obtruded the complex and intricate criminal laws of England on the populous nations of Bengal, Bahar, and Orissa, whose law, religion, and habits, were particularly abhorrent to them ; that a native of Bengal, of high rank, had been tried and convicted on a capital law of England for an offence punishable in the place where it was committed by fine only ; that the Court which had tried him had no jurisdiction over his person ; that he was brought within the limits of the jurisdiction by force, and in that state that the Court adjudged that its jurisdiction had attached upon him ; and, to sum up all, in the words most deservedly odious to an English ear, he was finally executed under that which, if a law at all, was an *ex post facto law.*"

He complained that all kinds of calumnies had been propagated through the press, not merely in daily papers, but in laboured treatises, in histories, in books of travels, fabricated for the sole purpose of disseminating and perpetuating libels of this and a similar tendency, with a more certain effect because less suspected. These authors had dared to make use of the high and respectable names of Sir William Blackstone and Lord Mansfield, as condemning the illegality of the proceedings in the case of Nuncomar, the latter being made to call the execution " a legal murder." He read a letter, dated Jan. 30, 1779, written by Blackstone, who was recently dead, to express his admiration of the high reputation which he (Sir Elijah) and his colleagues had acquired, *among all dispassionate men in England,* by their prudent and impartial administration of justice " on very delicate and important occasions." My father prided himself on enjoying the favourable opinion of Lord Mansfield, who was living, and in full possession of his faculties, though at a very advanced age; and he assured the House that, so far from using any such expressions, that noble lord had declared that he had never formed any opinion upon Nuncomar's case—that the assertion was an absolute falsehood, and that his lordship authorised him so to contradict it.* The name of another great lawyer, Lord Ashburton (Dunning), had also been introduced to add to the weight of the popular condemnation. He read a letter from that nobleman expressly to the point, and containing his full approbation of Nuncomar's trial. It was dated January 5, 1776, and ran thus:

"The publication of the trial has been of use, as it has obviated abundance of ridiculous and groundless stories. I see nothing in the proceedings to disapprove of, except that you seem to have wasted more time in the discussion of the privileges of ambassadors, than so ridiculous a claim deserved."

Dunning, like Blackstone, was in his grave, and Lord Mansfield, as full of honours as of years, had recently retired from the bench.

"These," said Sir Elijah, "were not men who would hold correspondence with judges guilty of a legal murder; these were not men who would be volunteers in applauding such conduct. They were great lawyers in their day; they are gone, and almost a new generation has succeeded them. Though it has been given out authoritatively, and propagated in print to prejudice my cause, I shall not, till I am convinced by fatal experience, be induced to believe that the gentlemen of the same profession, now in this House, can so totally differ in opinion from them, as to have reprobated my conduct, and pre-judged me unheard. . . . . . . My defence depending chiefly on matters of law, my reliance is on no personal favour, but on their professional ability to determine on matters of law, and their characteristic habit, not to condemn, not to reprobate without a hearing. '*Audi alteram partem*' is a maxim acknowledged to be equitable by all who know what justice is; but it is engraven on the heart of every honest lawyer."

* After the termination of these proceedings in May, 1788, my father called upon Lord Mansfield, who, shaking him cordially by the hand, exclaimed, "So, Sir Elijah, you have passed safe over the coals." This anecdote was related to me by a near relation of the venerable Earl, and an intimate friend of my own, who, being then a boy at Westminster School, somewhat above my own standing, happened to be present at the interview, and appeared to retain a distinct impression of what passed between the parties.

" My arrival in England," continued my father, "renewed the subject, and the papers have every day teemed with fresh libels. I resolved—and I have kept my resolution—that I would not myself publish, nor, as far as I was able, suffer any publication to be made on my account. . . . . I disdained to defend myself by the arts by which I have been attacked—to write, or suffer anything to be written *anonymously*, I never would condescend. To the conscience of every individual who forms the body of that public, whose sense is alleged to be against me, I would put these questions : Whether, if he has formed any such opinion, it has not been from the materials which I have stated? Whether he has been informed of the truth of the facts? Whether he has read the Act of Parliament and the Charter giving jurisdiction to the Supreme Court? Whether he knows the state of the town of Calcutta? Whether he knows what the law there was before the Charter? Whether it has been at all, and in what manner, altered by it? Whether he has examined the evidence at the trial, and all the circumstances under which the law was carried into execution? Whether he now knows on what the legality or illegality of the conviction turns? If he does not, whether, before his opinion thus formed should operate as the foundation of a *criminal* charge, he should not have full information on those points? That information I hope to give to the House."*

After recapitulating the several articles contained in the charge about Nuncomar, as, that he had illegally brought the Rajah under the jurisdiction of his Court; that Nuncomar had been committed on false and insufficient evidence; that all the proceedings were the fruit of a confederacy between him and Warren Hastings, for the purpose of screening the Governor General from a just accusation by accomplishing the death of his accuser, &c., Sir Elijah said,—

" If the premises are true, they warrant a more severe conclusion ; if the premises are true, I am guilty, not of misdemeanours, I am guilty of murder; if for the purpose of ' screen-

---

* Here, in the original speech, for which I must refer to the publication by Stockdale, in 1788, follows a copious analysis of the Regulation Act and Charter, which I have already abstracted : next, a revision of the Articles, where various objections are taken to the application of them relative to those articles : then a comparison of the Act and Charter of George III., with those of 13 George I. and 16 George II., and lastly, a detection of the fallacy by which it was attempted to substantiate these objections, &c., &c.

ing the guilty from a just accusation,' I have made the law of England the engine and instrument of a confederacy to accomplish the death of the accuser, I have been guilty of a murder of the basest, foulest, and most aggravated nature. From such premises *that* is the only *true* conclusion. I do not decline it. It would have been justice to have drawn it. My life would then have been forfeit, had I been found guilty. It would have been mercy to have sacrificed that life, as an atonement for these enormous crimes ; which, if I am convicted of, or am to lie under the public imputation of having perpetrated, would become a burden too intolerable to be dragged to a distant grave. The substance of this Article has long been before the public, but brought before it in a manner which afforded me no means of answering it. The weight of it has, indeed, borne so heavy on me, that nothing but the consolation of my own conscience, indignation for unworthy treatment, and the expectation that the truth would at some time or other be revealed, could have supported me under it. With an overflowing heart I return my thanks to God, and his immediate instrument, my accuser, that he has been pleased to afford me this opportunity, now first given, of disclosing the true state of this so long misrepresented case, and of vindicating my own honour, and the conduct of the much injured judges of the Supreme Court."

After reciting the powers and the extent of the jurisdiction of the Court, as established by Act and Charter, he positively averred, that from the establishment of the Court, till he left Bengal, in December, 1783, there had been no indictment tried against any person who was not an inhabitant of Calcutta, nor for crimes not committed in Calcutta. He insisted that Nuncomar was a settled inhabitant of Calcutta ; that he was not ignorant of the law, but well acquainted with it ; and, that the crime with which he was charged was committed in Calcutta.

"An Hindu inhabitant of Calcutta," said he, "was as much amenable to the English law in Calcutta, as if the said Hindu had been an inhabitant of London. He might, with equal propriety, object to being tried by any law but that of his native country at the Old Bailey, as at the Court House in Calcutta. Gibraltar, in the kingdom of Spain, is,— Calais, in that of France, was,—part of the dominion of this realm : admitting the laws of England to have been introduced into those towns, a French inhabitant of Calais, or a Spanish inhabitant of Gibraltar, having offended against the law under which he dwelt, might, with equal reason, complain that he was not tried by the law of the place of his nativity, as an Hindu in Calcutta, because that town is situated in Bengal. There is nothing in the quality of an Hindu that makes the law of the country wherein he was born more attached to him, than to a Frenchman, or a Spaniard; all must be obedient to the law that protects them. It was not till since the seat of government, and the collection of the revenue, have been brought to Calcutta, that it has become populous, by the influx of black inhabitants. The laws have not been obtruded on them, they have come to the laws of England."

He affirmed, that long before his time the laws of England, statute and common, had been indiscriminately put in force at Calcutta; that murders, highway robberies, burglaries, felonies of all kinds, had been tried in the same manner as at the Old Bailey, and convictions and executions had on them, as well against Hindus, Mussulmans, Portuguese, and other foreign inhabitants, as against those who were more especially called British subjects. Copies of the records of the old Court were in the India House, and must be full of such trials. Besides records, and the precedents they established, he had been guided by the Charter, and by instructions sent out by the Court of Directors, showing the new Court how to proceed against prisoners not understanding English; how to proceed when any Portuguese, Hindu, or other native of India, not born of British parents, should happen to be prosecuted for any capital offence; which, according to the instructions, *would "probably often happen."*

On legal conclusions and precedents, the Supreme Court would have been justified in trying Nuncomar as an inhabitant of Calcutta for a crime committed in Calcutta; but before proceeding to the trial he made a still more particular search, and found that this specific statute of forgery had been acted on, and most completely published, to all the inhabitants of Calcutta, and to the Hindus more especially; for he found that, in 1765, Radachund Mettre, an Hindu, had been tried, convicted, and received sentence of death by the former Court, for the forgery of the codicil of a will of one Cojah Solomon, an Armenian. He admitted that this Hindu had not been hanged, but that was because it was the first condemnation for such a crime.

"I found," said he, "that the native Hindu inhabitants of Calcutta had petitioned the President and Council for his respite, not pretending that they were not subject to the laws of Calcutta, but chiefly on this ground : that, till that trial, neither they nor the prisoner understood the crime to be punishable by death, it not being so by the country laws. Their petition is solely for mercy *in that instance*, without any complaint of the law, or desire that it should not *in future* be executed. In consequence of this application the President and Council resolved to recommend the prisoner to mercy in these remarkable expressions: ' in hopes *that the condemnation will be sufficient to deter others from committing the like offence.'* It appeared by the records, that the East India Company had sent his Majesty's pardon ; all my diligence could not furnish me with any comment made on this proceeding ; and finding no censure passed upon it by the Court of Directors or the King's ministers, to whom the case must have been submitted to obtain the pardon, and that the whole passed in the ordinary course of business, and accorded with the other proceedings of the Court, I esteemed it a full precedent, more especially as there had been a plain intimation from the Governor and Council, if *the condemnation should not be sufficient to deter* the natives from the commission of forgery, that the law would be enforced in future."

It was alleged in the present articles of charge, that Nuncomar had been brought to Calcutta by force, and was there detained as a prisoner at the time of the commission of the crime.

"I deny the truth of the fact," said Sir Elijah, "and those gentlemen who were Members of the Council when Nuncomar was tried, and are now Members of this House, must well know the fact is not true. Had it been true, yet, before it could be matter of objection to the judgment, it must be shown it was in evidence at the trial ; it then would have been made part, and a material part of his defence : it would have been decisive in his favour ; but the contrary was in proof ; he was proved to be a *settled inhabitant* of Calcutta ; no such objection was ever suggested, nor was any attempt made to take him out of the jurisdiction of the Court as not being an inhabitant of the town."

He said he could trace the story of Nuncomar's being conducted to Calcutta, and detained a prisoner there until the arrival of the Supreme Court, to no better authority than that of a libellous letter in a book entitled " Travels in Europe, Asia, and Africa," published in 1782 ;* that the author of that book, from his known connection, might have received more true information ; and that book, like every libel published on the subject, uniformly endeavoured, as the articles of charge were now doing, to advance the character of Sir Robert Chambers at the expense of his own. As to the part of the charge that alleged that Nuncomar had been convicted on false and insufficient evidence, he requested the House, before they assented to the truth of that proposition, to peruse the whole trial and judge for themselves. As to the mode of execution by hanging, the laws of England left nothing to the discretion of the Court ; the sentence for the felony being, that the convict be hung by the neck till he is dead. To vary was treated by our law-books as criminal in the highest degree.

" Some," said Sir Elijah, " go so far—though certainly too far—as to say that this is not in the power of the King himself ; that he may indeed pardon part of the sentence—as in high treason all but beheading—but, that he cannot order execution to be done in a manner variant from the sentence."

He declared that, before Nuncomar suffered, he had the most authentic information, that Hindus of all castes, Brahmins included, had been executed by hanging.

" I was particularly informed," said he, " by a gentleman formerly a Member of the Council in Bengal, and now of this House,† who has this day repeated to me the same information, that he had himself carried such sentence into execution against two Brahmins, without any disturbance, and even with the consent of the Hindus themselves. The prosecutor who sued for the execution in this case, was an Hindu ; many of the witnesses were Hindus ; what the sentence must be, was well known to the prisoner, the prosecutor, and all the Hindus in the settlement ; yet, no objection was made by the prisoner, or his counsel, before or after the sentence was pronounced, to the mode by which he

---

* The book referred to, is, I suppose, " Macintosh's Travels in Europe, Asia, and Africa ;" 2 vols. 8vo., 1782 ; of which a French translation appeared at Paris the same year, and a German translation at Leipsic in 1785.
† Mr. Barwell.

was to suffer death; no evidence was given of its being shocking to the religious opinions of the Hindus; no mention is made of it in the address of the Hindus."

The articles alleged in the broadest manner, that there was a conspiracy between him and Mr. Hastings, in order to destroy so dangerous a witness as Nuncomar; and inferences to support the assertion, were drawn from these circumstances :—that the forgery had been committed five years before Nuncomar was brought to trial before the Supreme Court; that it had been, and was at the time, the subject of a *civil suit* in the Dewannee Adaulut, a country court; and, that no steps had ever been taken to make it a matter of *criminal* prosecution, much less of a capital indictment, until Nuncomar had become the accuser of the Governor General. General Clavering, Colonel Monson, and Mr. Francis, had even deposed that, in the interval between the forgery and the trial, Nuncomar had been protected and employed by Mr. Hastings; and this deposition had been inserted in the report of a Committee of the House of Commons. Now, in defending himself, Sir Elijah Impey not merely admitted, but insisted upon, the fact asserted by Clavering, Monson, and Francis; and he even cited the evidence of Mr. Hastings himself, when examined upon oath, on the trial of Joseph Fowke and others, for a conspiracy against him. This course, if it proved that Nuncomar could not have been tried for forgery before he *was* tried, proved also, that the Governor General had, at least in this case, put himself above the law for temporary political purposes,—proved that the guilty could not be prosecuted, previously to the arrival of the Supreme Court, so long as Mr. Hastings extended his protection. Mr. Hastings's evidence *upon oath*, which Sir Elijah read to the House, contained, however, a denial of his ever having, directly or indirectly, countenanced or forwarded the prosecution against Nuncomar. When asked whether he had not had connections with that Rajah, he had said he certainly had; that he had employed him on many occasions; had patronized and countenanced him; though he never had any opinion of his virtue or integrity, and believed the Rajah knew he had not.

"It was in evidence," said Sir Elijah, "at the trial, that Mr. Palk, judge of the adaulut, had confined him for the forgery. It was notorious that Mr. Hastings had ordered him to be released. This, of itself, was sufficient to prevent any native inhabitant of Calcutta from commencing a prosecution against him, for there was then no other criminal court to resort to, but that in which Mr. Hastings presided. It was in evidence also, that the prosecutor had it *not in his power* to commence a criminal suit, even in the court in which Mr. Hastings presided, or in any other court, *before the time at which the indictment was actually preferred ;* for the *forged instrument* was deposited in the Mayor's Court, and *could not be procured* from thence. It was not restored to the party entitled to it, till after the records and papers of the Mayor's Court had been delivered over to the Supreme Court. One main cause assigned for erecting the Supreme Court was, that the Company's servants either presided in, or could influence the other courts. . . . . The Supreme Court, the only Court where Mr. Hastings's influence could not extend, sat, for the first time, towards the end of October, 1774. . . . . . In June, 1775, at the first effective court of oyer and terminer, and gaol delivery, held by that Court, the indictment was preferred and tried. That the endeavouring to procure the papers from the Mayor's Court was intended as 'a *step* taken' towards a criminal prosecution, before Nuncomar became the accuser of Mr. Hastings, I have no evidence to prove; but that no *effectual steps* could have been taken, I have given satisfactory proof. As there had been no delay in the prosecution, as the point of time when the prosecution was brought was the *first possible point* of time when it could be brought, no presumption whatsoever could arise from lapse of time, or the coincidence of the prosecution of Mohunpersaud* with the accusation before the Council, or from the unavoidable accident of the prosecution not having been commenced until he had become the accuser of Mr. Hastings. . . . . . That the accusation was the cause of the prosecution of Nuncomar by another person,—that it had been the subject of a civil suit in the Dewannee Court,—there was no legal evidence: the proceedings themselves, or authenticated copies, ought to have been shown; parole testimony was not admissible; it did not lie on the *prosecutor* to produce them. Had they tended to the defence of the prisoner, *he* should have produced them; his *not* doing it, at least induced a strong suspicion that they would *not have made for him.* That suspicion was strengthened by the evidence given, that he had

* The prosecutor of Nuncomar.

been imprisoned by Mr. Palk, the judge of the court in which the proceedings were supposed to have been had. The matter, therefore, having been in a civil court, as he made it no part of his defence, but chose to keep back the evidence, furnishing a fair presumption against him, it could not, with justice, have been applied by the Court, to fling an imputation on the prosecution; nor did it give any appearance that the prosecution bore any relation to the accusation against Mr. Hastings.''

All this may prove that the Supreme Court could not have tried Nuncomar sooner than they did; but it may not fully prove that the Governor General had not chosen the moment for letting loose the proofs of Nuncomar's guilt. But, at the same time, there was nothing in the circumstance of Nuncomar's being in the character of an accuser of Hastings, that could stop proceedings against himself upon a separate and unconnected charge, brought forward by a different prosecutor, with different witnesses, and with everything about it different and distinct.

"The prosecutor," said my father, "had a right to demand redress; to have refused it, would have been a denial of justice. Had I taken so decided a part as to have flung out the indictment on the ground of the prisoner having been the *accuser of Mr. Hastings*, how could I have justified the casting that imputation on the prosecution, without any evidence being laid before the Court that any accusation existed? Had there been evidence of an accusation, with what justice to the community at large, could the Court have adjudged that to be a sufficient cause for not putting the prisoner on his trial? If such indemnities were held forth to informers, what man would have been safe in his property, liberty, fame, or life? What kind of informers were likely to be brought forward? Those who, by their crimes, were subjected to the laws, and had been thereby taught that, by simply preferring accusations, they would be protected from the justice of the laws."

After mentioning what was set forth in the charge—as that Nuncomar had accused Mr. Hastings of various peculations, and other corrupt practices, before the Council at Calcutta, and that Mr. Hastings, instead of confronting his accuser, thought proper, under pretence of dignity, to decline all defence, and to dissolve the said Council at various times—Sir Elijah asked how this could affect him, as nothing of the sort had

been before him and the Court when they were proceeding against Nuncomar? He said that the circumstances were not only not in evidence, but were not
known to him and the other judges; that by rumour,
and by rumour only, it was known in Calcutta, that
Nuncomar had preferred some accusations against Mr.
Hastings,—accusations, which, so far from being public, were preferred to the Council in their private department, where each member was under an oath of
secrecy.

"If the prisoner Nuncomar was an object of the special
protection of the Court, from the circumstances in which he
stood as an accuser, that claim should have been laid before
the Court, in evidence, and formed part of the defence: they
were all matters capable of proof: they were proper subjects
to go to a jury. Why were they kept back? Why were not
the Court and jury acquainted therewith? . . . . . .
If they could leave no doubt in the mind and opinion of
the jury, the jury could not have hesitated to acquit the
prisoner. If the judges *must* have been convinced, it would
have been their duty to have directed the acquittal. This
was the only mode by which protection could have been given
to Nuncomar: they were not thought sufficient to produce
that conviction when the transactions were recent; if they
had been, they would have formed a material part of the
defence. Why, then, is it averred they must produce such
conviction now, at the distance of thirteen years from these
transactions?"

It was inserted in the charge, and Sir Elijah allowed
it to be true, that Mr. Chambers had made a motion
from the bench for quashing the indictment; but the
Chief Justice urged, that this was done more in *favorem
vitæ*, and from the natural lenity of Chambers's disposition, than from any sound reason in law. Sir Robert
Chambers had wished to try Nuncomar on a statute
that did not inflict capital punishment for forgery—the
5th of Elizabeth,—thinking it optional in the Court to
adopt that statute, instead of the statute of George II.,
which made forgery capital.

"That it was optional in the Court," said Sir Elijah, "to
choose the statute which it liked best, I thought impossible;
for I understood it to be an undoubted maxim in law, that,
whenever a statute constitutes that offence which was a misdemeanour to be a felony, the existence of the misdemeanour

is destroyed and annihilated; or, as lawyer's express it, the misdemeanour is merged in the felony.   The 2nd George II. became the only law by which forgery was a crime; the Court, therefore, must have proceeded on that statute, or not at all. If forgery was not a capital offence in Calcutta, it was no offence there.   If the statute could not have been put in force, it would have operated as a pardon for the offence, which the legislature intended it to punish with more severity.   This, as most other arguments with which I have troubled the House, were made use of by me in Court to support the indictment. By these, I then understood that Sir Robert Chambers was *convinced ;* he most certainly *acquiesced ;* I never understood him to have been overruled, and his *subsequent conduct*— if any doubt could be entertained—proves most manifestly that he was not : for he not only sat through the whole trial, but concurred in overruling every objection in arrest of judgment; assented to the summing up of the evidence; was present, and concurred in the sentence."

My father then read a paragraph of a letter written to the Court of Directors, shortly after the trial, and signed by Chambers, the two other judges, and himself, and in which they all asserted that they had in every instance been unanimous, whatever representation might be made to the contrary.   Sir Elijah Impey further showed, that all the judges, Chambers included, signed the calendars, which were the only warrants for execution in Calcutta.   He showed, moreover, that Chambers, on the same day, and only a few hours after the execution of Nuncomar, proposed carrying the consequences of the conviction even beyond the execution ; he read a letter, in which Chambers suggested that the sheriff should be immediately ordered to seal up, not only the books and papers of the malefactor, but also his house and goods ; and that a commission should issue under the seal of the Supreme Court, to inquire after his effects at Moorshedabad, and elsewhere.*   But on this

---

* Mr. Chambers said in this letter, " among his papers, it is said, there will be found bonds from many persons, both black and white, against whom I conceive that writs of *scire facias* should be directed by us, as Supreme Coroners."

Mr. Macaulay, in the Edinburgh Review and in his Essays, says, " The Mussulman historian of those times assures us, that, in Nuncomar's house, a casket was found, containing *counterfeits of the seals of all the richest men of the province.*"   I have never fallen in with any other authority for this story, which, in itself, is by no means improbable.

occasion, the Chief Justice alleged, that, as the Charter had not appointed any officer to secure escheats and forfeitures, he did not consider it to be the duty of the Court to act as escheater for the Crown; and that, therefore, he had declined giving any such orders. He asked whether Sir Robert Chambers, after his public concurrence, and his zeal to prosecute the effect of the conviction, to its utmost consequence, could wish to be defended by a denial of his approbation both of the judgment and the execution?

Sir Elijah had no recollection of any appeal; but he had reason to believe, that a petition delivered by the prisoner, desiring to be respited, and recommended to his Majesty's mercy, had been, after a long lapse of time, confounded with an appeal. If there had been an appeal, it must remain on record, and be capable of proof. He quoted the clause of the Charter respecting appeals; by which clause, the Supreme Court had full and absolute power to allow or *deny* appeals.

He next quoted the clause relating to respites; by this last clause, the Supreme Court were empowered "to reprieve or suspend execution of sentence, in cases where there shall appear a proper occasion for mercy;" but in such cases, they were demanded to transmit to the Sovereign a state of the case, of the evidence, and of their reasons for recommending the criminal to mercy.

Hereupon he argued, that neither the law nor the Charter required the judges to assign reasons for carrying the judgment into execution; that it was only in case of *not executing* it that they were bound to *assign their reasons*. He maintained that there were no reasons to be assigned for respiting Nuncomar.

"Could it," said he, "have been stated as reason to his Majesty, that Nuncomar had preferred an accusation against Mr. Hastings? Who was the accuser, and who the accused? It was notorious to all India, that Nuncomar had been the public accuser of Mohammed Reza Khan, without effect, though supported by the power and influence of Government. He had been convicted before the judges, of a conspiracy to bring false accusations against another Member of the Council. Against whom was the accusation? Not against Mr. Hastings, censured by this House; not against Mr. Hastings, impeached by the House of Lords;

not the Mr. Hastings for whom the scaffold is erected in Westminster Hall; but that Mr. Hastings whom I had heard the Prime Minister of England, in full Parliament, declare, to consist of the only flesh and blood that had resisted temptation, in the infectious climate of India; that Mr. Hastings, whom the King and Parliament of England had selected for his exemplary integrity, and entrusted with the most important interest of this realm. Whatever *ought* to be my opinion of Mr. Hastings *now*, I claim to be judged by the opinion I *ought* to have had of him *then*. What evidence had the judges that the accusation of Nuncomar was true? How could they know they were screening a public offender in the person of Mr. Hastings, so lately applauded, so lately rewarded, by the whole nation? Ought the judges to have taken so decided an opinion on the guilt of Mr. Hastings, as to grant a pardon to a felon, and assign as a reason that the convict had been *his* accuser? With what justice to Mr. Hastings could this have been done? With what justice to the community? Who could have been safe, if mere accusation merited indemnity?"

Sir Elijah insisted that neither he nor the other judges had prejudiced Nuncomar, or acted unfairly towards him or his witnesses; that, while there was no reason that could justify the Court in recommending the prisoner to mercy, there were many against it; that the defence, in the opinion of both the judges and jury, was a fabricated system of perjury; that the jury requested that the prisoner's witnesses might be prosecuted; that, after the trial, it became matter of public notoriety that the defence had been fabricated, and witnesses procured to swear to it by an agent of the prisoner; and that one of the judges, Mr. Justice Lemaistre, had declared, that a large sum of money had been offered to him to procure a respite.

In the next place, my father alluded to the attentions and honours paid to Nuncomar while in prison, by General Clavering, Colonel Monson, and Mr. Francis; stating, that the secretaries and aides-de-camp of those Members of Council, visited him after his commitment for the felony, and that the ladies of the families of General Clavering, and Colonel Monson, were in the habit of sending their compliments to him in the prison. He affirmed, what already had been affirmed upon oath in another place, that Nuncomar, cheered by these

flattering attentions—very unusual in such a case—
conceived hopes of being released, through the influence
of General Clavering and Colonel Monson, even to the
day before his execution, when he wrote a letter to the
Council for that purpose. After reading the affidavit
of Yeandle, the jailer, he read two other affidavits made
at the time, by two gentlemen at Calcutta, who were
connected with the native inhabitants, and who swore
that it was an opinion prevalent among them, that the
Rajah would be released by General Clavering, or the
Council. One of these affidavits was that of Mr.
Alexander Elliot, a younger brother of Sir Gilbert
Elliot, the present accuser of Sir Elijah Impey. Mr.
Alexander Elliot, who held at the time a civil office at
Calcutta, had been conversant with the whole business,
and had even interpreted at the trial of Nuncomar.
He left India not long after to return to England; and
was *then* intrusted with a discretionary power from the
Chief Justice, and his brother judges, to publish the
trial if he thought it necessary : it being known to
them that very unfavourable representations were
current in England.

" *He*," said my father, " had collated the notes, and had
undertaken to bear testimony to the authenticity of them;
he had served voluntarily as interpreter through the whole
trial. He pointed out the prevarications of the witnesses;
he could have verified the narration from his own memory ; and, what is material to this point, he could have
spoken as an eye-witness to my particular conduct at the
trial. He lived in that intimacy with me, that I may
almost say he made part of my family; and as no secret of
my heart was unrevealed to him, he could have given the
fullest and most unequivocal account of my sentiments with
regard to carrying the sentence into execution. The calumnies propagated from Calcutta, by minutes of Council,
secret there, but published, and meant to be published, in
England, made him use the discretion intrusted to him to
refute them. He printed the trial; his testimony could have
supported the truth of it; if it could not, no consideration
would have prevailed on him to have published a trial with
such gross misrepresentations; and, by undertaking the vindication of the judges, to have been instrumental in deceiving
the King, his Ministers, and the public, in the most abandoned manner. He is unfortunately no more. But, though

I am deprived of his living testimony, yet his acts and his character still bear evidence for me."

Sir Elijah then read a letter from another gentleman, eminent in the civil service in India, to show the sense entertained of Alexander Elliot's excellent qualities, and the impression made by his premature death ; and he otherwise dwelt on the subject in a manner to embarrass Sir Gilbert Elliot, the brother of the deceased.

" Inventive malice," said my father, " can do no injury to his memory, except the prosecutor, by maintaining the foul motives charged on me, should, by necessary consequence, fix them on him, and thereby blast his fair fame with unmerited infamy, for the zealous part he took in the investigation of truth."

In his correspondence with the Secretary of State, Sir Elijah had referred to Mr. Elliot, and to the papers of which he was the bearer, for the proofs that nothing relating to the trial was intended to be hid from the English nation. In the same letter to the Secretary of State, a copy of which he read at the bar, he affirmed that, on a detection of gross practices on the part of the prisoner to suborn witnesses, made before Mr. Justice Lemaistre, and Mr. Justice Hyde, a band of witnesses sent down from Burdwan to give evidence at his trial, immediately disappeared ; and, that it would be seen, on perusal of the trial, that the guilt of the prisoner was proved as strongly from the case he attempted to make out, as from the evidence on the side of the prosecution.

Sir Elijah likewise read a letter addressed to himself by Mr. Alexander Elliot, in which that gentleman spoke of the disputes, misrepresentations, and falsehoods, of the majority of the Supreme Council, and pledged himself to be warm in defending the judges. In this letter, Mr. Elliot said, that no expressions could be harsher than what the Council deserved,—meaning hereby, Clavering, Monson, and Francis.

Sir Elijah complained that there had never been an instance of so extraordinary a charge against any judge in England, even on a recent cause ; and that his own case was the more perilous and extraordinary, in his being accused on account of acts done thirteen years before the time at which, and in a country sixteen thou-

sand miles from the place in which he was now called
upon to answer for them; and that not only without
receiving any notice of the charge, but after having
been misled into a security that no such charge would
ever be made against him. He reminded the House
that his prosecutor, Sir Gilbert Elliot, had not even
asserted that he could produce any evidence to show an
illegal communication between him and Mr. Hastings,
or his partisans; that he was without evidence even
that Mr. Hastings, or his partisans, were in any league
or combination against the prisoner; that they had any
communication with the prosecutor, or were in any
manner instrumental or privy to the prosecution. He
said that Mr. Hastings had been purged on oath on
that subject; that the only proof assumed, was an inference drawn from the single circumstance that Nuncomar was not capitally indicted till after he had accused Mr. Hastings—a circumstance which had been
satisfactorily accounted for; and he insisted that,
though the fact had been for eleven years the subject
of parliamentary investigation, and Mr. Hastings's conduct had been most critically scrutinized, nothing had
been, or possibly could be brought to light to prove any
combination against Nuncomar.

" From this sole circumstance," continued Sir Elijah,
" standing as it does, it is asserted, that such a notoriety has
arisen, as to produce an *universal necessary conviction* that
the whole proceedings were for the purpose of screening Mr.
Hastings from justice.

" That no such universal conviction did ever actually exist,
I have the most infallible proofs; or, if it did exist, that the
whole body of Armenian and Hindu inhabitants of Calcutta,
that all the free merchants, all the grand jury, all the petit
jury, Sir Robert Chambers and all the judges, the Governor
General and all the Council, must have been united in the
same horrid combination. For I have in my hand, the addresses of all the Armenians, of all the Hindus, of all the free
merchants, and of the grand jury, which authorised part, and
heard all our proceedings, when those proceedings were
recent."

Sir Elijah insisted that these Calcutta addresses had
proceeded spontaneously from the good opinion of those
who drew them up and signed them. He said,—

" To the addresses I know objections have been made, and perhaps will be revived, that they were procured by power and influence. How such power or influence could be derived from the Court, cannot, I believe, be easily accounted for. In whom the power and influence of Government was then vested, every act of power and every record of the Company have fully published. The Company's servants, on whom such power and influence must act most immediately and forcibly, formed the only body that did not join in the addresses. And that the gentleman* whose name stood first on the address of the free merchants, who had been president of the settlement, and then enjoyed the office of Superintendent of the Police, for which a knowledge of the manners and habits of the country was particularly necessary, and for which his long residence in the country had pecularly qualified him, was, immediately after presenting the address, without any fault objected to him, discharged from his office, and his place supplied by a gentleman who had not been many months in the settlement, is a fact which will not be controverted.† My portraits now hanging, the one in the Town Hall, the other in the Court House— the one put up soon after this trial, the other on my leaving the settlement—if this notoriety be true, are libels against the inhabitants, the settlement, the judges, advocates, attorneys, and officers of the Court, who subscribed no small sum for the preserving my memory amongst them."

If the existence of a plot or combination against Nuncomar had been notorious, as described in Sir Gilbert Elliot's charge, how was the conduct of numerous and respectable classes of men to be accounted for? Was it a universal conspiracy in favour of the Governor General? Was there no man left in all Calcutta with conscience and courage enough to interpose, in order to prevent this alleged legal murder?

"The alleged notoriety," said Sir Elijah, "could not have had any operation on the minds of the grand jury who found the bill, nor of the petit jury who convicted him ; nor of Sir Robert Chambers, and the other judges, who sat through the trial, agreeing and assenting to all the acts of the Court ; who

* Mr. Playdell. He had been formerly President of the Council. Every man who knew him in India, must bear his testimony to the respectability of his character, and the peculiar propriety with which he conducted that office.

† The gentleman thus thrust into the office of Superintendent of the Police, was Mr. Macrabie, brother-in-law to Mr. Francis.

concurred in giving sentence, in disallowing the appeal (if any there was), in refusing the respite, signing the calendar, and carrying the sentence into execution. Had my conduct been profligate, as it is stated to have been, should not the other judges, instead of concurring, have opposed me in every step? If Sir Robert Chambers had really, as is asserted, thought the proceedings illegal, if this notoriety had produced this conviction in him, if he deemed my conduct iniquitous, was not he particularly bound to have taken an active part? Should he not have given a counter charge to the jury? Should he not, by exposing my corruption, and detecting my partiality, have held me up—if I had not sufficiently done it myself—to the detestation of the jury and the whole settle-ment? This has, under similar circumstances, been done by honest puisne judges in England; could passiveness and si-lence in such a case be reconciled to honour and conscience? That this notoriety did not influence the Governor General and Council, or that which is called the majority of the Council, I am able to give still more convincing proofs from their direct unequivocal official public acts; and by *those acts* I desire it may be determined whether their opinions are in support of, or in opposition to, the prosecution on this article."

My father then related one of the most startling cir-cumstances in the whole affair. On the 30th of August, 1775, several days after the execution of Nuncomar, the Governor General and Council ordered a paper to be burned by the hands of the common hangman, as containing libellous matter against the judges. The paper was a petition or representation from Nuncomar to the Council; but its contents were not published. The judges knew that both this paper, and the pro-ceedings on it, *ought* to be transmitted to the Directors, and the King's Ministers; and, that the paper, though kept secret in Calcutta, would be made known in England. They therefore applied for a copy of the libel: this reasonable request was refused by the Coun-cil; but Sir Elijah Impey had at last, and by other means, obtained a copy of the libel, and of the proceed-ings of the Council upon it; and these he now read to the Commons.

He informed the House, that, on the 14th day of August, just nine days after Nuncomar had been hanged, General Clavering told the Council that, on the 4th of that month, the day before the execution of the Rajah, a person, calling himself the servant of Nuncomar, came to his house, and sent in an open paper. In presenting the paper for a respite nine days after death, Clavering said,—

"As I imagined that the paper might contain some request that I should take some steps to intercede for him, and being resolved not to make any application whatever in his favour, I left the paper on my table until the 6th, which was the day after his execution, when I ordered it to be translated by my interpreter. As it appears to me that this paper contains several circumstances which it may be proper for the Court of Directors, and his Majesty's Ministers to be acquainted with, I have brought it with me here, and desire that the Board will instruct me what I have to do with it; the title of it is, 'A representation from Maharajah Nuncomar to the General and Gentlemen of Council.'"

Mr. Francis thought the paper ought to be received and read. Mr. Barwell, who also voted with Mr. Hastings, could not understand by what authority General Clavering thought he might, at his own pleasure, keep back, or bring before the Board, a paper addressed to them; or how the address came to be translated for the particular information of the General, before it was presented to the Council.

"If the General," said he, "thinks himself authorised to suppress a paper addressed to the Gentlemen of Council, he is the only judge of that authority; for my part, I confess myself to be equally astonished at the mysterious air with which this paper is brought before us, and the manner in which it came to the General's possession; as likewise, at the particular explanation of every part of it before it was brought to the Board."

The astonishment expressed by Mr. Barwell must be felt by every one that reads these strange transactions; nor will it be diminished, by the explanation given by Clavering. The General said, in reply to Mr. Barwell, that until he had put the paper into the hands of his translator, he could not know what it meant; that the first day the Council met after knowing its contents— that is to say, after Nuncomar had been hanged—he brought the paper to the Board, but, the Board not having gone that day into the *secret department,* he did not think it proper, at that time, to introduce it. Colonel Monson thought that the paper ought now to be received and read. Mr. Hastings said,—

"I do not understand this mystery. If there can be a doubt whether the paper be not already before the Board, by the terms of the General's first minute upon it, I do myself insist that it be produced, if it be only to give me an opportunity of knowing the contents of an address to the Superior Council of India, excluding the first Member in the title of it, and conferring that title on General Clavering; and I give it as my opinion, that it ought to be produced."

General Clavering replied, that the address did not bear the meaning which Mr. Hastings gave it; and that, at all events, he was no more answerable for the title of the paper, than he was for its contents.

It was then resolved, that the paper should be received and read. Mr. Hastings then moved that, as the petition contained expressions reflecting upon the characters of the Chief Justice and judges, a copy of it should be sent to them.

Mr. Francis objected that to send any such copy would be giving the thing more weight than it deserved.

"*I consider,*" said he, "*the insinuations contained in it against them as wholly unsupported, and of a libellous nature; and, if I am not irregular in this place, I would move that orders should be given to the sheriff, to cause the original to be burned publicly, by the hands of the common hangman.*"

Mr. Barwell had no objection to the paper being burned by the hangman; but, he agreed with the Governor General, in thinking that a copy ought to be delivered to the judges. Colonel Monson, on the contrary, apprehended that the Board, by communicating the thing to the judges, might make themselves liable to a prosecution for a libel. He added :—

"The paper I deem to have a libellous tendency, and the assertions contained in it are unsupported. I agree with Mr. Francis in opinion, that the paper should be burned under the inspection of the sheriff, by the hands of the common hangman."

General Clavering also agreed with Francis, that the paper ought to burned at once, without saying anything to the judges about it. Mr. Hastings, on the other hand, urged, that the people of Calcutta formed but a very small part of that collective body commonly called the world.

"The petition itself," said he, "stands upon our records, through which it will find its way to the Court of Directors, to his Majesty's ministers, and, in all probability, will become public to the whole people of Britain."

Mr. Francis begged leave to observe, that, by the same channel through which the Directors, Ministers, and British public might be informed of the contents of the paper, they would also be informed of the reception it had met with, and the sentence passed upon it by the Board.

"I therefore *hope*," said he, "by its being destroyed in the manner proposed, will be sufficient to clear the character of the judges, so far as they appear to be attacked in that paper; and to prevent *any possibility* of the imputations indirectly thrown on the judges from extending *beyond this Board*, I move that the entry of the address from Rajah Nuncomar, entered on our proceedings on Monday last, be expunged."

The will of the majority was acted upon; the entry was expunged; the translation was destroyed, and the original, without any copy being sent to the judges, was publicly burned with all due solemnity, not by the common hangman, for there was none in Calcutta, but by the common gaoler. After reading all these minutes, Sir Elijah Impey said, that notwithstanding the anxiety of Mr. Francis that every memorial of Nuncomar's petition or representation should be destroyed, he possessed an authentic copy of it, with the translation, corrected by Mr. Hastings, who had given him the copy.

"Mr. Hastings," continued my father, "thought it no more than common justice to the judges to give it to me, and as it was in the secret-department of government, he delivered it to me under an oath of secrecy, not to disclose it in India except to the judges; except to them it has not been disclosed to this day, when it is called forth by necessity for my defence."

At the desire of the House, Sir Elijah Impey afterwards delivered in a *fac-simile* copy of the original translation of the paper, with Hastings's interlineary corrections. The paper after enumerating the rank, honours, and high employment of Nuncomar, said, that many English gentlemen had become his enemies, and having no other means of concealing their own actions, revived an old affair which had repeatedly been found to be false; that the prosecutor was a notorious liar, and had been treated as such by the Governor General, who had turned him out of his house; that the English gentlemen had become the aiders and abettors of this notorious liar, and that Lord Impey and the other justices had tried and condemned the writer, Nuncomar, by the English laws, which were contrary to the customs of the country, &c.

Sir Elijah argued, that General Clavering's sense of the propriety of allowing no respite, must appear from the whole of his conduct, and from the mode in which he treated that paper after he received it. He also cited Clavering's testimony upon oath; by which, it appeared, he did not consider that the prosecution of Mr. Hastings at all depended on the evidence of Nuncomar.

If General Clavering thought there were circumstances in the case which ought to render Nuncomar a proper object for mercy, could he have defeated the petition of the unhappy convict, by detaining his paper until it could be of no possible use to him? That paper was no private address to the General, but an address to the Board at large, whose sense he would not suffer to be taken on the propriety of recommending him to mercy, as he never produced the paper until nine days after the execution! If the paper was unsupported then, what new matter had arisen to support it now? If it was not good to obtain mercy for Nuncomar, how could it be good to bring down impeachment and punishment upon Sir Elijah Impey? What could make that a just accusation now, which was held to be false and libellous then?

Towards the close of his speech, Sir Elijah Impey thus pointedly reflected upon Francis :—

"That the paper itself should have survived, is hardly more providential for me, than that the gentleman who moved for the condemnation of it, and who expressed *his hopes* that it would prevent *any possibility* of the imputations indirectly thrown out against the judges, *from extending be-yond that Board,* is the surviving member of that majority. From him, who, to prevent its extending beyond that Board, had, with so much solicitude, procured the paper to be expunged from the proceedings, I hope I may be thought to have some claim to expect that these imputations will not be encouraged in England; should, nevertheless, such imputations have been suggested by any Member or Members of the Council—and I am sorry to say that their secret minutes show that there have—I am in the judgment of the House, whether it would not be a precedent of dangerous tendency to admit *secret communications and private informations,* in evidence, from any persons whomsoever, to disavow and contradict their own *solemn official unanimous acts,* entered upon public records,—on records *required by Act of Parliament to be transmitted to his Majesty's ministers, as authentic information, both of their acts, and their reasons for their acts.*"

Sir Elijah then said, that, as he had been charged as an individual, so he had defended himself as an individual.

"But," added he, "though called to answer as for acts done by me singly, those acts not only were not, *but could not* have been, done by me individually; I was one member sitting in a Court consisting of four members; *all the four members concurred* in the acts imputed to me; my voice singly and by itself could have had *no operation ;* I might have been over-ruled by a majority of *three to one.* I was not *more* concerned in the proceedings than any other judge; I was *less* so than two.[*] Informations had been laid against the criminal before two of the judges [Lemaistre and Hyde], who, by committing him for felony, *had applied this law* to his case, without my knowledge or privity. I was, indeed, applied to by the Council, as to the mode of his confinement; I had no right *to revise the acts of the judges ;* their authority was equal to mine; I did what humanity required; I made the strictest inquiries of the pundits, as to the effect of his imprisonment on his caste and religion; I learned they could not be hurt. I gave directions to the sheriff that he should have the best accommodations the gaol would afford; the jailer and his family quitted their apartments, and gave them up to him; I directed that every indulgence, consistent with his safe custody, should be granted him. *These only, were my individual acts,* and these appear on the report of your Com-

---

[*] Mr. Justice Lemaistre and Mr. Justice Hyde.

mittee.   If it had been just so to do, it was not I, but the
Court, which must have *afforded protection* to the criminal because the accuser of Mr. Hastings;   it was not I,
but the *Court*, that must have *quashed that indictment* ; it
was not I, but the *Court*, which *retained the prosecution;*
had Sir Robert Chambers been overruled, it was not I, but
the *Court*, that could have *overruled* him; it was not I, but
the *whole Court* that rejected *the appeal*—if there was an
appeal—that *refused the respite*, and *carried the sentence
into execution.*   ALL signed the calendar ; I executed no act
of authority as a magistrate, but sitting in *open Court*, assisted *by all the judges;* even those acts which are *peculiarly* objected to me, as *mine individually*, though I was the
proper channel of the Court to pronounce them, are not my individual acts; as Chief Justice, I *presided* in the Court,—was
the *mouth* of the Court ; *all questions* put, or *observations*
made by me, *were with the judges sitting on my right hand,
and on my left ;* those questions and those observations were
not mine, but the questions and observations of *the Court.*
I did not presume to make observations in my summing up to
the jury, without having first communicated with the judges,
and taken their unanimous opinion, on every article.   .   .   .
As no *act* is imputable *solely* to me, so there is no *motive*, in
the whole charge, assigned for my conduct, that is not *equally*
applicable *to every other judge;* nor is there one allegation that
exonerates the other judges, and applies them specifically to
me: if they are true with regard *to me*, they are true as applied *to every judge of the Court.*   The notoriety of the injustice of the proceedings applies to *all*, and gives an equal
ground of conviction, that *all the judges were in a combination
to sacrifice an innocent man, for the purpose of screening Mr.
Hastings from justice ;* ALL must have shown *an equally determined purpose against the life of the criminal ;* ALL had
equal knowledge of the accusation, the proceedings in Council,
and the conduct of Mr. Hastings; ALL knew equally the credit
of the witnesses, and the infamy of the un-named witness.
There is no stage of the business where they are not *all* as
much implicated in the motives as I could be;   yet *I alone*
am called to answer, whilst *they*, if this charge be true, are
*administering justice in Bengal, notoriously branded with
infamy,—and still judging on the lives of men, with hands
stained with blood !*   Though I say this as necessary to my
defence, I most solemnly protest, and most anxiously request,
that it may clearly be understood, that I do not entertain the
most distant wish that any judge of the Supreme Court should
meet with the same fate which I have experienced, after long
and faithful services in so inhospitable a climate, in their de-

cline of life, and be dragged from their tribunals, to appear as
criminals at this bar. Respect for their character, and friendship for their persons, whom in my conscience I know not to
deserve so harsh a treatment, would reprobate so unjust and
so malignant a wish. But I may, without prejudice to them,
deplore, that though *aided by their reasons for concurring in
the proceedings of the Court*, thus *separated* from them, and
called upon, as I am, *I cannot be armed by their reasons in my
defence*. Though *my* arguments feebly enforced may fail of
success, yet if urged more forcibly *by them*, and with such
addition of others, as *their* learning and ability might supply,
they might operate to conviction on the minds of my judges ;
and should I be so unfortunate as to be thought *impeachable*
for these JOINT ACTS, *they*, on better reasons shown, may be
exculpated. Had *they* been joined with me, I should have had
a right to avail myself of *their reasons* as well as my own. It
is hardly conceivable that any man, whose constant habits of
life have been known to be such as mine have been—and there
are not wanting members in this House who know both how
and with whom the earlier part of my life, down to the time I
quitted this country, had been spent—that I, a man, I will
assume to say, who left this country with a character at least
unimpeachable, who maintained that character till May, 1775,
should, in the course of the next month, have been so totally
lost to every principle of justice, every duty of office, every sense
of shame, every feeling of humanity, to have been so deeply
immersed, and hardened in iniquity, as to be able deliberately
to plan, and steadily to perpetrate murder, with all the circumstances with which it is here charged and aggravated.
Nemo repente fuit turpissimus. But if the minds of men, be-
sieged by constant repetitions of the same slander, laboured
into them daily and hourly, by perpetual and unremitting
libels, assailed by base whispers in private, and the malicious
clamours of faction in public, can, with regard to me, an individual, have been prepared to admit the belief of a fact so
strange and so unnatural; yet had four judges been now ranged
at this bar, all men of unimpeachable characters, down to the
same period of time, all charged with the same sudden loss of
virtue, and violent precipitation into the most abandoned guilt,
all charged with the same deliberate purpose, the same steady,
cool, unrelenting execution of so foul a crime ; it would have
struck the eyes, as well as the reason of the House ; common
sense would have revolted at it; it must have been pronounced
impossible! After what I have disclosed to the House, I trust
in my single case also it will be pronounced impossible. I
have been too long—I have had great indulgence—I fear I
have abused it too much—I will make no recapitulation : but,

if the judgment was legal, if no justifiable grounds could be assigned either of grievance to allow an appeal, or of favour to recommend to mercy ; if the matters of the reports do not supply competent evidence to support the article ; if the public opinion formed on libels, and misled by false authorities, is no ground for impeachment ; if the opinions of the Court of Directors, and the majority of the Council in Bengal fairly discussed, operate not in support, but to the defeat of this accusation ; if I am accused of no act, but what was a judicial joint act of the whole Court consisting of four judges; if no act is charged on me but what is equally chargeable on the other three judges ; if no motive is imputed to me but what is equally imputable to all the judges ; if the whole was in the ordinary course of justice, and there be, after every scrutiny, no evidence of any undue motives ; I now, Sir, finally submit, with perfect resignation to the judgment of the House, whether, at the distance of thirteen years, during nine of which, after the commission of the supposed offence, I have been permitted to preside in the Supreme Court, when by lapse of time, I must necessarily have been deprived of material living evidence, and by just inference, from the having been called to answer a *specific* charge of a less heinous nature, for a fact *subsequent* to this by seven years, I have been prevented from bringing evidence from Bengal, under all the circumstances with which I have fatigued the House, it be consistent with its candour, wisdom, and justice, to put me *alone* at the bar of the House of Lords, to answer criminally for the JUDICIAL ACTS OF AN UNANIMOUS COURT."

This, my father's triumphant defence, together with the vouchers produced to support every part of it, occupied two days in the delivery. It produced a deep impression on all who heard it. Mr. Pitt, the Premier, affirmed that, if he had been placed in the same situation, he could not say but that he should have acted precisely as Sir Elijah Impey had done. Other men, less cautious than the Prime Minister, expressed their indignation that a charge at once so atrocious and so absurd, should ever have been brought against a man of established character,—a man of honour and feeling, —against an upright and enlightened British judge. It was quite clear, from the effect produced by this oral defence alone, that the prosecution of my father would speedily be dropped. His enemies could not but feel that they had miscalculated his strength ; nor could

Sir Gilbert Elliot, the leader of the attack, defend himself from the humiliating conviction, that he had been frustrated and exposed, and placed in a position which no man laying claim to the charities of our nature, to fraternal affection, and gratitude for family services and friendship, would willingly occupy.

Sir Elijah had delivered his defence as an extempore speech; not reading it from a prepared and corrected manuscript as Mr. Hastings—who was no orator—had done : accordingly, when asked whether he would leave the House a copy of it, he said he could not, as he had not written it out, and had spoken hurriedly and under great agitation of feeling. Neither by law, nor by usage, was my father bound to act, in this particular, otherwise than he did. Precedent was rather in favour of his oral speech than of Hastings's written defence; and, even if he had committed his speech to writing—which he had not—he was free to give in or to withhold his manuscript, or any copy of it;* yet, both Fox and Burke angrily expressed their regret that the charges upon the table of the House had not been met by a *written* defence, which might remain in the hands of the House, and so save it much trouble and inconvenience.

But, very shortly after, my father's defence was given to the world. It was printed from very accurate shorthand notes, which were taken by a competent person while it was being delivered at the Commons' bar. With the very copious appendix of documents and vouchers—for the most part taken upon oath—it fills an octavo volume of 423 pages. It was published by John Stockdale, Piccadilly, and bears the date of 1788, in the month of February of which year the defence was spoken at the bar. Either a small edition was published, or care was taken by the calumniators of Sir Elijah Impey, to buy it up and destroy the copies. It is now among the rarest of books ; except the copy from which I have made the copious extracts contained in this chapter, and here and there another in the possession of one or more of my imme-

---

* For some of Sir Elijah's own reasoning on this point, see extracts from his own pamphlet, in reply to Francis, in the ensuing Chapter of this volume.

diate relatives and friends, I know not of a single impression extant; there is no copy in our national library, where nearly everything which appeared on the other side is to be found; there is no copy in the library of the East India House; there is no copy in any place where I have sought for it; and the many and long-continued searches made by myself, and, for me, by my friends, among book-stalls and dealers in old books, have all been fruitless. The much-prized copy I possess, will soon be lodged in the library of the British Museum, together with other materials which may, in future, enable the candid and industrious inquirer to form juster notions of the character of Sir Elijah Impey, and of an important part of the history of our Indian Empire, than have hitherto been conveyed by professed historians of India, compilers, and essayists. I have only to regret that, through circumstances which occurred in my early years, and over which I could exercise no control, my collection of MS. letters is not so full and complete as it might easily have been, and as, in fact, *it was*, a short time before the death of my beloved and venerated father. Still, however, the collection is of value. There will be found in it many interesting and highly characteristic letters of the great Hastings, which his biographer, Mr. Gleig, was compelled, by his limits, to omit.

I have repeatedly called Sir Elijah's speech before the Commons a "triumphant defence." Every attentive reader of common feeling and impartiality, will bear me out, and justify me in this expression,—

" Χάρμα δ' οὐκ ἀλλότριον νι-
κα φορία πατέρος."

CHAPTER XIV.

REPLY OF SIR ELIJAH IMPEY TO A PAMPHLET BY MR. FRANCIS.

Sir Elijah's persecutors were greatly embarrassed and irritated by his manly and convincing defence before the Commons, and by the very visible impression it made upon the House. Francis felt his character so seriously implicated by the revelations made by my father, with regard to that mysterious business, the suppressing, and then burning the Nuncomar petition, that he could not but attempt a reply. This he did with his customary vehemence and cunning—for Philip Francis, like some other men, could be cunning and vehement in the same breath—from his place in the House, on the 27th of February, 1788, or twenty-three days after Sir Elijah had spoken his defence at the bar. And, not resting satisfied with his speech in Parliament, and such abridged report of it as appeared in the newspapers, he published his oration as a separate pamphlet. To that production my father considered himself bound to reply. His " Refutation " is now before me; and this *brochure,* of only 54 pages,* and his defence at the bar of the House,

---

* The full title of the pamphlet is,—"A Refutation of a Pamphlet, entitled, The Answer of Philip Francis, Esq., to the Charges exhibited against him, General Clavering, and Colonel Monson, by Sir Elijah Impey, Knt., when at the bar of the House of Commons, on his Defence to the Nuncomar Charge. To which is added a *fac-simile* Copy of the Petition of Nuncomar, burnt as a libel by the hands of the common hangman, in consequence of a motion of Mr. Francis; with the proceedings relative to it in Council, at Calcutta." London: John Stockdale, 1788.

are the only things Sir Elijah ever published on his own hard case. The pamphlet, like the volume, is exceedingly rare : there has hitherto been no copy of it in our National Library, at the British Museum, where may be found nearly every pamphlet which proceeded from the other side, or assailed the reputation of Sir Elijah Impey or Mr. Hastings. When my present task is over, the pamphlet will be deposited in the Museum with the volume, and such of my family manuscripts as bear upon the question.

When taxed with publishing the pamphlet containing his speech of the 27th of February, Francis *denied the fact*. This was not forgotten by Sir Elijah in his " Refutation," which began thus :—

"To make *any* publication pending judicial proceedings, that may influence the minds of those who are to decide on them, or of the community at large, be it favourable or adverse to the party accused, is certainly censurable ; but in a higher degree, when calculated to prejudice the person under accusation. It was hoped that a stop would have been put to such outrages on justice by the public prosecution ordered by the House of Commons; yet a pamphlet has since appeared of the same nature, calling itself a Speech of Mr. Francis, delivered on the 27th of February, 1788. From the solemnity of the introduction, the public would be induced *to believe it to be genuine*, but it is well known that gentleman *has disavowed it*. Had he not, the futility of the reasoning, the falsehood of the assertions, and its not fulfilling the promise *of ' disclosing such scenes of iniquity as would astonish and shock the House,'* to which Mr. Francis had ' *most solemnly pledged' himself*, give it internal marks of spuriousness, which prove it had no right to boast of being his legitimate offspring; but as the production, frivolous as it is, does not want malice, it is due to justice to detect its falsity for the purpose of obviating its effects.

" It calls that part of Sir Elijah Impey's speech, which is supposed to have given offence, *a charge brought against General Clavering, Colonel Monson, and Mr. Francis ;* and then proceeds to state what that charge was—laying the fault on Sir Elijah Impey, in not having reduced his speech to writing, if it is not stated fairly. In one particular, it is not only stated unfairly, but *falsely :* he did not mention the secret minutes of the Council, which were in contradiction to their public acts, as being made *before and after* the execution of Nuncomar; in fact, none existed *before*. The fair way of stating the case, would have been, to have given the proceedings in Council, on the the 14th and 16th of August, 1775, at large, together with the paper which was the subject of them; and then, the minutes which were asserted to be contradictory to the public acts, being thus confronted with them, every reader might, on inspection, determine, whether such contradictions did exist, without attending to arguments necessarily perplexing, when the *materials*, on which they are grounded, are withheld."

Thus, as the reader will observe, not only the recent defamers of Sir Elijah Impey, but the very men who brought the original accusations against him, dealt in the *suppressio veri*,—in the withholding of *materials*, in the contempt of evidence, and in the ingenuity which perplexes, and the rhetoric which dazzles the uninformed mind. But my father, after the words last quoted, says, " here are those proceedings ; " and he goes on to give, in his " Refutation," those " Extracts of Bengal Secret Consultations," of the 14th and 16th of August, 1775, which I have already quoted,* and which fully prove the manner in which Francis, Clavering, and Monson, dealt with Nuncomar's petition, *after* the execution of the Rajah. After these Extracts, which Francis would fain have *buried*—

" Deeper than did ever plummet sound,"

Sir Elijah gave a *fac-simile*† copy of the paper which had been the subject of those proceedings in Council,— namely, the Nuncomar petition,—and extracted, from a very accurate report of his own speech at the bar of the Commons, taken in short-hand at the time it was delivered, the reflections he had really made on the conduct and motives of General Clavering, in withholding the petition until the Rajah was hanged, in declaring it to be a libel, &c.‡ These quotations from his speech at the bar, were followed up by extracts or copies of the secret minutes—complained of, and asserted to be contradictory to those proceedings—of the 21st March, 24th April, 15th September, 21st Novem-

---

* See ante, p. 94—98.
† For copies of this *fac-simile*, see the " Speech of Sir Elijah Impey," &c. &c., printed for J. Stockdale, Appendix, p. 158—161 ; the " Refutation," p. 11—14 ; and the Appendix to the present volume.
‡ See the preceding chapter, p. 316.

ber, 1775, and 21st March, 1776. Some of these minutes I have given in a previous part of this volume.

Francis, in his speech of the 27th of February, and in the pamphlet to which my father replied, said, among other reasons why Nuncomar's petition was treated as a libel, and burned,—

" It included *all* the judges; concerning two of whom— Mr. Justice Hyde, and Sir Robert Chambers—they * never had any suspicion of corrupt motives, and concerning another of whom—Mr. Justice Lemaistre—they had then no ground of suspicion, except his intimacy with Sir Elijah Impey, his acting on all occasions as his instrument, and the notorious violence of his deportment; they, therefore, treated it [the petition] as a libel against a whole Court of Justice ought to be treated."

To this my father rejoined,—

" It was, then, a libel, because it imputed guilt to *all* the judges collectively, and did not distinguish them from Sir Elijah Impey, to whom, alone, the whole guilt was to be imputed. Every publication, therefore, which attributes the guilt to them collectively, and not to Sir Elijah Impey, *is a libel*. . . . . To support this position, several minutes are produced. This is said to be his—Mr. Francis's —defence against the charge, as it affects the Council collectively. The minutes cited for this purpose, are from the Secret Consultations of these dates, March 21st, 1775, April 24th, 1775, September 15th, 1775, November 21st, 1775, March 21st, 1776. Now, those of the 21st of March, 1775, and 24th of April, 1775, cast no imputation whatever on the Court, or Sir Elijah Impey; they are, indeed, before any proceedings were commenced against Nuncomar; the other minutes are directed *against the whole Court, against the judges collectively ; not one of them discriminates the conduct of Sir Elijah Impey from that of the other judges, by the most distant allusion ;* not one of them has the least tendency to exculpate any of the judges. These, therefore, by the admission of Mr. Francis himself, are *libels*. The writing of those minutes is absolutely irreconcileable with the idea of condemning Nuncomar's petition as a libel, *because it included all the judges*, for the minutes themselves, equally *include them all ;* these must be libels, if that was, and *they* ought to be treated—to use Mr. Francis's words—' *as a libel against a whole court of justice ought to be treated.*' It

* The majority in Council,—Francis, Clavering, and Monson.

does not yet appear to be true, from anything that has been said or published, that Mr. Francis ever *did* charge Sir Elijah Impey singly; at present, therefore, it carries every suspicion of being, what it is denied to be,—' a new distinction, an after-thought, an *ex-post-facto* vindication.' Can Mr. Francis say, that, before the paper was produced at the bar of the House of Commons, he had ever revealed the contents of it to his most confidential friends? Can he say, that he ever before made this defence? The manner in which the attention of the public has been called to this subject, makes it now highly incumbent on him to produce *one* minute, *one declaration*, at least, in which he has charged Sir Elijah Impey *singly*, as is asserted, with ' *this political measure of the most atrocious kind.*' It is the act of a friend to advise him to do it; his friends and the public expect it. He is in time, yet, to urge it against Sir Elijah Impey; no decision has yet passed on the first article [the Nuncomar charge]. He would not have asserted it, if he could not do it, and he will not shrink from it. Let him produce *one*.

" It will be an extraordinary case, indeed, if one judge was able to execute so atrocious a measure, two of the other judges being admitted to be under no suspicion of corrupt motives, and the third only suspected from being intimate with the corrupt judge, from acting as his instrument on all occasions, and from the notorious violence of his temper.

" The latter are bold assertions against a judge who is no more; and, not to be expected from the mouth of him [Francis] who professes to be so tender of the fame of his deceased friends [Clavering and Monson], from the man who claimed favour and indulgence to one of them [Clavering], ' *as due to a person of high character, to a person who is not here, who is not only absent, but dead, and who died in the service of his country.*' To this indulgence, and on the same account, Mr. Justice Lemaistre, was equally entitled, with that gentleman, for whom it was claimed; this wanton and indecent attack might surely have been spared against a man answering to the *same* description. Mr. Justice Lemaistre left behind him a widow, a son, daughters, relations and friends, who may feel as keenly for an injury done to his memory, though, perhaps, not with the same public ostentation, as Mr. Francis may for that of the persons with whom he has been connected. His living in a particular intimacy with Sir Elijah Impey, has been positively and pointedly negatived, before the Committee, by one witness:* his clerk was also before them, and might have been examined to the

* Samuel Tolfrey, Esq.

same point; he could have informed them with *whom the midnight social hours* of that gentleman were spent. * What is meant by the dark innuendo, where it is said, 'of *him* we had *then* no other ground of suspicion,' is not explained; the friends of Mr. Justice Lemaistre have a right to an explanation of it.

"Mr. Justice Lemaistre was so far from being the instrument of Sir Elijah Impey, that his opinions with regard to the jurisdiction of the Supreme Court, differed materially from those of Sir Elijah: he was an honest and a warm man; he was not contented with opposing Sir Elijah Impey on the bench, which he thought his duty required, but protested against his conduct in a public letter. That he openly opposed Sir Elijah Impey in many instances in which the East India Company, and the Council, were materially concerned; and, that the opinion of Sir Elijah Impey was in those cases prevalent, by virtue of the casting voice, given to him as the Chief Justice,—being aided by Sir Robert Chambers only,—must be within the knowledge of Mr. Francis. Will he say, he did not know this to be the case, when a mandamus was applied for, to restore Mr. Stewart to the office of Secretary to the Council, in the action brought by Cummaul O'Deen against the Calcutta Committee, and in the instance of the rule formed by the Court, to support the right of the Company to detain prisoners on account of revenue? If he does remember those oppositions by Mr. Justice Lemaistre, ought he to have been made to say, that Mr. Justice Lemaistre *acted on all occasions*, as the instrument of Sir Elijah Impey?"

Again, admitting, for the sake of argument, that the author of the pamphlet, to which my father was replying, and Francis, who had delivered the speech of the 27th of February,† were not one and the same, but two distinct persons, he continued,—

" But Mr. Francis's character is treated with still greater freedom by this author, who makes him declare, with the most complete *sang froid*, 'that he did not hesitate to declare, in the most explicit manner, that the *private motive* of his standing so forward as he did, for the destruction of the copy, and translations of the petition, sent by Nuncomar previous to his execution to General Clavering, was not the public one assigned.' Does he esteem it a trifling matter to put false reasons on a record, which the Parliament has re-

* Supposed to have been Francis himself.
† The said pamphlet was nothing but a full report of the said speech.

quired to be laid before the King's Ministers, as official authentic intelligence of the acts of the Council, and the special reasons of those acts? After such an avowal, who is to distinguish, on the public records of the Company, what are his true reasons, from those which he may afterwards, 'in the most solemn and explicit manner,' 'on his honour,' and 'on his oath,' 'not hesitate,' when pressed, 'to declare not his true reasons,' 'but that he was really actuated by some private motive?' What a door does this open against him! What private motives of ambition and revenge, after such a declaration, had it been advanced by himself, might not those, who are not inclined to think well of him, assign for many public acts, of which he has himself, perhaps, given the true and honest reasons?

" Let us now suppose the reasons assigned on the record to have been only ostensible; let them be expunged, and every memorial of them be destroyed; let the true operative motive be substituted in their place. 'It was his fear for the safety of General Clavering; Colonel Monson and he observing that the judges had gone all lengths, that they had dipped their hands in blood for a political purpose, and that they might again proceed on the same principle.' This was a reason totally incompatible with that assigned for condemning the paper as a *libel*: this was *an unequivocal accusation of all the judges collectively*, and of the whole Court, *not of Sir Elijah Impey separately*. The judges, not Sir Elijah Impey, had gone all lengths, for *they*, not Sir Elijah Impey *only*, had dipped their hands in blood for a political purpose, and the fear was, that *they*, not *he only*, might again proceed on the same principle, and commit another legal murder on the person of General Clavering. What is become of their want of suspicion of Sir Robert Chambers and Mr. Justice Hyde now? Was all this fear for the safety of General Clavering, on account of Sir Elijah Impey alone? Mr. Justice Lemaistre was then suspected only from his intimacy with Sir Elijah Impey: was it thought, that he was so much an instrument of Sir Elijah, as to have aided him *in inflicting a capital punishment on the General?* And for what? *For what was esteemed publishing of a libel!* 'What he—General Clavering —had done, was, in truth, a most rash and inconsiderate action: namely, the bringing the petition at all before the Board; *the man was dead*, and General Clavering made himself the *publisher of the libel;* he put himself in the power of his enemies, who infallibly would ruin him.' This, let it operate as it may, Mr. Francis declares, 'on his honour', and that he shall, if necessary, *on his oath*, was a strong con-

current motive with Colonel Monson and him, for getting the paper destroyed.' In the same page it is said to be, not the concurrent, but the ' *the sole motive.*' Had this been the reason on record, would even the names of General Clavering and Colonel Monson—so continually insisted on by Mr. Francis as props to his reputation—added to his own name, have procured credit to it from one man in England, *let him be ever so much addicted to party?*''

My father then goes on to expose the monstrous absurdity of Francis's *pretended* belief, that the life of General Clavering was in danger, and that the judges of the Supreme Court at Calcutta,—in the opinion of the Members of Council,—had power over the liberty and life of a Member of Council.

" It was impossible that they should be ignorant, that the publication of a libel, the supposed offence for which it was feared the judges would again go all lengths, and would again dip their hands in blood for a political purpose, could by no strained construction of any law be made a capital offence. Did they fear that the General might be committed ' to the common gaol of Calcutta, *so miserable and so horrid a place, that the bare commitment to it was equal to death?*'* They must have known that in England it was a bailable offence. They knew the special protection which the Charter gave them; ' *That the person or persons of the Governor General, or any of the Council, shall not, nor shall any of them respectively, be subject or liable to be arrested or imprisoned, upon any action, suit, or proceeding, in the said Court, except in cases of treason or felony; nor shall the said Court be competent to hear, try, or determine, any indictment or information, against the said Governor General, or any of the said Council for the time being, for any offence, not being treason or felony, which the said Governor General, or any of the said Council, shall, or may be charged, with having committed in Bengal, Bahar, and Orissa, anything herein contained to the contrary notwithstanding.'* †*

"Was it expected to be believed, that the majority of the Council, with the whole executive power in their hands, would be so tame and submissive to a court of justice, as to suffer the General to be punished in any manner enormous and outrageous ? Could fears arising from the expectation of

---

* With the very extreme of exaggeration, the prison-house of Calcutta had been so described by Francis.

† See Regulating Act and Charter, ante p. 37—43.

such impossible acts, be assigned on the record, as causes for condemning the paper and destroying the memorial of it? If such causes, entered on record, would not have gained credit, they surely do not come with greater authority from the oral testimony of Mr. Francis alone, even with the addition of *his oath*, and of *his honour*, to sanctify them: no man's oath can be received in any court of justice, to falsify a record, much less to falsify *his own act*, recorded solemnly by himself. What would have been the indignation of the majority of the Council, if Sir Elijah Impey had attempted to falsify *their* reasons solemnly entered on record? Let us hear, what they themselves say on a similar occasion, in a minute of the 15th of September, 1775: 'As to the dismission of Mr. Playdell, we have *assigned* our reasons, and disclaim any *right* in Mr. Hastings to attribute our conduct to other motives.' Then what *right* has Mr. Francis *to attribute their conduct to other motives than what they have assigned;* and to throw so gross an imputation on the memory of his deceased friends, as that of having recorded themselves *liars?* Can common sense endure that his testimony should be received to prove, that the panic operating on the minds of him and Colonel Monson, had force sufficient to induce them to condemn a paper as a libel, which, in their consciences, they then thought true, and which Mr. Francis still thinks true, and to add a stigma to the memory of a man, whom they knew to be falsely condemned to death, because he had justly remonstrated against the iniquity of his sentence?

" Was this a cause that could produce such effects? Was this a fear, *qui cadere potest in virum constantem?* The assigning of such a fear as a motive, had those gentlemen been alive, might have been the cause of more real danger to Mr. Francis, than the supposed publication of the libel could have been to the General. Would either of those gentlemen have borne that such a defence should be set up for him with impunity? Would that brave man,* whom Mr. Francis represents as dying in the service of his country, 'not in an honourable, but an odious service; not in the field of battle, where his gallant mind would have led him, but in an odious unprofitable contest;' would he have suffered himself to be protected from such a danger in such a manner? Would the Colonel † have borne to hear such a concurrent motive assigned to himself? Would he have thought it honourable to the General to have falsified the record for his protection against such a fictitious danger? If their fears were so predominant on the 16th of August, as to produce these

---

* Clavering.   † Monson.

extravagant effects, how came they so far dissipated, that the same persons should, on the 15th of September following, adopt in their own name what through fear only they had condemned in the petition of the convict? If it was dangerous on the 16th of August, why was it less so on the 15th of September? Their fears in August were, that they were betrayed by a Member of their Council, to Sir Elijah; had that suspicion ceased in September? "

It had been attempted in the pamphlet to which my father's answer was a refutation,—

" To prove that the minutes and the reasonings on the proceedings are *not* contradictory, because it would have been an act of folly, had they been so, to have entered them on the same record,—that, no men, 'not absolutely idiots,' could have entered such contradictions on the same record, without placing ' themselves in a point of view before the Directors, which must utterly have annihilated their confidence in them.' "

To this flimsy reasoning, my father opposes a train of syllogistical arguments, from which he draws conclusions so plain and convincing, as to leave no single fallacy undetected, no assumed fact disproved. For evidence of this, I refer the reader to the pamphlet itself, from page 37 to 44; the rather, as I have already encroached too far upon the limits allotted, in the present volume, to topics which will be found elsewhere, very copiously discussed.*

But, though I despair of doing justice, in this place to the " Refutation," from whence I have been quoting, yet I cannot, even here, dismiss it altogether, without some further notice of its remaining topics.

" There is one assertion," continues my father, " of a serious nature, indeed, if it has truth and sound reasoning for its foundation. It is asserted, that the paper [i. e. the *fac-simile* of the Nuncomar petition] 'must have been obtained by means the most unjustifiable:' 'by means which prove that they—the Council—were betrayed to Sir Elijah Impey by one of the Members of their Board;' ' which prove to demonstration, a collusion and confederacy between him and Mr. Hastings.' . . . . .

" Before the communication of this paper is admitted to be

---

* Namely, in the documents which I repeat my promise of depositing in the Library of the British Museum.

damning proof, let us see what was communictated, and what was the occasion of the communication. The majority of the Council had, by gross insinuation on their secret minutes, accused both Mr. Hastings and the judges of a combination to take away the life of his accuser, and thus to defeat accusations which had been brought against him. If Mr. Hastings had not been joined in the same charge, ought he, as a man of honour, to have refrained from informing Sir Elijah and the judges of that unjust attack? Which was the dishonourable part of the business, the making these insinuations, as far as they respected the judges, matter of their secret consultations, and by that means transmitting them to England; or, the communicating them to the judges for the purpose of their repelling the injury? Mr. Hastings being in possession of this paper, which was a complete refutation by the Council themselves of the insinuations by them thus despatched to Europe, would Mr. Hastings have done more than common justice by putting it into the hands of one of the judges? But Mr. Hastings himself was personally interested in the vindication of the judges. He was charged as a confederate with them; he was become a joint defendant; it was necessary to him that the defence should be joint; they could not be guilty without his being involved in the same crime; the act which enabled the judges to defend themselves, was, as done by Mr. Hastings, in the nature of self-defence—that was the cause of the communication of the paper; and the paper itself was put into Sir Elijah Impey's hands, as much for the purpose of defending himself, as for the defence of Sir Elijah and the other judges. The Council were *betrayed* to Sir Elijah Impey, because Mr. Hastings put it in the power of the judges to defeat their secret attack; because he did not confederate and conspire with those who accused, to disarm the judges from making a defence, as necessary to his own safety and honour, as it was to that of the judges. This was the criminal intercourse; this was the instance in which they suspected themselves to be betrayed. This intercourse, this communication, did not exist till these minutes made it necessary for the mutual defence of all the parties who had been calumniated; no such communication was ever carried on, but on that occasion: no such had been at the time the paper was condemned; it is an *ex-post-facto* vindication that suggests it.

"The point of honour, on this subject, is carried for Mr. Francis to a most extravagant pitch; these are the words that are given him in speaking of the communication of the paper: '*Even if there had been no oath*, Mr. Hastings was bound by his own agreement; in my breast, I hold *such an agreement* to be equally binding as an oath.' If there *had* been such agreement, was it not *virtually*, was it not *completely* cancelled, when the very matter which was condemned in the paper, had been made matter of accusation against Mr. Hastings? Had not the majority of the Council equally agreed that the paper should be considered as a libel? Had not Mr. Francis—who first denominated it so more especially—agreed to esteem it so? Was not *he*, who had been the first mover in destroying all memorials of it, more particularly bound in honour, if not by his oath, after he thought all memorials actually destroyed, not to have set up that matter, which he had agreed with the Council to consider as false and libellous, as a true accusation against Mr. Hastings? Who was guilty of the first breach of faith, if Mr. Hastings can be supposed to have been ever bound by an agreement? Was it binding on one side and not on the other? Could any point of honour oblige him to submit to the consequence of so foul an accusation, without making use of the means of defence which were in his own hands? It would have been a most refined stroke of policy to have cajoled Mr. Hastings into such an agreement, and such a construction of the point of honour."

Mr. Francis—or the author, as he is called throughout the " Refutation,"—had attempted to account for the Council having refused to apply to the judges for a respite in behalf of Nuncomar; to this my father thought it necessary only to observe,—

" That all the applications of the Council which met with any opposition from the Court, were acts of direct interference with the province of the judges, and *pending the proceedings before the trial.*

" They could not possibly be considered as reasons for not laying such a case before the judges, as they might think reasonable cause to respite the sentence. The Court appears very properly to have resisted the receiving letters and messages concerning matters *in suit before the Court ;* it did not therefore follow, that applications private or public, might not be made to the judges, collectively or individually, for the purpose of a recommendation to mercy."

Here my father quotes the minutes in Council, dated June 25th, and the answer of the Court two days after, to prove that—

" The pamphleteer " had " been guilty of a most gross misrepresentation, by applying an answer of the Court to a subject different from that to which it was given. . . . .

That answer was not given, as is stated in the pamphlet, to any application made *in favour of Nuncomar;* it was a frivolous claim to the right of an ambassador, to which Lord Ashburton, as appeared by Sir Elijah Impey's defence, properly blames the judges for having paid too much attention.*

"No application was made in favour of Nuncomar by the Council *after* his conviction: the *former* applications were never assigned as reasons for not making them, by any of the Council."

It had been alleged, that my father, in his defence at the bar of the Commons, had made " *a wanton attack on the memory of General Clavering and Colonel Monson, and that he had been guilty of a breach of gallantry, in reflecting upon their ladies,* on account of their ceremonious visit to the convict, while he lay in prison under sentence of death :" " But," says my father, "the foppery of gallantry would have been ill-adopted by a judge pleading for everything that is dear;" nor "was Sir Elijah Impey under any such personal obligations to those gentlemen as to give up a material part of his defence to an accusation, which might affect his fortune, fame, and liberty, while living, as well as his memory, and the happiness of his posterity, after his death."

In answer to the pamphleteer's attack upon the *truth* of his defence, my father retorts thus :—

"No man has a right to call Sir Elijah Impey's veracity in question, because a Member of the House of Commons has thought fit to prefer articles against him. Before such an accusation, surely, some ground should have been laid for it."

Then glancing at Francis, he proceeds :—

"Had Sir Elijah given public reasons for a proceeding on record, which he afterwards *disavowed to be his true reasons,* and had *he* attributed *his* conduct to any other *private* motive, he would have no right to complain that the truth of any of his assertions should be publicly denied: till that or some other just cause of suspicion be ascertained, he [Sir Elijah], will do right to treat the attack and the attacker with the silent scorn they merit."

Mr. Francis, it is well known, had professed a neu-

---

* This ambassador had been sent from the Nabob of Bengal. See "Refutation," page 40, for the minutes omitted here. See likewise Lord Ashburton's letter, page 295 of this volume.

trality during the prosecution of my father; and it is equally notorious that he publicly professed *" never to sit in judgment on him, nor ever to give a judicial vote in any cause in which Sir Elijah might be a party,* unless he could safely give it *for him."* * How far Mr. Francis preserved this neutrality, or redeemed this pledge, is sufficiently apparent to all who have attended to his behaviour during these proceedings: and the conclusion fully justifies my father's words towards the end of his " Refutation":—

" The zeal and activity of a professed enemy satiating his vengeance as a prosecutor, ever acts on a generous people in favour of the party prosecuted. This Mr. Francis has already experienced."

And again :—

"Passions do not argue logically, or make metaphysical distinctions; they do not distinguish accurately the cases that are favourable or unfavourable to those against whom they have been excited. After *that declaration,* notwithstanding the qualification annexed to it, he [Mr. Francis] is most certainly to be dreaded by Sir Elijah Impey, should he ever become his judge. There is another character, in which he may, for the same reason, be feared,—*that of a witness.* If neither of these characters be assumed, his friendship or enmity must be matter of indifference."

The pamphleteer, alias Francis himself, in spite of the above profession of *neutrality,* &c., had rather inconsistently vowed " eternal hostility " against my father ; to this my father replies :—

" It is not Sir Elijah Impey who has marked him [Mr. Francis] as an enemy; *he* has, by his public declarations, marked *himself* as the enemy of Sir Elijah, who only gives credit to those declarations, in asserting that *he is so.* From the picture of his own heart, delineated by the pencil of Mr. Francis himself, when he made them, Sir Elijah Impey's must be deformed, indeed, if it does not appear to advantage, when placed, where Mr. Francis desires it should be, in opposition to *his.* Let Mr. Francis really desist from assuming the character of a judge, or a witness, and there is no reason that Sir Elijah Impey should not treat his '*eternal hostility*' with everlasting contempt."

* See Mr. Nicholls's testimony to this fact, in his " Recollections," quoted page 174 of this volume.

In a postscript to this cogent and closely logical pamphlet, my father reasoned upon the vehement eagerness of Francis and his party, to possess a written copy of the speech at the bar, which Sir Elijah had never com-committed to writing; and upon the malevolent uses to which Francis would have applied such written copy, if he and his friends had succeeded in extorting it.

" May it not be his object to procure something under the hand of Sir Elijah, which by glosses and constructions may be turned against him ? Why else that anxiety to get his defence delivered in at the bar of the House ? Why those observations to prejudice him for not doing it ? Why should that which was done by the desire of Mr. Hastings, be used as a compulsory precedent for the conduct of Sir Elijah ? He was heard by *himself;* he might have been heard by his counsel : was it ever thought just, that instructions given to counsel, should be called for, to be used as evidence against the party defended? If they were called for, could any strictures be with justice made to the prejudice of his client, for not delivering them ? What difference is there whether the materials were in the hands of Sir Elijah Impey or his counsel? The *evidence* he was ready to produce.

This remarkable pamphlet, and the printed copy of his defence at the bar of the House, may be taken as substantial proofs of the manner in which my father—as a learned lawyer, a first-rate logician, an accomplished orator, and an energetic though plain writer—could plead his own cause, and cast defeat and shame upon his assailants.

Great penman as he was, the author of the Letters of Junius never attempted to reply to this pamphlet. He knew that he could not refute this refutation ; he felt that the best way to deal with it, was to take no notice of it, or, if any, such only as was taken of the books in the Alexandrian Library by the exterminating and incendiary Saracen.* Still, this convincing pamphlet, and the triumphant defence remained upon record, and must, for a time at least, have been accessible, not only to public men, but also to private readers. Both remained *unanswered,* and *unanswerable.* Nevertheless, the eminent men, who had heard my father's defence, had looked upon his humane countenance, and had witnessed

* See Introduction.

z

his true English bearing at the Commons' bar, could
persevere, through a long series of years, in representing him as the judicial murderer of Nuncomar! As if
he had not shattered the foul charge, and heaped shame
upon those who raised it—as if he had never delivered
any defence at all—Burke, Fox, Sheridan, and the other
managers of Mr. Hastings's impeachment, continued,
session after session, to proclaim in the Houses of
Parliament, and in Westminster Hall, that the Indian
Rajah had been murdered by the Chief Justice, to
screen the Governor General; and that, in nearly all
the state crimes *imputed* to Hastings, Sir Elijah Impey
had been an accomplice or tool. That *some* of the
brilliant rhetoricians who inculcated, and enforced this
belief upon others, had, themselves, any faith in the
facts, I much doubt. But no such doubt was ever entertained by the unreflecting, uninformed, or only partially
informed *many*, who made up one of the two great
political parties into which this country was then
divided. To believe in the delinquency of Sir Elijah,
became a primary article of faith with the collective
body of Whigs,—a party-badge which every man must
wear, who followed the banners of Edmund Burke. Sad
—sad, and most cruel—was it, that a man so utterly
disinclined, so alien in his nature, to the spirit of faction,
should have been thus sacrificed to its utmost rancour!

"A furious party spirit," says Addison, "even when under
its greatest restraint, breaks out in falsehood, detraction, and
calumny; it fills a nation with spleen and rancour, and ex-
tinguishes all seeds of good-nature, compassion, and humanity.
A man of merit, holding different political principles, is like
an object seen in two different mediums, that appears crooked
or broken, however straight and entire it may be in itself.
For this reason, there is scarce a person of any figure in England,
who does not go by two contrary characters, as opposite to
one another, as light and darkness. There is one piece of
sophistry practised on both sides; and that is, the taking *any
scandalous story*, that has ever been whispered or invented,
*for a known undoubted truth, and raising suitable speculations
upon it.* Calumnies, that have been never proved, or often
refuted, are the ordinary postulatums of these infamous
scribblers, upon which they proceed, as upon first principles,
granted by all men; though in their hearts they know they
are false, or, at best, very doubtful."—*Spectator*, No. 125.

CHAPTER XV.

THE PATNA CAUSE—APPEAL THEREON—AND DISMISSAL
OF THE APPEAL BY HIS MAJESTY IN COUNCIL.

THE result of Sir Elijah Impey's defence on the Nuncomar charge, at the bar of the House of Commons,
was, that on the 9th of May, the House having divided
on Sir Gilbert's motion—that the first charge had been
made good—the motion was lost by a majority of 18;
the numbers being 73 against 55.

On the 27th, the day appointed for the Committee
to sit again, upon the usual motion that the Speaker
do now leave the chair, the Attorney General opposed
it, on the ground that the next article of charge, the
Patna Cause, was then depending before the Privy
Council. It would occupy too much space to quote
the debates which followed. A very partial report of
them will be found in the *Daily Advertiser* and the
Annual Register ; the one published by Woodfall,
formerly *the editor of Junius,* and, at that time, super-
intended by *Francis;* the other by Dodesley, and under
the revision and controul of *Mr. Burke.* These gentlemen could not conceal the facts that the motion was
negatived, even without a division, and that the further
consideration of the charges was adjourned to that day
three months. But they had not the candour to state,
what nevertheless was notorious, that in the course of
the " short conversation," which they allow to have

taken place at the close of these proceedings, Mr. Pitt declared that, "had he been placed in the same situation, he was not prepared to say, that he should not have acted as Sir Elijah Impey had done." They are, of course, equally silent as to the opinion expressed by Mr. George Grenville, who concurred with Mr. Pitt.

With the exception of the *first*, or Nuncomar charge, and the *fifth* charge, about the acceptance of the Sudder Dewannee Adaulut, the Patna charge involves and includes within itself, all the charges brought against my father. It involves the general question of the jurisdiction of the Supreme Court, from 1774 to 1782, accusing the Chief Justice, separately from his brother judges, who always concurred with him, of having illegally and arbitrarily extended the jurisdiction of the Court. This charge and appeal are of the very highest importance to the object I have in view; for, the result of the appeal before the Privy Council was the immediate cause of the abandonment of the whole prosecution. Not that I can believe otherwise, than that Sir Elijah's manly, eloquent, and triumphant defence, on the only capital charge—which was the most horrible and striking, and, indeed, the only one that ever excited the popular mind—mainly contributed to make his enemies relinquish the contest, and withdraw sullenly and silently from the field. That defence, must, at least, have convinced them, that they had fallen upon a man, who could prove himself a powerful adversary; upon one, who was strong not only in his conscious innocence, but also strong in forensic eloquence, strong in logic, and overpoweringly strong in law. It was through this discovery, and through alarm at the visible effect my father produced, when at the bar, that they put an interval of three months and four days, between the delivery of Sir Elijah's defence, and their motion that the Nuncomar charge had been made good. Throughout the proceedings, they endeavoured to make up for their deficiency in moral strength, by manœuvre and cunning.

The Patna charge occupies a vast number of folio pages in the Commons' Reports;* but the nature of it,

* Vol. V.

and its bearings, may be explained in a very few words. It involves, as I have already said, the general question of the jurisdiction of the Court; but it refers particularly to a sentence pronounced by the Chief Justice, on the last day of term, in 1779, in a cause of action, called Nanderah Begum *versus* Behadre Beg and others. The trial of this cause, like that which gave rise to the Cossijurah charge, may be considered as a test of the question at that time unhappily at issue, between the Supreme Council and the Supreme Court of Bengal, relative to their respective jurisdictions, which, by the ambiguous wording of the Act of Parliament, and of the Charter, had been rendered disputable from the first. I have sufficiently shown with what violence the dispute for authority was maintained by the Council, who went the length of employing an armed force to prevent execution of the writs of the Court. "We find," said the Commons' Committee of 1781, "that the differences between the judges of the Supreme Court and the Governor General and Council, which have lately broken out into an open and avowed resistance *by a military power*, began very early after the arrival of the judges at Calcutta." * Chiefly on account of the frequent revenue cases up the country, which came before the local Courts, wherein the native judges were appointed by the Council itself, the Council resolutely aimed at maintaining these Courts, and enforcing their decisions.

In 1776, Shabaz Beg, a native of Cabool, but *a military servant of the Company*, died at Patna, where he had long resided. He left no children, but his inheritance, which was considerable, was disputed by his widow, Nanderah Begum, and his nephew, Behadre Beg ; the widow claiming under a will and other deeds, alleged to have been executed by the deceased; and the nephew claiming as his adopted son and heir. On the 2nd of January, 1777, Behadre Beg, the nephew, preferred a petition to the Company's Council, or Dewan, at Patna, setting forth his claim ; and, after stating that the widow was removing and secreting the effects, concluding with a prayer, that orders should be given to prevent the removal of the goods, and to recover such

* Report. Printed in 1781.

as had already been carried away; and that the
cawzee—the Mohammedan judge—should be directed
to ascertain his right, and acquaint the Council therewith. The Patna Council precipitately gave directions to the cawzee, and other Mohammedan law
officers, to take an account of the estate and effects,
to collect them together, and to take charge of them
jointly with the parties, till a division could be made
to allot the share of each claimant, strictly adhering to
the Mussulman law of inheritance. In obedience to
this precept, the cawzee and muftees proceeded to the
house of the deceased ; and, after some resistance on
the part of the widow, executed their orders. On the
20th of January, 1777, the Mussulman law officers
delivered in their report; in which, after stating evidence, &c., they delivered their opinion, that the property of the deceased should be divided into four shares;
whereof three should be given to Behadre Beg, the
nephew, and only one to Nanderah Begum, the widow.
The council forthwith adopted this opinion, and directed the officers who had given it, to carry it immediately into effect. This was done ; and, apparently,
with much violence and harshness. The widow complained of injustice, and partiality, in the local court
and council.

In 1779, seeing that others frequently appealed from
the local courts to the Supreme Court, Nanderah
Begum commenced an action of trespass, *vi et armis,*
against the three Mussulman law officers of Patna,
and Behadre Beg, in the Supreme Court. The action
was for assault and battery, false imprisonment, breaking and entering her house, seizing her effects, and
for other personal injuries. She laid her damages at
600,000 sicca rupees, or about £66,000. Sir Elijah
Impey proceeded to trial and judgment. Behadre Beg
pleaded, that he was not within the jurisdiction of the
Court, and added a plea of not guilty. The other
three defendants, without attempting to challenge
the jurisdiction of the Court, pleaded generally, not
guilty. Behadre Beg's plea was overruled : for it
was proved, that he, as well as his uncle before him,
"was employed by the Company," and the Act and
Charter gave the Supreme Court jurisdiction over *all* the

servants of the Company, whether native or European.* The ground on which the cawzee and two muftees relied, was, that the Provincial Council of Patna had ordered them to do all that they had done ; that the said Provincial Council had authority, derived from the Governor General and Council, to sit and act as a court of justice, and to hear and determine suits between Mussulman and Mussulman, subject to an appeal to the Governor General and Council at Fort William, and also to enforce their decrees. The Supreme Court set aside this justification, as insufficient on the face of it ; seeing that the Provincial Council of Patna, having only a delegated authority themselves, had delegated that authority to others, contrary to an established maxim of the law of England—*Delegatus non potest delegare.*

The proceedings lasted *many* days. At last, on the 3rd of February, 1779, judgment was given for the plaintiff, Nanderah Begum, against all the defendants, with 300,000 rupees damages, and 9208 rupees 10 annas, costs, making together, 309,208 sicca rupees 10 annas, or about £34,000 ; and execution was sued out accordingly. As execution was resisted, the defendants were all arrested by writ of the Supreme Court. The Governor General and Council resolved to undertake the defence of the prisoners on the part of the Company, and also to put in bail for all of them. In the end, an appeal was granted to defendants, the East India Company being bound to prosecute the said appeal within five years, under a penalty of £30,000.

But the Company was in no hurry to do that which it was bound to do ; and the appeal does not appear to have come to a hearing until the 12th of June, 1788, or more than *nine* years after judgment was given by the Supreme Court. The enemies of my father, however, did not wait so long to put their own injurious constructions upon the sentence given, and the means adopted—in strictest conformity with English law—to carry that sentence into effect. They, at once, sent secret reports over to England, that Sir Elijah Impey had, most unwarrantably, extended the jurisdiction of

* For Abstract of Act and Charter, see ante Chapter II.

the Court; that he had displayed a shameful partiality on the trial; that he had granted such excessive damages as would keep the defendants in perpetual imprisonment. Then, after a short time, followed a petition to the House of Commons, usually styled and referred to as "Touchett's Petition;" wherein the whole conduct of the Supreme Court, not merely with relation to the Patna cause, but in every other matter which it had tried, was severely and indecently arraigned. The Committee of the House of Commons, to which this obstreperous petition was referred, presented and printed, in 1781, a report, as loud and unmannered as the petition itself. *

Yet, it is to be especially noted that this Report, in all its main bearings, presses not on the Chief Justice separately, but on the whole Supreme Court; on the inexpediency of the original institution of that Court; and on the expense of its proceedings. The drift of the Report is, that no such court ought ever to have been erected. The paper ends with an absurd comparison between the annual expense of the Mayor's Court, at Calcutta, and the annual expense of the Supreme Court, which had superseded the Mayor's, with an immensely extended jurisdiction. It never took into consideration that the Mayor's Court, filled by servants of the Company, who had other places and emoluments, administered law, or something that was made to pass for law, in Calcutta only; and that the Supreme Court was bound, by Act and Charter, to administer the law to three wide provinces—Bengal, Bahar, and Orissa—each as large as a European kingdom.

When the Committee's Report reached Calcutta, my father sate down, and, on the same day, wrote to Chancellor Thurlow, Attorney General Wallace, Sir Richard Sutton, and Dunning. These several letters were nearly in the same words. I extract from the last.

---

* This Committee was appointed on the 15th of February, 1781. It consisted of General Richard Smith, C. W. B. Rous, Robert Gregory, Thomas Farrer, *Edmund Burke*, Dudley Long, Hon. John Townshend, John Elwes, George Dempster, Lord Lewisham, William Graves, Frederic Montague, William Pulteney, *Sir Gilbert Elliot*, Sir Walter James.

"Calcutta, June 6, 1782.

" Dear Dunning,

" Sir R. Sutton has acquainted me with the event of the petition against the Court, together with the written examinations, the Report, etc. It is not worse than I expected, from the turn the business had taken, from the politics of the ministry, *and the constitution of the Committee.* He likewise apprised me of the part you will take ; for which I cannot be sufficiently thankful. In the Report, Appendix, etc., I see many things I never heard of before ; many things which excite my ridicule as well as indignation. That the Patna cause should, by any temper, be turned against the Court, astonishes me. *It is sufficient to damp the zeal of any man ;* but it is useless to comment on a business that is passed. The Indian scene, thank God ! is nearly closing with me. Though I still wish a door to be left open to my returning in case my private affairs should make it necessary. The very severe and quick returns of my nervous disorder, with aggravated symptoms, makes my long stay impossible."*

These eminent lawyers, my father's correspondents and life-enduring friends, could not be deluded by a one-sided Parliament Committee Report, even though the warm-tempered Burke had been deluded by it. They concurred in opinion that the conduct of the Supreme Court had been irreproachable, and strictly legal ; both Thurlow and Dunning voluntarily pledged themselves to stand forward in my father's defence. But Thurlow was dilatory, and Dunning was dead ere Sir Elijah reached England, and long before his impeachment was attempted by men who pretended that the world ought to take those scandalously partial Reports for proven and irrefragable facts ; and who had no other evidence to offer, except such as they drew from the *black* book, and blacker heart of Philip Francis.†

It would be tedious to the reader, and difficult for me, to go any farther into the merits of the Patna cause. I, therefore, proceed directly to the issue and fate of the Appeal on that cause, the pendency of which before the Privy Council was, on the 27th of May, 1788, urged by

---

* MS. Letters in my possession.

† On the 27th of February, 1788, Mr. Francis, then in Parliament, read, from his place in the House of Commons, his evidence against Sir Elijah, out of a MS. book, which was commonly referred to as the *black book*.

the Attorney General in bar of the further sitting of the Committee.

That Appeal came to a hearing on the 12th of June, 1788, when a motion was presently made to dismiss it altogether. The members of the Privy Council took time to consider what order to make. On the 24th, they agreed to report to the King that the Appeal should be dismissed. On the 26th they resolved to petition his Majesty to restore it.* But, on the 24th of March, 1789, they confirmed their first resolution; and, on the 3rd of April of that year, it was finally dismissed by the King in Council, *for want of prosecution.*

These facts, together with the following document, I have derived from the records preserved in Her Majesty's Privy Council. The inestimable value of this document is, in my mind, infinitely enhanced by the consideration that I owe it to the personal favour of the late Honourable Clerk of the Privy Council; an obligation which I have the greater pleasure in acknowledging, as it revives the memory of an hereditary friendship. To Lord Chancellor Bathurst my father was indebted not only for his recommendation to the appointment in India, but also for his Lordship's steady support in Parliament, both before and after his return to England : the Honourable William Bathurst, late Clerk of the Privy Council, is grandson of that noble Lord and eminent Chancellor.

EXTRACT FROM MINUTES OF PROCEEDINGS IN THE PRIVY COUNCIL.

" *At the Court at Windsor, the 3rd of April,* 1789.

" Present,—The King's Most Excellent Majesty,

Lord President	Earl Howe
Lord Privy Seal	Earl of Courtown
Duke of Richmond	Lord Sidney
Duke of Montague	Lord Amherst
Lord Chamberlain	Lord Dover
Earl of Ailesbury	Mr. Chancellor of the Exchequer
Earl of Leicester	[Mr. Pitt] †
Earl of Chatham	J. C. Villiers, Esq.

* See also Law Proceedings, registered at the East India Company's Office, in Draper's Hall.

† The fact of Mr. Pitt's presence at this Council, is important.

" Whereas, there was this day read at the Board, a Report from the Right Honourable the Lords of the Committee of Council for hearing Appeals from the Plantations, &c., dated the 27th of last month, in the words following, viz.—

" ' Your Majesty having been pleased by your Order in Council of the 28th July, 1784, to refer unto this Committee the humble petition and Appeal of Behadre Beg, Muftee Barraktoolah, and Muftee Gullaum Mackdoom, from a judgment pronounced in the Supreme Court of Judicature at Fort William, in Bengal, on the 3rd of February, 1779, in an action of trespass at the suit of Nanderah Begum, widow—the now respondent—against the appellants, and one Cauzee Sadhee —since deceased,—and whereby the said Court did, amongst other things, adjudge that the appellants and the said Cauzee Sadhee, were guilty of the said trespass laid to their charge, and that the said respondent, Nanderah Begum, should recover against them three hundred thousand sicca rupees for her damages sustained in that behalf, and nine thousand two hundred and eight sicca rupees, and ten annas for her costs : praying that your Majesty would be pleased to reverse the said judgment, or for other relief.'

" The Lords of the Committee were this day attended by counsel on both sides thereupon ; and the counsel for the respondent having prayed that in regard to the great length of time which has elapsed since the said judgment was pronounced, and the appeal therefrom allowed by the said Supreme Court, the said appeal might be considered as abandoned, and dismissed for non-prosecution accordingly : And their Lordships having fully heard all that the counsel on both sides had to offer thereupon, do agree humbly to report as their opinion to your Majesty, that the said appeal of the said Behadre Beg, Muftee Barraktoolah, and Muftee Gullaum Mackdoom, from the said judgment of the Supreme Court of Judicature at Fort William, in Bengal, of the 3rd of February, 1779, ought to be dismissed for non-prosecution, without costs.

" His Majesty taking the said Report into consideration, was pleased, with the advice of his Privy Council, to approve thereof, and to order that the said appeal of the said Behadre Beg, Muftee Barraktoolah, and Muftee Gullaum Mackdoom, from the said judgment of the Supreme Court of Judicature at Fort William, in Bengal, of the 3rd of February, 1779, be, and the same is hereby dismissed for non-prosecution, without costs. Whereof the Governor or President and Council of Fort William, in Bengal, for the time being, the Judges of the said Supreme Court, and all other persons whom it may concern, are to take notice, and govern themselves accordingly.

The event of this appeal equally proved the innocence of the accused, the sagacity of counsel, and the justice of Mr. Pitt's early administration. It quashed the whole proceeding.

> " Ibi omnis
> Effusus labor, atque immitis sæva *tyranni*
> *Fœdera*."

So much for the infernal confederation of *King* Francis, at least for thirty years to come : that is to say, till 1818, which is the date of Mill's first edition of his History of British India. But, alas!

> "Pretium chartis quotus arroget annus ?"

Fifty-five years after the event just recorded—namely, the proceeding quashed in Parliament—that confederation has been revived ! as if, in defiance of the well-known mathematical axiom,* falsehoods added to falsehoods could, in the end, be anything but false ! As if, by dint of mere repetition, they could ever multiply into truth ! As if facts proved by vouchers in 1788, could be disproved in 1841 and 1843 by no evidence at all ! As if, in other words, the real truth, and nothing but the truth, which I now advocate, having thus passed into legitimate English history, can be cancelled by a confederacy of self-constituted historians, such as Mr. Mill, and self-convicted falsifyers of record, like Philip Francis ! or, lastly, as if it is to be defeated by this more modern combination of critics and essayists, the Whig agents of an anonymous *Review!* Is that *Review*, however brilliantly conducted—yet avowedly on principles of party politics—to be read as impartial history ? and is history itself, with all its legal and parliamentary proofs, to be vilified, obliterated, suppressed, and sneered down as no better than " an idiot's dream" ?

We have too long witnessed the baneful consequences of reiterated slander ; let us now see what may be done by equal reiteration on the opposite side, that of justice and truth. This principle, I trust, will palliate the frequent and perhaps fatiguing repetitions in my narrative. They are to be considered as so many

---

* " Equals added to equals," &c.

protests against that besetting sin of political writers—*Punica fides.* *He* was no unwise or inexperienced public Censor, who never ceased to repeat in the ear of the Roman senate " *Delenda est Carthago ;*" nor was *he*, of all mankind, the least acquainted with the examples of history, the evidences of law, common sense, and human nature, who wrote, " *Magna est veritas, et prævalebit.*"

CHAPTER XVI.

SIR ELIJAH IMPEY'S LIFE AFTER THE PERSECUTION—
PRIVATE ANECDOTES AND CORRESPONDENCE.

APPROACHING, as I now am, to the termination of the task imposed upon me by a most awful and imperative commandment,* I cannot but hope that I have sufficiently interested my reader in the subject of this narrative, to meet with approbation if I conclude my work in the manner in which I began it, and in the spirit of a passage, which has always appeared to me replete with feeling, truth, and tenderness, though taken from a writer not often quoted for his pathos :—

"Διὸ καὶ ὅταν καὶ λύπη προσγένηται τῷ μὴ παρεῖμαι, καὶ ἐν πένθέσι καὶ θρήνοῖς ἐπιγίγνεταί τις ἡδομη. Ἡ μεν γαρ λύπη τῷ μη ὑπάρχεῖν, ἡδονη δὲ ἐν τῷ μεμνῆσθαι καὶ ὁρᾶν πως ἐχεῖνον, καὶ ἅ επρὰττε καὶ, οἷος ἦν."— Arist. Rhetor. lib. i. ii.

So true it is, that "in the midst of our lamentation at the loss or disappearance of a beloved object, there arises a sort of pleasure in its indulgence. We grieve, indeed, that he exists no more, but feel a certain melancholy pleasure in looking upon him, as it were, and in remembering what he did, and what he was."

I shall, therefore, venture to conclude with attempting, briefly, to describe what my father did in his last days, and what manner of man he really was.

Sir Elijah survived his defence at the bar of the House

* Exod. xx. xii.

of Commons, and his virtual acquittal from all charges whatsoever, for well nigh a quarter of a century ; and I have always considered it fortunate for his reputation that he had, thus, abundant time and opportunity to appear before the world in a very different light from that in which he had been so long exhibited. The injustice of his enemies never kindled a rancorous feeling in his generous nature, nor could persecution and defamation sour his cheerful temper. After the storm had blown over, yet scarcely more than when its fury was at its height, he stood forward—

> " As one who, suffering all, yet suffers nothing :
> A man who Fortune's buffets and rewards
> Had ta'en with equal thanks."

Indifferent to the obstinacy of vulgar prejudice, he was, nevertheless, desirous, as became him, to conciliate the good opinion of all whose estimation was of real value.

His first and most earnest object, therefore, as an officer of the Crown, after landing in England, was, as soon as possible, to do homage to his Sovereign. It has been seen that his Majesty George III. had not prejudged his case, that his letter of recall was written in gracious terms, and that it contained no expression of censure or displeasure, still less any intimation of dismissal.* The reader will also bear in mind, that my father was never dismissed ; and that, after a long, interval he voluntarily resigned a post to which his Sovereign wished him to return. He retained the rank and title of Chief Justice† up to the 10th of November, 1787, and, in that capacity, he was presented, in 1784, by the Lord Chancellor, at the first levee held in Buckingham Palace after his arrival in London ; he then having the same character, and wearing the same professional garb, as when he took leave in 1773, eleven years before.

His reception, like that of Mr. Hastings, who was presented at Court the year following, was honoured with very marked distinction. It was not until three years after this, that my father sent in his resignation ; and, full twelve months after he had so resigned, I find

---

* Ante p. 270. † Ante p. 285.

Government intimating to him, through a proper channel, that he might even yet return to Calcutta, as Chief
Justice, and with that seat in the Supreme Council
which he had so earnestly and so vainly solicited while
in India.

But, disheartened by the treatment he had before received, deterred by the advance of old age, and anxiously
engaged in the education of a young and numerous
family, he respectfully declined the honourable offer. Of
the above facts there scarcely needs proof more authentic
than the date of the appointment of my father's successor, Sir Robert Chambers, which did not officially take
place until 1789, more than five years after Sir Elijah's
arrival in England.

But the very appointment of Sir Robert Chambers to
succeed the late Chief Justice, proves more than this :
for it has been shown that Chambers unanimously, with
the rest of the judges, had consented to every judgment
and sentence pronounced in the Supreme Court, during
Sir Elijah's tenure of office. Furthermore Sir Robert
had been under the threat of censure in Parliament
for an alleged offence against the Regulating Act and
Charter, similar to that for which—and for which *only*
—his predecessor, Sir Elijah, had been recalled. But,
upon that charge neither Sir Robert, nor Sir Elijah, were
ultimately questioned : therefore the appointment and
promotion of Chambers amount to sufficient proof that
both he and my father were virtually acquitted of any
offence in accepting the Company's judgeships.

Sir Elijah continued, at due seasons, to pay his respects at Court, and to receive marks of his Sovereign's
gracious consideration. Well do I remember the following little incident—the time, the place, the person
of the good old King, and those of my honoured parents,
are all, as it were, before me at this moment :— In
the autumn of the year 1789, after the King's recovery
from his first unhappy malady, the royal family resorted to Weymouth, a place to which his Majesty was
much addicted. It was their custom, while there, to
appear on the public esplanade; where his Majesty, as he
turned round at either extremity of the walk, would
pause to address a few familiar words to such persons
as chanced to be near him, or as he was pleased to

notice. On one of these occasions, my parents, being on the promenade with some of their children, attracted the King's attention; and his Majesty, on inquiring the age of the youngest of our family party, was amused by the quick and lively manner in which the boy took the answer out of his father's mouth, and replied to his King, in defiance of paternal authority, and courtly etiquette! The frank, good-natured countenance of George the Third impressed my memory ever after with a feeling of loyal affection.

It was shortly after this that my father turned his thoughts towards a seat in Parliament; or, rather, that he resumed a project, which had been entertained by him many years before; for, as early as 1780, when he and Mr. Hastings were contemplating their return to England, I find many passages in their private correspondence expressive of an intention to "face their enemies upon equal ground." They had even sent instructions to friends at home to open a negotiation for that purpose.*

How far a revival, on the part of my father, of the same project ten years later, may be attributed to a similar motive, can now afford only matter of conjecture: but he had, undoubtedly other reasons of a less personal kind. From his enemies in Parliament, he had nothing more to fear: his spoken defence, and the dismissal of the Patna appeal, had secured him safety and honour. But a desire to devote part of his time and talents to the service of his country, and to the support of a minister in whom he confided, may fairly be supposed to have operated in his mind, equally with a determination not to shrink from any conflict, "*upon equal ground*," with an Opposition whose principles he could not be expected to adopt—with that factious, rash, and inconsiderate Opposition of *new* Whigs, whose violence was not to be abated, even by the imminence of the most terrible of foreign wars, and the chance of internal trouble and discord, if not of anarchy and rebellion.

The French revolution had, at this period, already assumed a ferocious, subversive, and sanguinary cha-

* Letters to Sir Elijah's brother, and to Mr. Masterman, in MS. letters, dated September 14, 1780, and August 22, 1782.

racter; the propagandists of its dogmas had already
penetrated into every European country, and clubs, in
imitation of the Jacobins of Paris, had been already
established in England. It was time for every man
who loved his country, his king and constitution, his
faith and his family, to step forward, and, according to
his degree and ability, to put forth his strength for the
defence and preservation of them all.

At the general election in the year 1790, my father,
by means of a committee, canvassed the borough of
Stafford, resolving to contest it, albeit, the stronghold
of one of his bitterest assailants, Mr. Richard Brinsley
Sheridan. On this occasion, as might be apprehended,
every electioneering expedient was practised to exasperate the popular mind against the new candidate.
Regardless of the recent decision of the House of Commons, the Sheridan party carried in their processions
the effigy of a black man hanging on the gallows; nor
did his unscrupulous competitor hesitate to placard the
late Chief Justice as the object of all his exploded calumnies.* Sir Elijah had been summoned to the poll,
from his country-house at Boreham, in Essex; but had
proceeded no farther than London, when he met the
news of his defeat, procured by the unworthy means to
which I have alluded. Nothing disheartened, however,
he soon afterwards took his seat as Member for New
Romney.

During several sessions Sir Elijah regularly attended
his duties in the House, and on private committees,
where he rendered much assistance on legal questions.
In general debate he seldom took an active part;
mostly divided with the Ministry, and always encoun-
tered his full share of Opposition malice. In one instance, though then but a young and negligent reader
of newspapers, I remember being interested by the report of some debate in which my father drew down
upon himself the whole phalanx of his former persecutors, with the formidable Charles James Fox at their
head. This was enough to dispirit the most practised

---

* I am indebted for this information to the retentive memory of my
highly-valued friend and schoolfellow, the present Colonel of the Stafford
Yeomanry, Edward Monckton of Somerford, Esq., eldest son of Sheridan's
respected colleague at the period of these events.

senator, much more one who had not entered upon that career till late in life; and who had nothing to oppose, practically, to long experience, and early initiation into those habits, but legal forms and forensic oratory, which are generally considered—with some splendid exceptions—rather as drawbacks than aids to parliamentary eloquence. One superiority, however, he certainly had over his hot antagonist—that of perfect calmness, temperance, and self-possession : nor was he a man easily to be discountenanced, or rudely set down. He, therefore, replied with becoming spirit; and as the attack seems to have been unprovoked, and quite foreign to the question before the House, it was soon silenced by the deep-toned voice of Mr. Addington.

Contemporary, and of like continuance in Parliament with my father, was Nathaniel Brassey Halhed,* a name never to be mentioned by me but with reverence and affection. Our family friendship, and, subsequently, my own personal intimacy with that extraordinary man, enable me to confirm all that has been recorded of the versatility of his talents.† In my long walk through life, I have seldom met the man who knew so much of so many things, or who had so ready a command of all he knew. In him the brightest of intellects was accompanied by the kindest of hearts. His principles were as sound as his erudition, and his friendship not less steady and enduring than his conversation was attractive and admired. Halhed's acquaintance with Mr. Hastings and my father began in India, where he held very important employments, and where his ability and zeal were of incalculable service to the Governor General and to the Company. To Hastings he always professed personal obligations, but it was not singly by the tie of gratitude that he was bound, for life, to that great and good man : he revered Mr. Hastings as an eminent statesman who had saved and enlarged an empire—and none knew better than Halhed the difficulties with which he had had to contend—also he loved him as the friend of letters, the patron of every elevating pursuit, the pleasantest of companions, the

* Mr. Halhed sate for Lymington.
† See Life of Sir William Jones, by Lord Teignmouth, and Memoirs of R. B. Sheridan, by Mr. Moore.

kindest and the easiest man to live with, that might be found in the wide world.

Sheridan and Halhed had sate on the same form at Harrow School; and, after their schoolboy days, the closest intimacy had subsisted between them. After a separation of very many years, which had been spent by Halhed in the East, they met again in England at the moment when Sheridan, with an entire ignorance of the subject, was preparing his oration on the Benares charge, and acting with the foremost of the enemies of the two men whom Halhed most loved and venerated, Mr. Hastings and my father.

The generous, warm-hearted, and enthusiastic Halhed, hoped he might yet be in time to serve, not only his Indian friends, but also his Harrow schoolfellow—for Halhed was a scrupulously conscientious man, and, as such, believed that no service could be greater than that which saved a friend from the commission and propagation of falsehood and defamation. So guileless was he, and so little versed in the practices of mere party men, that he fondly imagined, if he could but once demonstrate to Sheridan, from his own knowledge, that the charge he had undertaken to maintain against Hastings was founded upon false grounds, the associate of his youth would thank him for the revelation, and instantly throw up the charge, and consign his oration to the flames. The elegant, but inaccurate biographer of Sheridan, describes the interview which took place,* but he does not tell *all* that passed at it; and is wholly silent as to one of its results.

Halhed, than whom nobody was capable of conveying surer information, entered, at that meeting, into full particulars relative to the Benares charge. He opened the discussion with a heart overflowing with candour and conciliation. He was met with an artificial reserve, and an evasive arrogance which at once closed the door to all negociation. From that moment Halhed and Sheridan never met or spoke with each other upon amicable terms.

The attachment between my father and Halhed was mutual; it lasted till dissolved by death, nor was it for a moment interrupted by a strong divergency of opinion on some important subjects. On one point, and only

* See Mr. Moore's Memoir, vol. 1, p. 461.

on that one, Halhed's imagination was too strong for
his judgment. I would speak with the utmost delicacy
of this foible of my highly-gifted and long-lamented
friend ; nor would I speak of it at all, were it not already
a matter of public notoriety. Among other obstruse
questions, Mr. Halhed had devoted much time to the
study of prophecy, and the awful mysteries of the
Apocalypse. The amount of European, as well as
Asiatic lore, which he brought to bear upon these subjects, was immense, nor in a less degree was the ingenuity
with which he applied it all. But his head was heated
by this one absorbing and inexplicable subject. At this
juncture another very inoffensive enthusiast—Richard
Brothers, commonly called " Brothers the Prophet"—
began to utter his wild predictions. Halhed listened,
examined, and became more than half a believer in them.
This was during the early part of the French revolution,
when the British Government and people naturally took
alarm at every suspicious circumstance. Brothers was
constantly announcing the fast-approaching subversion
of all states and kingdoms ; but in a far different sense
from that maintained by the Republicans of France.
Government, however, chose to couple his religious in-
sanity with their political madness ; and Richard
Brothers, for some supposed seditious words, was
apprehended and committed to Newgate, as one guilty
of high treason. Halhed, who rightly thought that he
had been committed on a very irregular and foolish
warrant, resolved to stand forward as his champion
in the House of Commons, and gave notice of a
motion for his discharge.

My father, fearing that his friend would not confine
himself to the question of law, and the loyalty of the
prisoner, but that, growing warm in debate, he might
give vent to his peculiar opinions, and, in a manner,
identify himself with Brothers, remonstrated in private
with Halhed, and left no effort untried, to dissuade
him from making his speech. But all was in vain.
The day before that fixed for the motion, Halhed wrote
the following note :—

" Dear Sir Elijah,
" I must make my motion. I cannot help it. You undoubtedly, will answer me, if you like. Be assured I shall say

nothing offensive to anybody, and, that my motion will not be so objectionable, in point of matter and business, as that we discussed last night; for which discussion I hold myself most truly obliged to you.

"Yours sincerely,
"N. B. HALHED.

"Tuesday morning.
"You will have the goodness to excuse me, if I cannot be at home this morning." *

Having thus shut his door to his friend, Halhed, with much diligence and deliberation, prepared his speech. What followed is but too well known. On Wednesday, March 31st, 1795, Halhed made his motion in the House, and delivered his extraordinary oration. Extraordinary, indeed, and startling, and extravagant in its premises, was the greater part of the speech; yet, so ingeniously and systematically was it constructed, and so eloquently was it delivered, that it was listened to in profound silence for three long hours. My father often described that silence, by saying, "You might have heard a pin drop in the House." The motion was lost for want of a seconder; and, in a very few days, London was ringing with jokes, and more weighty censures, against Halhed,—even as his friend had gently predicted. Unfortunately, the hallucination was not to be dissipated. This remarkable man, so clear-sighted on other subjects, most unaccountably adhered to the extravagant opinions he had formed on this; and, before long, it was announced, that he was preparing to follow the pseudo-prophet and king of the Hebrews, to Jerusalem! Then, to use an expression of Horace Walpole, "it rained squibs and satires!"

Let me not be understood to join in any unbecoming ridicule of matters, too serious to be laughed to scorn, if I am tempted to copy one harmless piece of raillery, which proceeded from no unfriendly pen, and was so far from being taken amiss by the object of it, that Halhed himself joined in the smile which it excited, and gave the original note to my father; who, though he might continue to expostulate, never allowed himself to laugh at his friend, or to treat such subjects with any levity.

* From Halhed's MS. note to Sir Elijah, now in my possession.

The note was written by one who had been schoolfellow and playmate with Halhed and Sheridan.

" Bath, February 12, 1796.

"Dear Halhed,

"Without inquiring how *you* come to be the chosen of the chosen, the ingenious smith to make the ' key to the lock,' I will tell you I am satisfied of its mechanical aptitude, and am happy to be, like Ursula, acquainted with every ward of it. Meanwhile, through the aperture of the door, I cannot envisage the interior with much glee. Heavens ! must it be, that while your poor schoolfellow shall be left a prey to the miseries denounced on this ill-fated country, you, under the blessed auspices of your prince and prophet, will be singing, —

'Hail Judea ! Happy Land ! ' . . . .

. . . . Oh ! happy Hebrew ! Yes, Richard Brothers is right. And sure it is, I *did* remark, now so many years past, a brotherly regard in you for *Dutchy*, the little cockle-selling Jew at Harrow. And oh ! attend to what may be considered my dying request. Should you meet that worthy Israelite on your way,—at Constantinople, for instance,—pay him, O ! pay him, three halfpence which I still owe ! ! !

"Heaven, and Mr. Brothers, only know, whether or not I shall ever revisit Babylon; but of this I am well assured, in case I do, that I will personally bear witness to your profound sagacity, and my unfeigned admiration of it.

With the greatest regard, yours,
Wm. Lutwyche." *

Yet, apart from this one aberration, Halhed was as sound in mind, as he was good and generous at heart. His learning, fostered by industry and research, kept steadily on the increase; his intellect was comprehensive and commanding ; he ceased not to be consulted and referred to, by the most gifted and clear-headed of his contemporaries. As a guide and counsellor to studious youth, he was invaluable. I, who owe him much, and loved him well, would fain dwell longer on the merits, and manly virtues, of Nathaniel Brassey Halhed ; but must be contented, in this place, to express my regret,

* This letter was found among my father's papers, with a note in his hand-writing, purporting that it had been given to him by Mr. Halhed, the object of the witticism.

that he has left so little behind him, to rescue his literary character from oblivion.*

My father was attached to a quiet rural life. On quitting Parliament for good, he fixed himself almost wholly in the country, seldom visiting London. This was some time in the year 1792; but he did not entirely give up his house in Wimpole Street, until he went abroad, nine years later. The first country-house he rented, after his return from India, was, as I have said, at Boreham, in Essex, now the seat of Sir John Tyrrel, Bart., Member for the County. There, some of the happiest days of my childhood were passed; and there, my father, who acted as tutor to all his sons, smoothed the way to my classical studies; and, with the assistance of the Rev. W. Trivet, formerly an usher at Westminster, and then master of the well-conducted grammar school at Felsted,† prepared me for the earlier forms of Westminster School. Well do I remember the patient assiduity, and imperturbable good temper, with which my father imparted his instruction; making that clear to the capacity of a child, which many professed teachers contrive to make difficult to the comprehension of a youth. To him, and to the eminent professors under whom I was placed, by his parental care, I am proud to attribute whatever literary tastes and habits it is my happiness to have imbibed.

Upon giving up Boreham, Sir Elijah rented, of William, the fourth Duke of Queensberry—third Earl of March—Amesbury House, in Wiltshire. It was a noble villa, built in the best style of Palladian architecture, and pleasantly situated on the banks of the Avon, near Stonehenge. Pleasant, too, were its classical recollections; for there the poet Gay, one of the most single-minded of men, had probably written many of

* The late Nathaniel *John* Halhed, Judge of the Sudder Dewannee Adaulut, and nephew of my friend, inherited the papers of his uncle, by bequest of his widow, but died without publishing them, in 1836. They then fell into the hands of his friend and executor, Dr. John Grant, of the East India Company's Medical Establishment, a gentleman highly capable of editing them; so there is yet hope that, sooner or later, they may see the light.

† Felsted is an ancient endowment, and historically interesting, as being the school at which the sons of Oliver Cromwell were educated. Of my contemporaries, the most remarkable were, the two younger brothers of the late distinguished wit, poet, and scholar, John Hookham Frere.

his latest poems, and had spent much of his time loitering, as was his wont,—

" Where the tall oak his spreading arms entwines,
  And with the beech, a mutual shade combines; "

Or making merry, in some cool alcove,˙with his noble host, and goodly company:—

" While all the wondering nymphs around him throng,
  To hear the syrens warble in his song." *

In the hospitable Deanery of St. Paul's, where I have been honoured as an occasional guest, is a very pretty landscape, with figures representing Gay, even in such company, and in such an alcove; revelling, haply, with his choice companions, Pope, Parnel, Swift, Arbuthnot, in the ducal bowers of Amesbury.

While Sir Elijah was making arrangements for quitting London, to take possession of his new abode, he, being still in Parliament, was assaulted and knocked down in the street, as he was walking one night, after a late debate, from the House of Commons to his residence in Wimpole Street. The occurrence took place at the south-east side of George Street, Hanover Square, near the corner of Maddox Street. As nothing was taken from his person, it seemed as if robbery had not been the motive of the assault; but it is possible that the blows might, nevertheless, have been dealt with that intention; and, that the robber may have been frightened away from his victim, by the approaching footsteps of those who found him in the street, and conveyed him home. Others may, perhaps, have indulged in conjectures about old personal grudges; but my father never did. I can only remember the placidity and cheerfulness of his temper, while laid prostrate on the bed of sickness; the injuries received having been serious. He was attended by his much-esteemed friend, Mr. Adair Hawkins,† one of the most eminent surgeons of the day.

---

* Gay's " Rural Sports," canto I. The local tradition, in our time, was, that Gay wrote his fables in a grotto, which I well remember, at Amesbury; and it is recorded by Johnson, that he enjoyed " the affectionate attention of the Duke and Duchess of Queensberry, into whose house he was taken, and with whom he passed the remaining part of his life." He died on the 4th of December, 1732, the year of my father's birth.

† Father of the present learned and able physician, Dr. Francis Hawkins, with whom I claim a family friendship.

By this time, I was in the fifth form at Westminster, and busied upon what is called "the Horace Task." This admirable exercise consists in transmuting the different lyric metres, either into heroic or elegiac verse; or the metre of one ode into that of another.   The task given out on the present occasion, was the Alchaic ode to Postumus,* which I, being at his bedside, was labouring to turn into long and short.   Perceiving my difficulty, he turned in the bed, and, after a little thought, dictated the following graceful couplet, as a beginning :—

"Labitur hora fugax, heu ! Postume, Postume ! vitæ,
Nec morti pietas afferet ulla moram."

Mr. Adair Hawkins, who came in at this moment, admonished my father, that turning hexameters and pentameters, was rather too trying an occupation for a sick man.

Another little anecdote, of this period, I have also retained.   On Sir Elijah's convalescence, among the many distinguished men who visited him, was the first Marquess of Lansdowne ; who, as Lord Shelburne and Secretary of State, had signed the letter of my father's recall.   His Lordship spoke of the pleasure he anticipated in having Sir Elijah for his neighbour in the country, and made use of a compliment so characteristically elegant, that it sunk into my childish memory: —"The distance," said he, " from Amesbury to Bowood is but short, and nature has spread a verdant carpet beween them."

It must have been in the summer of 1792, that our family settled themselves at Amesbury ; and that my father resumed those habits of equitation which he had always loved, and which, no doubt, very materially contributed to preserve in him a green and vigorous old age.   The country about Stonehenge was most favourable to coursing ; and many, and exhilirating, were the canters we took together over Salisbury Plain, where both hares and greyhounds are said to be of the fleetest and strongest breed.   Two of my father's old Cambridge friends, Dr. Harrington, at that time the incumbent of Thruxton, not far from Amesbury, and

* Horace iv. lib. ii.

that eminent lawyer, and highly-esteemed judge, Sir James Mansfield, both being passionately fond of the sport, sometimes shared it with us; and, when Sir Elijah left Amesbury for Sussex, Sir James rented the manor, for the sake of its fine coursing ground.* I remember well Sir James Mansfield's favourite greyhound; it was hardly ever separated from him, followed him into court, and was painted with him in his portrait. But it is better worth remembering that we here find Sir James, who, as Solicitor General in 1781, had differed in opinion from Dunning and Wallace, on the Sudder Dewannee Adaulut question—about a dozen years after, the familiar companion of my father's field sports, and guest at his table. The fact is this: he had long been disabused as to the main fallacy, namely, the accept-ance of the salary. *He had voted against the recall.* "This," says my father in one of his India letters (see MSS. in the British Museum), "is the more handsome in Mansfield, as he was once of another opinion." Long after, as Chief Justice of the Common Pleas, and up to the period of his death, Sir James Mansfield was one of Sir Elijah's most intimate friends; and their children after them associated familiarly together for many years.

At Amesbury, as previously at Boreham, and as sub-sequently at Newick, the judges on the circuit invariably visited Sir Elijah, and were entertained by him with that hearty hospitality and playful humour, which, while it would often set the table in a roar, was never known to wound the feelings of a single individual. *These* were judges who wore unspotted ermine—*these* were men whose good fame was never questioned; *these* were the associates who steadily adhered to my father, and took pleasure and pride in his society, even at moments when the bitterest of factions was shaking St. Stephen's Chapel, and threatening the roof of Westminster Hall with their denunciations against him! *They knew* my father well—*they* had known him all his life—and *they* knew the spirit of his persecutors; *they* knew law, and were men not to be deluded by mere declamation. The last of those good and wise men have long been in their graves; but delightful and still vivid is the memory I

---

* The house was shortly after converted into a nunnery, and has since been pulled down.

preserve of them, as I saw them in their social hours, and heard their unpremeditated converse on men and measures, and on their own adventures and struggles in early life. And it is still my happiness to know, that amidst the many over-refinements of the present age, there yet exists a generation of plain, manly British lawyers, not inferior in worth or ability, in wit or learning, to any that have preceded them.

In the spring of 1794, my father removed from Amesbury to Newick Park, in the Weald of Sussex. Newick was, in our time, a spacious and comfortable old manor, the property of the late Lord Vernon. It was then surrounded by a park, containing many head of deer; it has been since disparked, but is still, under its present worthy occupant,* pleasant and picturesque, with extensive lawns, gardens, and plantations, beautifully watered, and looking upon the South Downs. Many of the recollections of my youth cling fondly to that spot; one of them is so identified and interwoven with a beautiful trait of my father's character, that I must record it here.

Mr. Richard Burke, the only son of the great statesman, and the object of all his earthly hopes, died on the 2nd of August, 1794, at the early age of 36.† The news reached us on the evening of the following day, at Newick, whither we had just returned from a visit to Mr. Barwell, at Stanstead. My father and I went out to walk in the park; and there, as we were sauntering through the venerable avenue of oaks by which the house was then approached, he stopped all at once, and laying his hand affectionately on my shoulder, said, "Poor man! God knows I owe Mr. Burke no obligation, but I feel for him—I pity him from my heart!"

By a merciful dispensation it was ordered, that an interval of many years was passed by my father in almost unalloyed enjoyment of health, in the bosom of his family by whom he was tenderly beloved, and in the interchange of decent hospitality with his Sussex neighbours. When Mr. Hastings became settled at Daylesford, our family paid him frequent visits there, which he

---

* James Slater, Esq.
† See the very touching account of this event in Mr. Prior's Life of Edmund Burke.

and Mrs. Hastings, almost every year, returned to us at Newick. My father and his oldest friend met also, occasionally, at other places; and their intercourse was never ruffled by any useless retrospection. Even when time had thrown his snow over their heads, their hearts glowed with a friendship as warm as that of youth.

In his Sussex retirement, the ex-Chief Justice of Bengal, became a busy and rather enthusiastic horticulturist and farmer. I hardly ever saw him, on the morning of a working day, at Newick, without a garden spud in his hand; and he took his full share in most of the gardener's active operations. Besides the spacious garden, and some three hundred and thirty acres of grass land, which supplied a large dairy, and fed about sixty head of deer, he now held three farms of arable ground, upon which he bestowed no little scientific skill. Of this I have proof in divers memoranda of experiments and calculations found among his papers.

" I now rent," says he, in one of these memoranda, dated February 27, 1805, "a farm (Tutt's) on lease, which expires in 1808, consisting of one hundred and five acres, at £68 10s. Besides which, I am tenant at will to Mr. Fortescue, of another small farm called Newnhams, rent £33, and also of one called Norriss's, rent £23 ; but these are distinct from Newick Park, and need not go with it."

In the interval of these pursuits he derived amusement from the theory, and, to a certain extent, from the practice of chemistry. He established a little laboratory next to his study, and purchased and perused that voluminous collection, entitled " Annales de Chimie." He showed his attachment to science by being one of the first promoters and earliest Fellows of the Royal Institution ; and, when in London, he was constant in his attendance on the chemistry lectures in that Institution. At Newick he was assisted in these favourite pursuits, by his friend and constant visitor, Tiberius Cavallo, F.R.S., who was the author of several scientific works that are still held in estimation.* Though

* Cavallo's principal works were, "A Complete Treatise on Electricity," 8vo. 1777 ; " An Essay on the Theory and Practice of Medical Electricity," 8vo. 1780; " A Treatise on the Nature and Properties of Air," &c., 4to. 1781 ; " The History and Practice of Aerostation," 8vo. 1785 ; " A treatise on Magnetism in Theory and Practice," 8vo. 1785 ;

he wrote in English, and published his works in this country, Cavallo was a native of Naples : he had come to England as an adventurer in the field of science and literature, under the auspices of the Corsican patriot, General Paoli, the friend of James Boswell and Samuel Johnson ; and by that distinguished foreigner he was introduced to our family, with whom he soon, and very deservedly, became a great favourite. I still cherish his memory ; he was a cheerful, modest, and obliging man, not overburthened with worldly wealth, but contented with his lot, unexpensive in his habits, yet always of an independent spirit, and even dignified in his demeanour. To us children he was a most amusing instructor, the promoter of all our little excursions abroad, active and hilarous, full of conversation at a party, essential at a concert—indispensable at a play. His name reminds me of more than one anecdote illustrative of my father's jocund humour. Among our intimate acquaintance was a wealthy and eccentric old dowager—Lady * * * * *—who prided herself on her station and ancient manor house, and who was a passionate admirer of theatricals. On one occasion, when my father had excused himself, Cavallo was invited to escort her ladyship and my sisters to the play. The philosopher was somewhat behind time and the party were kept waiting to the great discontentment of the dowager, who loved to see the curtain draw. It entered not into her conception of the fitness of things that a great dame should be delayed by a poor philosopher, and, at last, her pride and impatience found vent, to my father's no small amusement, in the following ejaculation,—as he told the story,—" Cavallo indeed ! Who is your Cavallo ? I wonder where he came from ? I wonder *where* his *country-house* is ? "

The same old lady was as enthusiastically fond of lapdogs as of plays. At the same time she entertained a constant dread of hydrophobia. Some mischievous neighbours, one day, nearly drove her to distraction by telling her that mad dogs had become very common;

" Essay on the Medicinal Properties of Factitious Airs," &c., 8vo. 1798; " Elements of Natural and Experimental Philosophy," 4 vols. 8vo. 1803. A short but very good account of this able and excellent foreigner will be found in the *Penny Cyclopædia*, Supplement, vol. 1, p. 301.

and that it was probable her own special favourite had been, or might soon be, bitten. Her ladyship, who had long been accustomed to consult my father, not only on matters relating to law or business, but on all other concerns whatsoever, drove off in a prodigious fidget to our house. "Oh! Sir Elijah," said she, "I fear poor Fop is going mad! do you think there is any danger?" "None," replied my father, putting on a serious face, "none! he can never be mad enough to bite so excellent a mistress. But, should he unhappily impart the malady to any one of the little insects which are familiar to dogs and men . . . I tremble at the thought of your ladyship's being bit by—an hydrophobious flea!" But it was not in this piece of drollery, or in many others, to relieve Sir Elijah from the dowager's consultations.

We had a cousin, an undergraduate at Oxford, who was ambitious of becoming a Fellow of All Souls. He wrote to Sir Elijah, as head of the family, to prove him of kin to the founder, Archbishop Chichley. We were at table when the letter arrived. It was difficult to decipher, but my father caught just enough of its meaning to turn it into a joke. So putting on his spectacles, and holding it at arm's length, he began reading it aloud, When he came to the words " Founder's kin," he hesitated ; and, at last, interpreted them—" Found in skin." " Our cousin," he added, with a quiet laugh, " wants to be found in skin !" However, being a good genealogist, he soon set seriously about reconciling the *stemmata Chichliana* with our family tree ; but found it impossible to graft one upon the other. Some time after, when I was at Christchurch, and our cousin still residing at —— Hall, my father came to see me, and we crossed over together to pay our kinsman a visit. He was out, but not at *All Souls*—so at least we guessed ; for, finding nothing but his gown, hanging on a peg, my father concluded that he could not yet be proved " Found in skin."

We had another cousin, whom we loved in spite of an unhappy foible, which made him not always producible in company. He was nevertheless a frequent guest at Newick when we had none. He drove his own gig ; but, being a nervous Automedon, he generally chose a season for his visit, when the roads were in their best condition ; and, sooth to say, our Sussex roads were ofttimes nearly impassable, by reason of many deep ruts ; for Mac Adam had not yet taken the field, and railways and steam carriages were not, as yet, so much as dreamed of.   Whenever, therefore, it was particularly inconvenient to entertain our somewhat exceptionable visitor, my father used to work upon his fears, by representing Newick, which was then a deer park, as rather dangerous in the *rutting* season.   There was, besides, a very rutty and precipitous hill to be surmounted, called " *Cinder* Hill ; "—and, according to my father's interpretation to our nervous cousin, it was so called " because many travellers had left their *ashes* there."

All this was afterwards versified in the harvest home ditty, to which allusion has been made.*   It is much too long, and not altogether good enough to copy, for it was the joint composition of several hands that were not equally skilful.   My father's contributions were by far the merriest and the best.   I will give one or two of them ; first prefacing that the song had a burden or chorus, which ran thus,—

> " Fun, boys! fun! our sports are begun;
> The wise ones declare after pleasure comes care,
> Why then after labour comes fun."

and this fun partly consisted in hitching in the names, of all manner of friends, in the fashion of poor Theodore Hooke's after-dinner improvisations, or in a style to remind one of

> " O Rourk's noble fair
> Which will ne'er be forgot,
> By those who where there,
> Or those who were not." †

Our absent cousin of the gig was thus *mis en scéne.*

> " Cousin * * * 's far away, for he likes not our clay,
> Now the season for rutting's begun,
> For our roads and our deer, at this time o' year,
> Are rutting and butting for fun.
>   Fun, boys ! fun ! etc.

* See foot note, ante p. 18.
† Swift.

" If he travels, he 'll drown in the pool o' Pilt Down,
  Or in Honey-pot Lane, ten to one ;
Or down *Cinder*-hill—so he'd best make his will—
He will scatter his *ashes* like fun.
                    Fun, boys ! fun ! etc."

We had a humourous Irish gardener who was said to have been educated for a Roman Catholic priest, and who had acquired a smattering of Latin; which, with his rich native brogue, not a little mystified and amused his less learned neighbours. He was an especial favourite with my father, who thus sang of him, in our harvest song :—

" The larn'd Master Ryan, you well may rely on,
  Will never our merriment shun ;
Though larned by natur, he's quite a gay cratur,
And bothers us all with his fun.
                    Fun, boys ! fun ! etc."

Among other old India friends who followed Sir Elijah into his retirement, and frequently partook of these hearty, old English merrymakings, was Samuel Tolfrey, who has been already mentioned in connection with graver subjects, but who could turn his epigram with the best of them, and joke and pun all through a harvest holiday.*

When Tolfrey and Halhed, and a few more congenial spirits met together, there was a collision of wit and a good fellowship at Newick Park, which could not easily have been matched elsewhere.

" Halhed, " said a forward young man who presumed to be too familiar with him, " What is your christian name ? " " *Mister,* " replied Halhed, " and I desire you will call me by it." He had once a black serving-boy, who understood no language but Bengalee. " Hand me the salt, " said Halhed inadvertently. The black boy stared and shook his head. " What a stupid fellow,"

---

* Mr. Tolfrey, long after his connection with the Supreme Court at Calcutta, obtained an appointment under Sir Elijah's distinguished relative Sir Edmund Carrington, Chief Justice at Ceylon. Subsequently to that appointment he was employed as a civilian under the governments of the Hon. Frederic North (Lord Guildford) and General Sir Thomas Maitland. Mr. North granted him a conisderable sum of money for his able compilation of a Cingalese Dictionary. Tolfrey was a man of great industry and research, and very rare natural abilities.

cried his master, looking hard at him as he pronounced the last word, "why it's as clear as *noon-day*." The lad instantly handed the salt-cellar, for *nún*, in the language of Bengal, is *salt*, and *da* means *give*.

I have said that Tolfrey could point an epigram. I subjoin two or three of them, which diverted my father, and were once universally known :—

> "Here lies William Curtis, late London's Lord Mayor:
> He has left this here world, and has gone to that there."

> "Of the Hottentot Venus this record we find,—
> She is dead,—and has not left her equal behind."

Tolfrey was living at Cheltenham when the Duke of Wellington paid a visit to that place. It had been rumoured that his Grace was coming to drink the waters, for the disease incidental to hot climates, and hard military service. All Cheltenham prepared to receive the great man as he merited ; the town was illuminated throughout, and all sorts of emblems, devices, and inscriptions, were invented and exhibited. Tolfrey hung out a transparency, on which was a portrait of the Duke, with these two lines, strongly illuminated, below :—

> "The hero who conquers wherever he fights,
> Though his liver may fail him, shall never want lights."

But my father's pleasantry was colloquial ; it lay rather in prose than in metrical impromptus ; and, was mostly of a sort that could win the smiles and sympathies of the fairer sex : for his wit was perfectly exempt from that grossness which was but too prevalent in his earlier days, not only among the gentlemen of the robe, but in other distinguished classes of society. A very accomplished and much admired lady of quality, one of our nearest neighbours at Newick, knew that Sir Elijah suffered frequently from an affection of the kardia, commonly called "heart-burn," and, fearing that he must have nearly exhausted his remedies, kindly offered, one day, to replenish his medicine chest; "I thank you," said he, "but," pointing to the chalk-cliffs between Newick and Lewes, "yonder, madam, is my medicine chest ! "

The same lady, while presiding, one evening, at her own tea-table, asked whether she should give him black tea or green ? " I am indifferent to the colour," said he, " but rather particular as to the quality : the cups may be China, but not the tea." His usual drink was a decoction of English herbs. For the same reason he abstained from wine and every other fermented liquor, but was as great an epicure in water as his friend Mr. Hastings. Sometimes, especially during the progress of my education, the object of my father's railleries was myself ; for he seemed to consider it no unimportant part of discipline to teach his children how to take a joke. When a boy, others flattered me, and, perhaps, I flattered myself, that I had a voice and some taste for music. One day, I was trying my powers by sundry repetitions of Handel's lively air :—

"O ! had I Jubal's lyre,
Or Miriam's tuneful voice."

" What a blessing, my dear boy," exclaimed he, " that you have neither ! "

By this time, I and my two youngest brothers had respectively reached the upper and middle classes of Westminster School ; then flourishing, to the number of four hundred, under the rod of Dr. Vincent. My two juniors had already been promised Bengal writerships ; and were trained accordingly, with extra lessons in arithmetic, and the Eastern languages, under their father's tuition. Sir Elijah, who has been impudently and ignorantly accused of knowing nothing of those dialects, carried his knowledge of them so far, as to be quite able to instruct his two sons *himself*, employing a native Persian, then in England, only " to teach them a more perfect pronunciation." * I have, in my possession, a Persian grammar, which he corrected and simplified, and many loose abstracts beautifully written, by his own hand, in the Arabic character ; and I am assured, by the surviver of those two brothers, that he studied out of a MS. compendium compiled by my father himself. I have said that Sir Elijah was an admirable teacher. With what effect his lessons in the

* Extract from a MS. letter.

Oriental languages were imparted to my brothers, Hastings and Edward, will best appear from a letter addressed to him, by the late John Herbert Harrington, Esq., then senior in Council :—

"Calcutta, 19th January, 1803.

"　.　.　.　.　.　. You will perceive by the inclosed, that Hastings left this College in the first classes of the Hindustance and Bengal languages, and in the second class of the Persian. He was appointed to take part in the Public Disputations, but was unfortunately prevented from attending by indisposition. He also obtained a medal of merit at one of the quarterly examinations. Edward was in the first class of the Bengalee, and third class of the Persian language. He also obtained a medal for the attention he had given to the Shanscrit. . . . . . ."

As for me, about five years before the date of the above letter, I find myself the subject of a correspondence relating to one of these writerships, parts of which correspondence seem to me too curious to be omitted :—

"Lord Liverpool to Richard Barwell, Esq.

"Addiscombe Place, January 6, 1798.

"Dear Sir,

"I am very much concerned to hear of your frequent disappointments in obtaining an object which I know you have had in view. You may be assured that I will earnestly apply to Mr. Dundas, and endeavour to induce him to make good his engagement as speedily as possible. I cannot answer for my success, for I last year obtained, with some difficulty, a writership for the grandson of Governor Watts, who is, by marriage, my nephew. If I find I am not likely to succeed with Mr. Dundas, I will apply to some of the Directors ; though here, also, I am doubtful of success . . . .

"Yours &c., &c.,
"LIVERPOOL."

"Richard Barwell, Esq., to Sir Elijah Impey,

"Stanstead, January, 1798.

"Dear Impey,

"I gave you my application to Lord Liverpool. I now give you his answer. This is the straightforward style in which he has always acted towards me : how differently the Englishman shews by [the side of] my professing Scotch friend ! . ."

"Lord Liverpool to Richard Barwell, Esq.
"London, January 21, 1798.
" Dear Sir,

" Since I came to town, I have had an opportunity of speaking to Mr. Dundas on the subject of young Impey's going out to India. You will easily believe I pressed him strongly. He did not give me a direct promise that he should be sent out this year ; but he held out the strongest hope that he should be able to do so. I am the more inclined to rely on those expectations, he having informed me to which of the Directors I could apply for the appointment. As a personal favour to *me*, he rather discouraged me from making the application, and held out reasons to induce me to think that I should not do it with success. I shall not, however, fail to make such application.

"I am, with sincere regard, &c. &c.,
"LIVERPOOL."

" Richard Barwell, Esq., to Sir Elijah Impey.
" Stanstead, January 24, 1798.
"Dear Impey,

"I hope my godson may now be assured of our object; and your mind, as well as my own, rely confidently on his success. . . . . Return the inclosed letter, and the one I sent before; as I mean to contrast them with my Scotch friend's professing epistles, whenever the opportunity offers, before a certain great character,* who is too partial, and whom he certainly impresses with disadvantageous sentiments and prejudices. . . . . . ."

The affair ended in my declining, after some hesitation, the proposed writership, which was transferred to my brother Hastings,† my father acquiescing in the arrangement, with his accustomed kindness and liberality. Another was procured for Edward,† through Sir Elijah's steady friend, the late highly respected Colonel Sweeny Toone, who was then a Director of the East India Company ; and, in due time, both my brothers successively proceeded to Bengal.

The agony which my father suffered in parting with them is not to be described. Though in the enjoyment of tolerable health, he was, by this time, far advanced in the vale of years ; and he had the melancholy fore-

* Evidently Mr. Pitt.
† Godsons—one of the Governor General, the other of Lord Chancellor Thurlow.

boding that, in this life, they were never to meet more. I have alluded, in an early part of this work to his parting with my brother Hastings, at the Isle of Wight.* That event took place in the summer of 1800 ; and, in the year following, my brother Edward sailed. After my dear father's death in 1809, there was found among his papers, on a single sheet, and in his own hand writing, the following earnest prayer, which he had never shown to us, while living.

"O God, the Ruler of all hearts, the disposer of all events, in whose breath are the fountains of life, whose hand scattereth abroad the arrows of death, in whose sight nothing is great, nothing is small, who in the desert raisest up mighty nations, and to deserts reducest proud cities; without whose permission not a sparrow perisheth; by whom the hairs of our heads are all numbered: Preserve, I beseech thee, my dear sons Hastings and Edward, from all perils by land and by water, from all assaults of our enemies, from all diseases, particularly those which are incident to hot climates; and from all distresses, calamities, and evils of this life, ghostly or bodily. Whatever is religious and virtuous in them, cherish and confirm; whatever hath a contrary tendency, correct and expel; and grant that the purposes of their going hence may be honestly and speedily accomplished; so that they may soon return in wealth and credit, health and happiness long to live ; and that my days may, by thy loving-kindness, be so graciously enlarged, that I may see them again, before mine eyes are closed in death. Bestow, I implore Thee, on my wife and on all my children, relations and friends, long life and prosperity in this world, and grant that they may finally enjoy everlasting life and felicity in the world to come. O God ! let thy mercy be extended unto all men. Hear me, O heavenly Father, of thy great mercy, through the merits and mediation of Jesus Christ, thine only Son our Lord."

My father had also the interests of his elder sons to attend to. Of these, one had entered the army, another the navy ; another, whom I have noticed before, as assisting his father at the bar of the Commons, in 1788,†

---

* See foot-note, Chap. I., page 4.

† See ante, p. 189, where an error has crept into the note appended to that page, which I now take this opportunity to correct. My brother Archibald, was not officially "*Counsel*" to the Honourable Court of Directors ; but, as I have always understood, he occupied, by their permission, an honorary seat within their bar. He died, July 9, 1831 ;

was bred a barrister. For Michael, so named from our uncle, and for John, the godson of Dunning, he was indefatigable in his exertions at the army and navy boards. Out of many letters, I select the following extract relative to my naval brother. It was addressed to me, then a student at Christchurch.

"Wimpole Street, 24th February, 1801.

" . . . . . I was yesterday with Lord St. Vincent, who received me in the warmest and most friendly manner. He told me he was glad John was in the West Indies, as at home he could do nothing for him for some months; that Duckworth was under great obligations to him, and that he would write to him to promote John as soon as possible. ' But,' he added, ' keep my secret, Sir Elijah, for if it should be known that I have done anything for *your* son, I shall bring the whole world upon me, whom I have been absolutely forced to refuse: therefore, *Tace !'* "

Without attempting any detailed account of my eldest surviving brother, Admiral Impey's services, I may be pardoned for stating generally, that they were distinguished, chiefly in the West Indies ; and, that I have often heard him attribute his skill as a navigator, and much of his success as an officer, to the care which our father bestowed on his early marine education, and to the instruction of that able sailor, Captain James West, with whom he made two voyages to India and back, before he entered the Royal Navy.*

But Sir Elijah was preceptor to all his children. In every higher branch of education, he was sedulously attentive to that of his daughters, whose accomplishments and conduct in society, did honour to his tuition. It does not become me to dwell longer upon my own progress, than is sufficient to exemplify the personal advantages which I derived from paternal instruction, and with due gratitude to acknowledge my father's ever-ready assistance.

and, being a Bencher of the Inner Temple, was interred in the Temple Church, near a tablet erected by his late widow. I have a melancholy pleasure, in giving my humble testimony to the merits of my late distinguished brother, Archibald Elijah Impey.

* He likewise sailed on board the *Providence*, with Captain Bligh, on his commission to transplant the bread-fruit tree from the Pacific to the West India Islands, in 1791.

With a view to being elected from the Westminster foundation to one of the Universities, I was admitted a King's Scholar, in 1794. About this time, partly stimulated by encouragement at home, and partly by the example of some clever contemporaries at school, I became much addicted to the composition of Latin verse. Robert Southey left Westminster just as I entered ; but had excited a spirit of emulation among his successors, the D'Oylys, the Murrays—Lord Stormont and his cousin William, Lord Henderland's son, whose sapphics were the object of my particular emulation— William Corne, Joseph Phillimore, and the rest of " Kidd's Golden Election." All these were a little my seniors. Among those on the same form, and of the same standing as myself, the most distinguished were, Lord Henry Petty, now Marquess of Lansdowne, Welbore Ellis Agar, since Earl of Normanton, the Honourable William and Charles Stuart, brothers of the late Lord Blantyre, and James Boswell, youngest son of the biographer. Then came Richard Edensor Heathcote, late M.P. for Coventry, John Symmons, who, at the age of eighteen, had translated the " Alexandra " of Lycophron, into blank verse ; and Henry Fynes —Clinton—the future author of " Fasti Hellenici." But I had fairly caught the inspiration from my more immediate predecessor, John Josias Conybeare—late Prebendary of York, and Vicar of Bath Easton—to whose memory it is ever my delight to pay the tribute of admiration and affection. He was my dearest friend and inseparable companion, both at Westminster and at Oxford. For many years he has been no more, but I feel his loss as though it were a recent sorrow. His genius, his research, his rare acquirements, are well known to the literary world, through his " Illustrations of Anglo-Saxon Poetry," which were ably edited by his brother, the distinguished geologist and divine,—my much respected friend, William Daniel Conybeare, now Dean of Llandaff. They were published in 1826.

The summit of my boyish ambition was, to translate Pope's " Rape of the Lock," into long and short verse. My father suggested hexameters as more appropriate to the subject, and was even *barbarous* enough to recommend the jingle of monastic rhyme. He pointed out Parnell's ingenious travesty of the second canto of Pope's mock heroic. But I was too deeply smitten with Tibullus and Propertius to condescend to any less classical metre. The consequence, of course, was, a sudden standstill at many a knotty point. At every such halt I applied to my father, and he generously set me going again. I remember several instances of his seasonable aid. I found it difficult to render Pope's two lines :—

> " Here living tea-pots stand, one arm held out,
> The other bent,—the handle this, and that the spout."

My father gave this version :—

> " Urna manum tendit dextram, curvatque sinistram,
> Fungitur hæc ansæ partibus, illa tubi."

And then, enlarging the idea, and borrowing Wilkes's joke, he added :—

> " Fit genetrix partura *Theam,* et *te,* Pronuba Juno !
> *Te,* veniente die, *Teque,* cadente, vocat."

I was again puzzled when I came to—

> " On various tempers act in various ways,
> Make some take physic, others scribble plays."

Here he dictated to me :—

> " Utque regis mentes vario moderamine, succos
> Illa bibit medicos, hæc Heliconis aquas.

In describing the game of Ombre, Pope has this couplet :—

> " Now move to war her sable Matadores,
> In show-like leaders of the swarthy Moors.

I could make nothing of it, even though told that matador, a Spanish word, was derived from the Latin, *mactator.* Laughing, and recurring to his monkish rhythm, my father thundered out,—

> " Nunc Mactatorum manus advolat atricolorum,
> More modoque Jubæ, cum sonuere tubæ."

He then threw up the cards, and left me and Pope to finish the game between us.

I cannot refrain, even at the risk of being thought tedious, from finding room here for some lines of a graver character. They formed part of a Christmas holiday's task, under the title of "Maria in diversorio;" where the virgin was made to prophecy and protest against the future Roman Catholic worship of her image.

> " Nam memini in fatis volventibus, affore tempus,
> Cum te, nate Deo, generis divine Redemptor !
> Posthabito, ventura colent me sæcula matrem,
> Ausa immane nefas.   ' Hoc, tu Romane ! caveto.' "

This, though nothing but a *cento,* was evidently beyond the conception of a junior in the second election ; and Vincent was far too sagacious to mistake it for mine. "Boy, boy !" said he, "these are no verses of yours, your father made them, and you may tell him I told you so."

Sir Elijah had always been partial to the scenes of his own childhood, and grew more and more so, as I proceeded in my career. He frequently visited the school, renewed his acquaintance with our excellent head-master, often begged our half-holidays, or *plays,* as they were called ; and, by repeated appearances in Dean's Yard, became well known to the boys, and a sort of favourite among them. He was, besides, a pretty constant attendant at our anniversaries, —the performance of the comedies of Terence in December, the Westminster Meeting, then always held on the Tuesday next after the fifth Sunday after Easter ; and the Election Dinner in College Hall, on the same Tuesday in Rogation Week. On the latter occasion, it has long been the custom to produce a certain silver cup, or "poculum," of which the history is this :—About the year 1777, there happened to be residing in India, many gentlemen who had been educated at Westminster; they were desirous of bestowing some testimony of their attachment to the school ; and, with that feeling, subscribed to a piece of plate for the use of the King's Scholars of St. Peter's College. This piece of plate assumed the form of a very noble, double-handed drinking cup, which was characteristically ornamented with elephant's heads, the proboscfs being bent into handles, and the sides engraved with the names of the donors.

The first name was that of "Warren Hastings," the second, "Elijah Impey." A part of the exercises which constitute the examination of the candidates for either University, consists, as I have noticed elsewhere, of Latin epigrams; and, sometimes, short copies of verses of a more serious turn, are recited. These recitations are not unfrequently made the vehicle of compliment to some one present at the Election Dinner, who may be considered a fit object of such an address. In 1801, two years after I had gone up to Christ Church, it being known that Sir Elijah would attend this anniversary, it was good-naturedly contrived by the under-master,* in whose department it lay, to greet my father's visit with a poetical compliment. Here are the lines, under an appropriate thesis,† alluding to the "poculum" before-mentioned. They were spoken by my late friend Edmund Goodenough, afterwards Dean of Wells, but, at that time, captain of the school.

Musarum reduci salvere jubemus alumno,
   Tamque diù notas nursus adire lares;
Ecce etiam, eöis præmissum pignus ab Indis,
   Hanc pateram! fidei te meminisse tuæ.
Ecce elephas rostrum tibi, flexile curvat in ansam,
   Dentis, in argentum vertere lætus, ebur.
Unde propinandum est in honorem matris Elisæ,
   Cujus in æternum floreat alma domus!‡
At te, merce datâ jamdudum, quòd nequiamus
   Immunem cyathis tingere, testis adest.
Quicquid in hôc pulchrum est, vel quicquid amabile dono,
   Illud in auctores muneris, omne redit.

Which may be translated thus :—

Welcome! old brother Westminster, to these
Time-honoured walls : our Lars and Lemures
Hail thee a pilgrim worthy of their shrine,
True to thy pledge : for lo! yon pledge is thine.
Wafted on Hooghly's tide, from far Bengal,
Yon tankard tells of old St. Peter's Hall;
Tells of thy plighted faith, and blameless truth,
In age redeem'd the promise of thy youth :

---

* The late Rev. Dr. Wingfield, afterwards Prebendary of Worcester.
† " . . . . Cum tuâ
    Velox merce veni."—Hor. Ode viii., lib. iv.
‡ Quod felix faustunque sit!

That mimic tusk, from elephantine bone,
Changed to a silvery lustre not its own,—
Those thinking heads, on solemn draughts intent,
Their lithe probosces into handles bent
Invite thy grasp.   Then toast Elisa's name ;
Drink deep : A " Floreat " to our royal dame !
Yet thou no more gratuitous canst share
The rich carouse : for lo ! 'tis *reckon'd* there,
Whate'er of glory in the gift may be
Graces the giver, and reverts to thee.

These verses, a few days after the dinner, were thus acknowledged by my father, in a letter addressed to me at Oxford, from Daylesford, where he was then visiting.

". . . . . Your friend, Hugh Jones,* will have told you I was at the Westminster Election, where I heard your verses, and was much pleased with them: though, if my ear served me right, there was an incorrectness in one syllable. But they were good, and I thank you for them. . . . . Goodenough did you great credit.   The Dean † told me he was always scolding you for such slips, and asked me if you did not say so ?   I answered the truth—that I heard from you of nothing but his kindness. . . . .   You are not to wait for any other invitation from Mr. Hastings; his attachment to you is truly parental, and I desire you to treat him as a parent.   You cannot conceive the pleasure and consolation which I derive from being again so close to Hastings. He likes your lines."

After this—indifferent as they are—I am not ashamed to own them.

In 1799, while I was yet at Westminster, though about to proceed to Christchurch, died Clayton Mordaunt Cracherode, Esq., one of the Trustees of the British Museum, a gentleman otherwise distinguished in literature, and very justly respected by all old Westminsters.   As a regular attendant at their meetings, he was deemed a fit subject for celebration at his death ; and I, as captain, was desired to furnish the verses.   Being discouraged by the unmusical sound of the name, I remonstrated against the hardship of harmonizing it in Latin.   My father, on the other

---

* Now Archdeacon of Essex.
† Dr. Cyrill Jackson.

hand, contended that there was no difficulty in the
case, that the name was wonderfully euphonious, and
that nothing could be easier than to make Cracherode
march to the music of melodious verse ; then, after a
twinkle of the eye, and one of his quiet smiles, he
suggested this hemistich,—

> " Musis Cracherodus amabile nomen ! "

Most fertile and ready was he in badinage of this
kind, almost to his latest moments.   Many more of his
jests still linger in my memory, but the samples I have
given will suffice.   In another style, more popular and
intelligible in general society, his success was great.
I never knew a better teller of a story, or one who had
more amusing stories to tell.   Many of them related to
the humourists with whom he had gone the western circuit, or practised in Westminster Hall, when several of
his professional brethren seem to have been great oddities.
He had a leash of tales about the facetious Serjeant Davy.
The whole budget, with his occasional illustrations and
commentaries, might afford materials for as pleasant a
picture of our old English men of the robe, as Sir Walter
Scott produced of those of the ancient school in Edinburgh.   And here—though I must as carefully separate
the venerated name of the late Sir Richard Sutton, as that
of my father, from any vulgar community with either—yet
can I not refrain from inserting an anecdote concerning
them, which has been kindly communicated to me by one
of the most valued and confidential friends of the Sutton
family.   The Rev. I. T. Becher, Prebendary of York
and Southwell, has lately furnished me with the following particulars ; and has added to the obligation by
allowing me to quote his own words, which I extract
from two valuable letters addressed to me from his
residence, " Hill House, Southwell, June, 1846."   After
stating that " the friendship between the late Sir R.
Sutton and Sir E. Impey was, from their boyhood, of
the warmest and most affectionate kind," that " Sir
Richard had travelled repeatedly over almost every
part of the continent, was such an admirable linguist,
that he could converse with every European in his native
language," and that " he was an excellent decypherer,"
Mr. Becher continues,—" One day after dinner your

father produced a manuscript in cypher, received lately by him from the East Indies, and applied to Sir Richard to decypher it, which he voluntarily undertook to do. However, to our amusement, it was found to be a collection of illegible words which Sir Elijah had taken out of different letters addressed to him by Sir Richard Sutton, whose handwriting, during his latter years, became, in many parts, quite unintelligible ; as he continued to write with his usual rapidity, though his fingers were severely contracted by the gout."

But it is time to leave these humourous trifles. Yet will I not leave them, without asking whether these, my father's pastimes, this my father's cheerful old age, could characterise a man of rancorous passions, or betoken a heart perverted by ambition,—a soul debased by bribery, a conscience burthened with blood ? Can the reader, by any possibility, imagine, that Sir Elijah's life at Newick Park, could be that which I here most conscientiously describe it, if it had been such as his defamers represent it to have been at Calcutta ?

The year 1801 was a disastrous one in the annals of my dear father's life. In the autumn, after his return from that happy visit to Daylesford, mentioned in a preceding page, I received from him this mournful letter, directed to me at Oxford.

" Wimpole Street, October 28, 1801.
" My dearest Elijah,
" Pity me that I am forced to communicate to you—having nobody with me but your mother--the cruel intelligence of the death of your brother Michael. I learned it from a kind letter of Prince William of Gloucester,* which I found after my return from the Admiralty this morning. . . . . . I will write again, being now too much occupied with your dear mother, to whom I have just broke the sad tidings. I trust she will soon bear it with greater fortitude than can be expected from her at this moment; nor can I yet bear to impart the horrid particulars—you know I am not a good comforter. We think of returning to Newick next Saturday. . . ."

Major Impey had most unhappily fallen in a duel at Quebec. He had previously served with distinction under General Sir Charles Grey at the capture of the

---

* His Royal Highness the late Duke of Gloucester, then Colonel of the 6th Regiment of Infantry, to which my brother belonged.

French islands in the West Indies; * He left behind
him the reputation of a gallant officer.

On the very day after writing his first sad letter, my
father wrote to me again.

" I have this morning been with Prince William, from whom
I have experienced every attention, kindness, and humanity.
He read to me the paragraph of a letter from the 6th regiment
which contains the whole account of this most melancholy
event,—more melancholy as it was caused by a duel with an
officer of the same regiment, a Lieutenant * * * * * * It originated in a dispute at the mess after a review. On the next day,
September 1st, he received a mortal wound, and died the day
following. On that day, Lieutenant Colonel Scott wrote to me
a letter which I received this morning. He describes himself
as an intimate friend of my poor Michael, and as his executor.
.   .   .   Your dear brother's behaviour was manly and chris-
tianlike ; and it is a substantial comfort to me that I can cherish the strongest hopes of his eternal happiness, from knowing
the spirit in which he died. I am assured that he endeavoured
to avoid the duel, and resolved not to hurt his antagonist.
He never fired his pistol."

Sir Elijah returned to Newick, and remained there
about six weeks, when he hurried up to town again, to
meet and provide for his widowed daughter-in-law ;
who, by that time, had arrived from Canada with her five
infants. He could know no rest or tranquillity of spirit
until he saw them lodged under his own roof. At the
moment of their arrival, he was preparing for a journey
to Paris, upon very pressing business, which involved
the recovery of considerable sums of money ; but
the journey to France was postponed, and for some
weeks, not a thought of his money-business appears to
have entered into his mind. He occupied himself, early
and late, upon one absorbing object,—how to secure the
welfare of this afflicted family—the wife and children
of the son who had perished in his prime. I have now
before me a letter he wrote at *midnight* on the 27th of
November, to tell me the journeys he had gone, and the
preparations he was making.

" In a day or two," said he, " they will be all safe under
my roof and protection. When we go to Paris, they will be at

* My surviving eldest brother, now an Admiral, served with distinction
as a naval officer in the same expedition under the command of Sir John
Jervis, afterwards Earl St. Vincent.

Lovibonds, whose generosity and affection cannot be surpassed.* . . . . I must apologize to you for not having
written as soon as I came to town, but every moment has been
taken up with endeavours to soothe the sorrows of the afflicted
widow and orphans."

Henry, the eldest of these children, was early educated by his generous uncle, the present Sir Robert
Affleck, Bart., of Dalham Hall, husband of my lamented
sister Maria. Sir Elijah procured for him a cadetship
to Bengal. As ensign he afterwards distinguished himself in the war with Nepaul, under General Ochterlony.
On the 27th of October, 1816, he gallantly maintained
his position at Mukwampoor, in a manner for which he
was publicly thanked in the general orders. See Mac
Farlane's Indian History, vol. ii. p. 199.

* My brother-in-law, the late excellent George Lovibond, Esq., of Man-
chester Square, then residing at Park House, near Maidstone. He married my late beloved sister Martha, christened after Sir Elijah's " pious
mother," Martha Fraser. See ante, Chap. I. p. 4.

CHAPTER XVII.

SIR ELIJAH AT PARIS—IS DETAINED AS PRISONER OF WAR
—DEATH OF SIR ROBERT CHAMBERS—ANECDOTES AND
CORRESPONDENCE.

AT this time Europe was enjoying the delusive truce
which goes by the name of the "Peace of Amiens." The
preliminaries had not yet been signed; but General
Andreossi had arrived in London from Buonaparte, our
Government had sent Mr. Jackson to Paris, and a
friendly intercourse was allowed between the two countries. In consequence of Mr. Pitt's truly liberal and
enlightened commercial treaty with France, in 1786, and
of the brilliant financial schemes of M. Necker, which
it was fondly expected would bring about *reform* in
France, without *revolution,* my father, like many other
Englishmen, had invested some of his fortune in the
French funds. He had also placed money in the hands
of the Parisian bankers, Messrs. G ********* and
M ****, in the intent, I believe—for I am not very well
informed about these matters—of investment in public
securities. When the tremendous revolution broke out,
these bankers held some of the cash, for which they
now showed no disposition to account. The French republicans, by a very simple and summary process, had
expunged the whole of their national debt, and
refused any compensation to the creditors of the State,
whether native or foreign. But now something like
a system of order and law being established, under
Buonaparte, and his brother consuls, Cambaçares and

2 c

Le Brun, it had been mutually agreed by the diploma-
tists of both nations, that French subjects having
claims in England, should have justice done them
here, and that English subjects having claims in
France, should have like justice there—according to
the spirit and meaning of a clause always inserted in
treaties of peace. My father's agents at Paris had
written a pressing letter, urging him to lose no time in
taking steps to recover his property.

On the 4th of December, 1801, we obtained our
passports, and a few days after were landed at Calais.
Our party consisted of my father and mother, my
youngest sister, and myself. At Amiens, we found
Lord Cornwallis in negociation with Joseph Buonaparte,
for the settlement of the definitive treaty; and, at Paris,
we were one of the first English families that had yet
arrived. The peace was then exceedingly popular there.
In nearly every class of society there seemed to be a
disposition to welcome the English; and *we* certainly
had no reason to complain of a want of hospitality.
Mr. Jackson had already fitted up his residence; and
we were soon comfortably established in the Hotel
Caraman. After delivery of letters of introduction we
were admitted, at the Tuileries and elsewhere, into the
first circles of Parisian society.

After the fearful storms of revolution and war, internal
and external, which had strewed the political shore with
so many wrecks, and which had so altered the fortunes
and relative position of thousands, it was a common
occurrence in Paris, at this first subsidence of the
tempest, for personages of the most opposite principles,
to find themselves side by side, or crowded and whirled
together in the vortex of the same *salon*. Yet, I doubt
whether Paris, even at this time, witnessed a stranger
re-union than that which I am about to describe.

Among the persons whom we met in the very mixed
society of Paris, was the *ci-devant* Mrs. Le Grand,*
who had lately been married to M. de Talleyrand, then
Minister for Foreign Affairs. My father renewed
his old acquaintance with her; and, through the lady,
he became sufficiently intimate with the extraordinary
diplomatist, her husband, to be one of the Englishmen

* See ante p. 174.

most frequently invited to his table. The *soirées* and *petits-soupers*, of Madame de Talleyrand, at her charming villa of Neuilly—now in the possession of his Majesty Louis Philippe—were, at this period, about the most select in France ; being rivalled only by those of the Consuless Josephine, the literary Madame de Staël, and the fashionable and fascinating Madame Recamier. They united not only the *corps-diplomatique*, but all such as were distinguished by their station or talents.

At Neuilly, were to be met foreigners from every country and court in Europe. At one of these assemblies, myself being present, this remarkable rencontre took place, of persons not likely ever to have met beneath the same roof, under any circumstances less fortuitous. These persons were—Mr. and Mrs. Fox, Sir Elijah and Lady Impey, M. and Me. de Talleyrand, Sir Philip Francis, and—Mr. Le Grand !

Between Mr. Fox and my father, there had been " foregone conclusions " too notorious to make it possible that they should meet upon friendly terms ; yet, far from there being anything of personal antipathy in the disposition of either, I am inclined to believe, that, if they had known each other earlier, and under circumstances of less public heat and animosity, there was that in the generous nature of both, which might have attracted each to the other. In this instance, it was pleasing, at least, to observe, that the ladies of either family seemed to like each other, though the gentlemen stood quite aloof. As for Francis and Sir Elijah, they were, like Hessians and Hanoverians, in the same camp,—though, of course, without any discourtesy. How Sir Philip and Le Grand looked and felt in their present false position with M. le Ministre des Relations Extérieures and his elevated wife, it matters not much to inquire ; but, I can well imagine, that the whole group must have been amusing enough to some of the by-standers, who were acquainted with the Indian history of Madame de Talleyrand.

The object of poor Le Grand's visit to Paris was to solicit some profitable appointment under the French government. This he attempted—wonderful to relate—

through the interest of the fair *divorcèe*, whom he addressed by letter as his "*chere et ancienne amie*," and by whom, as well as by her present husband, he was in the meantime very politely received; but his efforts ended in a signal disappointment. The particulars have been recently related to the public.*

As for the business which had carried us to France, it proceeded very, very slowly. The bankers, Messrs. G * * * * * * * * * were to be moved to the painful duty of refunding only by process of law; and from one tribunal the cause was removed, by appeal, to another and another.

Although my own stay at Paris was this time but short, by the considerate advice of my father I took up my abode at a *pension*, for the purpose of improving my pronunciation of French. A better establishment could hardly have been chosen. M. Le Comte, an experienced teacher, and a worthy man, presided over it. Its numbers were considerable, and consisted of French youths of good family, though now all levelled to the republican rank of *citoyens*. It had been recommended to us by the Earl of Lauderdale, whose son, Lord Maitland, was the only countryman I found there. Their lordships, by the way, father and son, in point of citizenship and republicanism, appeared to be no exceptions at Paris, for they both constantly wore the tri-colour cockade.

If I remember right, it was at M. le Comte's that I formed an acquaintance with a real living Greek,—a man of a very picturesque aspect, and of rather lofty

---

* See "Our Indian Empire," by Charles Mac Farlane, vol. 1, p. 219. Sir James Mackintosh relates that he met Le Grand at the African Club, at the Cape of Good Hope, in 1812, and describes him as "a gentlemanlike old man, a native of Lausanne,"—"Memoir of the Life of Mackintosh," edited by his son. Part of the sequel of Le Grand's history I can supply:—After the Peace of Paris, in 1815, he came to London; so did Madame la Princesse de Benevento. His object was to publish the particulars of the lady's life at Calcutta, in revenge for his disappointment at Batavia—her's to seek redress for the publication. I saw it; it was a paltry book, printed at the Cape. They both applied to me. I advised the author to suppress his work, and the Princess not to go to law. This advice, of course, was very unpalatable to both : the lady took a legal opinion, and the gentleman *took* himself off. What became of him since I know not; but the libel shortly disappeared, and the matter seems to have ended as amicably as before.

literary aspiration. He presently possessed me of the idea to study the modern Greek language; and while I remained in the land of Latin,* as they call that quarter of Paris, near the University, where my *pension* was situated, the venerable descendant of the ancient Achaians and I became rather intimate. His name was Polizioii.

So long as I was there, my father communicated with me in French, as he had heretofore done in Latin and Greek.

On the 28th of January, 1802, I left Paris to return to my college at Oxford. I had only been a day or two at Christ Church, when I received from him the following letter, which re-produces my Greek acquaintance, and shows the constant playfulness of my father's disposition :—

"Paris, Feb. 2, 1802.

"The morning of the day you left us, before I was dressed, your friend Polizioii paid me a visit. He talks of being in England in a month. He has a work in the press, which I fear will not secure him much profit; no less than a heroic poem on the late war, in Homeric verse. What do you think of my giving him a letter to Dr. Vincent? To the Dean of Christ Church I dare not, without his leave. On parting, I found myself suddenly in the embraces of the venerable and bearded bard ! It reminded me of the tender scene between old Nestor and old Mentor in the Odyssey—only we had lost our Telemachus.

Last night Madame de Staël, General and Madame Marmont, and M. Perigaux visited me. Buonaparte returned from Italy on Sunday night; his arrival was announced by the discharge of cannon. He has accepted the Presidency of the new Republic, which has changed its name from Cisalpine to Italian. I am to be presented to him next Thursday. I left letters with Talleyrand yesterday. I cannot yet give you any favourable account of my affairs. The report here is, the definitive treaty is nearly concluded. Jackson tells me he sent you a turkey stuffed with truffles, a bottle of Burgundy, and a dozen of claret ; I hope, therefore, you did not stop between Paris and Calais. My best respects to the Dean, and the offer of my services about the maps and coins for Christ Church library. . . . ."

* Pays Latin. Rue Vielle Estrapade, Fauxbourg St. Jaques.

In a few days more came the following :—

"Feb. 10, 1802.

.   .   .   .   "When you write again let me know how all
goes on at Park House,—whom you met in London,—how you
were received at Christ Church.   It was not my fault if you
exceeded your time, or if the Dean was disappointed about
the maps and coins.   Be sure to let me have his farther
commissions.   I have little to write of myself that will interest you, except that we are all well, and that I was introduced last parade-day to Buonaparte and Madame.   We
dined with them.   I saw Talleyrand on Sunday—he desired
me to leave a memorial in English, and promised his answer
to Perigaux.   .   .   .   .   I have just received an invitation
to spend the evening of to-morrow with le Ministre de la
Police Generale de la Republique, M. Fouchè.   A few days
ago Lord Camelford came here without a passport, it having
been refused in England.   Buonaparte was immediately informed of it, and his lordship was instantly conducted out of
the Republic."

"Paris, March 16, 1802.

"I must still disappoint your expectation of my being able
to guess the time that my business will permit me to return
to England; but you may depend upon my not delaying it
beyond necessity.   .   .   .   .   Your friend Lusignan was
present when I opened your letter, and was pleased to find
himself remembered in the paragraph which I read aloud.
You are right about Polizioii, but neither you nor the Dean
need be under any apprehension of exhibiting him in the
walks and quadrangles of Christ Church.   If you give me to
understand that Vincent would be flattered by producing a
real living Greek poet, a second Homer, in Dean's Yard, I
shall be proud to play the Pisistratus, and usher him into the
literary world of Westminster.   .   .   .   .   I do not think
you will carry off the prize of pun from your sister University,
to whom it hath been adjudged for time immemorial.   I
don't think a Cantab could pun worse.   I am interested,
however, in your account of the controversy concerning public
and private education, having always been a strong partisan in the cause of which my old friend has become the
champion.*   .   .   .   .   ."

* This alludes to "A Defence of Public Education, addressed to the
Most Reverend the Lord Bishop of Meath, by William Vincent, D.D.,
in answer to a Charge annexed to his lordship's Discourse preached at the
anniversary in St. Pauls," &c. &c.   London, 1801.

Other letters followed in rapid succession. The two subjoined extracts may have some little interest.

Paris, May 25, 1802.

" I do not yet know that I have much reason to congratulate myself on the late judgment pronounced in my favour against G * * * * * * * * * and M * * * *. They have been attempting to play the same game in England as they have done here; but they will find difficulties there, as our laws are not so complaisant to frauds as those of France. My memorial is before the Ministre des Relations Exteriéures; I have lately received much civility from him, but do not think for that reason my affairs are likely to be more prosperous. There is a proposition adopted by the Senate, that Buonaparte be nominated Consul for life: it will not stop there; the succession will be fixed. . . . . I do not think it right to discuss politics by the common post, especially as all things are not as I could wish. . . . . I have reason to believe, that instead of passports being now more easily procured, they will be more difficult to get: I cannot explain the reason, because I do not know that it is not a State secret. . . . . ."

" Paris, May 26, 1802.

" I forgot to tell you in my last, that if you keep your resolution of returning to Paris, you must come as early as possible. Buonaparte will be absent on a tour between the 15th and 20th of next month, and I wish you to be introduced. . . . . Your mother is become a complete Frenchwoman, gay as a butterfly, busy as a bee, and extending her acquaintance on all sides. . . . . The old Dowager Duchess of Deuxponts, whom * * * proposed for *King of the Romans*, is her most intimate friend. With Her Royal Highness the old Duchess of Cumberland, and the ever-blooming M * * * * * * * * * * of A * * * * * * *, with Madame Buonaparte, Messrs. Le Brun and Cambaçares she is *chair et ongle*. . . . The settlement of my affairs is as uncertain as ever : my case cannot, of course, be separated from those of others. . . . ."

These delays and obstructions, and the want of common honesty in the bankers, were sufficiently vexatious, but they could not ruffle my dear father's temper.

Early in the summer of 1802, I returned to my old quarters at Monsieur le Comte's, in the Rue Vielle Estrapade, and remained there during the ensuing long vacation—dined with the three consuls, and renewed my acquaintance with Mesdames Talleyrand, Recamier, and de Staël. In the following autumn, having left my family still at Paris, I received letters of which these are extracts :—

Paris, Nov. 16, 1802.

" . . . . I am harrassed by the delays of the President of their Tribunal, whom I cannot get to pronounce a judgment. Lord Whitworth arrived on Sunday last. I called on him on Monday; as it was a visit of mere ceremony, I do not know what instructions he has brought out, but do not expect he has any relative to matters which concern private claims. . . . I am nearly come to the resolution of wintering here, you will therefore probably pass over the sea again, I hope more pleasantly and safely than when you went by Dieppe. . . ."

After passing the Christmas vacation once more at Paris, I received the following on my return to Oxford :—

"Paris, Feb. 13, 1803.

" I thank you for your punctuality—your letters from Calais, Dover, Park House, and Oxford. . . . . The season for the last fortnight has been extremely severe, but what is worse, an epidemic disease has prevailed ever since your departure, and has proved fatal in many instances: Mademoiselle Charlotte, whom you must remember as dancing so exquisitely, Princess Castel Forte, the beautiful and inseparable companion of Madame Gallo, a daughter of Chaptal Casti the Italian poet, and La Harpe the celebrated author, have fallen victims to it. . . . . We have been more fortunate; for, I thank God, I can now pronounce that your dear mother, who was attacked—but about whom I would not frighten you—is now well, no symptoms having returned for five days. . . . . Your schoolfellow, the citizen Lord M * * * * * * *, has suffered from another cause: his foot slipped while he was dressing, and he had the misfortune to fall on the fire stove, by which means he broke the three bones which connect the two last fingers of the left hand. They have been well set, and he is doing well. I am very much rejoiced that you left Paris uninfected by the disorder. Thank you for your comfortable news regarding dearest Hastings and Edward. . . . ."

"Paris, Feb. 27, 1803

" . . . . I have letters from Harrington, in Calcutta, dated August 20 and 21. The accounts of my dearest fellows are so pleasant, that I must transcribe his words. ' Hastings, who is living with me, is as attentive and diligent as you could possibly wish. Both he and Edward are as steady and regular in their conduct, I verily believe, as any two young men in the College, and I have the greatest satisfaction in being able to give you this assurance ; they are both in good health. . . .' What you say of the charming Miss Macdonald surprises, alarms, and grieves me very much. God send she may receive benefit from Lisbon. How I pity the poor Chief Baron and Lady Louisa! . . . ."

"Paris, March 25, 1803.

" My cause was finally pleaded on Wednesday. Judgment passed yesterday, and that of the Tribunal of Commerce was reversed. . . . . This is still subject to an appeal to the Tribunal of Cassation, which passes sentence, not on the merits, but on the errors of the judgment. . . . . At Cambaçares's, where I was last night, Segnier, the President of the Courts of Appeal, addressing himself to a friend of G * * * * * * * * * * said, "Nous avons aujourd'hui vengè l' honneur de la justice Française scandaleusement compromis par un jugement inique du Tribunal du Commerce." So this matter rests at present. But since what passed in that Tribunal, nothing can make me sanguine on the business. . . . . The rumours of war have induced John* to tender his services. He left us by the diligence of Wednesday. War is not, however, talked of here, so much as in London ; the French think that peace will continue. I confess I have long thought otherwise ; yet at present I see no immediate necessity for quitting Paris—how soon it may press, is uncertain."

"Paris, May 27, 1803.

" I write merely to prevent your being alarmed by the propagation of any exaggerated accounts of the situation of the English here. . . . . An order was made on Monday last to arrest all British subjects, belonging to the militia, or commissioned by our King, who are within the age of 18 and 60 years. . . . . Being under none of these descriptions, I conceived myself to be exempt. I have been called upon, nevertheless, as a prisoner of war, to sign my parole of honour not to quit Paris. . . . . All other Englishmen who are not, like me, permitted to remain at Paris, are ordered off to Fontainbleau. The order is said to be made by way of reprisals for the capture of two French ships, sailors, and passengers, before the declaration of war. You will

* My brother, then a Master Commander.

see by this that our return home is more uncertain than ever. . . . . Let the good Dean know I have the new coins for him.* . . . ."

Before the date of this letter, Sir Elijah's colleague and friend, Sir Robert Chambers, who had returned from India about the year 1800, died at Paris, after a short illness. My father attended him in his sickness, arranged his funeral, followed him to his foreign grave, and did his best to assist and console his widow and youngest daughter. Other sorrows gathered fast around my father during these inauspicious years. In a letter, dated June 13, 1802, he wrote to me,—

"The letters I receive from England are filled with the deaths of my friends: Kenyon, Walker, and General Adearn, are in the list of the dead. Poor Dehaney and his wife are dangerously ill; two of the Shuttleworths are in the same state. I never have, in so short a space of time, been deprived of so many old friends. Kenyon and Walker are of the number of my best and oldest. I open my letters with fear and trembling. Yours always have—God send they always may—give me comfort and pleasure."

In a subsequent letter without date, but evidently referring to that above quoted, he writes,—

"I complained to you of the losses I had suffered by the death of my friends. I have, I fear, suffered one in addition, that goes very near my heart. I have two letters from Mr. R. Sutton, acquainting me that my old and attached friend was at the point of death, on the 6th of this month. These things, and no prospect of success in my money matters, weigh heavy on me. . . . . Get a letter from Lord Hawkesbury to the Minister here. Captain West will, I know, do this, and apply to Mr. Taylor, who will procure it."

Sir Richard Sutton died, very shortly after, at his seat, Norwood Park, in Nottinghamshire, in the 69th year of his age ; and grievously did Sir Elijah lament his inability to pay the last act of respect to his constant life-long friend. On the 21st of June, 1802, he was

---

* They were sent by a safe hand—my late friend James Shuttleworth, Esq., and finally deposited in the library at Christ Church.

buried in the parish church of Averham,* where a monument is erected to his memory, and inscribed with an epitaph, written at the request of his relatives, by the Rev. I. T. Becher, whom I have already mentioned as acquainted with both our families. It is, therefore, with the greater readiness that I avail myself once more of that gentleman's authority for these additional facts.

"Sir Richard Sutton held the office of Under Secretary of State during the Administration of Lord North, when Lord Rochford was Principal Secretary for the Southern Department. He was also Recorder of St. Albans, and served in several successive Parliaments, chiefly for Boroughbridge, on the nomination of Henry Duke of Newcastle.

"Sir Richard's two dearest friends were, Sir Elijah Impey and Dr. Hinchliffe, Bishop of Peterborough.† . . . Their mutual attachment originated in early youth, and continued unbroken till dissolved by death. . . . In his will, which was proved in Doctor's Commons about the year 1803, he appointed Sir Elijah Impey one of his trustees, with powers extending over the Sutton estates and the very valuable London property."

If my father had not been able to obtain justice at Paris during the semblance of peace, it may be expected he could entertain small hopes of success, when open war was breaking out, and Buonaparte insulting our brave English ambassador, and making prisoners of all the British subjects travelling or residing in France and Upper Italy. The processes of appeal and re-appeal, which had been so irksome, were now stopped altogether; and instead of getting his money, my father was well nigh losing his liberty for the rest of his life. The French procedure, at that time of day, seemed to excite contempt and derision in our English-bred lawyers. I have heard that the late Lord Ellenborough, whom my father numbered among his friends, attended a trial in one of the courts, either of Cassation, or Commerce; that his lordship listened very attentively

---

* For this intelligence, conveyed to me in a very obliging note of the 2nd of July, 1846, I am obliged to the Rev. Robert Sutton, grandson of the late Sir Richard, and Rector of Averham cum Kelham, in the county of Nottingham; and to the present baronet I am grateful for the kind interest with which he has honoured this publication during its progress through the press.

† Mr. Becher remembers their full length portraits for many years hanging on the walls at Norwood Park.

to all the pleadings, and that, when they were over, and
he was leaving the court, deliberately, with his hands
held behind him, he uttered a very significant, and
by no means gently modulated—" Pooh !"

Even when involved in all these troubles, and dis-
quieted by the idea that he should be kept—as so
many Englishmen were—to pass the remnant of his life
under the surveillance of Buonaparte's police, separated
from his family, and surrounded by uncongenial and
inimical objects, I find him devising all manner of
means to contribute to the comforts of us who were in
England, and of my two youngest brothers, who were
in India; and, in his correspondence with me, he mostly
managed to maintain a cheerful, hopeful tone.   In one
of them he is even jocular : it requires a word or two
of explanation.   Up to about this time, Sir Elijah had
worn a wig, which in those days was called a " Bob,"
but he left it off because it was of the same fashion as
those which characterised the priests, and were never
worn by the laity at Paris.   He had no disrespect
whatever for the members of the Gallican Church, but,
nevertheless, objected to be mistaken for a French Abbè.
He preferred, therefore, wearing his own hair; and
having made acquaintance with a very worthy eccle-
siastic, M. Boccauf, he made him a present of the dis-
carded coëffure.   This happened at a moment when it
was most acceptable; and is alluded to, among various other subjects, in a letter, of which the following
is a fragment :—

    .   .   .   .   "I want your Lent verses to shew to little
Boccauf ; who, by the bye, honoured my bob-wig by making
it part of his decoration at the grand Te Deum.   Tickets
were sent to us for Notre Dame; where, at eight o'clock yesterday morning, the said bob marched in solemn procession."

Poor Boccauf! he was the humblest, mildest, and most
courteous of men.   His history, as far as I remember
it, is this : during the dreadful Septembriares he had
narrowly escaped the massacre of the priesthood, and
had subsequently fallen into the most abject poverty.
In that state he became dependent on the bounty of the
celebrated rich banker R———— ; who, like a proud
upstart as he was, treated him far worse than any gen-

tleman would have treated the most menial servant. He had once the brutality to browbeat him in my father's presence, for leaving the door open. My father quietly shut it, and at the same time shut himself out, never to return to the counting-house of M. R————; but poor Boccauf from that moment became a constant guest at our hotel. This paragraph of a letter to me soon after, mentions him once more, and for the last time.

"Paris, May 25, 1803.

". . . . I wish I could give you as good an account of poor Boccauf. He was seized nine days ago with a putrid fever, and died last night. It is an event very grievous to us. The gentleness of his manners had gained upon our affections, and every day more and more confirmed them."

To such as have a real notion of the pathetic, and of the way in which it may be entwined with, and enhanced by the familiar, the homely, the trivial, and, at times, even the ridiculous, this and the following little circumstances will excite any emotion rather than that of derision. My brother had written very earnestly from India for some English dogs; and in the same letter where my father laments the loss of Kenyon, Walker, &c., and speaks almost despondingly of his return home, he adds,—

"As to the dogs for my dearest Hastings, you know the impossibility I am under to procure them. Act for me in the business, and get such as you think will please him; but you must consult Captain West about the mode of transporting them. Let the dear fellow be satisfied. Write to him and tell him the situation I am in, but in a manner to give him no alarm, only to quiet him and my dearest Edward on account of my not being able to correspond with them and answer their wishes. Edward—I learn from Mr. Harrington —has drawn on me for money to buy a horse. Let him know I have ordered the note to be paid according to his wish."

And all this occupied his thoughts, evidently at a time when they must have been much perplexed by his own situation ! and all this was imparted to me in a manner plainly meant to disguise the depression of his own spirits, in order to alleviate mine ! But what gave my father additional uneasiness, was a report that the

Consul intended to put an interdict upon all correspondence and communication whatsoever between
France and England; but, a few days after the date
of the preceding letter, he wrote to me—

" I have the pleasure to inform you that our correspondence will meet with no interruption, as a communication will
be kept open by the way of Bremen.   This is a great comfort
to me.   A letter will be five days on its way from Paris to
Bremen ; how long after to England, I do not know, but it
will arrive some time. . . . . I wish you to abate your
anxiety about us.   It is a great consolation to me that you
are not here, as I think the obtaining *your* return would be
more difficult than mine.   I feel no difference of any kind in
my situation, except that I show myself once a week at the
bureau of the police.   Cambaçares, as soon as the arrest took
place, applied to the officer who had it in charge, to treat me
with every kind of attention ; and I experienced it.   I attend
his levées as usual, and he continues his politeness.   *The*
levées of the First Consul I have not attended.   He is absent
on his tour to Bruxelles, &c.   Talleyrand is with him, and
Madame T. is gone to visit a new purchased estate in
the neighbourhood of Blois. . . . . Remember the
dogs for my dearest Hastings. . . . . I say nothing of
my return, as I would not flatter or disappoint you.   I need
not say that I shall not delay it one moment after it is in my
power to effectuate it.   Communicate to my dear friend
Hastings every thing concerning me that you think will be
satisfactory to him and Mrs. Hastings. . . . . Write
to your dear brothers in India *directly*.   There are ships and
packets going every day."

CHAPTER XVIII.

THE ENGLISH SENT TO VERDUN, ETC.—SIR ELIJAH ALLOWED
TO REMAIN AT PARIS—CORRESPONDENCE CONTINUED—
HE RETURNS HOME—ANECDOTES—DEATH.

BEFORE the close of this year the friends of the English
detenùs in France were thrown into consternation by
hearing that Buonaparte, in a vindictive humour, had
ordered all those prisoners to be shut up at Verdun and
other places. To remove our anxiety my father wrote
to me,—

"Paris, December 9th, 1803.

"At a crisis like this, supposing that exaggerated accounts
will be propagated in England, with regard to the late order
respecting all the English iu the French territory, and perhaps,
with regard to me in particular, in performance of my promise
which I gave you last week, I write to-day. It is true that
an order has been issued to remove them all, without exception,
to Verdun, Charleroi, and Biche—the last two are *fortresses*.
The cause I know not ; but I have great reason to believe,
from the representation that has been made to government of
my partcular situation, that it will not be carried into execution
against me. The friendship and protection we have met is
beyond what we could possibly expect. Your mother turns
out to be the most zealous, active, and adroit solicitor that I
have seen ! . . . . . . But it is *impossible* at this
present moment to obtain a passport.

"Postscript, December 16.
"By the influence of my friends, I remain at Paris, but
don't know *when* I shall get a passport."

Three long months after the date last quoted, I received the copy of a letter from General Berthier, Minister of War, to M. Talleyrand, Minister for Foreign Affairs, who had interested himself in my father's behalf. It was this :—

"Paris, 22 Ventose, An. 12.

"Le Ministre de la Guerre
"Au Ministre des Relations Extèrieures.

"J'ai soumis au Gouvernement, Citoyen Ministre, la demande formèe par M. le Chevalier Impey pour obtenir son retour dans sa patrie. On n'y a pas jugé que cette autorization peut-être accordèe á M. Impey dans les circonstances actuelles. Je vous prie de faire connaitre la decision á cet etranger en faveur du quel vous m'avez fait l'honneur de m'ècrire.

"J'ai l'honneur, &c. &c.
"[Signed] BERTHIER."

Underneath this copy of Berthier's letter, which is officially short, and cold enough, my father wrote,—

"Thus my hopes are frustrated for the present. What change of circumstances may be favourable to my demand, I do not at present see ; but events lately passed here, and the state of the war, certainly are very untoward. I shall lose no opportunity of trying again, but cannot be sanguine in my expectations of success. I am grieved and alarmed at not hearing from England. My apprehensions increase for your mother and sister. If any accident happens to me—and, at my age, it cannot be an unlikely event—what a forlorn situation must they be in !"

On the same day he wrote to that steady and most useful old friend, Mr. West, the worthy captain of the Indiaman, who had brought us home from St. Helena. To him he said,—

"For my own person I have little concern, but confess I am very uneasy when I think of any accident that may happen to me here. What a state my wife and daughter would be in !"

At last my dear father recovered his liberty, and thus announced the fact to me :—

"Paris, June 20, 1804.

"This is the shortest, but perhaps the most agreeable letter I have written to you from France. It is only to announce that I have procured passports to Hamburgh by

Rotterdam, so that this, possibly, may not be the earliest intelligence you may get of my being in England. All well !
all send love."

Travelling with all expedition, as may be supposed,
with his wife and youngest daughter, through Brussels,
the Netherlands, and a part of Holland, Sir Elijah halted
at Breda ; and then embarked at the nearest seaport, in
the first vessel he could find.

This vessel was little better than a boat : it was so
ill-stored, that provisions fell short during the delays
occasioned by contrary winds and stress of weather.
The party suffered much inconvenience; but the recovery
of their liberty compensated for every drawback. Their
precipitous land journey on the continent, had been
marked by no impediment or occurrence beyond the
sensation caused at every barrier between France and
Holland by the inspection of their passport ; for this was
a special passport, and the very first which bore the
name of any English family, *and the autograph signature
of Buonaparte*, since his iniquitous tyranny over our
countrymen detained after the so-called "Peace of
Amiens."

Uncertain how soon, and at what port they might
arrive, I had been advised to wait for them in London ;
when, at the old house in Wimpole street, I had at last
the happiness of embracing them early in July, 1804,
and shortly after I conducted them to Newick Park.

The event of my dear father's arrival and reception
there, lives still fresh and joyous in my memory. As
the old family coach-and-four, which had met us at East
Grinstead, drove through the Newick turnpike, and, roll-
ing over the beautiful rural Green, passed the scattered
hamlet, in its approach to the church, we were greeted
from the steeple by a merry peal of bells ; handkerchiefs
waved from every cottage window, and we were accompanied up Fount Hill, and through the Park lodge, by
a band of honest peasants, who ran at each side of the
coach, shouting a hearty welcome to the good old man
who had so often encouraged their labours, and assisted
at their pastimes. He did not allow his horses to be
taken from the carriage : the attention, marked, as it
was, proved already too much for his nerves. For, in
the very midst of this merriment, it cast a dash of me-

2 D

lancholy over his spirits, which reminded me of the well-
known sentiment of Lucretius :

> " . . . . medio de fonte leporum
> Surgit amari aliquid quod in ipsis floribus angit. "

I was struck at the alteration in my father's personal
appearance, which had taken place since our last parting
at Paris.

He had now exceeded the limit of man's appointed
age by nearly two years ; and though his constitution
appeared not to have suffered materially by the shock,
yet, in addition to the accumulation of years, there was
visible in his whole expression a trace of unwonted
pensiveness, which told a tale of by-gone sorrows.

Something, however, of this effect might be attributed to the alteration of his dress ; for Sir Elijah, as I
have said, now wore his own grey hair.   On this occasion, his person still erect, his eye still lighted up with
calm intelligence, presented altogether the aspect—
such as it continued almost to the conclusion of his
days—of a most venerable, hale, and hearty old English
country gentleman.

Alighting from his carriage, and surrounded by part
of his family assembled to meet him at Newick, it
would be impossible, as he smiled upon us, to have
imagined at that moment, a countenance more indicative of benevolence and paternal love.   In a few days
he was welcomed home, in turn, by all his respectable
neighbours, in a country where an occurrence like this
could never fail of exciting a sentiment of heartfelt
congratulation.

It must have been about this time that, hearing of
his return from France, his old fellow-traveller, Master
Popham, wrote to him, proposing to make him a
gratulatory visit.   It was, of course, most joyously
accepted ; but whilst we were all anticipating the merriment of the meeting—on the very day when he was
expected—came news of his sudden death.   He had
mounted his horse—for such still was the manner of
his journeying—and fell from his saddle in an apoplectic
fit.   Thus was dissevered the last link of that chain
which had held together three congenial spirits, which,
for forty years, nothing but the necessary separations

of life could have placed at a distance from each other, and which nothing but death could ultimately disunite.*

Irreparable as these bereavements were, my father mourned as one not insensible to many remaining comforts and consolations, and hailed as he had been to his happy home, by other objects so deservedly dear to him, he soon shook off this transient sorrow, and easily fell into his old familiar employments in the garden and the farm. But, alas! this was a state of happiness not long to last without alloy; it was a prelude only to the bitterest family affliction—severe as others had been—which it was his lot ever to endure,—the premature death of his *favourite* son. I use the word advisedly: there was no undue or inequitable preference in Sir Elijah's treatment of one child over another; yet, by an irresistible impulse of nature, and a fondness well warranted by merit as well as instinctive affection, he was attracted to *one* in particular, and marked *him* as his "*best beloved.*" I have already twice mentioned the melancholy foreboding with which Sir Elijah parted with my brother Hastings in 1801; but I have not yet alluded to the many endearing qualities by which Hastings especially had won upon his father's heart; mildness of disposition, accompanied with rare comeliness of person†, and a singular modesty of manner, were, perhaps, the most prominent of these characteristic endowments; but the latter was often carried to such an excess of diffidence, as to create a painful apprehension, lest it should impede his advancement, and frustrate the object of his going to India. In allusion to this anxiety, my father wrote to me just

---

* See ante, Chap. I. p. 11. The reader may remember the name of Alexander Popham, as one of my father's fellow-travellers on the Continent in 1766-7, when they all sat for their busts to Nollekens. They were executed in terra cotta, and two of them are preserved in our family; the third, which was Popham's, I have lost sight of; but I have been told by my friend, the eminent conveyancer, Henry Bellenden Kerr, Esq., that he remembers it, not many years since, in the possession of the representatives of his grandfather, the late John Gawler, Esq.

† My father was a good Homeric scholar, and seldom omitted to apply some passage of his favourite author, wherever it was appropriate to his subject. In allusion to my poor brother's personal beauty, he would often quote these lines,—

Μή μοι δῶρ ἐρατα πρόφερε χρυσῆς 'Αθροδίτης.
Οὔτοι αποβλητ ἐςι Θεῶν ἐρικυδέα δῶρα
'Οσσα κεν αὐτοι δῶσιν, ἑκων δ' οὐκ αν τις ἐλοῖτο.—Iliad, iii. 64.

2 D 2

before he left Paris, a letter, from which I extract this
short paragraph :—

"Letters have reached me from India. Sir Henry Russell,
one of the judges at Calcutta, says, that dearest Hastings
dined with him *once* soon after his arrival; but that no attentions or solicitations could allure him to come a second time.
Sir Henry speaks most handsomely of his general demeanour;
God send that the spirits and activity of my dear fellow Edward, may be instrumental in conquering a timidity so op-
pressive to my poor boy, as to be a serious drawback on his
advancement !"

But another, and a sadder letter, from India, by the
friend and constant correspondent of our family, John
Herbert Harrington, announcing the death of my
brother, came to my hands in England, though not
until many months after my father's return from Paris.
More than one had, unhappily, been addressed there,
giving an account of my brother's declining health, but
had never reached my father.   This is part of Harrington's letter to me :—

Calcutta, Feb. 14, 1805.
". . . . . Not knowing whether your father may
be in England or in France, when this reaches you, and wishing to convey the sad intelligence it contains to you, and
through you, to the rest of your family, I think it advisable to
send the enclosed for your father, open for your perusal; and
beg you will either forward or deliver them to him in such a
manner as may appear to you proper.

"I will not repeat the melancholy tale they relate, but
rely on your firmness of mind to support both yourself and
your dear relatives.   I further inclose what I think of having
inscribed on our dear Hastings's monument. . . . ."

Disconsolate at first, my poor father could not, for
many months, speak of his heavy loss save in *prayer
and fasting*.   I speak not figuratively, for, to the end of
his days, on every anniversary of this mournful event,
my father strictly *fasted*.   Among his papers, after Sir
Elijah's death, together with the prayer already noticed,* was found a relic, which he had never shown to
any of us.   It is an elegy, consisting of some eighty
couplets.   I shall copy a few only at the conclusion, to

* Ante p. 392.

show that, like many elegant scholars, and men of feeling, he had vented the first paroxysms of grief in pathetic verse :

.　.　.　.　. Ah! then, farewell to thee,
My best beloved ! this unavailing tear
Adorns my grief, as sable plumes thy bier :
And lo! fast fleeting hitherward, I feel
The shadowy forecast of their darkness steal
On this hoar head, that thrice hath told its score,
And whitens now with twice seven winters more.—
*　*　*　*　*　*　*　*　*
O, ever hovering in my fancy's sight—
My dream by day, my vision in the night !
Know—for 'tis sure in heaven no sin to know
Some touch of sorrow for a father's woe—
Know, that I bless'd thee with my dying breath,
Bless'd thee in thought—the *"small still voice of death;"*
Know that in pious hope I sank to rest,
And blessing thee, am numbered with the blest.
*　*　*　*　*　*　*　*　*
For thus I reason'd with my faltering heart:
Let not despair give death another dart;
Nor vainly grieve, as hopeless mourners use;
Be firm in faith, nor dally with the muse.—
All bliss on earth is borrow'd, not our own;
Shall man repine, if heaven resume the loan?
But there's a lasting treasure-house—a store
Once freely given, to be reclaim'd no more.

Thus mingling hope, grief's bitterest dregs among,
I thank my God that thou wert lent so long;
That lost awhile, *my best beloved* shall be,
For aye restored, mine own eternally.

In the meantime I had been instructed to answer Harrington's letter; but so soon as Sir Elijah had sufficiently recovered his composure, he thus addressed him himself:—

"　.　.　.　.　. Think everything that gratitude and paternal affection, under the heavy blow that oppresses me, can dictate, as hereby expressed, for all the obligations which your kindness has imposed upon me.　.　.　.　. My son Elijah has, by my desire, written to you; for it was at a time when it was too much for me to write myself; and ill am I qualified to do it now.　But to prevent misunderstanding, it is absolutely necessary to make the effort.　.　.　. I am told there is a bond to Sookmu Roy for 17,000 sicca rupees, with interest at 10 per cent.; oblige me by taking up, as soon as possible, sufficient to discharge the debt with interest.* . . My son wrote likewise about my dear boy Edward: but let not anything which escaped me, in the agony of my grief, operate either on him or you so as to influence your advice or his conduct to his prejudice. . . . . My senses have recovered sufficient calmness to see that this fatal accident does not increase the chances of danger to him. Should he, however, feel himself unhappy where he is, still more, should he sicken, or be likely to suffer seriously from the climate, let him by no means waver or lose time in returning. He will be entitled, at my death, and that of his mother, to an equal share of my property with my other children ; and during my life I will make him as comfortable as I can: but do not estimate the provision, either now or ultimately, beyond a very moderate annual sum, or in any degree equivalent to his present pecuniary condition. What I mean is, supposing him to be anxious to return, from whatever cause, that he should not consider himself, poor boy! a prisoner in India. Staying or returning, I have provided, so that he shall not want the utmost it is in my power to bestow. . . . ."

About the same time, my father likewise addressed a letter to his surviving son in India, couched in such pious and affectionate terms, that I could never pardon myself for not alluding to it, though it is far too long and personal for me wholly to transcribe. The following is a very short extract :—

"How little did I expect that I could ever feel reluctance in sitting down to write to you! But the fatal event conveyed to me by letters from India on the 4th of last August, has so depressed my mind, that though I have, still remaining in you, so dear an object of affection there, yet have I not been able to turn my thoughts to Bengal, without emotions which have quite paralysed my endeavours to express myself with any tolerable consistency. . . . . I have not—perhaps never may—recovered from this shock. But I kiss the rod with which it has pleased the Almighty to afflict his sinful creature. . . . . Should any symptom of disorders incident to the climate attack you, take instant alarm—lose not a moment—haste to your affectionate parents and friends. . . . . You have now attained to an age when your understanding must be sufficiently mature to require no

* Ante, Chap. I. p. 17.

peremptory advice; yet, listen with patience to the counsel of
a fond and anxious father. . . . . I see by my most
admirable friend Harrington's correspondence, that a debt
contracted by your poor brother to a native, was an ingredient
in his consideration against the propriety of leaving India for
the recovery of his health—a mistaken, yet a most honourable
motive! This makes me the more restlessly anxious on your
account. . . . . The ease with which money can be
procured from native brokers, may, I fear, make you less
scrupulous in applying for it. . . . . There is another
consideration, which I must assuredly have enforced in many
of my preceding letters. O, my dear boy! read and reflect
over them, call to mind all the injunctions which I endeavoured to impress upon you both—alas! how ineffectually
in one instance—before you left this country. Once more
observe : being indebted to a native, you are ever after in his
power. It has repeatedly happened, in my own knowledge,
that the master, thus embarrassed, has been urged by the influence of his banyan, to do, or permit to be done, things very
unjustifiable, and which nothing but such coercion would have
made him consent to. . . . . Let me conjure you, by
the affection you bear to me, by the value you set upon your
own credit, honour, and virtue, should you ever be so involved,
set about disengaging yourself at once from fetters so dis-
graceful, lest they jeopardise your fortune, fame, and even
your existence. . . . . That God may bless you, that
He may sanctify to you every means of honest, active industry, to accelerate your return, and to bless my eyes, ere
they close in death, is my constant prayer. . . . ."

But the efficacy of my father's religious resignation—
his fastings and his prayers—was best demonstrated, to
the few who witnessed them, by the calm which ultimately succeeded them. Time likewise administered its
wonted relief; and the same merciful Providence which
had endowed him with fortitude to surmount so many
other trials of life, supported him in this. About a year
after, Sir Elijah had so far regained the composure, if
not the perfect command of his spirits, as to write to
me at Oxford, where I had resumed my residence, almost as cheerfully as before ; but his epistolary wit was,
ever after,

    "Sicklied o'er with the pale cast of thought."

"I do not think," he writes, June 20, 1806, "that you
have just cause for censuring me as a bad correspondent.
What are the subjects that a retirement like mine can suggest?

The most agreeable circumstances that can attend it are
peace, tranquillity, and a succession of quiet enjoyments, that
can have little variation, and therefore, few objects to be detailed by post ;   yet I can rejoice in some few topics of
interest to us both.   I have lately heard that dearest Edward
is well, and pleased with his new appointment.   I owe the
intelligence to the kindness of Col. Toone; but the pleasure is
sadly abated by my having now only one son in India to hear
of . . . .   I thank you for your epigrams, but cannot
answer your challenge :   *I have no points left, even my shoes
are square toed.*"

From a series of subsequent letters, and from personal intercourse afterwards—almost constant up to
the autumn of 1809—I collect that, during the three
remaining years of his life, till within six weeks of his
dissolution, my father enjoyed his usual health and
spirits.   He had once more rallied, and was himself
again, resuming his customary habit of communicating
with his friends, both far and near.   The early part of
the preceding year had been spent in a round of social
visits ; first to Daylesford, next to the Priory, in the
Isle of Wight, at that time the seat of his old contemporary at the bar, Judge Grose; thence he crossed over,
to Southampton and skirting the New Forest, made a
detour to Melchet Park, near Rumsey, the delightful
residence of Major and Mrs. Osborne.   The Major
was an old India acquaintance, remarkable in his attachment to Mr. Hastings and my father.   To the
former he had raised a beautiful memorial in his park,
in the form of a Hindu temple.   But to both these
friends he had adhered through all their troubles, with
the same steadiness and perseverance which distinguished his own most arduous military career.   His
indefatigable friendship followed them into their retirement, nor ceased till it was dissolved by death.   His
testimony outlives both him and them ; for at his decease, Major Osborne left a large collection of papers,
bearing witness to their merit.   Many years since, I
was honoured by a commission from the Major's
amiable and still surviving widow, to deposit those
documents in the Library of the East India House.
Some of them consist of autograph letters from persons of the first eminence, chiefly in honour of Mr.

Hastings; the most prominent of them, perhaps, is a letter from the late Lord Chamberlain, the Earl of Morton,—the more valuable, as it bears record of his lordship's never having omitted to attend the trial of the Governor General for a single day. The noble earl, as is well known, sat among the Peers of England, as Baron Douglas, of Lochleven ; and, at Mr. Hastings's acquittal, on the 23rd of April, 1795, voted him " not guilty of any one charge."

I pride myself on my acquaintance with the present Dowager Countess of Morton, and have heard the facts attested by her ladyship, with an affability which adds another grace to the value of these testimonials.

I cherish the remembrance of my father's last visit to Melchet Park; nor will I leave it, without recommending to *certain historians,* a careful perusal of Major Osborne's papers at the India House.

From Melchet Park the travellers returned through Salisbury and Chichester, &c., to Newick, where I joined them at Christmas, the last which my dear father ever celebrated, as was his custom, with the festivities of that season. The company then assembled at Newick Park, besides the family residents, were Mr. and Mrs. Hastings, the Halheds, my especial friend James Boswell, and Tiberius Cavallo.

The worthy philosopher had by this time become an almost constant inmate; and had he now been questioned by any inquisitive dowager touching his country-house,* he might, with some colour of truth, have pointed to Newick Park. He was still our master of the revels, and, into these Christmas gambols, had introduced one of Italian origin, grafted upon the Dutch concert. It was enacted after this wise : the players seated round a table pretended to play upon various musical instruments, each confining himself to some particular one, and, with suitable action, accompanying them with a *sotto voce* imitation of their respective sounds. But the ingenuity of the amusement lay in the leader—Cavallo— whose province it was to elicit forfeits from the rest. This was done by pointing with a scroll of paper, in the fashion of a Maestro di Capella, to every mock musician

* See ante, Chap. XVI. p. 366.

in turn, who was thereby summoned to perform a solo; while the rest, who had before been playing in chorus, were to remain quiet. These signals were purposely made in such rapid succession, as to perplex those to whom they were addressed; and if the performer, so applied to, did not instantly respond to the summons, or if, in his hurry, he assumed an instrument not his own, he forfeited a pledge, redeemable by a penalty imposed upon him by the party whose instrument he had assumed. It was *concerted* that Mr. Hastings should play the organ, Sir Elijah the violoncello, Halhed the Jew's harp, and Boswell the bagpipe; but, either by mistake, or contrivance, Boswell and my father interchanged instruments; so when the forfeits were cried, Bozzy called upon my father for a Greek or Latin speech. This he obeyed, *ore rotundo*, by repeating " *Barbara celarent Darii Ferio Baralipton;*" but, in revenge, Jemmy was presently commanded to translate it. How my friend got out of the scrape I do not exactly recollect, but I remember that he began by declaring, " It would be *barbarous* to *conceal* the meaning of those mysterious words." This is, perhaps, the last pleasantry of the sort in which my dear father was known to take a part.

The decline, however, of these and similar harmless habits, was very gradual in him; and as, in like manner, his strength and inclination to bodily exercise declined, he resorted more and more to his books. Besides the current publications of the day, he now renewed his acquaintance with the classics; and while his old school companion, Mr. Hastings,* was quoting Young, and translating Lucan, Sir Elijah was refreshing his memory with Homer and Virgil. In the evening he used to read Shakspeare aloud for our entertainment: but when his voice grew feeble, and his spectacles no longer served him by candlelight, a game at whist or chess sometimes supplied their place. In

---

* I have omitted to mention that Mr. Hastings was an admirable epigrammatist. It was on the occasion of this visit that he amused us with the following :—

    " A serpent bit Francis, that virulent knight:
    What then? 'Twas the serpent that died of the bite !"

Which I translated thus :—

    Dente venenato stimulatur Zoilus anguis.
    Quid tum? mordet adhúc Zoilus, anguis obit.

the daytime, his favourite Homer, now more and more frequently, gave place to the Greek Testament; and I have before me an old Dutch edition, which he was latterly in the habit of comparing with Paley's "Horæ Paulinæ," and Le Clerc's "Harmony of the Evangelists." They are all well worn, and scored with his marginal notes. I find also scattered among his papers, and in the library which I inherit, fragments written in a beautiful Greek hand, and a ponderous commonplace book crowded with extracts, in different languages, under various heads.

The mention of Homer reminds me of a remarkable instance of my father's humanity to animals, coincident with his approaching end. Sir Elijah had a favourite house-dog—Hector—a noble animal of the St. Bernard's breed. It is a well known peculiarity in that species, that they often attach themselves exclusively to their owners, and as often take capricious dislikes to other people. Hector was beyond measure fond of my father, but could not bear his bailiff. For this reason he was, during the day, chained up, but regularly admitted to take leave of his master every night, just before he retired to rest. Latterly this custom had been discontinued, owing to his boisterous caresses, which grew more and more troublesome, as my father's illness increased. This the poor animal seemed to resent, grew sullen, refused his food, and was thought to be dangerous. Sir Elijah ordered his servants to watch and secure him, but by no means suffer him to be destroyed. One day my father had been looking into the "Iliad," and when he came to a passage in the 23rd book, he sighed, and murmured to himself, " poor Hector!" Supposing him to allude to the Hector of Homer, I looked over the page, and found that the lines related to the dogs which the poet describes as lying, αλύσσαντες περὶ θυμῷ*—*fretting in mind*—before the

---

* " Αὐτὸν δ' ἂν πύματόν με κύνες πρώτῃσι θύρῃσιν
  Ωμησαὶ ερύ8σιν, ἐπεί κέ τις ὀξέϊ χαλκῷ
  Τύψας, ἠέ βαλὼν ρέθέων εκ θυμὸν ἕληται,
  Ους τρέφον ἐν μεγάροῖσι τραπεζῆας πυλαωρ8ς,
  Οἵ κ'εμον αἷμα πιόντες, ἁλύσσαντες περὶ θυμῷ
  Κεισοντ 'εν προθύροισι."
Which last words Pope incorrectly translates—"*famished* dogs late guardians of my door."

gates of Priam's palace—when the good old king was prophecying his own death. On the morning after Sir Elijah's decease, poor Hector was found dead in his kennel.

It was not till September, 1809, that my father was seized with alarming symptoms of his mortal malady. In tenderness to our feelings, he had made light of his complaint; though, there is reason to believe, that he was well aware of his danger. He consented, at last, that I should accompany him to consult Dr. Baillie, in London. The Doctor, to test the steadiness of his pace, desired him to walk across the room; when, as if to convince us that there was little the matter with him, the dear old man assumed a sturdy gait, and laughed at his own efforts at activity. But Baillie, who never disguised from his patients their real state, and who was accustomed to explain it by some ingenious simile, compared my poor father's condition to that of a man that had received a blow from a giant, who stood over him, in an attitude which threatened a repetition of the attack. He defined the nature of the disorder to be an effusion of serum on the brain, not uncommon with those whose mental powers had at any time been too severely tasked. The reader will here remember, that, in an earlier part of this volume,* I have alluded to the occasional return of the symptoms of my father's illness at Calcutta, in 1778-9,—a numbness in the hand, and an indigestion, which never entirely left him. On our return to Newick, Sir Elijah rapidly declined; yet, in more instances than one, he manifested, even in this state, an extraordinary preservation of intellect, and correctness of memory: the first showed itself in the dictation of a difficult letter, to an attorney, on the renewal of the lease of Newick Park, which terminated in this year; the second occurred in the quotation of a line in Horace,† while we were applying leeches to his temples. But the last and most affecting trait of his character, while sense and sensibility yet remained, was displayed in the tenderness with which he treated, in his very last moments, a female servant, who assisted in removing him from the sofa to

* Ante page 269.
† " Non *missura* cutim nisi plena cruoris hirudo."

his bed. He had leaned upon her bosom, so as to produce a slight ejaculation of pain,—" Did I hurt you, my dear ? " were his last distinguishable words.

Sir Elijah Impey expired about midnight on the 1st of October, 1809, in the seventy-seventh year of his age, surrounded by an afflicted family, in perfect charity with all men, and in communion with the HOLY PRO-TESTANT CHURCH OF CHRIST, established in these realms. His remains are interred in the family vault at Hammersmith, where a plain monument is erected to his memory.

I shall attempt no summary of my father's character. If it has not been sufficiently elucidated in these pages, all that I could add would be worse than superfluous. But, if, after a fair examination of this book, it shall appear to the candid reader, that Sir Elijah Impey was not only *not* the man, but *the very reverse* of the man, he has been represented by his enemies to have been ; if I have succeeded in establishing, upon *good evidence,* facts, which it has been attempted to controvert upon *no evidence at all;* if, upon such examination, it turns out that none except the *un-candid* remain *unconvinced;* then shall I have accomplished the object of this Memoir; for then, I shall have fulfilled a double duty,—my duty to God, and my duty to man : to *God,* in obedience to an injunction, not the least solemn upon the decalogue; to *man,* in the vindication of HISTORIC TRUTH AND JUSTICE, not the least sacred of all worldly obligations.

But whether I succeed or fail in the main object of this work—an appeal to the *public* against a *public* wrong—at least I shall have completed a secondary, but no unimportant one,—the satisfaction of my own CONSCIENCE.

" *Liberavi animam meam.*"

APPENDIX.

No. 1.

EXTRACTS from a "Copy of the proceedings of a general quarter session of the peace of oyer and terminer, and general gaol delivery, holden for the town of Calcutta, and precincts thereof, on Wednesday, the 27th day of February, 1765,

"BEFORE

"Charles Stafford Playdell, Esquire, President.

John Burdett, } Esquires.
George Gray, }

"Opened the Court, and the Sheriff delivered in the precepts: Swore in the following gentlemen to serve on the grand jury :—

"James Amyatt, Esq.,	Foreman,
Messrs. Robert Gregory,	Russel Skinner,
Jas. Lister,	Patk. Maitland,
Archibd. Keir,	Nichs. Grueber,
John Gould,	Willm. Maxwell,
Robert Dobinson,	Hugh Baillie,
John Charnier,	Alexander Scott,
Thos. Woodward,	Jas. Whyte,
William Magee,	John Holme.

"Swore in Randall constable, to attend the grand jury: Sent an indictment against Radachund Mettre for forgery— The grand jury returned it a true bill.

"Set Radachund Mettre at the bar, and arraigned him on the following indictment :—

"Town of } The jurors for our Sovereign Lord the Calcutta, ss. } King upon their oath do present, that Radachund Mettre, of the town of Calcutta inhabitant, on or about the 21st day of November, 1764, in the fifth year of the reign of our Sovereign Lord George the Third, King of Great Britain, &c., at the town aforesaid, did feloniously forge a codicil to the will of one Coja Solomon, late a merchant of

Calcutta, with an intent to defraud the said Coja Solomon's estate of the value of six thousand Arcot rupees, and did feloniously present the said codicil, against the peace of our Sovereign Lord the King, his crown and dignity, &c.

" Witness,
" Andrew Carapet,
Coja Assim,
Maria Matruse.

" To which he pleaded not guilty.

" Swore in the undermentioned persons to serve on the petit jury:

" Messrs. William Smith,	Matthew Miller,
Geo. Scott,	——— Whitall,
William Dobbins,	George Sparks,
George Moore,	——— Paddey,
Benjn. Randall,	Joseph Panton,
William Swallow,	Jno. Martin.

" Proceeded to trial, and swore in Andrew Carapet evidence for the King," &c. &c.

[Here follows the trial, printed at length in the Appendix No. 2 of Sir Elijah Impey's Speech, &c. London: Stockdale, 1788. It is unnecessary to recite more than the issue of this trial.]

" The court summed up the evidence to the petit jury, and they withdrew.

" Swore in Smith, constable, to keep the petit jury.

" The petit jury came into court, and returned the following verdict :

" That Radachund Mettre is guilty of the forgery laid to his charge.

" The prisoner being set to the bar,

" The chairman pronounced the sentence of death on him in the usual form.

" Ordered him into the condemned hole.

" The business of the present sessions being over, dismissed both juries with thanks for their services; and adjourned the sessions to the 27th day of May, upon a fresh summons.

" (A true copy.)
" EDWD. BABER,
"Clerk of the Peace."

This trial and sentence of death of a native for forgery, on the 27th of February, 1765, supplies a full precedent for the proceedings against Nuncomar, in 1775. It proves also the complete publication in Calcutta of the law, 26 Geo. II.

No. 2.

FAC-SIMILE Copy of the translation of the Petition of Nun-comar, delivered at the desire of the House, by Sir Elijah Impey, during his defence at the Commons' bar. The original translation is printed in the common type ; the words printed in italics are inserted in the original in the hand-writing of Mr. Hastings.

" To the Governor General and Council.

" WITHIN these three soubahs of Bengal, Orissa, and Bahar, ~~from~~ the manner in which I *have* lived and the ~~character~~ *honor* and *credit which I have possessed.—** ~~reputation I enjoy.~~ Formerly the Nazims of *all* these soubahs *afforded attention and aid to my good name* upon ~~my good name bestowed some consideration and regard,~~ and from the *presence of the* king of Hindostan I ~~have a~~ *received a* munsib of five thousand, and from the ~~first~~ of the company's ~~government,~~ *administration* ~~looking upon~~ *in consideration of* my good wishes to the king, the gentlemen who ~~were in power here, and the present~~ *had the direction of the affairs of this place, and at this time the* governor, Mr. Hastings, who is at the head of affairs, ~~respected me, and do~~ *did hold and do hold me in* respect ~~me. I was~~ never ~~disloyal to~~ the state, ~~nor com-~~ *did occasion any loss to* ~~mitted any~~ oppression ~~upon~~ the Ryots. For the fault of *of* *proceed from me* representing ~~some~~ facts which ~~I just made known~~ for the *at this time a* *just* (*true*) *in a small degree* interest of the king, and ~~welfare~~ of the people, many English *the* *relief* *I in a small degree made known* gentlemen have become my enemies ; and, having no other means to conceal their own actions, deem*ing* ~~it highly politick~~ *of the highest* for themselves ~~to make an end of me.~~ An old affair of *my destruction of the utmost expediency* *revived*

* Something is wanting to complete the sense.

Mohun Pursaud's which had *formerly been* repeatedly ~~been declared~~ *found to be* false; and the governor, knowing Mohun Pursaud to be a notorious liar, turned him out of his house; ~~they have now~~ ~~revived,~~ and ~~granting him their aid and assistance, and~~ *themselves becoming his aiders and abettors and* ~~joining with~~ Lord Impey and the other justices, have tried me by the English laws, which are contrary to the customs of this country, in which there was never any such administrations of justice before; and taking the evidence of my enemies in proof of my crime, have condemned me to death. But, by my death, the king's justice will let the actions of no person remain concealed; and now that the hour of death approaches, I shall not for the sake of this world, be regardless of the next, but represent the truth to the gentlemen of the council. The forgery of the bond, of which I am accused, never proceeded from me. Many principal people of this country, who were acquainted with my honesty, frequently requested of the judges to suspend my execution till the king's pleasure should be known, but this they refused, and unjustly take away my life. For God sake, gentlemen of the council, you who are just, and whose words are truth, let me not undergo this injury, but wait the king's pleasure. If I am unjustly put to death, I will, with my family, demand justice in the next life. They put me to death out of enmity, and from partiality to the gentlemen who have betrayed their trust; and, in this case, the thread of life being cut, I, in my last moment, again request that you, gentlemen, will write my case particularly to the just king of England. I suffer, but my innocence will certainly be made known to him."*

* The original petition was first laid before the Governor General and Council by Sir John Clavering, August 14, 1775, nine days *after* the execution of the convict, and burned, by their order, under the inspection of the Sheriff of Calcutta, on the 21st.

No. 3.

EXTRACTS from Copies of the Addresses presented to Sir Elijah Impey, and to the Supreme Court of Judicature, 14th and 27th July, 1775.

"To the Honourable Sir Elijah Impey, Knight, Chief Justice of the Supreme Court of Judicature.

"My Lord,

"We, the grand jury for the town and districts of Calcutta, beg leave, before we separate, to offer in a body, through your lordship, our sincere acknowledgments to the court for the great attention they have been pleased to show us, through the whole course of an unusually tedious sessions, in accommodating our business as much as possible to our convenience, and in affording us every remission from it of which the nature of our service would admit.

"Allow us further, my lord, to express on this occasion the satisfaction we feel in possessing in your lordship a chief justice, from whose abilities, candour, and moderation, we promise ourselves all the advantages which can be expected from the institution of the Supreme Court.

"May you long continue at the head of the court, to add to that esteem for your character which your conduct has already acquired.

"Town Hall, July 14, 1775.

"(Signed)   G. HURST,
CHA. BENTLY,
ALEXR. VAN REXTEL,
&c. &c. &c."

"To the Honourable Sir Elijah Impey, Knight, Chief Justice of the Supreme Court.

"My Lord,

"We, the free merchants, free mariners, and other inhabitants of the town of Calcutta, deeply affected with a sense of the manifold benefits which are derived to this settlement from the institution of the Supreme Court of Judicature, beg leave to wait on your lordship, to testify before you, in this public manner, our gratitude to our most gracious sovereign, and to the legislature of Great Britain, for the inestimable obligation they have thus conferred upon us. Far distant from the mother country, and necessarily deprived of a constitutional protection, which other colonists enjoy in the assembly of the people, we were also left under a feeble and incomplete administration of the laws of England till your arrival in Bengal; we then had the happiness to see the power of the law firmly established above all other powers, and an equal measure of justice distributed to all men.

"At the same time, my lord, that we address our warmest expressions of thanks to your lordship for the security to our persons and properties, which we enjoy under the protection of the court, it is with unfeigned acknowledgments we do justice to the merits, integrity, and abilities of your brethren. The eminent station to which your sovereign has been pleased to call you, puts you in a point of view more exposed to the observation of the people, and renders your talents and virtues more conspicuous. We have all of us had occasion, many of us as jurymen, to observe, through the course of the full exercise of the various jurisdictions vested in your court, the candour, wisdom, and moderation with which you have conducted all their proceedings. It is not alone that intimate acquaintance with the laws, which you display on these occasions, that attracts our admiration, or that superior sagacity in detecting the sophims which are advanced under their colour; but the steady unshaken conduct which you pursue in maintaining the dignity and independency of the King's court, unawed by opposition of any sort, in impartially granting to every man, under all circumstances, the protection to which he is legally entitled, and in repressing the spirit of litigiousness, and the chicanery and quirks of practitioners.

"We particularly felt our breasts glow with the warmest sentiments of gratitude when we heard you, from the highest seat of justice supported by the unanimous voice of your brethren, reprobate with every just mark of indignation, the insidious attempt to introduce into practice the granting of blank subpœnas for the attendance of witnesses; so detestable an instrument of oppression, in the hands of wicked or powerful men, might have produced the full effects of the edicts of the inquisition, or the *lettres de cachet*, the most arbitrary state. Our reputations, our fortunes, and perhaps our lives, would have been in that case left at the mercy of every profligate informer, who might have been detached into the country, loaded with blank subpœnas, to fish for evidence in any suit or prosecution, among an abject and timid people, ignorant of the nature of these writs, who would have considered them merely as mandates from authority, to swear as they were directed, and being ready to sacrifice truth, honour, and religion, to the dread of power.

"We cannot also refrain from declaring how much we esteem ourselves indebted to the pains you bestowed during the course of the late tedious and important trial, in patiently investigating the evidence, and tracing the truth throughout all the intricacies of perjury and prevarication, and in finally detecting and putting in the way of condign punishment the cloud of false witnesses, who seem to have acted from concert, and to have had hopes of introducing into the court, under the shelter of an unknown tongue, and concealed forms of oath, a general system of false swearing, to the total subversion of all reliance on evidence, and to the utmost danger to the life and property of every man in these provinces.

" Permit us then, for our own sakes, and for the sake of all his Majesty's subjects in Bengal, to express our most hearty and sincere wishes for your health and prosperity, and that you may long continue among us to fill that chair where you now sit, with much lustre, and so much to our advantage, and to that of the whole settlement.

" Before we withdraw from your presence, we have one suit to prefer, which we hope in kindness will not be denied us : we request your lordship, that you would be pleased to sit for your portrait at full length, to the painter whom we shall appoint to draw it; we propose to put it up in the town hall, or some other public room, merely as a gratification to our own sentiments of esteem and respect for you, well knowing that your virtues, and the services you render to the public, will erect a much more durable monument to your name and character in the memories of the latest posterity.

"C. S. PLAYDELL,
JOHN ROBINSON,
JOS. PRICE,
&c. &c. &c.

" A true copy."

" To the honourable Sir Elijah Impey, Knight, Chief Justice of the Supreme Court of Judicature, and the Judges thereof.

" My Lords,

" We, the Armenians of Calcutta, in full conviction of many salutary effects already resulting from the administration of English laws in this settlement, and in certain expectation of still more advantageous consequences, beg leave to express our warmest sentiments of gratitude to that power by whose interposition they were introduced, and to those hands by which we see them so impartially executed.

" Ever mindful of the abilities and of the candour displayed

by all the members of the bench, we think it our duty to
signify our thankful sense of them to your lordship, as the
president, and through you to the rest of your brethren; who,
as they have uniformly exerted themselves for the public
good, are also entitled to a share in our respectful acknowledgments.

"We must confess our fears, upon the introduction of
English laws into this country, to have been neither light nor
groundless; where our fortunes, our lives, our honour, and
our religion might be at stake, we could not but shudder at
the consequences of justice distributed in an unknown language, and upon principles of which we were totally ignorant.
It is to you, my lords, that we owe the obligation, not only
of a release from those terrors, but of a comfort and satisfaction proportionably more solid, as our causes of uneasiness
had been substantial.

"We are now convinced that chicanery, subornation of
evidence, perjury, and forgery, will never, by any particularity
of circumstance, or exertion of influence, escape with impunity; and severe warnings, which have been given to all
offences so injurious to society, are most ample pledges for
the protection of the peaceable subject in his property, his
person, and his reputation.

"We are also told, that by your timely interposition, an
attempt to introduce *blank warrants** for summoning any persons from all parts of the provinces, has been most effectually
precluded. By this step your lordships have probably
rescued an extensive kingdom from absolute destruction;
for what man, independent either in his fortunes or his principles, would have resided one moment in a country where he
was perpetually liable to be harassed by vexatious and expensive journeys, and by a painful attendance upon a court of
justice, at the folly, the pique, or the caprice, of every litigious
individual?

"We have now experienced, within the space of a few
months, a total removal of every serious solicitude, and the
most comfortable assurances of security in the possession of
all we hold valuable, in these striking specimens of the ex-
cellence of the British law, and the impartiality of its administration; we are, therefore, very earnest in our wishes, that
its salutary influence may be yet wider extended, and its es-
tablishments (if possible) more effectually secured. Calculated as it is for a people whose climate, whose religion,
manners, and dispositions, differ totally from those of India,

---

* See this word observed upon in the minute of Bengal Secret Consultations, September 11, 1775: the context shows that it was not meant
a blank warrant to apprehend, but a blank subpœna.

there must necessarily be many parts of it which materially clash with our sentiments and our prejudices, though we have the most exalted opinion of its general advantages.

" Give us leave, then, my lords, to hope, that it may hereafter be so modified and blended with the immediately national and constitutional peculiarities of this country, as to leave us no possibility of apprehension from its most extensive exertion, or excuse for undervaluing the obligations we receive from it—that so our gratitude may be still more warmly excited towards our most gracious monarch, who, in this first exercise of his authority, has given us so wonderful an instance of the wisdom of his government, and so respectable a representative of the British legislature.

" We must heartily unite in wishing, that your lordships may long continue to preside in that court from whence all our future security is to be derived; and that we may have the satisfaction of knowing that our fortunes, our lives and our reputations, equally unexposed to attacks of private artifices, and the fluctuation of arbitrary authority, stand inviolate upon the unalterable principles of equity.

"PETRUSE ARRATOON,
MINAS ELLIAS,
OWENJOHN THOMAS,
&c. &c. &c.

" A true copy of the translation delivered with the original address, which is in Armenian."

" To the Honourable Sir Elijah Impey, Lord Chief Justice of the Honourable the Supreme Court of Judicature, and the Judges thereof.

" My Lords,

" The King of England, regarding with an indulgent eye on the subjects of this kingdom, formed a new law; and conferring on you, gentleman, the administration of justice, sent you to this country. When we heard this news, our hearts were filled with various doubts concerning the manner in which the new law would operate; but some months have now elapsed since your arrival in Calcutta, during which, in all such causes as have come before the court, you, gentlemen, in every way attentive to the welfare of this country, by receiving complaints, by forming regulations for issuing warrants, by weighing the representations of the plaintiff and defendant, by investigating the evidence on both sides, by distinguishing the characters of the witnesses, and in every way by a complete examination, have established the new law : upon this, doubts which we before entertained being removed, confidence and joy sprang up in our hearts, and we are thoroughly convinced that the country will prosper, the bad be punished, and the good be cherished. May the God of Gods ever preserve you in health, and may you long continue to administer justice in this country !

" The law of you, gentlemen, may differ in sundry points from the usages of this country, the Shaster, and the Beblar (or religious customs). We will examine into these points, and represent them; and our prayer is, that in the usages of this country, the Shaster, and the Bebhar, and in giving and receiving (i. e. in matters of property), it may be so ordered, that our welfare may in every respect be promoted, and our religion preserved.

" (Signed)   MAHA RAJAH NUBKISSEN,
RAJAH HUZROO MULL,
RAJAH RAMLOCHUN,
&c. &c. &c.

" A copy of the translation delivered together with the original Hindoo address, which is in the Bengalee language, on the 27th July, 1775."

The address of the grand jury is subscribed by twenty-three names; that of the free merchants, free mariners, and other inhabitants of Calcutta, by eighty-four ; that of the Armenians by forty-three; and that of the native inhabitants of Calcutta, Burdwan, Currapurrah, &c., &c., by above one hundred.

The foregoing addresses were enclosed together with a letter addressed by the judges to the Court of Directors, which the Supreme Council were requested to despatch. They sent *the letter*, but declined sending the *addresses*.

No. 4.

" ANSWER to the Addresses of the Grand Jury, and Free Merchants and Mariners of the town of Calcutta, delivered by Sir Elijah Impey, then Chief Justice.

" Gentlemen,
" I know nothing that can give me greater satisfaction than that which I received, by your thus testifying your due sense

of gratitude to his Majesty, for erecting an independent court of justice in this settlement, and thereby extending the full protection of the English laws to the natives of this country, and to his British subjects at this distant extremity of the British empire.

"The protection of the laws is the only constitutioual protection that can consist with a free government. Protection by power only is capricious; it may shelter the guilty as well as the innocent.

"We can assume no great merit in not allowing the blank subpœnas to issue in the case you allude to. They were moved, for the purpose of being sent high up into the country, though the fact charged was committed in Calcutta, expressly to bring down such witnesses as might come in, though the party applying neither professed to know what the witnesses were to prove, or that such witnesses actually existed. Such subpœnas would be considered by the timid natives as mandates, and, if suffered to have been made use of by wicked men of power and influence, you most truly say, that your reputation, property, and lives, could not be safe; it would have subverted that justice which it is our duty to enforce. There is little doubt, had they been granted, instead of having those witnesses produced, most of whom you know, and so justly reprobate, we should have had a new troop of false witnesses.

"Neither can we assume to ourselves any extraordinary merit or sagacity in detecting the falsehoods of the witnesses produced at the trial. The subject matter of the evidence, the manner of delivering it, and the persons who delivered, made the imposition attempted to be put on the Court, too gross to deceive either the Court, or such bystanders as did not through prejudice wish to be deceived.

"Two things operate to make our stations easy to us: the one, that we have a strict rule for our conduct, the law; the other is, that we do not administer justice privately. The eyes of all the inhabitants of the settlement are upon us; they by that means become judges of our conduct, and will bestow on us censure or confidence, in proportion as we deserve either the one or the other.

"In the present unhappy state of the settlement, we are most sensibly affected, by receiving the public approbation of two such respectable bodies of men, as the grand jury, and the free merchants and mariners of this town; of a grand jury elected by ballot from all the Company's servants below the Governor General and Council, and from all the substantial inhabitants of this place; of the free merchants and mariners, a body of men from their situations independent

and unbiassed by interest or fear. The voice of the grand
jury so elected, and of the free merchants and mariners,
is the voice of the settlement.

" I entertain the highest sense of the great honour done
me by the marks of esteem which you are pleased particularly
to address to me. The first and great satisfaction which I
feel in my present situation is, the approbation of my own
conscience; the next, that those to whom I administer justice,
bestow their approbation on my conduct, and put full confidence in the rectitude of my intensions.

" It is with the greatest alacrity that I accept of the honour
proposed me; for being unconscious of either exerting or possessing any peculiar talents, I understand it is at least as
much a public testimony of gratitude to his Majesty, for
adopting the measure of erecting an independent court of
justice in this town, as a personal compliment to the humble
instrument of carrying his gracious intentions into execution."

" ANSWER to the Hindoo Inhabitants of the town of Calcutta,
delivered by Sir Elijah Impey, Knight, Chief Justice.

" Gentlemen,

" It is a great consolation to us, that having been under
the unhappy necessity of inflicting a capital punishment on a
person of an high cast in your religion, we receive this general
and public approbation of our distribution of justice from so
numerous and respectable a body of Hindoos, among whom
it gives us inexpressible satisfaction to see, there are many of
the most principal Brahmins.

" It was natural, when you heard that a new law was
formed in a remote country, by a legislature differing most
widely from you in religion, laws, and customs, for the administration of justice in this, that you should be filled with
doubts concerning the operation of it, and be strictly observant
of the conduct of those who were appointed to carry it into
execution: we are happy that your observation of our proceedings has created that just confidence in us, which has so
soon caused your doubts to subside, and we feel ourselves the
more obliged to you for it, as it hath not escaped us, that
some evil-minded persons, disaffected to the establishment of
an independent court, have wickedly and maliciously endeavoured to destroy that confidence, and to disturb your minds
with apprehensions of the most alarming nature, by attempting to persuade you that your laws and usages, formed on
your religion and government, interwoven into your manners
and sentiments, and sanctified by the experience of a long

succession of ages, were instantly to be over-ruled, abolished, and superseded by the authority of a foreign law ; to alienate your minds from the court of justice, and to alarm you in the most sensible manner, you have been told that your marriages with more women than one, would subject you to severe penalties ; than which nothing can be more false.

"It is true, that in England it is considered as criminal; but the reasons which make it so in England do not exist here. It is considered as criminal there because the religion of England allows but one wife to one man, and the laws there confer certain rights and privileges on that wife only, and suffer her children alone to inherit the estates of their parents: He, therefore, who in England marries another woman during the life of his wife, abuses his wife, who has a right that no other shall share in his affections; commits a fraud on the second woman, who cannot enjoy the rights and privileges she was taught to expect; injures his offspring by her, and is guilty of a breach of the laws, and a violation of the religion of his country. It would be absurd, cruel, and unjust to treat such an act as criminal here, where no injury is done by it to any person, and where the laws and religion of the country give a sanction to it. I dwell longer on this subject, and am more desirous of dissipating all doubts that either you or the Mussulmauns have entertained on it, as I know this has been particularly urged, because calculated to sink deep and make a lasting impression on your breasts, as it must universally affect you in your domestic happiness, and in your nearest and dearest concerns.

"The pleasure which we feel from these public expressions of your sense of the manner in which we have discharged our duty, grateful as they are to us, is small in proportion to that which we receive from their giving us an opportunity of vindicating our most gracious Sovereign from the calumny of treating you rigorously and harshly in the very instance of his extending his fatherly influence and goodness to you, and of assuring you that the new Act of Parliament is with respect to you no new law, otherwise than in giving you an additional security for your lives and properties, by placing the execution of the law, which is to protect you, in an independent court of justice. It makes no alteration in your religion, laws, and usages, or in those of the natives of this country; it leaves them in every respect the same as they were when the new law took place.

"For your greater ease and peace of mind, I make this public declaration, that whenever occasion shall require, I hold myself bound to make strict inquiry into, and to pay due attention to the customs and usages of the different natives of

this country; and you may depend on the highest respect
being had in our decisions to the Shaster and Bebhar, those
sacred deposits of your religion and laws : we have already,
in the only case which required our being informed of your
religion and law, called in and consulted with those venerable
oracles, the pundits, and were guided by their decisions,
drawn from the text of the Shaster.

" It will be a great ease to us in the farther discharge of
our duties, to be furnished with your observations on those
points in which you apprehend any innovations likely to be
made, that being apprised of them we may be more cautious
in our judgments, if those points should come before us.

" The protection of you, gentlemen, and the other natives
of this country, was the first and main object that induced
his Majesty to place the administration of justice in our hands;
and I am sure we shall all esteem ourselves guilty of a criminal breach of trust, if we do not in cases of property, and
in all other matters, which may come under out cognizance,
labour to the utmost of our power to promote your welfare
and to preserve your religion.

" Mr. Justice Chambers, and Mr. Justice Lemaistre, will
be sorry that their absence from the settlement has prevented
them from receiving this address personally from you: but I
will, with the utmost expedition, convey to them the satisfaction they must enjoy from being addressed by persons of your
rank and estimation."

———————

"ANSWER to the Address of the Armenians, delivered by Sir
Elijah Impey, Knight, Chief Justice.

" Gentlemen,

" It is by no means surprising, understanding as you did,
that new laws were to be introduced among you, formed to
rule a nation differing so wide in climate, manners, and religion, from you, that you should take an alarm.   It will be
with the highest satisfaction I am enabled to acquaint his
Majesty, through his ministers, with what cheerfulness you
submit to his laws, and with what gratitude you acknowledge
his royal care, extended to these regions so remote from the
seat of his empire, and with what warmth you wish, that the
salutary influence of his laws may be yet wider extended, and
their establishment (if possible) more effectually secured.   I
will likewise most faithfully transmit your hopes that the
laws may hereafter be modified and blended with the immediate national and constitutional peculiarities of this country.

" We enjoy great happiness from finding that our administration of those laws has tended to remove the prejudices

which you so naturally entertained; and it rejoices me to have it in my power to inform you, that the same gracious wisdom and goodness that prompted his Majesty to extend the benefit of his laws to this country, has prescribed to us, by his royal charter, in what manner and how far we are to introduce them, thereby providentially guarding against any inconvenience that might arise from a promiscuous and general introduction of them.

" The principles of laws relating to property are universal; to give to every man what is his due, is the foundation of law in all countries and in all climates; it is a maxim that must be acknowledged by men of all religions and persuasions : religion, custom, and prejudice, do, indeed, make the same act criminal, or more or less so, in one country than in another.

" But his Majesty has already most graciously consulted your religion and customs, and the climates which you inhabit, and has with most fatherly tenderness indulged even your prejudices; it is his royal pleasure, that only such of his laws shall be enforced, as are conformable to your customs, climate, prejudices, and religion.

" We cannot but be sensibly affected by this public approbation of our conduct, given unanimously, by so opulent, so respectable, and so independent a body of men, as the Armeneans resident in this town.

" Did our consciences not co-operate with that approbation, we should feel these expressions of your sentiment as censures, not praises.

" We are confident, that if the laws of England are honestly and conscientiously administered, you cannot be disappointed in the effects which you so sanguinely expect from them; and we pledge ourselves, that it shall be our constant study, to administer them in such manner, that you may derive from them the greatest benefit, and the fullest protection, which they are capable of bestowing."

This is as much as I have thought it necessary to extract from the " Appendix to the Speech of Sir Elijah Impey, published by Stockdale, in 1788." It contains 244 8vo. pages, to which the reader is referred, particularly for the evidence of Thomas Farrer, Esq., before the Committee of the House of Commons, from the 11th to the 20th of February, 1788, p. 105 to 164. To the evidence of Samuel Tolfrey, Esq., from p. 170 to 215. And to the evidence of Philip Francis, Esq., given from his place as Member of Parliament, on Wednesday, the 16th of April, 1788, from p. 222 to 244.

No. 5.

This was originally presented as a *Petition*, which having been refused, it is my purpose now to put it once more on record as a *Memorial*, together with the answer of the Directors, and my letter to Lord Fitzgerald thereunto annexed. It has been slightly corrected for the press, and the alterations are printed in italics.

To the Honourable the Chairman and Court of Directors of the East India Company, &c. &c.
The Memorial of Rear-Admiral John Impey, and of Elijah Barwell Impey, Esquires,

Sheweth,
That your memorialists are the two eldest surviving sons of the late Sir Elijah Impey, Knight, formerly Chief Justice of the Supreme Court of Judicature at Fort William, in Bengal, &c. &c.

That, in that character, and as representatives of a family, many of whose members have been, and still are, employed in the service of your Honourable Company, your memorialists appeal to you for protection against a very unprovoked and injurious libel on the memory of their said father, lately published by your Assistant Secretary, Mr. Edward Thornton.

That the said *libel*—and your memorialists use the word advisedly, and in its legal sense—is contained in the second volume, page 152, of a book entitled, "The History of the British Empire in India." It relates to Sir Elijah Impey's acceptance of the superintendence of the Sudder Dewannee Adaulut, in 1780, and runs thus:—

" To the reputation of the Chief Justice the appointment was more injurious than even to the Governor General. It was deadly. Had Sir Elijah Impey died before he accepted the fatal gift, he would, by impartial observers, have been regarded as a man of narrow mind, headstrong passions, and overbearing temper; but no imputation, based on sufficient evidence, would have shaded his judicial integrity. His own act effected that which the ingenuity of his enemies failed to accomplish. He inscribed upon his own brow the record of his disgrace, in characters deep, broad, and indelible."

Your memorialists beg leave most respectfully to state, that the libellous matter contained in this, and many other passages of a similar tendency, have acquired a greater weight and credit, from having been written by a gentleman, who, from the office which he holds, is generally supposed to be possessed of better information, and supported by higher authority, than any other ordinary writer on the same subject. That the book, from its having been printed by Mr. W. H. Allen, of Leadenhall Street, who is reputed to be the Company's bookseller, and from its having been gratuitously presented to many of the proprietors of India Stock, has thereby obtained a wider circulation, than if it had issued from any other shop; and that the indulgence thus afforded to the author and publisher, has been by them abused and perverted to an unworthy purpose: resulting in consequences which your memorialists are convinced were never contemplated by your honourable Court; namely, the defamation of a public functionary, long deceased, and an outrage on the respectability of his descendants.

Unwilling to obtrude themselves upon your notice otherwise than on public grounds, your memorialists abstain from all expression of private feeling; nor will they encroach upon your time farther than is necessary to rebut what may possibly be objected to this appeal—viz. "*That in the fair and impartial examination of a public character, Mr. Thornton is amenable neither to your memorialists, nor to his official superiors.*"

But your memorialists undertake, in a few words, to detect the fallacy of any such plea; by demonstrating, first, That Mr. Thornton's examination *has not been impartial*. And secondly, That the circumstances under which he has conducted it, inasmuch as they equally apply to your honourable Court as to your memorialists, render him *alike responsible to both*.

First, That Mr. Thornton's examination, if it can so be called, *has not been impartial*, but, on the contrary, peculiarly uncandid and unfair, is evident from more than one remarkable fact. For while Mr. Thornton, by the general spirit of his work so far as it relates to Sir Elijah Impey, scruples not, unwarrantably, to revive many unfounded calumnies, he studiously suppresses all evidence of his established defence; so that not even the word itself should once occur in the whole course of the narrative, in a sense conveying the slightest intimation of a fact, which, nevertheless, is notorious, and has become a part of authentic history; namely, that Sir Elijah Impey *did*, on the 4th day of February, 1788, defend himself at the bar of the House of Commons, to the effect of completely annulling the threat of a Parliamentary impeachment, moved by Sir Gilbert Elliot, Bart., on the 12th of December, 1787. The bare omission of such a fact, is, in itself, sufficient generally, to betray the *animus* with which Mr. Thornton wrote. But in the case particularly referred to, namely, Sir Elijah Impey's superintendence of the Sudder Dewannee Adaulut, Mr. Thornton has, in like manner, withheld all the existing vouchers in

vindication of that transaction; while he prominently exhibits
every partial opinion *against* it In reference, for example,
to the question as to the legality of that measure, submitted
to counsel in 1781, Mr. Thornton quotes only the answer of
Mr. Rous, the Company's Barrister, and totally conceals
those which were delivered by Mr. Dunning and Mr. Wallace,
both great lawyers in their day. He likewise omits the important fact, that the opinion of the former was founded on
expediency alone, and those of the two latter upon law. With
the same view, Mr. Thornton parades the remarks and comments of Sir John Day, *the partisan of Mr. Francis*, but is
quite silent in regard to the sentiments of Thurlow, Wal-
singham, Pitt, Grenville, and many others who supported the
conduct of Sir Elijah Impey in either House of Parliament.
But if, in regard to personal opinions, Mr. Thornton has been
thus partial and unjust, no less disingenuously has he dealt
with those written documents, by which Sir Elijah Impey is
equally exculpated, or, at the very least, capable of defence.
For, had Mr. Thornton merely consulted and made known the
memorials deposited in the Company's offices, not many steps
removed from his own, he would have discovered, and might
have shown, that in a letter addressed to the Governor General and Council, dated July 4, 1781, "the Chief Justice
declined accepting the salary annexed to the Sudder Dewannee
Adaulut, until he should hear from the Lord Chancellor and
the King's Attorney General, to whom he had written on the
subject." And that, "on the 15th of November, 1782," on
his resignation of the appointment, "Sir Elijah Impey transmitted to the Governor General and Council, by the hands of
the Accountant and Treasurer, a true copy of account of all
money, as well received from the Mofussil Adauluts as in
the Sudder Dewannee Adaulut, on account of all deposits
from April to September, 1782;" that is to say, for the
whole period during which those Courts had been in active
operation under his controul. *Now the truth, divested of
all partial colouring, is this: In 1780, before any salary
was proposed, the Chief Justice accepted the appointment as
a provisional measure only, to put an end to a conflict which
had unhappily arisen between the Council and the Court, in
consequence of an imperfect Act of Parliament, the 13th of
George III. cap. 63., which had given supremacy to both, but
left the jurisdiction of either undefined. In 1781, when it
was proposed to annex a salary to the office, the Chief Justice
declined accepting it unless approved by the Government at
home.* The crown lawyers, with the exception of the Solicitor
General, Mr. Mansfield, who first agreed, and afterward revised his opinion, authorised the appointment. The Com-

pany's standing counsel, Mr. Rous, disapproved of it, on the same plea which Mr. Mansfield had assumed. Pursuant to that opinion, the Court of Directors rescinded it, and the Chief Justice, *having, in the mean time, laboriously conducted the office—for it was one of real business*—refunded the proceeds, not one shilling of which he had ever appropriated to his own use.

In the statement of these facts, your memorialists are confirmed by official documents at the India House, registered in the minutes of your Councils abroad, and attested by a " Memorandum " of the Directors at home—from the latter your memorialists extract the following words: " *It could hardly have been expected that the Chief Justice should give up his few hours of relaxation, and enter on a fresh scene of labour and perplexity without compensation. The offer of a salary was at once a necessary and judicious sacrifice, but the property of the Company has by no means been wantonly lavished. £8000 bore no proportion to the sums which must eventually be saved. Perhaps they were ten times the amount, and of this salary we are yet to learn that a single shilling has ever been received ; though the appointment was passed in Council in October,* 1780." And again, at the conclusion of the same document, your memorialists find the following paragraph: " *Whatever plan may be adopted for the better arrangement of the judicial office in Bengal, it may be affirmed, that considerable advantage will still be derived from the professional assistance afforded by the Chief Justice, to the Sudder Dewannee Adaulut. His regulations and instructions —for he has already proposed many—will probably continue the standard of practice ; his decisions will be firm precedents for future judges, and his example stamp respectability on the office. No weak, indolent, or undignified character, will readily find admission into the vacant seat of Sir Elijah Impey.*"

Such is the testimony which Mr. Thornton has thought proper to suppress. That upon which he grounds his accusations proceeds exclusively from the same source whence the Select Committee of the House of Commons derived their information, and whereon they founded their report—the evidence of *ex-parte* witnesses, notoriously collected for the very purpose of crimination. Had Mr. Thornton drawn his conclusion from premises fairly stated on both sides of the question, whatever might have been its severity, he would have been then entitled to the plea of *impartiality*, he might *then* have insisted on his right of discussing the merits of a public character with all the acknowledged liberty of the press, to its full extent, and your memorialists would *then* have been debarred of their plea. But he has done no such thing. It suited his purpose to falsify, not to discuss the conduct of Sir Elijah Impey; *therefore it is that Mr. Thornton revives the factious opinions of more than half a century ago ; therefore it is that he confines his researches to the Annual Register, and Daily Advertiser ; therefore it is that he republishes the libels of Woodfall and Debret, but cautiously abstains from divulging any one of those numerous exculpatory documents which lay ready at his hand, based upon the testimony of your own Board, and enrolled among the archives of your own repositories.*

Your memorialists having thus, as they humbly conceive, established their first proposition, namely, that Mr. Thornton has no right to the plea of an impartial historian, proceed secondly to show, that Mr. Thornton has made himself responsible, not only to your memorialists, but also to your honourable Court, under circumstances alike offensive to both.

The facts are these. Shortly after the publication of Mr. Thornton's first volume, aware that the author was approaching that period which would comprise the proceedings in the Supreme Court, during Sir Elijah Impey's tenure of office in India, and apprehending that Mr. Thornton might fall into the mistakes and prejudices of some who had preceded him, one of your memorialists called upon that gentleman, and, in the presence of another of your officials, offered him a copy of Sir Elijah Impey's Defence before the House of Commons, a publication, which, from lapse of years, has become scarce, and which Mr. Thornton confessed he had not read or even heard of; he nevertheless declined the offer, and accompanied the refusal with a positive assurance that "full justice should be done to the character of Sir Elijah Impey." *It is only necessary to compare these words with the libel above recited, to prove that they must have been meant either to deceive or to insult your memorialist ; they were either false or sarcastic; in either case unworthy of a gentleman, and especially one upon your establishment.* For at the time of this interview, on or about the 9th of June last, Mr. Thornton was apprised that your memorialist had solicited and obtained leave from your honourable Court, to search the Company's records, in order to refute the calumnies of another author; * a purpose which, in a letter communicated by your Secretary, Mr. Melvill, had been very graciously countenanced by your honourable Court; *yet Mr. Thornton has done all he could to thwart that purpose, by adopting the very errors against*

* Mr. Macaulay.

which he had been warned, and which your memorialist was labouring by your aid to correct.

In counteracting a purpose thus authorised and approved by his superiors, with a full knowledge of the fact, it is respectfully submitted, that Mr. Thornton has, in like manner, presumed to counteract your beneficent intention towards your memorialist; that he has aggravated his offence to the latter by a breach of promise; and that, by manifesting an equally culpable disregard and contempt of the former, he has brought himself under the cognizance of your authority.

Your memorialists, confining themselves to the two propositions which they undertook to prove, refrain from entering any farther into the merits of a case, which they have never denied to be open to *fair* discussion, but which, if not already set at rest by long and scrutinous proceedings in Parliament, above sixty years ago, and if not sufficiently established on proofs recorded in your own councils, both abroad and at home, will assuredly gain nothing from the advocacy of your memorialists; yet, on the other hand, as little ought it to lose from the injurious comments of Mr. Edward Thornton.

Let each, then, it is humbly suggested, be called upon to produce his vouchers, before either is suffered to prevail over the other, under the apparent support of your patronage.

Your memorialists, on their part, are prepared with abundant evidence, to disprove the allegations above quoted, and willing, if allowed that honour, to produce them at any court that may be named for that purpose; or to deposit them in the hands of the Company's Solicitor, for the inspection of any Director or Committee of Directors deputed by your honourable Court.

Should this be thought informal or unnecessary, your memorialists are content to refer to the following documents. They have been collected, for the most part, with no little assiduity of research, from various authentic sources, and verified by official signatures.

They consist:—

1. Of a large collection of letters, private and official, bequeathed by Sir Elijah Impey to one of your memorialists.

2. Extracts from the folios in Leadenhall Street, entitled "Bengal Revenue Councils," particularly those beginning in September, 1780, and ending in November, 1782.

3. Of a transcript by one of your clerks, from a manuscript volume inscribed "Miscellaneous," in which is registered (page 533, B 447), "A Memorandum on the Judicial Establishment of India, vindicatory of Mr. Hastings and Sir Elijah Impey."

4. The registration of processes issued by the Supreme Court, 1774 to 1779, kept at your Solicitor's office at Draper's Hall; particularly relative to appeals against the judgments of the court, which have been dismissed by the King in Council.

5. An authentic document, procured from the Privy Council Office, of the issue of an appeal brought against a judgment given in 1779, which was dismissed for want of prosecution in 1789.

6. The book alluded to as having been offered to Mr. Thornton, and by him declined: viz., "The Speech of Sir Elijah Impey, &c., delivered by him at the bar of the House of Commons, on the 4th day of February, 1788," &c. &c. "London: Printed for John Stockdale, MDCCLXXXVIII."

All these documents were equally accessible to Mr. Thornton as to your memorialists, *for had he not refused a part, he would have been welcome to the use of all in their possession.* Had that gentleman examined them with half the labour that has been bestowed upon them by one of your memorialists, he might have grounded his history upon far less equivocal authority *than that of a political faction, prompted and impelled by Sir Elijah's bitterest and most inveterate enemy.** *He might have considered the formidable array of talent thus instigated and brought into action against the unassisted efforts of the accused, and the triumphant result of those efforts in one instance, as a fair presumption of a like issue in others, had opportunity been allowed. He had better, in short, have been silent on a subject of which he was either wholly ignorant, or but partially informed.*

But Mr. Thornton has not been silent, except to the effect of concealing the truth; for it has been proved, that he has been equally regardless of the documents within his own reach, as of those to which one of your memorialists in vain solicited his attention. If, therefore, knowing both to exist, he has carelessly omitted, or designedly suppressed them, then is Mr. Thornton manifestly guilty of one or other of these offences—unpardonable negligence, or wilful misrepresentation. From this dilemna Mr. Thornton cannot escape; for this conduct Mr. Thornton ought to be rebuked; and by whom so properly as by his own honourable masters?

On these grounds, your memorialists rest their claim for such redress as in your wisdom and sense of justice you may think fit to afford; and although they do not presume to dictate any particular mode or measure of its application, yet they venture, in all humility, to implore, that it may be such

---

* The late Sir Philip Francis.

as to mark the disapprobation of the libel by your honourable Court, so that it may be put on record in justification of their plea. And in thus appealing to your authority, as the legitimate vehicle of censure to your immediate dependent, they trust that you will deem them to have acted in a manner more indicative of respect for your honourable Court, and more consistent with their own age, education, and condition, than if they had sought their remedy elsewhere, or by any other means.

Your memorialists have no vindictive feeling towards Mr. Thornton, of whom they personally know nothing more than that his name is affixed to a work generally believed to be authorised by the East India Company, and circulated at their expense. They desire no more than to be placed by your favour, as vindicators of their father's reputation, on an equal footing with Mr. Thornton, his defamer. *In other words, all they require is, the same liberty to publish the truth, as Mr. Thornton has assumed in propagating what is false.*

Lastly, if, in the course of this appeal, they have been betrayed, by the excitement of a distressing subject, into any unbecoming warmth of expression, they rely on the known candour and liberality of your honourable Court for every due allowance.

(Signed)   JOHN IMPEY, Rear Admiral.
     ELIJAH BARWELL IMPEY.

4, Middle Scotland Yard, Whitehall,
     December 2, 1842.

To this appeal the memorialists received the following answer:—

"East India House, January 12, 1843.

"Gentlemen,

"I have laid before the Court of Directors of the East India Company, your memorial relating to certain passages in a History of the British Empire in India, now in course of publication by Mr. Edward Thornton, and in reply, I am commanded to inform you, that although their patronage has been given to the work in question, the Court must disclaim being in any degree responsible for opinions expressed in it.

"I have the honour to be,

"Gentlemen,

"Your most obedient humble Servant,

"J. D. DICKINSON,

"Rear Admiral Impey, and   "*Deputy.*
"Elijah Barwell Impey, Esq."

A draft of the foregoing memorial had been submitted to the inspection of the noble President of the Board of Controul, before it was presented to the Directors; and a copy of their reply, soon after its receipt, was likewise communicated in the letter subjoined, addressed to his Lordship.

2, Saville Row, Bath, January 19, 1843.

My dear Lord,

Having had the honour of laying before your Lordship a copy of my memorial to the Court of Directors, I think it my duty to communicate their reply. How far they are justified in their declaration, that " *although their patronage has been given* to the work in question, the Court must disclaim *being in any degree responsible for opinions expressed in it,*" I do not presume to decide; leaving the issue to your Lordship's determination, upon public grounds, and with an implicit reliance on your honour, wisdom, and equity. With my private sentiments, I have no right or inclination to trouble your Lordship, beyond the expression of my gratitude for the kind interest which you have taken in the object of my present pursuit.

I have the honour to be,

My dear Lord,

Your obliged and faithful humble Servaut,

E. B. IMPEY.

To the Right Honourable
President of the Board of Controul.

To this letter no answer was returned. How far his Lordship's silence may be attributed to his last illness; to what degree the subject may have engaged his thoughts; or whether he may or may not have considered it a fit object for interference, it is useless now to inquire.

London: Printed by D. Batten, Clapham.

By the same Author,

ILLUSTRATIONS OF GERMAN POETRY.

2 vols. 8vo. Price 16s.

SCHILLER'S LAY OF THE BELL.

Illustrated by RETZCH, with a Translation of the Poem, and an Analysis
of the Outlines to face each Plate. Second Edition, German and English,
4to., elegantly bound in Morocco, in Hayday's style. Price £2 2s.

The Poem, Translation, and Analysis, may be had separate, in cloth
boards, price 7s. 6d.

GOD'S PASTORAL CARE OF HIS PEOPLE, AS SET FORTH IN PSALM XXIII.

A Course of Lectures delivered during Lent, 1843, at. St. Matthew's
Chapel, Denmark Hill, by the late T. E. HANKINSON, M.A. 12mo. cloth.
Second Edition. 2s. 6d.

THE VISION OF ISAIAH CONCERNING JERUSALEM,

From Chapter XL. to the end. Rendered into verse according to
BISHOP LOUTH'S Translation. Cloth, gilt edges. Price 2s. 6d.

SHORT FAMILY PRAYERS

For every Morning and Evening of the Month, and for particular occasions ; Selected and Arranged from the Liturgy, Psalms, and various
Eminent Writers. By WILLIAM SOLTAU, Esq. Second Edition, enlarged. 12mo. Price 3s.

VENITE EXULTEMUS, MAGNIFICAT, &c.

Pointed for Chanting. Stitched, 3d. And, also, with APPROPRIATE
CHANTS, arranged in Four Parts. By CHARLES KEMBLE, B.A., Wadham
College, Oxford. 18mo., embossed cloth, gilt edges. Price 1s. 6d.

THE MERCY SEAT UPON THE ARK.

Comprising a Prayer and Hymn for every Sunday in the Ecclesiastical
Year. Price 2s. 6d.

A HELP TO PRAYER.

18mo., printed in large type, cloth, gilt edges. Price 1s. 6d.

PSALMS AND HYMNS

Selected for use in Clapham Church by the late Rev. JOHN VENN.
Sixth Edition, much enlarged by the present Rector. 18mo. & 32mo.
Price 2s. 6d. 8vo. 5s.

Lightning Source UK Ltd.
Milton Keynes UK
UKOW06f1611050916

282241UK00011B/513/P